Public Finance

An introduction

Graham C. Hockley
Senior Lecturer
Department of Economics
University College, Cardiff

Routledge & Kegan Paul
London, Boston and Henley

First published in 1970
by Routledge & Kegan Paul Ltd
under the title of 'Monetary Policy and Public Finance'
39 Store Street,
London WC1E 7DD,
Broadway House,
Newtown Road,
Henley-on-Thames,
Oxon RG9 1EN and
9 Park Street,
Boston, Mass. 02108, USA
This completely revised edition
first published 1979
Set in IBM Press Roman by
Hope Services, Abingdon
and printed in Great Britain by
Lowe & Brydone Ltd
Thetford, Norfolk

British Library Cataloguing in Publication Data

Hockley, Graham Charles

Public finance. – 2nd ed., revised.
1. Finance, Public – Great Britain
I. Title   II. Monetary policy and public finance
336.41   HJ1001   78-41205

ISBN 0 7100 0148 7 (c)
ISBN 0 7100 0149 5 (p)

To my parents

Contents

Preface

This book continues with the same format as the author's earlier *Monetary Policy and Public Finance* but has been completely rewritten to take account of the many and substantial changes that have taken place in both the monetary and fiscal fields.

The unhappy financial history of the first part of the 1970s, leading to the 'lifeboat' operation of the Bank of England and extensive changes in monetary control, is detailed.

On the fiscal side there has been a great number of changes. Many have been of mere detail but there has been a number of substantial changes such as the abolition of selective employment tax (SET), the introduction of value-added tax (VAT), and the replacement of estate duties by a capital transfer tax. There are also substantial, though temporary, North Sea oil and gas revenues flowing in. These changes have not, unfortunately, led to many deletions in the list of faults in the tax structure: there is still a formidably complex tax structure that is far from equitable.

Chapter 2 ('The financial system') and Chapter 12 ('The social services') are additions. Also new is a substantial section (Chapters 19, 20 and 21) which looks at local government and regional finance. Chapter 19 deals with the present reorganised structure of local authorities and their revenue and expenditure. Chapter 20 looks at the issues involved in central/local relations, the types of fiscal arrangements that can be made, and has a considerable section on the important issues involved in equalisation. Chapter 21 considers local-government and regional-government sources of finance together: a common-sense but seldom-followed practice. It finishes with a discussion of the rating system.

Acknowledgments

I wish to record my great indebtedness to Professor J. Revell of University College, Bangor, for comments on Part I, to Professor A. B. Atkinson of University College, London, for his comments on the chapters on public finance, to Professor Sir Bryan Hopkin of University College, Cardiff, for his comments on Part III, and Dr I. Thomas of the Welsh Office for his comments on the chapters on local government. I also received invaluable assistance from M. Knights, a visiting economics teacher to Cardiff, who read most of the draft manuscript and made many improvements in style and content. Shortcomings and omissions, however, remain my responsibility.

The author and publisher would like to thank the following for permission to use copyright material: George Allen & Unwin for D. R. Denman, *Origins of Ownership*, 1958 and R. M. Titmus, *Income Distribution and Social Change*, 1962; The Bank of England for several issue of the *Bank of England Quarterly Bulletin*; the *Economic Journal* for A. Rubner, 'The Irrelevancy of the British Differential Profits Tax', June 1964 and G. L. S. Shackle, 'Recent Theories concerning the Nature and Role of Interest', June 1961; Longmans Green & Co. for A. J. Merritt, *Executive Remuneration in the UK.*, 1968; Oxford University Press for A. T. Peacock and Jack Wiseman, *The Growth of Public Expenditure in the United Kingdom*, 1961; Prentice-Hall Inc. for W. J. Schultz and C. L. Harris, *American Public Finance*, 1965; C. A. Watts & Co. for Joan Robinson, *Economic Philosophy*, Penguin, 1962.

Finally, as is proper, the last word goes to a woman – my wife – whose encouragement and forbearance greatly eased my task.

Introduction

This book is intended as an introduction to a university course in public finance and for use of students who are studying for professional examinations. Also, I hope, it will be intelligible, and of interest, to the general reader. In public finance most of us judge from a purely personal standpoint: a good tax is a tax that is paid by somebody else; wise government spending is spending that benefits oneself; correct monetary policy is regulation that protects one's own interests. The multitude of voices raised on almost every aspect of public finance, each claiming right on its side, but frequently each seeking its own ends, tends to drown out general considerations.

Essentially, a study of public finance is an attempt to break away from this Babel, to see through arguments based on the interests of this or that group, and attempt to establish rational principles on which policy can be based.

The scope of a public finance course is ill-defined. Government spending and revenue are central to it, but there is considerable overlap with monetary policy. The Government can, after all, merely create money to pay for the goods and services it requires, or it can borrow from its citizens as well as taxing them. This book takes the view that it is impossible to have a very realistic understanding of public finance matters without some understanding of the operation of the monetary system.

Part I is therefore devoted to the monetary system. Chapter 1 discusses the nature and attributes of money, how it affects the economy, and the value of money. The following chapters deal respectively with the financial system, the Bank of England, the discount market and the commercial banks. These institutions have a unique and long-established relationship with each other. Following this is a description of other financial institutions which in recent years have transformed much of the financial scene. Our concern is not so much with the detailed working of these institutions but with obtaining an understanding of their interrelationships and how they form the monetary system. Chapter 7 draws the previous discussion together in looking at the implications for monetary policy of a Budget surplus or deficit. This chapter therefore provides many of the links between the sphere of public finance and that of money, which will be taken up and developed later in the book.

A description of the monetary system, it will be clear, is a description not of a static framework but of an evolving structure. The rapidity with which change can take place is indeed one of the remarkable things about the collection of institutions labelled the 'British Monetary System'. As with many rapidly changing things, the spice of controversy is never far away.

Part II introduces the public finance section with four chapters which briefly outline how government expenditure and revenue have changed in this century. This background is essential for an understanding of the system as it exists today. In this context policy can be discussed from two angles: one approach is to look at reasons for government expenditure and its change over time; the other approach is to concentrate on ways of ensuring that expenditures, given that the decision to spend has been made, are wisely and not wastefully applied. This book has a number of things to say, relevant to this latter and important question, particularly on simplification of the system of tax and benefits, which could lead to large savings. But the detailed parliamentary and administrative procedures, and statistical techniques, that attempt to ensure efficiency in this narrow sense have been considered outside the scope of this volume. Changes up to November 1978 have been incorporated.

Chapter 12 looks at the system of social services. Payment for the bulk of social services is by means of a separate assessment. This, for most people, is at a proportional rate, with no allowance for differences in taxpayers' circumstances except for a distinction between employed and self-employed persons. This is contrasted with the elaborate provisions of the income-tax system. National Insurance benefits and supplementary benefits are given together with their overlap with the tax system.

Chapter 13 is a key chapter, setting out the accretion principle of income. This concept is used thereafter as a yardstick to evaluate the current system of taxes and benefits which is detailed in the following chapters. Chapters 19, 20 and 21, as outlined in the Preface, deal with local and regional finance. The National Debt raises complex monetary and fiscal issues, which are examined in Chapter 22. Chapter 23 gathers previous threads and looks at some alternative ways in which the system can evolve.

Part III does not attempt a detailed assessment of the use of policy in the post-war period: this has been well covered in recent publications; but it outlines the problems of using monetary and fiscal policy to control the economy.

Part I
The monetary system

1
The nature of money

But it is pretty to see what money will do.
SAMUEL PEPYS, 21 March 1667.

Essential properties of money

To make a comprehensive list of all the items which have been used as money at various times and in various places would be tedious. What do the following items used as money have in common: cattle, rice, bark-cloth, women, gold, iron, stone and cigarettes?

These and all items used as money have the common intangible property of *general acceptability*. Within the community concerned, money is accepted because it is confidently believed that it can be in turn passed on for goods and services. The item serving as money in many communities is often scarce and therefore valuable in its own right, but this is by no means necessary. A look at a one-pound note will make this clear. It says: 'Bank of England. I promise to pay the bearer on demand the sum of one pound. Chief Cashier'! It is of itself just a piece of printed paper. If you do demand one pound, you can have another one-pound note with a different number on it or a handful of coins whose intrinsic value – the cost of the metal – is only a few pence. The note is worth having, not because the paper on which it is printed is valuable, or because the printing on the note has intrinsic worth, but because it is generally acceptable in Great Britain: that is, whatever goods or service are desired can be obtained by the exchange of a sufficient number of notes. The 'promise to pay' engraved on the note is a reminder of the origin of bank-notes: at one time they were receipts for precious metals deposited with goldsmiths and it was expected at any time that the note or receipts could be returned and the metal repossessed. It is only in this century that 'backing' for notes, in the form of gold or silver, has been effectively done away with for purposes of transactions internal to a country, Bank-notes and coins are not the only form of money in a modern society – for example, most transactions are carried out by means of drawings on current accounts with the commercial banks. More will be said later on the types of assets which should be considered as money, and also on the factors which determine the quantity of money in the economy.

What are the reasons for all but the most primitive of societies singling out some item that becomes generally acceptable and called 'money'? A first answer is summed up in the phrase 'the sheer inconvenience of double coincidence of wants', i.e. the need to find a seller of the item you require who at the same time needs what you have to offer. In recent years some economists have dug rather deeper than this, for money is not the only answer to the inconvenience of double coincidence of wants. It is possible to imagine a barter society developing where middle-men would act to pool goods. They would accept goods that they themselves did not require for their own use, with a view to future exchanges. Alternatively the individual can engage in a series of transactions to obtain the item he requires. Yet a third possibility would be a kind of barter-credit system where goods were obtained now in return for a promise to return other goods in the future. Following Brunner and Meltzer (1971), such arrangements are held to be inefficient for two main reasons: first, such barter arrangements may well involve longer transaction chains, and second, greater uncertainty is involved. An alternative way of putting the last point is to say that more information is required in barter situations: information on the physical properties of the goods being offered and of particular goods' desirability for future exchanges; or in a credit system information on the creditworthiness of the transactor. Such inefficiencies would be paid for in terms of higher 'prices', i.e. good *A* would exchange for less of good *B* than would be the case if *A* could be sold for money and the money used to purchase *B*. The description so far has been in terms of money functioning as a means of payment.

The term 'a means of payment' is a narrower concept than the term 'a medium of exchange'. A means of payment discharges the debt obligation of the purchaser: the seller of the good, service or asset has no further claim. In contrast a medium of exchange is a broader concept which includes items which allows transactions to proceed but does not necessarily extinguish claims between seller and purchaser or leaves a claim between the purchaser and some third party. The most important example of the latter category is trade credit, but credit cards and similar arrangements are other examples; these are a medium of exchange but not a means of payment. A discusssion of these issues appears in papers by Clower and Shackle, reported in Clayton *et al.* (1971) and Goodhart (1975).

Money, by its nature, as well as acting as a means of payment also acts in some degree as a *store of value*. If money were like a day-return ticket on a railway, valueless after the day had ended, nobody would keep it. It is because money is expected to have general acceptability and more or less the same purchasing power the day after, and the day after that, that money is held, and this function is described as a store of value. It is unfortunate that the term *store of value* is often taken to mean that the value is constant. What determines the 'value of money', that is the amount of goods and services for which it can be exchanged and the problem of its value over time, will be taken up again in this chapter.

Money usually also acts as a *unit of account* and as a *standard of deferred payments*. The unit of account refers to the fact that instead of valuing each and every article and service in terms of all others, it is valued in terms of a common denominator, the means of payment. In a similar manner, contracts for future payments are usually made in terms of the means of payment, but they can be made in terms of the value of gold, or a foreign currency, or a quantity of goods. It is usual for money to act in both these ways, but is by no means necessary; the guinea today sometimes acts as a unit of account, but it does not circulate as a means of payment.

Money and liquidity

The term 'liquidity' is a specialised economic term. Unfortunately the concept of liquidity has been used in a number of ways, and has come to have different meanings. Recently the term has been used to describe how an economic unit arranges its affairs to ensure that its cash inflow matches its cash outflow. An important part of such management is usually the liquidity of assets held by the institution. It is this latter use of the term that we shall have in mind, and regard it as *the speed and certainty with which an asset can be turned into money without loss, or into a known amount of money in relation to its face value.* Notes are completely liquid in that nothing more needs to be done to purchase a good than handing over the appropriate number of notes. Shares in quoted companies, gilt-edged securities and Treasury Bills can all be turned quickly into money – just pick up the telephone and call a stockbroker or bank. Equity shares and gilt-edged securities are, however, much less liquid than Treasury

Bills, for the amount of money obtainable by sale on the market is not known in advance, whereas Treasury Bills have only to be held to maturity, at most three months, to be paid at their face value; or alternatively they can be discounted straightaway at a rate of discount which is known in relation to the Bank of England rediscount rate. If the rediscount rate increased it would inflict a much greater loss on having to sell a gilt-edged security than it would on having to discount a bill.

A second distinction between these assets is that equity shares are the liability of various companies and therefore there is a possibility of default, whereas government securities are, in most countries, deemed to have a negligible risk of default. In a financial panic it is better to be holding liquid government assets than liquid private assets.

It is evident that assets can be arranged on a scale, at one end completely liquid, i.e. money, and at the other end illiquid, say an IOU from me to you, or a piece of real property. If liquidity, the ability to exchange an asset quickly for a known sum of money, were the only consideration governing the holding of assets, we should expect to find that the yield on securities would increase as the asset became more illiquid, the better yield being necessary to induce the public to hold the more illiquid securities. It is found that securities do, as a rule, follow roughly this pattern, although a number of other things have to be taken into account. Money, unless it is held in the form of a deposit account at a bank, does not earn interest, while the yield on short-term government securities will normally be lower than the yield on long-term securities. Business fixed-interest securities will normally yield rather more than government securities because of a higher risk of default. Equity shares, since they offer both the attraction of sharing in business profits and the risk of getting nothing, are likely to be more volatile as to yield, depending on the market assessment of their worth.

In the previous paragraph, the terms 'yield' and 'interest' have been used. A fixed-interest security is issued at a particular price and at a particular rate of interest. Say it is issued at £100 at 4 per cent. This means that each year the holder will receive £4 until such time, if the security has a redemption date, it is repaid at £100. The yield on this security is the market price of the security divided into the rate of interest paid. Thus, if the security in our example is sold on the market for £50, the yield is $100/50 \times 4$, i.e. 8 per cent. If it fetched £25, the yield would be $100/25 \times 4$ or 16 per cent. The yield on an equity is calculated in the same way, by dividing the market price into the face value of the security and multiplying by the dividend. It is important to grasp this inverse relationship between the price of a security and its yield. If the price of securities falls, the yield must increase, in both cases on the assumption that the rate of interest or dividend paid on the security remains unaltered. The stock of liquid assets (stock = assets in existence) is large, in particular it is large in relation to the flow of new liquid assets. Also, the stock of company securities is large in relation to new securities coming on to the market. For this reason a change in the price of existing securities (as we have seen, we are also saying, by definition, that yields have changed) is likely to affect the terms on which new securities will be taken up by the market. Many of the matters touched on in this section will be taken up later in more detail.

Definitions of money

It was a deliberate choice not to start off with a definition of money in our society. This seemingly simple question does not admit of a simple unique answer. A commonly quoted definition tells us that money is 'Anything generally accepted in final payment for goods, services and settlement of a debt.' This definition, while it is useful, needs further clarification.

The following distinctions will be found useful. The first between *money* and *liquid assets* is based on the function performed by the asset in question. On this definition money is used for assets that act both as a medium of exchange and as a store of value, while liquid assets are used for securities which, while acting as a store of value, do not circulate in exchange. Money consists of the liabilities of the Bank of England, i.e. coin and notes and Bankers' Deposits (i.e. deposits of commercial banks at the Bank of England), together with deposits by the public at commercial banks. Liquid assets are items such as deposits at the National Savings Bank and Trustee Savings Banks, deposits in building societies, in local government and finance houses. These differ from money when the moment for payment arises; they must first be turned into money, rather than exchanged directly for commodities. It should be clear from this distinction that what is money at any particular time is a matter of law and custom. In practice, some assets overlap the money/liquid asset dichotomy. Deposit accounts, often called 'time deposits', at commercial banks are not transferable by cheque and formally require at least seven days' notice before withdrawal. In practice, a cheque on a current account, sometimes called 'demand deposits' or 'sight deposits', would be unlikely to be dishonoured if the current account has insufficient funds to meet it, provided it was covered by a balance in a deposit account. The National Giro system started in 1968 and is a means whereby the payer can pay cash into any post office, or have his special account debited, and the sum is credited or paid to the payee. Facilities for transfer between Giro and Savings Bank accounts are provided; such accounts have therefore moved toward the more liquid end of the spectrum.

Money itself, as defined above, can be split into primary and secondary money. *Primary money* consists of coin, notes and Bankers' Deposits, often simply referred to as 'cash'. Deposits at commercial banks on both current and deposit accounts are, in this country, what constitutes *secondary money*.

Money should not be confused with legal tender. Only notes, and coin up to a small amount, are legal tender. In spite of this the value of payments by cheque are many times the value of payments by cash and notes. The risk of default by major banks in Great Britain and most other developed countries is nowadays considered so small, i.e. confidence is so great that transfer of deposits to third persons will be honoured, that deposits are included with notes in the definition of money. In Great Britain also, the definition of money known as M3 makes no distinction between current and deposit accounts. As we have seen, deposit accounts can usually be drawn on with almost as much ease as can current accounts. An added reason for not distinguishing between these two accounts is that British banks, unlike, for example, American banks, do not have to observe different reserve ratios for each type of account.

Quantity of money and liquid assets

At the end of 1976, in approximate figures, notes and coin outstanding in the economy amounted to £6,714 million, while current and deposit accounts in banks in the United Kingdom were £45,302 million. Savings certificates, premium bonds, defence bonds, National Saving and Trustee Savings accounts amounted to £12,350 million. Short-term deposits with local government authorities amounted to over £4,349 million and shares and deposits with building societies to some £26,279 million.

This list of liquid assets is not intended to be a complete one. For some purposes, deposits with finance houses, accumulated funds in insurance companies and others may be included. It can be seen that notes and coin are small in relation to bank deposits, and in their turn liquid assets are bigger than bank deposits.

Liquid assets perform some of the functions of money. They act as a store or value, and, while they cannot be used directly as a medium of exchange, they affect the demand for money. Coin and notes, together with current-account deposits at banks, do not generally earn interest; deposit accounts earn a small rate of interest; liquid assets, as a rule, earn rather more. So a change in interest rates may cause the public to switch some money from bank deposits to liquid assets. Alternatively, the public can switch from liquid assets to money by, for example, demanding repayment of some of their National Savings certificates. The amount of money in the economy is thus not necessarily a good guide to the spending power of the public.

The monetary authorities work with two main concepts of money: M1 and M3. They also use a concept called Domestic Credit Expansion (DCE), which will be explained (see pp. 9–12). M1 = notes and coin in circulation with the public, plus UK private-sector sterling current-account deposits with banks, less 60 per cent of transit items.[1] (M2 = M1 plus time deposit accounts. This money aggregate is no longer used by the Bank of England, which now confines its attention to a narrow and broad definition of money, namely M1 and M3.) M3 = M1 plus deposits (including certificates of deposit) held by UK residents in both the public and private sectors. In 1977 the definition of M3 (and therefore DCE) was divided into two categories. Sterling M3, as the name implies, includes only sterling deposits. The sterling concept of M3 is thought to be more relevant in analysing the monetary demand for goods and services in the home economy, as such purchases are made in sterling. A broader definition also includes foreign currency deposits. The figures given in Table 1.1 are for the broad definition of M3. They include foreign currency deposits, which have varied from some 3 per cent of the total in 1970 to 8 per cent in 1976.

As the Bank of England said (September 1970), 'There are no clear rules for deciding which of these totals is most appropriate: there can be alternative definitions of the stock of money encompassing a wide or narrow set of components.' A considerable literature has grown up on the substitutability of money and near-monies which is surveyed in Feige and Pearce (1977); no strong conclusions yet emerge from the data.

The idea that there is a simple relationship between GNP and the money supply receives a shock from the last three columns of Table 1.1, which give the percentage increases in GNP, M1 and M3. There is first of all the point that M1 and M3 behave very differently: in some years they had much the same increase, in 1975 M1 increased much more than M3, while the reverse was the case in 1972 and 1973. Any attempt to link GNP and the money supply in this period would need to explain the

Table 1.1

M1 and M3 4th quarter totals (unadjusted £m.)

Year	M1	M3	Money GNP	% increase in GNP	% increase in M1	% increase in M3
1968	8,784	16,092	37,723			
1969	8,812	16,596	39,836	5.6	0.3	3.1
1970	9,635	18,175	43,924	10.3	9.3	9.5
1971	11,088	20,541	49,656	13.0	15.1	13.0
1972	12,657	26,245	55,492	11.8	14.2	27.8
1973	13,303	33,468	64,815	16.8	5.1	27.5
1974	14,739	37,260	74,958	15.6	10.7	11.3
1975	17,495	40,555	93,978	25.3	18.6	8.8
1976	19,467	45,129	110,259	17.3	11.3	11.3

Source: Bank of England Quarterly Bulletin.

different behaviour of these magnitudes. There appears to be no obvious simple relationship either between the changes in M1 and M3 taken separately and the behaviour of changes in GNP.

Domestic credit expansion

DCE was a concept introduced in Britain in 1969 at a time when she was involved in negotiating a loan from the International Monetary Fund (IMF). It is an attempt to adjust the money-supply figures to take account of any change in money balances directly caused by an external surplus or deficit.

In a closed economy any change in the quantity of money must work its effect on the home economy. With an open economy a change in the quantity of money, as well as influencing the home economy, can lead to a change in imports and to a change in foreign capital flows. Thus taking the case of an increase in the money supply, this may not only lead to a price increase but also to a balance-of-payments deficit. As the balance of payments deteriorates, foreign exchange reserves fall, i.e. the Exchange Equalisation Account acquires sterling and this sterling is used to hold Treasury Bills. In static terms a reduction in reserves leads to a reduction in bank deposits and bank holding of Treasury Bills (as the Exchange Equalisation Account holds more). This has the effect of reducing the money supply. For example, a £500 million increase in the quantity of money and a fall in reserves of £100 million would show up as a measured change in the quantity of money of £400 million.

A good many assumptions would have to be made for an exact relationship of the kind outlined above to hold but the basic assumption of the strong relationship between the two magnitudes is straightforward. Hence the use of the concept of DCE which concentrates on the original change in the money supply whether this results in offsetting changes in the balance of payments or not. The change in DCE over a period equals the change in the quantity of money plus the change in the balance of payments. It is measured as follows: total bank lending plus the increase in non-bank holdings of currency (= the change in the money supply) plus overseas credit to the public sector. The public sector includes the central government, local authorities and public corporations.

In December 1976 agreement was reached with the International Monetary Fund on credits to ease the crises of confidence which Britain was then experiencing. As part of the deal a definite target was set for DCE for 1977–8, and a provisional target for 1978–9. These targets are to be monitored by the IMF and achievement is a condition of the credits. Thus recently, although M1 and M3 are not forgotten, prime emphasis has been placed on DCE.

The formal relationship of M3 and DCE

The formal relationship of the new definitions of M3 and DCE, which exclude foreign currency deposits, is shown in Table 1.2. Table 1.2 does not establish cause and effect but shows that DCE is composed of the net changes in the public-sector borrowing requirement (PSBR), the private-sector holdings of National Debt and bank lending. When, from the DCE figure, we allow for the net changes in the four items shown, which takes account of foreign flows of finance, we are left with the sterling definition of M3.

Does money matter?

An intense debate on monetary matters has been carried out over the last twenty years. For survey articles see Johnson (June 1962), Barro and Fischer (April 1976) and Nobay and Johnson (June 1977). Not surprisingly, people have been concerned with different aspects of money and have given rather different answers to the question: 'Does money matter?'

There is general agreement that, in contrast with a barter economy, a money economy has advantages in facilitating exchange, encouraging the division of labour, reducing search and transactions costs, and decreasing

Table 1.2

Sterling M3 and DCE: unadjusted figures, first half of the financial year 1976–7 (£m.)

Public-sector borrowing requirement (PSBR)		+5,321
Purchase (–) of public-sector debt by the UK private sector (other than banks)		–2,122
Bank lending in sterling (increase +) to:		
UK private sector (including official holdings of commercial bills)		+1,765
Overseas		+ 467
	DCE	+5,431
External and foreign currency finance of the public sector (increase –)	–2,131	
Overseas sterling deposits (increase –)	+ 48	
Banks' foreign currency deposits, net foreign currency assets (increase –)	+ 32	–2,051
Banks' non-deposit liabilities (increase –)		– 477
	Sterling M3	+2,903

Source: Bank of England Quarterly Bulletin, *vol. 17, no. 1, March 1977.*

the need for information. There is also widespread agreement on the price that has to be paid for these benefits. In Professor Shackle's words (1961):

> In a barter system or one where money serves only as a numeraire, knowledge is effectively bound to be perfect. For nothing can be sold except by the concomitant purchase of some other resource embodying thing. Without money we cannot put off deciding what to buy with the thing we are in the act of selling. If we do not know precisely what use a thing will be to us, we are compelled nevertheless, by an absence of money, to override and ignore this ignorance. It is money which enables decision to be deferred.

The presence of money destroys Say's Law of the equality of total supply and total demand. The intellectual credence of Say's Law, an idea which dominated economics for over 100 years, was shattered by Keynes (1936) in chapter 2 of his *General Theory*. The implications of discarding Say's Law and of working with a money economy are difficult to come to grips with and work out, as this chapter indicates.

Money is therefore both a blessing and a curse. The advantages that have been outlined are so powerful that practically all societies have developed forms of money. The dark side of money lies precisely in the fact that it enables decisions to be deferred. Production can take place for which there is no current demand, and thus general overproduction and slump is possible. Money that is not spent may be held for the ultimate purchase of some commodity or service but money that is not spent conveys no signals to suppliers and manufacturers.

The answer to the question 'Does money matter?' is that it matters profoundly if we are comparing an economy with and without a monetary system. Other aspects of this question have more controversial answers.

We have seen that there is some ambiguity about which assets should be defined as money. Answers to questions in this area are less clear cut and have been subject to intense recent debate. As far as monetary policy is concerned there is a need to know if the sub-set of assets we choose to call 'money' is sufficiently differentiated from other assets. If the authorities change the quantity of money, will this affect the economy in a predictable way? To have most effect should the authorities operate to change a much wider range of financial assets? If so, how wide?

Much of the debate on these matters has been conducted in terms of two stereotypes which have been labelled Keynesian and Monetarist. The model labelled Keynesian should not necessarily be identified with the ideas of J. M. Keynes. It is an important part of much recent research that those who call themselves Keynesian have departed in crucial ways from the ideas of Keynes expounded in *The General Theory* (1936) and his earlier *Treatise on Money* (1930), and that these have been retrogressive departures. For a critique on these lines, see Leijonhufvud (1968), Shackle (1967; 1972; 1974), Clower (1969), and Hines (1971).

The Keynesian emphasis is on the close substitution of money and liquid assets, with little substitution between money and goods. On this view an increase in the quantity of money brought about by open-market purchases of securities by the Government would, on the whole, be reflected in the purchase of alternative liquid assets. This would raise their price and lower their yields. In turn, the change in the most liquid assets would be expected to ripple along other financial assets and influence their yields in the same direction. Real investment effects would follow if the expected returns from real investment were unchanged, but the rate of interest (cost of borrowing) had changed. The implication of this line of argument is that monetary policy should seek to influence rates of interest directly, rather than indirectly by changing the money stock. Keynesians predict a high interest elasticity of demand for money, so that it would take a substantial change in the money supply to cause a significant variation in interest rates.

The Monetarist position is to argue that the direct effect of money will be felt on a wide range of assets (Friedman, 1974b, p. 28):

> We, on the other hand, stress a much broader and more 'direct' impact on spending, saying, that individuals seeking to dispose of what they regard as their money balances . . . will try to pay out a larger sum for the purchase of securities, goods and services, for the repayment of debt, and as gifts than they are receiving from the corresponding sources!

The extreme Monetarist position would predict a zero interest elasticity of demand for money.

Different positions can be illustrated as shown in Figure 1.1.

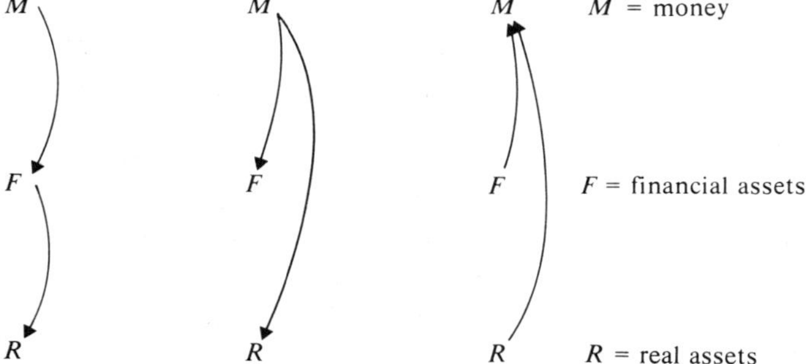

Figure 1.1.

Is the effective chain of transmission as illustrated in the first column from money to financial assets and from financial assets to real assets? Or, as illustrated in the second column, is money expected to affect both financial and real assets directly? The third column illustrates another possibility, i.e. that the money supply itself alters because of prior changes in real or financial markets or in both.

The empirical evidence is surveyed in Laidler (1977) and in the *Bank of England Quarterly Bulletin* (June 1970; March 1972; and September 1974). The conclusion reached is that the evidence supports neither extreme version. A significant negative relationship has been found in nearly all studies between movements in interest rates and money balances; so that given the level of money incomes the higher the interest rate, the lower will be the level of money balances. The elasticity found was low but always statistically significant.

In terms of the question we set out to answer, 'To influence the economy, should the authorities operate on the quantity of money or a wider range of assets?', the empirical evidence points to both having important effects.

A third answer to the question 'Does money matter?' is provided when we specify what we mean by an increase or decrease in money. In textbooks it is common to start from what, at first sight, seems a satisfactory position: 'Now consider what happens if we double the quantity of money.' In fact this statement is meaningless unless and until the means whereby the quantity of money is doubled is specified, as has been shown most rigorously by Patinkin (1965).

If we conceptualise, and imagine that starting from an equilibrium position everyone's holding of money is doubled, or changed in an equiproportional manner, it is not surprising that prices will also double or change in a similar proportion. Professor Tobin (1963) has labelled such a miraculous events as 'manna from heaven'. In practice, we know that an event like decimalisation, where from a certain day it is declared that there will be 100 new pence to the pound instead of 240 old pence, and most importantly all existing contracts are deemed to the rewritten in the new currency, is essentially an event without real effects on the economy. However, money does not appear as 'manna', nor is it distributed from a helicopter, as imagined by Professor Friedman (1969), it comes into existence either by: printing notes; an increase in bank deposits, or open-market operations. There are important differences in these cases. Apart from the case of printing notes, an increase in money is accompanied by a change in the debt structure of the economy.

The printing of notes is purely inflationary since the real resources of the economy are not changed and the Government (in a fully employed economy) just bids up prices if it tries to buy resources directly; alternatively, those it passes the money to, by way of transfer payments, bid up prices. For this reason notes in a well-regulated economy are not used as a source of finance by Governments, except as a by-product of supplying notes on demand to the economy.

An increase in bank deposits is accompanied by an increase in debt since those who are in receipt of a loan have an obligation to repay. In a fully employed economy similar effects on prices can be expected, as happened with an increase in the note issue, which explains why banks are subject to various regulations.

When the Government purchases or sells its own debt various effects can follow. Let us take a few examples. If the Government is able to sell its debt to members of the public, this will decrease the quantity of money (as bank deposits are transferred to the Bank of England to pay for the debt). A very different situation arises if the sale of government debt is accompanied by an increase in the money supply – which can happen if the sale of securities is made to the discount houses or banks. The Government can always increase the money supply by purchase of some of its securities. What is not directly under its control, as the depression in the 1930s showed, is the ability to ensure that the extra money is spent or used by the banks to expand their loans. When, as in this section, we consider how a change in money is brought about, it is clear that the change is initially felt in different sectors of the economy and is likely to have a disproportionate effect on some prices. In particular these changes do not cause debts to be rewritten, so any price changes, as a result of the money changes, will have a differential impact on debtors and creditors. Again we have different answers to the question 'Does money matter?', depending on how the change in money is brought about.

The value of money

The term 'relative price' means the amount of one good which will exchange for another. In contrast the term 'value of money' means the amount of goods and services that money will buy, compared with what it would buy, say, last year. When it is said that the price level has gone up, the same idea could be expressed by saying that the value of money has fallen. As such the term 'value of money' is the inverse of the price level and is a more difficult and ambiguous concept.

In the words of Professor Hicks (1939), 'If we have equi-proportional changes in all prices, all commodities can be considered as a single composite commodity with price p, where p = the absolute price level.' Putting the matter in this stark form brings out the difficulties of using the terms 'price level' or 'value of money'. If prices do not change in an equiproportional manner, we have no unambiguous measure of the value of money. This was elegantly expressed by Modigliani (May 1975) as 'money has as many prices as there are commodities, current and future, for which it can be exchanged'. Everyday habits of talking about the 'cost of living' or 'fall in the value of the pound' may hide, but do not solve, this problem. They get round it by a more or less arbitrary system of selecting the components to go in the index and weighting of the components, once these have been selected.

We are faced with a number of variables that interact with one another;

we need a general equilibrium system to solve for any variable. A change in the amount of money in the economy is likely to change output and prices in the economy. However, changes in output and prices can occur independently of changes in the amount of money, but they will nevertheless affect the value of money. Talking of a change in the amount of money in the economy, as we have just done, without specifying how the amount of money comes into the economy, can also hide important differences. If the public desire to hold more money, this can come about, for example, by their exchanging some assets for money. If the assets exchanged are National Savings securities, no great effects may be apparent. The net effect is that the Government has issued more notes and fewer securities. If the public attempt to obtain the money by selling securities on the market, this does not (unless the monetary authorities themselves buy the securities) increase the amount of money in the economy (the public will be exchanging the same quantity of money and securities amongst themselves), but it has the effect of driving down the price of securities, i.e. increasing the yields. The initiative for the increase in money may come from the monetary authorities, who buy government securities in the market. If the public's desire for money has not changed, then this increase in money will be spent on securities or goods with probable effects on prices, interest rates and output. When the desire for increased money holdings comes from the public, we should not expect a direct effect on output and prices; the money we have postulated is required by the public to hold, not to spend. When the increase is brought about by the monetary authorities, we may expect direct effects on spending. Increased spending in times of unemployment is more likely to result in increased output than in increased prices, while in times of full employment, by definition, output cannot be increased without changing techniques of production.

THE QUANTITY THEORY OF MONEY

There are a number of concepts in economics that, like land-mines, seem to exist for the purpose of trapping the unwary. The Quantity Theory of Money is one of them. In the hands of skilful practitioners, the theory is a useful one in explaining the role of money; in less careful hands, it degenerates into a mechanical formula that conceals rather than reveals the truth. Below is set out the theory very briefly.

Money has been defined as coin, notes and bank deposits; this (as with any other definition of money) is a *stock* concept, i.e. at any particular time there is a certain amount in existence; it has a definite magnitude.

Now, money can change hands many times in the course of a year; we can measure the money value of the annual flow of final purchases of goods and services, the Gross National Product (GNP), and by dividing it by the amount of money in existence find out the average number of times money turns over in the period, i.e. its velocity of circulation.

In the example above, money was divided into GNP to arrive at the income velocity of money. This concept relates money to final purchases of goods and services. If money is divided into the value of all transactions in the economy, the transactions' velocity of money is arrived at. The latter relates to all purchases in the economy and includes intermediate purchases by firms of raw materials and fabricated parts, whereas the former relates only to finished goods.

Money (M) times its transactions' velocity of circulation (V), or MV, can be equated with the total flow of the things that are purchased for money, i.e. the volume of trade, T, multiplied by the price level, P. So we obtain

$$PT \equiv MV, \text{ or } P \equiv \frac{MV}{T}$$

This is an identity. That is, the statement is true by definition. The number of transactions times the price level must be equal to the quantity of money times its turnover.

A different interpretation can be put on this expression if we assume that V and T are constant because we assume a fully employed economy and a fixed level of imports. We can write

$$M\overline{V} = P\overline{T}$$

From this we can infer that M and P are related. The direction of causation, whether it is an increase in money pulling up prices, or an increase in prices sucking up the money supply, cannot be determined by this simple model.

An alternative way of expressing this is the so-called cash-balance equation $M \equiv kPT$. Here k is the reciprocal of V and expresses that fraction of the period's expenditure on goods and services which on average is held in the form of money. If V is 10 in a period, then average money holding is $\frac{1}{10}$.

These identities can be misleading if figures are substituted and conclusions drawn. Working with $P \equiv MV/T$, it is not legitimate to draw the conclusion that it is always the case that the price level varies directly with the quantity of money and its velocity of circulation, and indirectly with the volume of transactions. The reason for this is that we cannot assume that *M, V, P* and *T* are independent of each other. For example, it may be that, as has already been pointed out, as *M* is increased, *V* decreases because people wish to hold more money; or the increase in money could go to the company sector, which in depressed times may not want to use it; or during a depression the increase in *M* may not lead to higher prices but to rather more output and sales, i.e. an increase in *T*. It has also been pointed out that prices can increase independently of a change in the money supply or a change in the velocity of circulation.

A MORE SOPHISTICATED QUANTITY THEORY

Professor Friedman in a famous article which has been extended subsequently (1956, 1968) has attempted what he terms a 'reformulation of the quantity theory of money'. Patinkin (1972) argues that it is misleading to describe Friedman's work as a reformulation, seeing it rather as 'an elegant exposition of the modern portfolio approach to the demand for money'. Friedman sets out to explain changes in money and national income (GNP), rather than prices in general as in the old Quantity Theory.

We will not enter into the disputes mentioned above. The essence of Friedman's Monetarist approach is to state the demand for money as a function of the price level, the rate of change of prices, various interest rates and a number of other variables. The advantage of this approach is that the income velocity of money is not, as under the old Quantity Theory, a constant, but rather a variable. Given the price level, rate of change of prices, etc., the velocity of money can be predicted from the equation. The essence of the dispute between the Monetarists and others is whether the prediction of the velocity of circulation is sufficiently stable to justify the use of monetary policy to try and stabilise the economy. Because of long and uncertain time lags the Monetarists do not advocate the use of monetary control as a means of short-term control over the economy; rather they envisage some target rate of growth of money supply in line with the expected growth of the economy.

VALUE OF MONEY CONCLUSION

The seemingly innocent question of 'What determines the value of money?', or its equivalent 'What determines the general level of prices?', is, as we have seen, one that involves a description of how the economy works, and that is not a simple task. A direct linking of money and prices is now rejected, but intense debate still continues over the part that money plays in general price rises.

Summary

The inconvenience and expense of barter has led to nearly all societies using money. Barter is inefficient because it involves a double coincidence of wants, or longer transactions' chains. Barter means greater uncertainty, or alternatively more information is required. Money has taken the form of a very wide variety of items at different times and in different places, having only one thing in common, the intangible property of common acceptability within the community concerned.

The term 'money' is used for assets that act both as a means of payment and as a store of value. The term 'liquid' is the name given to assets which, while acting as a store of value, do not circulate in exchange, and in addition have the property that they can be turned into money without loss, or into a known amount of money in relation to face value. Examples of liquid assets are Treasury Bills and deposits at the National Savings Bank. The distinction between money and liquid assets is not a rigid one but will depend on law and custom in the society concerned.

In Great Britain the term 'primary money' is used for coin, notes and Bankers' Deposits at the Bank of England. 'Secondary money' consists primarily of deposits at banks. Once again what constitutes secondary money will depend on prevailing law and custom in society.

All economists are agreed in rejecting the crude Quantity Theory of Money which states that a change in the quantity of money of x per cent will necessarily lead to a like change in prices of x per cent. The effect of changes in the quantity of money on prices is not direct and proportional: there is, in the words of Keynes, 'many a slip, twixt the cup and the lip'.

The manner in which a change in the quantity of money may influence prices is a complicated one which is likely to vary at different levels of employment, according to how the increase comes about, according to the division of the increase between people with different incomes and wealth, and many other complicating interactions and relationships.

The above remarks are particularly relevant to the short run, which is our main concern. The long-run relationship between money and prices may have some simpler relationship. Keynes (1936, p. 306) regarded this as a question for historical generalisation, rather than pure theory. He saw the tendency for the long-run course of prices to be nearly always upward as due to the fact that when money is relatively abundant, wages rise, and when money is relatively scarce, some means is found to increase the effective quantity of money.

Note

1 The bank's gross figures for deposits and advances are adjusted to allow for sterling transit items. These transit items appear in an individual bank's balance-sheet both as credit items (e.g. Standing Orders) and debit items (e.g. cheques in course of collection). When banks' figures are aggregated, these items may give rise to double-counting. It is assumed that 60 per cent of the total value of debit items less credit items affects deposits and this proportion is therefore deducted from gross deposits with the remaining 40 per cent added to advances.

2
The financial system

I want to stress one very important point – often neglected or glossed over in abstract discussion. This is that monetary policy is conducted within a particular framework of institutions and markets. This framework provides opportunities, of course, but it also creates constraints.
The Jane Hodge Memorial Lecture by the Governor of the Bank of England, reported in the *Bank of England Quarterly Bulletin*, March 1971.

This chapter aims to give a broad background to the financial system and details of recent changes. It starts with the economic meaning of saving and investment and the part played by financial intermediaries in these processes. It then looks at changes that occurred in the 1960s, leading up to the new arrangements introduced in 1971, and outlines some of the consequences of the new arrangements. The final section looks briefly at the statistical information that is available.

Saving and investment

Saving is commonly thought of as a positive act: a person purposely puts aside so much of his income in a particular savings scheme. The economist defines saving rather differently, and this has been the source of much confusion. The economic view of saving is to regard it as *the act of not consuming out of current resources*. Thus if a person spends £4,000 out of an income of £5,000 in a particular year, his savings in that year will be regarded as £1,000. This is so even if the person intends to spend this £1,000 as soon as the new year has started. In year one £4,000 was spent and £1,000 was not spent, i.e. saved; in year two in this example the £1,000 of expenditure will be added to his other outlays in that year and when deducted from his income will give a new figure for savings. This figure may well be negative, indicating that in year two expenditure exceeded income: either previous savings were run down, as in this example, or borrowing took place.

Investment can also be used with different meanings, and in particular may refer to buying financial securities or buying capital goods. In economics the word 'investment', used without further qualification, usually refers to buying capital goods and will be so used in this text.

The act of saving and the act of investment need not be performed by the same sets of people, or from the same motives. One of the main functions of financial intermediaries is to bring savers and investors together and to marry the interests of debtors and creditors. We are all to some extent debtors and creditors. If you pay rent or rates in advance you are a creditor, if in arrears a debtor, most households are in debt to the milkman if they settle weekly, and so on. Debts and credits of this type are not of great economic significance; it is when we come to bank loans, hire purchase, house loans and a host of other financing that the importance of intermediaries becomes apparent. These are important functions, and one of the problems of developing countries is to try and build up this financial apparatus. It is not easy, as the history of financial failures and crises of developed countries shows. Many developing countries have an outflow of capital from their wealthy citizens partly because the mechanism whereby this money can be invested safely at home is lacking. The complete absence of financial intermediaries would mean that investment can only be undertaken on a direct basis – lending to an individual for use in his business – and that is very risky. It is relatively easy to duplicate the structure of financial intermediaries, much more difficult to duplicate the web of confidence and trust that gives such a system stability.

Two basic methods of financial intermediation can be distinguished. The first method is a brokerage operation whereby the assets of the lenders are passed on to the borrowers. When the transaction is complete the intermediary ceases to have an interest. Thus government securities and company securities are of this kind, with stock exchanges performing most of the matching operations. In the case of some government securities these may be purchased through a post office or other institution, but again these institutions are merely acting as brokers.

The other method of intermediation is where the institution forms a cushion between the borrower and the lender. The lender places money with the institution and in return receives some claim against the institution. In its turn the institution lends in various ways to the ultimate borrower. Banks, insurance companies, building societies, pension funds and unit trusts are important examples of this kind. A lender to a financial intermediary of this type has no say over the disposal of his money – he is buying the expertise and honesty of management. Lending to a bank or building society has the important property of increasing the liquidity of the lender, and of the economy. To lend a person £1,000 towards the purchase of a house can mean that your money is tied up for a very long period. The bank or building society will normally repay your deposit on demand, although they may have lent long term, since they arrange their affairs so as to meet demands for withdrawals.

The advantages of financial intermediation

The outstanding advantage of intermediation is efficiency. Without it investment must largely depend on the resources of the individual owner; borrowing, where it is possible, is likely to be at extremely high rates of interest.

From the lender's point of view efficiency is due to the institution being able to spread its resources and so reduce the risk of a complete loss of capital.[1] The collapse of a company in which a saver has invested all his capital can result in the total loss of his savings, whereas the financial intermediary has a portfolio of other investments to cushion the loss. Financial intermediaries can also bring economies of scale in purchasing assets and in building up expertise.

For the borrower efficiency is due to being able to tap a wider market for funds at lower cost. He is able to arrange his borrowing closer to the optimum.

No real distinctions have been made so far between different kinds of financial intermediary; in particular banks have been treated as just another intermediary. In future chapters we shall examine the justification for doing so, and see if there is something special about banks that merits special attention. This question has its mirror image in Chapter 1, where it was asked whether money was special and therefore merited separate attention, or whether it was necessary to have regard to a much wider range of financial assets. If money is in some sense 'unique' we need to pay special attention to banks since the liabilities of banks are part of the money supply; if it is the wider set of financial assets that are crucial to the welfare of the economy, then the set of institutions concerned with issuing these assets needs to be considered.

Changes during the 1960s

Banking in the 1960s underwent considerable change. There was a tremendous growth of foreign banks setting up branches in Great Britain – partly to service international companies and partly to operate in the Euro-currency markets. When the Committee on the Working of the Monetary System (1959), the Radcliffe Report as it is known after its Chairman, reported, it was able to say that the domestic business of these foreign banks was negligible, but by the end of a decade it was rivalling that of the clearing banks. There was also the growth of new 'banking-type' institutions and the enlargement of the functions performed by established financial intermediaries. In general it was only the clearing banks that were subject to controls by the Bank of England, although requests were extended to all banks and finance houses in the late 1960s. Undoubtedly this fact helped to account for the relative stagnation of the clearing banks while many of the competing institutions showed rapid expansion. In practice, matters were more complicated as the clearing banks adopted many of the practices of their rivals by using subsidiary companies.

A distinction must be made between clearing banks, or more widely, deposit banks; they have been labelled retail banks and non-deposit or wholesale banks. The former are concerned, *inter alia*, with the operation of the payments mechanism, whereas wholesale banks have little to do with the payments mechanism, being mainly concerned with the financial intermediary side: accepting deposits which cannot usually be transferred by cheque and making loans. The term 'wholesale banks' covers a variety of institutions.

There was, until the 1970s, a fairly sharp division between the way clearing and non-deposit banks operated. Clearing banks, in a way that will be outlined in greater detail in subsequent chapters, maintained cash and liquid asset reserves and used the discount market to accommodate surplus funds and to ease cash shortages. The Bank of England stands in the background as lender of last resort. The non-deposit banks in general held much lower reserves of cash and liquid assets; they sought safety in matching the maturities of deposits and liabilities so that if nobody defaults it is a self-liquidating process. In this 'Christmas tree' version, as it has been labelled, an institution seeks some degree of matching between the term deposits which it seeks to attract and the length of time it is willing to make loans. The longer the length of time needed to claim a deposit, the higher the rate of interest the institution will offer. Non-deposit banks make little use of the discount market, either when they are short of funds or when they have surplus funds; instead they tend to operate in the parallel money markets where yields (and, as it turned out, risk) are higher. The term 'parallel money markets' covers deposits with local authorities, balances with other UK banks, inter-bank loans and a newer and growing system of negotiable certificates of deposit. The latter, as the name implies, are term deposits made with banks which may be negotiated to a third party in the event that the original depositor requires funds before the term of the deposit has elapsed. Rates of interest in the parallel money markets are extremely volatile, depending on the day-to-day supply and demand for funds – on occasions the rate for overnight money has worked out as over 100 per cent when expressed on an annual basis.

With the change in 1971, details of which are given below, some of the above distinctions have become blurred. Clearing banks, for example, now accept term deposits and make use of the inter-bank market. A wide range of financial institutions have been brought under more formal control of the Bank of England and all banks are subject to the 12½ per cent reserve-assets ratio (see below).

'Competition and Credit Control'

The new arrangements which came into force in 1971 had two aims (*Bank of England Quarterly Bulletin*, June 1971; September 1971). The first aim was to encourage competition in the banking system and between the banking system and the rest of the financial system. The consultative document which formed the basis for the changes acknowledged that competition and innovation had been impeded by the old system.

This competition was to be fostered by ending the agreement on quantitative limits agreed between the Bank of England and the clearing banks, the abandonment of collective agreement on interest rates and the application of a reserve ratio and Special Deposit scheme across the whole banking system.

The new methods of control applied to all banks and, with slight modification, to large finance houses. At the same time changes were made in the operation of the discount market.

Under these arrangements London clearing banks are required to keep a day-to-day total of 1½ per cent of eligible liabilities in the form of cash at the Bank. All banks are required to keep a day-to-day minimum ratio of reserve assets to liabilities of 12½ per cent. Special Deposits may be called for which in effect makes the 12½ per cent ratio variable. In general the eligible liabilities are sterling deposits, so that foreign banks are controlled only in respect of their sterling business and not their business conducted in foreign currencies. The move from a 28 per cent liquid asset ratio to a 12½ per cent ratio was not as dramatic as it sounds, as the crucial consideration is the definition of assets which the Bank allows to be counted as eligible paper. In particular till money of the banks can no longer be counted as reserve assets. Details of these changes will be found in later chapters.

The second aim was to usher in a new era of monetary policy. This seems to be part of the see-saw that we have seen in the post-war period of primary reliance either on monetary policy or on fiscal policy.

These monetary aims were to be achieved in the main by allowing interest rates to respond more readily to market forces: the Bank would no longer automatically intervene to stabilise rates.

Changes since 1971

First, we have now begun to see the clearing banks pay market rates of interest for large sums of money acceptable on a time basis. These may be either straight deposits or by the issue of negotiable certificates of deposit. The acceptance of large deposits for a longer term than seven days is taking a leaf out of the non-deposit banking system and could herald a movement towards a balance-sheet banking concept whereby loans and deposits tend to be matched by maturity.

Second, commercial banks are moving away from their traditional overdraft system (where interest is only payable on the day-to-day balance outstanding). Before 1971 they ventured into personal loans and, usually with some pressure from the monetary authorities, into the finance of investment in agriculture and industry, together with export and ship-building finance. Sometimes this lending was done by bank finance channelled through special institutions, for example the Industrial and Commercial Finance Corporation (ICFC) and the Finance Corporation for Industry (FCI). There has been a further extension of lending to business since 1971 but, perhaps inevitably, this is still criticised as inadequate. The provision of term loans is not necessarily disadvantageous to industry, as overdraft limits, particularly to small companies, were sometimes subject to drastic curtailment in a credit squeeze. It may also be the case that a term loan may be easier to tie in with fixed capital investment since the terms of the loan may be geared to the expected cash flow of the project. In this way companies' borrowing powers can be increased.

Third, there has been a big increase in the clearing banks' sterling certificates of deposit and activity in inter-bank loans. These activities concerned both money borrowed and lent. They have also increased their activities in foreign currency deposits.

Fourth, the ending of the agreement on common interest rates by the commercial banks has resulted in the hoped-for greater competition, both between the banks and between banks and other financial institutions.

Fifth, on the money market as a whole we have seen a sharp increase in interest rates and greater variability.

Sixth, there was a financial crisis in 1973–4 of very serious proportions which brought down a number of major secondary banking concerns and property companies, and but for massive Bank assistance could have led to widespread financial collapse. Inflation accelerated in the period after 1971, reaching an annual rate of 25 per cent in 1975. Of course the financial ills of the 1970s cannot all be blamed on the changes that have been outlined. There is now general recognition that mistakes were made in this period and a number of changes have been made as a consequence (to be outlined later).

Statistical information

The amount of financial information available since the Radcliffe Report of 1959 has shown a large increase – it is still woefully inadequate. It is no surprise that economic management of the economy has such a bad record in the post-war period. For much of the time we have been in the position that is analogous to judging a company by looking at its profit and loss statement and ignoring the balance-sheet and other information.

The equivalent of the profit and loss statement for the economy is the Blue book of *National Income and Expenditure*, published by HMSO. This is the sum of all incomes accruing to the inhabitants of a country, whether as wages, salaries, profits, interest or rent, from their contribution to production. The interest is not so much in the aggregate totals as in the detailed breakdown in the many pages of the Blue book. The importance of these tables should not be overlooked – they were first produced in time of war in 1940 as an emergency measure.

But the Blue book tables are only a part of what has come to be termed social accounts. Rudiments of this other information is beginning to appear, some in the Blue book and some in other sources, but the accounts have still to be integrated and produced so that they cross-check with each other.

Another way of looking at the economy is via input–output tables which retrieve the flows of intermediate products in the economy which get washed out of the Blue book tables. Occasional tables have been produced for Britain, but they are so out of date and irregular as to have little practical use.

Figures for the distribution of income and wealth are required. Income figures do appear in the Blue book, both before and after tax, but they have to be interpreted with care since the figures are based on income-tax returns, and some income does not get allocated. Wealth figures hardly exist; those that do are based on mortality multiplier methods using death statistics – a method subject to a great deal of uncertainty. The recent work of the permanent Royal Commission on the Distribution of Income and Wealth has led to improvements in this area which will, it is hoped, be incorporated in the official statistics.

The financial counterpart to an input-output table is a flow-of-funds statement which retrieves the financial transactions made between the various sectors of the economy. Some information on flows is appearing but much remains to be done.

Finally, we have national balance-sheets. Information on the stock of assets and their ownership at a point in time would round off the social income accounts. An official account of the progress being made with balance-sheet data can be found in Reid (November 1976).

Social accounting, as opposed to national accounting, is used to denote the activity of designing and constructing a system of accounts which will embrace all the ramifications of an economy, as far as these are measurable, and so would include all the accounts mentioned. While work has been done on the theoretical problems and parts of some of these accounts are in hand, there is clearly a long way to go. The effort to get consistency between the parts, with cross-checking of results, would of itself be valuable. If one looks at any science it is often the case that advances were made as a result of observations spread over long periods of time, or of immense effort put into the collection of data, for example Newton's revolutionary work had a couple of centuries of prior observations to build on. Current weather prediction (reasonably accurate on a macro scale) is based on thousands of observations taken every few hours all over the world. Our own economic data sources are puny in comparison. In the words of Stone and Stone (1964, p. 113), who have done so much to produce our own *National Income and Expenditure* tables, and have advanced the work of social accounts:

In other words, for a theory to be meaningful it must have empirical consequences and for it to be useful these consequences must relate to observable phenomena. Thus useful theories cannot be developed independently of what can be observed any more than useful facts can be established without some regard to theoretical considerations. Facts and theories meet in analysis. The combination of the two is essential if economics is to progress, since it is neither a pure subject, like mathematics, of which one does not ask that the theories should be applicable to actual phenomena, nor is it a collection of facts, like the object of a junk heap, of which one does not ask how they are related. For 'balanced growth' in economics it is necessary to keep the facts and theories in line so that they can be related to one another.

Summary

Financial intermediaries act to bring savers and investors together and to marry the interests of debtors and creditors; they do this either by acting as brokers or more usually in a developed economy by offering depositors liquid claims against themselves. The outstanding advantages of intermediaries are efficiency and cheapness. Changes leading to the new policy of 'Competition and Credit Control' in 1971 have been detailed and some of the important effects listed. Finally, some of the shortcomings of current statistics were given.

Note

1 The reduction of risk comes mainly from the inclusion of securities and investments whose returns are relatively uncorrelated with those already held, not from an increase in numbers of investments *per se*. For example, a portfolio of 100 securities whose returns rise and fall together give little more protection than a single security.

3
The Bank of England

A catalogue of changes and developments in the position and character of the Bank of England, over, say, the last forty years, looks impressive; but it cannot conceal the fact that all too often, if not indeed typically, they have failed to match the pace of change in the external situation which they were supposed to meet.
M. J. ARTIS (1965), *Foundations of British Monetary Policy.*

Today the Bank of England (referred to as the Bank) together with the central government make up the sector termed the 'monetary authorities'.

Starting out as a joint-stock business venture of rather dubious quality in 1694, the Bank soon developed into the Bank of the Government and achieved a position of some importance in monetary affairs. Since relations between the Government and the Bank have therefore grown up as a result of long association, an explanation of these relations is not to be found by examination of legislation. This 'club-like' atmosphere is typical of the British monetary system; rules are obeyed not because of laws, but because of conventions. It can form a source of strength. Modifications can come about gradually without the need for changes in statutes which may confer on the change a dramatic character it does not warrant. The converse of this is that opportunities for the legislature to have full-scale debates on the institutions are removed.

The organisation of the Bank of England

The effective managing body of the Bank now consists of the Governor, the Deputy Governor, and four full-time Executive Directors. There are a further twelve part-time Directors. The Governor and the Deputy Governor are appointed for five years, the Directors for four years. All can be re-appointed.

The part-time Directors are apointed for their expertise in industry, commerce, banking or trade-union affairs, and may be called upon by the Governors for advice on any problem in which they have qualifications. In addition they attend a weekly meeting: the 'Court' as it is called.

The main work of the Bank is done through committees, of which the principal one is the Committee of Treasury. This committee is the policy-making body of the Bank and receives the reports of all other committees before they are submitted to Court. Membership consists of the Governor, his Deputy, and five other Directors.

No mention has been made of the Bank of England Act of 1946 whereby the State acquired the whole of the capital stock of the bank and brought it into public ownership. Formal powers are written into the Act whereby the Treasury may from time to time give such directions to the Bank as, after consultation with the Governor of the Bank, it thinks necessary in the public interest. In essence this provision has not changed the working of the system, which is one based on persuasion and discussion, and one in which the use of coercive powers is considered foreign. The Bank was, under this Act, also endowed with statutory powers to direct the affairs of the commercial banks. Again, compulsion is relegated to the background, and directives are issued only after consultation with the commercial banks.

Functions of the Bank of England

A look at a simplified statement of the Bank shows up many of its functions (see Table 3.1). The division between the issue and banking departments is historical. The number of notes in circulation is, as we shall see, whatever the public demands at any time. Notes are *not* issued to finance government expenditure. (This matter will be taken up in more detail later.) We note here the function of the Bank to maintain a sufficient supply of notes to meet whatever is the demand for them.

The function of the Bank, as banker, is brought out by items (2), (4) and (5) in the statement. The relative smallness of the sums appearing under these items should not mislead one into underestimating the importance of the banking function. The Bank is providing for its customers a wide range of services, analogous to those offered by commercial banks to their customers, with the difference that the main customers of the Bank are the Government, other banks (both home and foreign), some of the financial intermediaries and international organisations.

Bankers' Deposits refer to the accounts of the commercial banks. They

Table 3.1

Bank of England statement as at December 1976 (figures in £m.)

Issue Department			
(1) Notes in circulation	6,858	(6) Government securities	5,952
Notes in banking department	17	Other securities	923
	6,875		6,875
Banking Department			
(2) Bankers' Deposits	325	(6) Government securities	1,905
(3) Special Deposits	1,806	(7) Advances and other accounts	640
(4) Public Deposits	17	Premises, etc.	84
(5) Reserves and other accounts	499	Notes and coin	18
	2,647		2,647

Source: Bank of England Quarterly Bulletin, *vol. 17, no. 1, March 1977, table 1.*

form the commercial banks' cash reserves. Inter-bank indebtedness between London clearing banks will be settled by drawing on Bankers' Deposits, and more important transactions between the clearing banks (and their customers) and the Government will be reflected in withdrawals or replenishments of these deposits.[1] The cash reserve of the London clearing banks is kept at a figure of 1½ per cent of their eligible liabilities, so that the figure of Bankers' Deposits will not show great variation; a surplus of cash may be loaned to the discount houses at 'call or short notice', and likewise a deficit may be met by calling in some of these loans. Alternative use might be made of the inter-bank market. This should not be allowed to obscure the importance of Bankers' Deposits and the function of the Bank to exercise monetary control over the banks and other financial institutions.

The word 'public' has been used to denote all individuals and institutions outside the monetary sector. The term 'Public Deposits', item (4) in the statement, means, however, Government Deposits. Once again the smallness of the account should not be allowed to mislead the reader. The account is deliberately kept to a working balance. The Government does not as a rule borrow from the Bank, with the minor exception that small sums may be borrowed overnight, by way of 'ways and means advances', to meet residual requirements. A deficit will be made up by the issue of government securities, either Treasury Bills or bonds, and likewise a surplus will be used to buy securities, i.e. fewer securities will be offered on the market. The Bank itself manages the sale of purchases of these securities on behalf of the Government.

Special Deposits, item (3), are also deposits by banks, but in this case they are not allowed to treat these deposits as cash, or as liquid assets. This is a recent form of monetary control, which will be dealt with more fully later on.

Other accounts, item (5), covers the accounts of discount and acceptance houses, of overseas central banks and of such bodies as the International Monetary Fund. In addition the Bank keeps accounts for a few individuals, amongst them its staff, and for a few private and public companies – a legacy from the days when the Bank was active in general banking.

Item (7), 'Advances and other accounts', points the way to one of the Bank's crucial functions, that of lender of last resort. This means that any institution, with the privilege of access to the Discount Office of the Bank, with 'eligible paper' (e.g. Treasury Bills) knows that the Bank will accept them as collateral for a loan. The Minimum Lending Rate (MLR, called Bank Rate prior to 1972) is the rate at which the Bank normally offers assistance at last resort; it was announced by the Court of Directors, customarily on Thursday mornings, after the Governor had consulted with the Treasury and the Chancellor of the Exchequer. Since 1972 MLR is normally linked to the rate of discount for Treasury bills and announced on a Friday.[2] It is a key rate among short-term rates because it exercises a powerful influence on other rates. Commercial banks' rates were geared, by convention, to Bank Rate and can still be expected to move in the same direction as the MLR. When these important rates changed, market influences spread the impact through to other rates. In practice, rates given by local authorities on short-term borrowing change overnight, and financial institutions and intermediaries change their rates with different time lags, as the effect of higher rates to be obtained in the markets mentioned draws funds away from them.

Although MLR is the usual rate at which the Bank will lend at last resort, this is at its discretion. In recent years, on occasions, the discount houses have been charged more than this, and they can always be given assistance by the purchase of bills in the market by the special buyer.

Interest rates are also influenced by open-market operations in gilt-edged securities (*Bank of England Quarterly Bulletin*, June 1966):

The prices he [the Government Broker] bids in response to an offer are therefore seen as the expression of the Bank's current policy, and are closely watched by the jobbers for any sign of a change of emphasis in the policy, such as might lead the market to expect new movements in prices.

The Bank also acts as an agent for the Government in administering exchange control; it manages the Exchange Equalisation Account – which holds the reserves of gold and foreign exchange – and acts as registrar of government stocks, stocks of nationalised industries and of some local authorities, public boards and Commonwealth governments.

The size of the National Debt, the need to manage it to maintain a satisfactory structure of the debt between short-, medium- and long-term securities, together with meeting any fresh financial needs of the Government, means that the Bank has a significant monetary impact. The scale of these buying and selling operations means that whether or not the Bank is seeking to influence market rates deliberately, it will have an important impact.

The final function of the Bank is one that is not apparent from the statement shown in Table 3.1: that of financial adviser to the Government. Its leading position in the financial structure of Great Britain, and its activities and contracts abroad, mean that the Bank is in an unrivalled position to tender advice. It undertakes research to assist its advisory function.

Relations between the Bank of England and the Government

The relationship between a central bank and the executive is always a tricky one. Checks and counter-checks are needed to ensure on the one hand that the Government does not resort to the printing of notes to solve its fiscal problems, and on the other that the management of the monetary side of the economy, in so far as it is within the control of the central bank, shall be in accordance with the wishes of the Government. The personality of the Governor of the Bank, compared with that of the Chancellor of the Exchequer and his opposite number in the Treasury, is probably as good a guide as any to their influence at any one time.

Enough has been said to make it clear that the relations between the Bank and the Government are subject to change. One recent example to illustrate what has been said will be given. In the words of a former Governor, the Bank has 'the unique right to offer advice and to press such advice even to the point of nagging; but always, of course, subject to the supreme authority of the Government' (Committee on Finance and Industry, 1931).

What is not as yet clear is whether this right to offer advice should be confined within the circle of discussion of the monetary authorities, or whether the Bank should be free to make its disagreements known. The American practice in these respects is to have much fuller public discussion and to publish dissenting views. There is less search for a viewpoint on which all can agree.

Britain seems to get the worst of both worlds, in that the few times the Bank has moved to make its disagreements public may have helped to make the situation (it is usually one of confidence in the pound) worse, and in addition have had all the appearance of trying to coerce the Government to its point of view. Either the adoption of the convention that disagreements are fought out in private, or much fuller publication of information and views, would seem to be a better solution. The Bank, until the publication since December 1960 of its *Quarterly Bulletin*, was notorious for the secrecy with which it conducted its operations. The *Bulletin* has done much to enable an informed discussion of monetary issues to take place.

The supervision of the UK financial system

The unhappy financial history of the first part of the 1970s included the collapse of a number of non-deposit or fringe banks and other financial institutions, and high rates of inflation, reaching 25 per cent in 1975.

There were many factors contributing to this situation. Credit control in the 1960s had driven many sound borrowers to the secondary markets. After 'Competition and Credit Control', the banks were able to win many of these customers back, leaving less creditworthy borrowers for the fringe section. Another development was the widespread use by a wide range of institutions, both for surplus funds and borrowing, of the parallel money market, to be described in Chapter 6. Borrowing on these markets carries considerable risk that funds will dry up in a crisis, and as a consequence interest rates are driven to very high levels: rates equivalent to over 100 per cent expressed on an annual basis are not unknown. Most of the so-called 'fringe banks' were registered under Section 123 of the Companies Act, 1967, and formally registered with the Department of Trade, not with the Bank, although the Department of Trade had no formal powers to examine the quality of the registered business. Revell (1975, p. 8) puts subsidiary blame on the rapid expansion in the population of banks in London in the 1960s which had the effect of diluting the number of skilled staff, the inadequacies of staffing being exposed in the chillier financial climate of 1973–4. On top of these changes the Government tried to stimulate the economy by increasing the money supply and so making borrowing cheaper. As it turned out, industry responded very little to the stimulus and much of this money found its way into the property and stock markets. Over all there was a serious lack of information and data about these trends in the economy. When, at the end of 1973, the Government took action to contain the serious situation which was then apparent, principally by checking the growth of the money supply and placing restrictions on commercial rents, the weaknesses of the system were exposed. The threatened collapse of many secondary banks, with the possibility that they would pull down established banks and other financial institutions in their wake, led the Bank to organise assistance which came to be called the 'life-boat'. This operated so that a secondary bank which found itself unable to borrow on the markets to meet its maturing obligations could, through its main clearing bank, have funds channelled to it. In turn the business of an institution receiving assistance in this way was monitored. About thirty institutions were helped in 1974 and many more supported under individual arrangements from their clearing banks, the Bank or other sources.

While the assistance offered by the life-boat operation is expected to continue (from 1978) for a number of years, most of the supported institutions have been reconstructed in various ways to strengthen their position. More permanent measures have been introduced. Bank regulation has been changed in a way which will be outlined in this section and proposals have been made to licence and regulate all deposit-taking institutions. Details will be given in Chapter 6. An account of these developments, on which this section gratefully draws, is given in the *Bank of England Quarterly Bulletin* (June 1975 and June 1978) and George Blunden (1976).

We are concerned mainly with the role of the Bank in supervision of the financial system. This role, in this period, is not clear cut. There are those who would largely exonerate the Bank from blame on the grounds that formal management of the fringe banks was not, as we shall see, vested with them and information was inadequate. Opposing this point of view are those who hold that the Bank was implicated since it is one of the main partners in the sector labelled the monetary authorities which has responsibility for the over-all regulation of the financial system. As the Bank will now be formally concerned with the regulation of all deposit-taking institutions, the problem of divided control should not arise in the future and better information is now being collected.

The attitude of the Bank to control was stated as (*Bank of England Quarterly Bulletin*, June 1975):

Our subsequent acceptance of wider responsibilities in this field [of supervision] has been gradual and has, like our first move, been in response to market requirements or to events and has been recognised, sometimes grudgingly, as necessary or at least as tolerable by the organisations affected.

It would seem to be fair comment on this section that in this period the Bank seemed to regard itself as a fire-brigade to put out financial fires rather than fire-prevention officers to stop the financial blaze in the first place.

The preference for the 'Old Boy' approach is apparent: 'We believe that each bank is a unique institution which must be judged individually . . . our approach is personal.' This approach is contrasted with the rigid patterns and legislative sanctions of some other countries: 'The Principal's room [Principal of the Discount Office] has always seen a constant flow of visitors anxious to talk as freely and frankly as they would in the confession box or to a marriage guidance counsellor.'

There is of course a great deal to be said for flexibility of control, and the comparative soundness, until recent years, of the financial system is something the Bank can point to with pride. The other side of the coin is that informal control can, as we have seen, go seriously wrong, and it leaves the outsider with very little to go on in judging the performance of the financial sector. Secrecy, which some people see as the British disease, is maintained. However, this June 1975 article and a subsequent one (*Bank of England Quarterly Bulletin*, September 1975) are interesting in pointing out the way that controls are likely to be developed.

The need for more frequent and more comprehensive information about banks was recognised. They now institute 'prudential examinations', additional information which is not contained in the usual bank returns. These are obtained from virtually all banks registered in this country (with rather different arrangements for London and Scottish clearing banks and the British overseas banks), and includes some eighty deposit-taking institutions which include the members of the Finance Houses Association. As a rule these returns are on a quarterly basis, but in a few cases they can be monthly.

The Bank says if we had possessed the information which we now have from these returns 'a year or two earlier we would have been able – always assuming that we would have been wise enough, and that is a bold assumption – we would have been able to forestall some of the troubles to which I referred earlier'.

The final section of the June 1975 paper discusses various balance-sheet ratios. These were seen as valuable tools in forming individual assessments and for comparative purposes both at home and abroad; they reject assessment in terms of rigid balance-sheet ratios.

The first point was a distinction between capital and reserves needed to provide for the infrastructure and to protect depositors. Capital resources should normally cover infrastructure items on a one-to-one basis, although clearing banks with their many small prime sites which can be realisable easily have rather less restrictive conditions. The term *infrastructure* covers premises, equipment (unless leased), trade investments, goodwill and investments in subsidiaries.

Capital resources are defined as the total of paid-up share capital, reserves, loan capital and provisions against advances, deferred tax and minority interests.

Free capital resources are the capital resources less the book value of the infrastructure. Clearing banks, as noted, need not include the full value of premises.

The adequacy of capital may be assessed in various ways. A common method is to take the ratio of capital and resources to total deposits. The Bank prefers a ratio of free capital resources, thus excluding the infrastructure, to total deposits. It appears to have a figure of 10 per cent in mind as a basic guide-line for acceptance houses and similar banks, but it makes it clear that this is only a rough guide-line and a more satisfactory measure can be provided by sub-dividing capital according to risk. The risks that the Bank has in mind are that full capital values may not be obtainable in the event of a forced sale, and the risk of default. Accordingly the Bank came up with the following categories:

(1) *Risk-free*, e.g. cash and balances with the Bank of England, advances to, or guaranteed by, the UK public sector and advances to UK-listed banks.

(2) *Forced-sale risks*, e.g. Treasury Bills, local authority bills, British government and other public-sector stocks, eligible bank bills, certificates of deposit with UK-listed banks.

(3) *Credit risks*, e.g. balances with other banks, advances other than to the UK public sector.

(4) *Forced-sale and credit risks*, e.g. certificates of deposit with other banks, trade bills, leased assets and other portfolio investments.

Having spelt out the categories of risk, the next step might be to set minimum ratios for each kind of risk category for each kind of institution to observe. This step is not taken; the reason given may be labelled the 'esoteric' approach to bank control. We are told that the amount of capital needed to protect depositors against loss should first of all take account of the level of earnings – a dubious proposition since it may be argued that protection should be related to the likely worst results of the institution, *not* to its earnings at any one time. The argument then continues:

> The acceptable relationship of free capital resources to risk assets to be sought will vary for different categories of banks and even from bank to bank within a category. It will need to take account of each bank's historic experience, the spread of business and other special factors which might affect future profits.

The logical, and therefore readily understandable, approach of setting ratios for *each type* of institution is rejected in favour of ratios for *individual* institutions, with the implication that only the Bank has the knowledge and experience of individual institutions to apply these ratios. Informed criticism of monetary management is thus made extremely difficult except as an historic exercise, since the ratios to be observed by each institution, and whether these have been changed, will be unknown.

A distinction is drawn between the concept of 'capital adequacy' that has just been described and the concept of 'liquidity', although the closeness of these concepts is noted. It is possible to imagine capital resources adequate and matched but inadequate in the sense that, say, a shortfall in inward cash flow would leave the institution in a difficult position because its assets were not sufficiently liquid and had to be realised at a loss.

Evaluation of a bank's liquidity position will normally be done separately for sterling and foreign currencies. They regard an examination of liquidity as a vital part of the examination of any bank. As before, the idea of uniform ratios for classes of institution is rejected in favour of a piecemeal approach.

Discussion about profitability, capital adequacy and liquidity are to be held annually with each clearing bank and quarterly with all other UK-registered banks. The 'confessional' box looks like being very busy.

Summary

The effective management of the Bank is in the hands of a small group: the Governor and his Deputy, who are appointed for five years, and four full-time directors appointed for four years. They are assisted by twelve part-time directors.

The Bank manages the note issue, acts as banker to the Government, other banks and many financial intermediaries and international organisations. It exercises monetary control as agreed by the monetary authorities, of which the Bank itself forms an important part. One of its crucial functions is that of lender of last resort to the discount houses, which together with its large-scale operation in the financial markets gives the Bank influence over interest rates. The Bank manages the Exchange Equalisation Account and operates on the foreign exchange markets and acts as registrar of government, nationalised industries and a number of public authority stock issues. Finally, the Bank, because of its leading position in the financial structure of Great Britain, and its activities and contacts abroad, tenders advice to the Government on economic matters.

The Bank's management, or lack of management, of the financial sector outside the clearing banks is the function that has been most criticised in recent years. The steps that have been introduced to strengthen this control have been outlined.

Notes

1 For example, if Smith pays the Inland Revenue a £100 cheque for tax owed, the joint-stock bank will debit Smith's account and will in turn have its Bankers' Deposits account at the Bank of England debited in favour of the Exchequer.

2 In October 1972 the Bank made new arrangements for determining and announcing MLR. In normal circumstances this rate was to be set at ½ per cent above the average rate of discount for Treasury bills at the most recent tender, rounded to the nearest ¼ per cent above. The rate would be announced each Friday afternoon with the results of the Treasury Bill tender. This move was seen as one where MLR could respond to market forces without it being interpreted as signalling major shifts in monetary policy. The Bank could, with the approval of the Chancellor, go back to the old arrangements when it wished to signify a shift in monetary policy. It would then announce the rate on Thursdays independently of the Treasury Bill rate. The Bank has in fact used this power on a number of occasions.

4
The discount market

Because that is the way the market has always been, going back a long way.
Verbal evidence of the London Discount Market Association to the Radcliffe Committee of 1959.

It is easy to imagine the despair of people when they attempt to understand the British monetary system. Because it has grown up over so many years, it appears haphazard, full of illogicalities. If the system were being constructed afresh, the monetary system would probably appear simpler and more tidy. For example, the functions performed by the discount houses could be performed in other ways; it was, however, the considered opinion of the Radcliffe Report that they performed effectively and efficiently and it seemed unlikely that savings in cost or manpower would result from a change. With these preliminaries in mind, we will consider the organisation and functions of the discount houses.

Structure of the London discount market

In October 1976 the London Discount Market Association consisted of thirteen houses. In addition, there were also three smaller firms known as discount brokers, doing a similar kind of business, as well as six banks which had a largely autonomous money-trading department. Finally, there were six firms of stockbrokers known as money brokers who specialise as intermediaries between jobbers and institutions with stocks to lend; they also borrow funds to enable jobbers to carry stocks.

The discount houses stand as an intermediary between the Government and the Bank of England in the sense that we have seen that the Government borrows (other than overnight) not from the Bank but by issuing securities which are channelled chiefly through the discount houses. In a similar manner, the discount houses stand as an intermediary between the Bank of England and the commercial banks; funds required by the latter are channelled chiefly through the discount market rather than by the commercial banks borrowing directly from the Bank.

The discount houses are commercial bodies, and like banks they aim to make a profit by borrowing money more cheaply than they lend it. They operate for the most part in the short end of the market, and operate almost entirely on money which is borrowed on even shorter terms than they lend. They are able to do this in safety because the discount houses enjoy access to the Bank as lender of last resort.

Source of funds

Normally the cheapest source of funds for the discount houses is provided by borrowing 'money at call and short notice' from the clearing and other commercial banks. This money, as the name implies, can be recalled by the banks either immediately or at very short notice and explains how the commercial banks are able to maintain such a small cash ratio, in spite of differences, day to day, in the calls for cash. The banks safeguard their position by requiring the discount houses to pledge assets against these loans somewhat in excess of the discount houses' borrowing. This has two effects: one is to safeguard the banks against a fall in the capital value of the pledged securities; the second is to ensure caution in the discount houses' business since this margin of cover has to be provided out of their own resources. They also, as we have noted, have access to the Bank of England; funds borrowed from the Bank will normally be charged at the same rate as the MLR, which is a penal rate for the discount houses. However, in recent years if the Bank wishes to influence the money market in a particular way, it can charge the discount houses less or more than this.

Functions of the London discount market

The discount houses are important for smoothing flows of money, and in influencing interest rates. They undertake to 'cover the tender' of Treasury Bills issued weekly by the Government. This means that, however many Treasury Bills the Government decides to issue, they can be sure that, failing other buyers offering better terms, the discount houses will take them up. In turn the discount houses sell the bills to commercial banks in suitable maturities and to the Bank and other holders. The discount houses are only able to give this undertaking to cover the tender because they know that if they are unable to borrow funds from other sources, they can borrow from the Bank. The discount houses do not normally keep the bills they buy until they mature, but sell them, chiefly to the commercial banks, as and when the banks require them.

The discount houses, as well as channelling finance to the Government, provide finance to the private sector by discounting bills of exchange. They also act as jobbers in short-term government bonds. Historically, commercial bills should be mentioned first, because the discount houses grew up to provide discount for them. It was not until the 1880s that the Treasury Bill came into existence and much later before it came into widespread use.

The bill of exchange is an old device whereby the seller of goods draws on the purchaser of the goods an order for the sum of money involved to be paid on demand or at a fixed time in the future. Once the purchaser 'accepts' the bill by signing on the face of it, the seller is able, if the acceptor is sufficiently well-known, to rediscount the bill through the money market. The purchaser does not have to pay for the goods immediately and the seller, for a small discount, can obtain his money as soon as he sells the goods. The convenience of this in times past, when delivery of goods, particularly between countries, took months, is obvious. Hence also the growth of acceptance houses which specialised in accepting bills, that is adding their names to a bill and so making themselves liable to pay the bill if the original acceptor defaulted. Once a bill had been accepted by a reputable house, it became an easily negotiable instrument.

So convenient a device has been widely adopted by Governments, by means of Treasury Bills. These have no counterpart in the despatch of goods, but otherwise are similar to bills of exchange, being promises to pay a stated amount, usually ninety-one days from the time of issue. In amount the Treasury Bill outweighs the commercial bill in importance. The amount of the former outstanding in the market at any one time can rise to £4,000 million or more. Paradoxically, the commercial bill may become important during a credit squeeze. An obvious source of funds to certain traders if they are denied bank credit is to make more use of bills of exchange; that this was done is shown clearly in the figures of amounts of bills outstanding. The new regulations on 'Competition and Credit Control' in 1971 limited banks' commercial bills that could count as reserve assets, that is, those that were eligible for rediscount at the Bank of England, to a maximum of 2 per cent of total eligible liabilities.

The Treasury Bill market

It remains to outline briefly the market structure for Treasury Bills. These are issued weekly, tenders (minimum sum £50,000) are invited every Friday for the bills to be issued in the following week. In general, the highest tenders, i.e. those offering the nearest to the face-value of the bills, will receive them. The difference between the tender price and the face-value of the bill represents the discount the Government pays for borrowing money. The quantity coming on to the market depends on two factors: the requirements of government finance, which will be considered later, and the amount of surplus funds held by government departments. These surplus funds are used for Treasury Bills – the so-called 'tap issue' – and the remaining bills are offered on tender.

The discount houses used to submit a 'syndicated bid', that is they submit a common tender price between them. This 'price', or discount, at which they will take bills is fixed somewhere between the cost of their cheapest and dearest sources of borrowed funds, that is somewhere between the cost of funds borrowed from the commercial banks and the cost of borrowing from the Bank of England at penal rate. Since 1971 each discount house now makes it own bid for as many bills as it wants. In addition, in order to cover the tender, each discount house is allotted a quota of bills and this part of the bid is at a common rate agreed by the London Discount Market Association each week. The need for a common rate is to prevent individual houses putting in a low bid which would effectively leave the others to take up the bills. In turn the Bank of England continues to act as lender of last resort on eligible paper.

Control of the discount market

Since 'Competition and Credit Control' in 1971, control over the credit extended by the discount market has been by way of agreement to hold a minimum of 50 per cent of their funds in public-sector debt. The categories of debt included in this ratio are British and Northern Ireland Treasury Bills, company tax reserve certificates, local authority bills and bonds, and British government, British government-guaranteed and local authority stocks with not more than five years to run to maturity.

To stop any attempt by banks to engage in very short-term transactions designed to 'window-dress' their accounts in place of genuine observance of their minimum reserve ratio, the Bank has asked each house to give a firm undertaking that they would not in any circumstances be prepared willingly to engage in such transactions. The Bank reserves the right to call at any time for full information on the conduct of each house's book, as well as being concerned that the size of business bears an appropriate relationship to its capital and reserves.

Summary

The discount houses were set up originally to discount commercial bills. Today Treasury Bills and dealings in other government short-term paper form the major part of their business. There are now thirteen major discount houses enjoying access to the Bank as lender of last resort and there are a number of discount brokers and money brokers doing similar work. Access to the Bank of England enables the discount market to act as an intermediary between the Government and the Bank in the sense that the Government normally borrows not directly from the Bank but by the issue of securities which are channelled through the discount market. The discount houses also stand as intermediaries between the clearing banks and the Bank of England. The clearing banks normally replenish cash not by borrowing from the Bank but by calling in their loans to the discount houses.

5
The commercial banks

The approach to banking supervision in the United Kingdom has been somewhat different from that in other countries, partly because of the way banking developed and partly because of our traditional disposition to use unwritten, rather than codified, systems in some areas of our national life. . . . But, as you may have heard, the UK Government recently announced that they had decided in principle to introduce legislation which would enable the United Kingdom to provide for the prior authorisation of deposit-taking institutions, in line with the requirements of the proposed EEC directive on the harmonisation of the regulations relating to credit institutions.
Governor of the Bank of England, Speech at a Seminar on 'Banking Tomorrow', reported in the *Bank of England Quarterly Bulletin*, December 1975.

This chapter is primarily concerned with the domestic banks known as the London clearing banks. The term 'clearing banks' comes from the mechanism that has been developed for settlement of inter-bank indebtedness.[1] They operate the cheque-payment mechanism and have wide branch networks. Other types of banks, such as merchant banks or acceptance houses and overseas banks, are important and will be looked at in the next chapter.

Structure of the London clearing banks

The structure of British banking had been stable, apart from regrouping amongst some of the smaller banks, from the 1930s up to 1968. A system existed of eleven clearing banks, dominated by the 'Big Five': Barclays, Midlands, Lloyds, Westminster and National Provincial, with Martins coming next in size of total deposits. This stability was broken early in 1968 when a merger was announced between the Westminster and the National Provincial, the smallest two of the 'Big Five', and which put them at the top in size. Shortly afterwards, Barclays, Lloyds and Martins announced their intention to merge.[2] The merger would have made them, ranked by deposits, the second biggest bank in the world, exceeded only by San Francisco's Bank of America. This triple merger was referred to the Monopolies Commission and was advised against by a majority of six to four.

A number of reasons for these mergers and attempted mergers can be given. Banking has always offered economies of scale of a kind such as the ability to offer better security to depositors by having a larger geographical spread, being better able to withstand a financial crisis, to economise on cash holdings and to offer specialist services. These well-established reasons for merging were not likely to have been important in the British case, where these banks were already of a sufficient size to reap most of these benefits. Undoubtedly the success in attracting deposits in the 1960s of other types of financial intermediary and especially foreign banks put commercial banks on the defensive. Competition amongst commercial banks for deposits was restricted in this period and as banks had competed by way of proliferating branches, undoubted economies in sites and staff could be achieved by merging. Economies could also have been expected in the expensive computers banks were then installing. The banks stressed the greater financial resources that they would command which would enable them to meet the needs, at home and abroad, of the largest industrial organisations.[3]

Commercial-bank operations

The clearing banks are profit-making institutions, drawing their revenue from the difference in rates which they pay for borrowed money (generally nil in the case of demand deposits) and the return they obtain by lending, or investing in financial securities of various kinds. The commercial banks maintain an interest-rate structure which before 1971 was tied to Bank Rate. Banks now have discretion about changes in their rates but it remains true that they are likely to follow the trend of the MLR. In Chapter 1 it has already been explained that in the United Kingdom current accounts are counted in the M1 definition of money and both current and deposit accounts in M3.

The growth of term deposits and negotiable certificates of deposits complicates matters. Term deposits should perhaps be excluded from a definition of money, at least if the term is over a certain period. The case for excluding negotiable deposits is less strong.

Banks are not confined to lending out only the money which is deposited with them. They can create money by creating claims on themselves.

For example, they may allow a customer to overdraw his account, or make him a loan. With the active participation of commercial banks in the inter-bank market since 1971, it is also possible for a bank to borrow on the inter-bank market in order to increase its own lending or portfolio. A clear knowledge of the process by which banks create credit, the limits to this process, the influence and limitations of the monetary authorities in controlling it, and the similarities and differences of other financial intermediaries in creating credit, are essential and form our chief concern in this and the next two chapters.

Creation of credit

In order to make this process clear we start with a very simplified system. When this is understood it is relatively easy to bring in real-life complications. Let us assume an economy with only one bank, where any money lent by the bank is redeposited back in the bank. Further, it is assumed that this bank has found from experience that it need only keep 20 per cent of whatever sum is deposited with it as a reserve in the case of cash being demanded back by its customers (20 per cent has been chosen to make it quite clear that our system is not intended to be a replica of the current banking system).

Stage 1 starts, we will assume, with the injection of an additional £1,000 of cash in the bank. Of this, the bank needs to keep only £200 (20 per cent) as a reserve.

Stage 2 is the process whereby the bank lends out the remaining £800, or, what amounts to the same thing, purchases securities for this amount. (Our assumption is that the whole of this £800 is redeposited back in the bank.) If we assume that holder A obtained an overdraft of £800 and paid this to holder B by cheque, then the bank makes a simple book entry. Holder A is indebted to the bank for this sum, his liability has not decreased, while the deposit account of holder B has increased by £800.

Stage 3 is a repetition of stage 2, with the bank free to lend, or buy securities, to the value of £640, keeping the remaining £160 as a reserve; and so on. The ultimate value of the credit created is given by the formula:

$$\text{total deposits created} = \frac{\text{new reserves}}{\text{percentage reserve ratio}}$$

which in our example is 1,000 × 100/20 = £5,000. An initial deposit of £1,000 has led to a 'multiplier' process whereby total deposits have increased by £5,000. Table 5.1 sets out the process in detail.

Table 5.1

Hypothetical example of the creation of bank credit

Stage	Loans and investments made (£)	Total (£)	Deposits created (£)	Total (£)	Reserves required for deposits created (£)	Total (£)
1	–	–	1,000	1,000	200	200
2	800	800	800	1,800	160	360
3	640	1,440	640	2,440	128	488
4	512	1,952	512	2,952	62.4	550.4
Final	–	4,000	–	5,000	–	1,000

From Table 5.1 we see that stage 1 is the deposit of £1,000, of which the bank needs only £200 as a reserve. Stage 2 records that a loan or investment is made by the bank of the remaining £800. This results in a return of the £800 to the bank as a deposit by another party. The bank needs to keep £160 of this as a reserve and can therefore in stage 3 make loans or investments of £640. The final result of this process after many stages have been undertaken is recorded in the bottom line, where we see that total loans and investments made by the bank come to £4,000, so deposits are up by £5,000, £1,000 of which must be kept in reserve.

The assumption of our model, that there is only one bank, does not alter our argument in any essential way. A number of banks must make sure that they keep in step in their creation of credit, otherwise one bank would lose deposits to another.

The fact that the banking system is not a completely closed system of payments leads, as we shall see, to an ability to create credit which is much below that indicated by this simple model. Before examining this point, the methods by which banks establish confidence and their reserve ratios are described.

Confidence in banks

It was mentioned earlier that banks are profit-making institutions, but they must conduct their activities so as to maintain the confidence of the public.

The traditional way for a commercial bank to maintain confidence is to keep a reserve of cash and liquid assets. When these ratios are laid down by the authorities and, most importantly, the central bank acts as lender of last resort to ensure the liquidity of the assets, a stable system can ensue. But developments, particularly since 1971, have changed this in important ways. Commercial banks have moved some way in the direction of their competitors in taking in term deposits and making fixed-term loans. Liquidity of a bank can then be assisted in two ways. One is by, more or less, matching assets and liabilities so that, for example, one-year term deposits are matched by one-year loans to customers. Another possibility is to arrange the repayment terms of a business loan to coincide with the expected cash flow from the investment. These developments mean that it is not safe to judge the liquidity of a business from its conventional balance-sheet, which excludes information on terms of loans and deposits. The liquidity provided by matching deposits and repayment terms of loans does not preclude the monetary authorities insisting on minimum reserves as well, but it is clear that these developments add complications, particularly if the authorities do not want to penalise institutions with different practices.

A third development in banking is much more inimical to control by minimum ratios. It has been described by Revell as 'perhaps the most revolutionary change to occur in banking in recent years'. (See Revell (1975), on which this section gratefully draws.) This revolutionary change is the practice whereby banks can bid for deposits on the inter-bank money market and thereby lend to customers. At one time after 1971 one-third of deposits of banks came from this source.

The fringe banking débâcle of 1973 and its aftermath showed the vulnerability of this money market. In a crisis funds dry up or are only available at very high rates of interest. Concerns which have borrowed from the market and lent at longer term may find themselves insolvent.

The implications of these developments for control of banks and other financial institutions are slowly being worked out. Control by setting reserve ratios, described in the next section, still has an important part to play but, as was detailed in Chapter 3, this is being supplemented by means of 'prudential examinations' and looking at various ratios between assets and liabilities.

Bank multiplier

It is now possible to return to the simple model set up at the beginning of this chapter in order to arrive at a version of the credit multiplier. It would be the reciprocal of the reserve ratio of 12½ per cent, that is, eight times the change in deposits. This attempt to decide the ability of the banks to create credit by some mechanical formula relating to the reserve ratio of the banks is a misleading one. Expansion of deposits is in most circumstances likely to be far below this figure. Contraction of deposits is even more circumscribed. The advantage of setting out the credit multiplier, as we have done, is so that the process whereby credit is created in the economy may be clearly understood; it should not be used to derive a ratio. A better understanding is obtained by an analysis of leakages in the flow of money in the banking system, to which we now turn.

The limits to the process of creating credit

In the simplified example used, the multiplier, or limit to credit creation or contraction, is simply determined by the formula:

$$\frac{\text{change in deposits}}{\text{percentage reserve ratio}}$$

We will consider the case of an addition to deposits but, *mutatis mutandis*, it applies to a decrease in reserves. The higher the reserve ratio, the lower will be the amount of credit that can be created. The actual reserve ratios kept by the joint-stock banks will give us the upper limit of the banks' power to create credit.[4] This limit is of theoretical interest only, for the assumption of our simplified model, namely that any money lent by the bank is redeposited back in the system, must be subject to important qualifications. The circular flow of money from the bank to *A*, *A* to *B* and *B* back to the bank, which we envisaged in our simple model, is subject to 'leakages'.

Given below are some important leakages:

First, some recipients of bank money will require cash; for them, a deposit at a commercial bank is not an acceptable means of payment. The bank has no option but to 'pay for' the asset in cash, that is to run down its deposit with the central bank. From an aggregate viewpoint the more cash the public wish to hold, the less will be the amount of bank deposits.

Second, and more importantly, transactions between banks or members of the public (using their bank accounts) and the Government result in equal and opposite movements of Bankers' Deposits. This is so, as indicated earlier, because the Government does not bank with the commercial banks. It is this fact which makes open-market operations effective. Thus the purchase of bonds from the Government by banks, or purchases from the Government by the public, reduce Bankers' Deposits. Purchases of bonds from the banks, or the public, by the Government, increase Bankers' Deposits. In a similar manner, all payments to the Government, for example tax payments, reduce Bankers' Deposits, and payments by the Government to the public increase them.

Third, we have so far been implicitly talking about a closed system. As soon as we admit the possibility of payments to foreigners, we get another leakage, as these holders are unlikely to bank with the commercial banks.

Fourth, there are a large number of foreign banks with branches in Britain. Sums that find their way to these banks represent a leakage from the commercial banking system. However, from a monetary viewpoint this transfer of assets to foreign branch banks is merely a transfer of the power to create credit from the commercial banks to these foreign banks. This important difference will be taken up in the next chapter.

As a simple illustration of the difference between flows of money between the banks and the public, and flows between the banks and the Government, let us take the balance-sheet entries for the banks: first, when they extend a loan to a customer of £100; and second, when they purchase £100 worth of securities from the Government (see Table 5.2).

Table 5.2

Result of commercial banks making a loan of £100 to a customer

Liabilities		Assets	
Deposits (i.e. credit balances of customers: represent a liability to pay by the bank)	+£100	Loans (liability on the customer to repay; i.e. an asset of the bank)	+£100

Deposits created for the public are not lost to the banking system as a whole since members of the public bank with the commercial banks: *A*, who has the added deposit originally writes a cheque to *B* – from the banks' point this is a transfer of ownership – deposits and loans still remain at + £100, and the bank can extend further credit subject to the need for sufficient reserves and no leakages.

The purchase of a security from the Government results in no change in bank liabilities, but a rearrangement of assets. Cash is down, while there is a corresponding increase in securities (see Table 5.3).

When a member of the public purchases securities from the Government with a cheque drawn on his account, bank liabilities are down by this amount, with no corresponding increase in assets of the bank, a process described earlier as a leakage.

Table 5.3

Result of commercial banks acquiring assets from the Government

Liabilities	Assets	
No change	Cash (i.e. Bankers' Deposits at the Bank of England)	–£100
	Securities	+£100

The conclusion of this section is that an initial increase in deposits of the commercial banks as a whole sets in motion an expansion of the credit structure. The banks know from experience that the bulk of this increase can be used to purchase financial instruments (investments or advances) giving a positive yield. It is not possible to deduce the size of the ultimate increase in credit by a look at the reserve ratio of the banks. The expansion is limited in a number of ways, in particular by the whole complex of operations between the Government, the banks and the public sector. Chapter 6 takes up the story at this point.

Contraction of bank deposits

The monetary authorities may try to squeeze the liquid assets of the joint-stock banks to enforce a contraction of deposits on them (see *Bank of England Quarterly Bulletin*, June 1962). This will normally take the form of open-market operations to increase the amount of government debt held outside the banking system. As we have seen, this pressure can be applied by trying to induce the non-bank public to take up Treasury Bills, or, better still, long-term debt. Alternatively, the authorities can try to increase the public's holding of non-marketable debt by, for example, offering a better return on National Savings. Such sales reduce Bankers' Deposits as they are transferred to the Government's account. As the liquidity ratio must be maintained, this will initially cause a reduction in liquid assets and in the liquidity ratio. The reactions of the banks, first in the short term, and then in the long term, to this reduction in their liquidity is outlined below.

THE SHORT TERM

The commercial banks do not borrow directly from the Bank of England. If they wish to replenish cash, they would first of all recall some of the money at call and short notice from the discount houses, or alternatively since 1971 they may seek funds in the inter-bank money market.

If loans are recalled from the discount houses, provided that they cannot get the money from elsewhere, for example from foreign banks with funds in London, they will go to the Bank of England. The MLR is, as we have seen, a penal rate for the discount houses. The effect of this borrowing from the Bank on the discount houses is therefore to reduce their profits.

The discount houses can wriggle out of this in two ways: either by borrowing more from outside the banking system by offering better rates; or by raising their rate on Treasury Bills so that more will go to outside tenderers. The result is the same: a tendency for the Treasury Bill rate to increase and for other short-term rates to follow by the market mechanism of funds seeking, other things being equal, the highest return.

If the monetary authorities do not wish market rates to rise, they can stop the process right at the start by accommodating the discount houses at market rate. The 'Special Buyer' (one of the discount houses acting for the Bank of England) will be instructed to buy Treasury Bills on the market and so release cash into the system.

The implications should be quite clear: the monetary authorities can operate either on the rate of interest or on the quantity of money. Only fortuitous circumstances will enable both the monetary target and a rate of interest target to be achieved at the same time. The authorities' policy until 1971 had been to seek to establish the rate structure they would like; after 1971 they were more willing to see market-established rates.

If the commercial banks are able to borrow from the wholesale money market, then a similar chain reaction is set up – a tendency for rates of interest to be driven up.

The above account details the short-term reactions of the commercial banks and the discount houses to a squeeze. Below are detailed the longer-term reactions.

THE LONG TERM

The simplest method for the commercial banks is, if their liquid assets are above the minimum level, merely to acquiesce in the reduction of them.

Another method open to the banks is to try and replenish their liquid assets by running down their other investments. This was done during the 1960s to a considerable extent.

Attempts by the monetary authorities to reduce the number of Treasury Bills can be overcome by the banks if they are able to substitute alternative liquid assets such as commercial and other bills, although since 1971 commercial bills eligible as reserve assets have been limited to 1 per cent of eligible liabilities.

The above account is far removed from a mechanical formula which can be applied to give us the final adjustment which a bank has to make in order to compensate for a change in deposits. The process described above whereby the banks can compensate by running down their other investments is a complicated one which can have different results in different circumstances. In order to understand this, it must be borne in mind that these portfolios are largely gilt-edged holdings in short-dated stocks with less than five years to run to maturity. These stocks can normally be realised without substantial loss. The simplest, but slowest, way to reduce these portfolios is for the banks not to renew the securities as they come up for redemption. The effect of actual sale of the stocks before maturity will vary with the identity of the other parties to the transactions.

First, if the banks' sales are taken up by the monetary authorities (they may not wish to see the established pattern of interest rates disturbed), such sales will increase the banks' liquid assets by the proceeds of the sale, leaving deposits unchanged but, of course, the banks more liquid.

Second, the sales may be made to the discount market. The discount market can finance these holdings either by selling Treasury Bills to the banks or by borrowing more call money. The effect is the same as before; there is, however, a limit to the amount of stock that the discount houses are able, or willing, to hold.

Last, the banks may sell to the general public. This reduces bank deposits and leaves liquid assets unchanged and so improves the liquid asset ratio. From the banks' point of view (but not from the point of view of monetary control), it is a less satisfactory method than the other two ways. Even so, if the public finances its purchases of stock from the banks by holding less Treasury Bills or non-marketable government debt, its deposits will be unchanged and the final effect will be the same as if the banks had sold the stock direct to the authorities.

The conclusion to this section is that attempts to control the liquid assets of the banks is subject to important qualifications. It depends in particular on the attitude of the public to holding cash and government debt, the willingness of the banks to substitute assets, and the fiscal policy being pursued by the Government. Many of the factors noted that tend to offset monetary control may only operate at certain times and be of limited duration. But time is often the essence of the problem in monetary matters. It is not surprising that other methods of control have been devised to supplement control over cash and liquid assets; to these we now turn.

Other methods of bank control

MINIMUM LENDING RATE

The use of Bank Rate (now MLR) was for a long time considered as the proper means of controlling the banks. An increase was supposed to deter borrowing from the banks since their rates were, by convention, tied to Bank Rate. Similarly, a decrease was supposed to encourage borrowing. It is worth noting that since the commercial banks do not pay interest on current accounts, an increase in interest rates means greater profit for the banks. The term 'endowment' has been coined by the *Bank Charges Report* (1967) to cover this element in bank profit.

The effects of changes in interest rates will be examined in more detail in Part III on policy. It is sufficient to say now, that at least in the circumstances of inflation which have prevailed since the war, this effect seems so weak in most sectors of the economy as not to be an effective constraint. It has always been recognised in Keynesian literature that low rates, while helpful, were not sufficient to generate business confidence in a depression. It also seems that high rates, by themselves, may not be sufficient to deter expansion in inflationary conditions – at least, within the acceptable range of movements of Bank Rate. The above remarks apply to the dearness of money, not to its scarcity: a point which is frequently confused. If borrowing can be made more difficult, the effects are immediate. If a change in MLR is used for active open-market sales of government securities it causes depositors to switch from bank deposits to government securities with consequences for bank reserve ratios. The only other way in which changing Bank Rate can affect the scarcity of money is if there is a 'liquidity effect'. This refers to the fact that banks and other institutions may be deterred from selling securities by an increase in MLR, which, if it affects other rates, will move security prices down. It is argued that the fear of having book losses will particularly deter banks from realising investments and so recouping their liquid assets. There is no indication that this has happened in recent years. Banks have run down their investments dramatically in spite of historically high levels of discount rate. As we have seen, this is not surprising because banks' investments are in securities with less than five years to run to maturity.

SPECIAL DEPOSITS

Special deposits came into being on the recommendation of the Radcliffe Committee. If the monetary authorities call for Special Deposits, the banks are required to deposit a proportion of deposits at the Bank. These, unlike ordinary Bankers' Deposits, do not count towards either the cash ratio or reserve asset ratio of the banks. These deposits earn a rate of interest which is related to the average Treasury Bill rate. Thus if banks are unduly liquid and the monetary authorities wish to limit credit, they can call for Special Deposits. As with pressure on the liquid asset ratio by open-market operations, the banks may be able to overcome the effect of this type of squeeze in exactly the same way: namely, selling securities or substituting other assets. Like other pressures on the banks, it gives them a lever, if they wish to use it, to refuse advances politely.

Special Deposits were used only in a half-hearted manner until 1971 but since then have been seen as one of the main ways of achieving control over the financial sector.

In December 1973 the Bank announced a new system of supplementary Special Deposits which required banks and finance houses to place non-interest-bearing deposits with the Bank if the interest-bearing liabilities of the institutions grow faster than a specific rate which was set initially at 8 per cent. This 'corset', as it came to be known, was therefore a return to quantitative control. The specification that the arrangements apply only to the interest-bearing liabilities excludes the current accounts of banks. The scheme was intended to give the authorities improved control over money supply and bank lending. The system was in operation until February 1975 and was reactivated in November 1976.

The effect of the arrangements in 1976 was that if the average of an institution's interest-bearing resources on the make-up days for February, March and April 1977 were to exceed the average amount outstanding on the make-up days in August, September and October 1976 by more than 3 per cent, a non-interest-bearing Special Deposit would be required to be lodged at the Bank during May 1977. The amount of the deposit depends on the amount of the excess of the interest-bearing resources: up to a 3 per cent excess, the rate is 5 per cent; between 3 per cent and 5 per cent, the rate is 25 per cent; thereafter, the rate is 50 per cent.

DIRECTIVES, REQUESTS, OR EAR-STROKING

During the Second World War and up to 1951 the banks were obliged to hold Treasury Deposit Receipts. At one stage these amounted to 40 per cent of their deposits and were a method by which the assets of the banks could be maintained at the level desired by the monetary authorities. A process of 'forced funding' was used on one occasion in 1951 (for details, see the Radcliffe Report, 1959, para. 406). In effect, the banks had to exchange £500 million of Treasury Bills for the equivalent amount of short-term bonds.

Control of the banks by requiring them to hold specific assets, as outlined above, is regarded as an exceptional measure: the process is disliked by both the central and commercial banks. Instead a process has grown up whereby the Bank of England makes requests to the banks and, more recently, to the financial sector. The procedure is sometimes called issuing directives, or more familiarly 'ear-stroking'. These 'requests', as they will be called, are conventions which the banks observe even though they have not got the force of law. The legal powers which were given to the Bank of England under the Nationalisation Act could be used for the same purpose, but the use of such powers is not the way the system is operated. The Bank of England has said that if it had to use force to coerce the commercial banks, it would regard this as a breakdown of the monetary system. For our purposes the distinction is a fine one that need not trouble us. What matters is that these requests are carried out.

These requests must take a general form such as 'Do not lend more than last year', or 'Do not lend more to hire-purchase companies'. They cannot take the form of specific requests not to lend to a particular person or company. The banks are given guidance on the amount of lending; within this constraint they are free to select the happy or unhappy customers who get, or do not get, the loans.

PRUDENTIAL EXAMINATIONS AND RATIOS

We have seen that the financial crises in 1973, which (in 1978) is still having its repercussions, forced the Bank to reconsider its regulatory role of banks and other financial institutions. Details were set out in Chapter 3.

We may expect a very gradual use and extension of this form of control, but it would be surprising if in a few years it did not form one of the major means of control over banks and the wider financial system.

Summary

The structure in Great Britain of the London clearing banks had been stable for many years until 1968, when mergers took place. The need for mergers had been partly brought about by the success of other types of financial intermediaries and foreign banks in attracting deposits, partly by the introduction of a National Giro system, and partly because of the wish to make internal economies and rationalisations, both in the number of branches and use of expensive computing and other equipment. They also wished to have larger financial resources to meet the needs of large international companies.

Banks as a whole are able to create credit because when they re-lend money that has been deposited with them a portion of this money finds its way back into the banking system and can in its turn be used to make new investments or advances. The credit multiplier is not large; it depends in particular on the whole complex of operations between the Government, the banks and the public.

It has been shown that there are a variety of methods by which the monetary authorities influence the commercial banks. These are through MLR, open-market operations. Special Deposits, supplementary Special Deposits and requests. More recently, a system of prudential examinations and ratios has been introduced. The ease with which money control can be exercised depends intimately on the whole fiscal framework, and we pursue this point in Chapter 7.

Notes

1 Strictly, an account of domestic banks should give a separate account of the Scottish clearing banks and Northern Ireland banks, as there are minor differences between them and the clearing banks. For example, Scottish banks have limited power to issue notes and slightly different reserve requirements. In practice, the banks are not sufficiently large, or different in operation, to distort the picture and most of what is said about the London clearing banks applies to them as well.

2 Two Scottish banks, the Royal Bank of Scotland and the National Commercial Bank of Scotland, also announced their intention to merge at this time.

3 The emphasis in recent years is for British banks to extend their operations overseas, particularly in the USA. They are thus following the example of American banks which have made inroads in the domestic markets of Britain and other continental countries.

4 The economic journals have for some years contained a recondite debate over the cash and liquid asset ratios of the banks (for example, Newlyn, June 1964; Crouch, December 1964 and August 1965). A criticism of points of view expressed in these articles is given by Cramp (June 1966; and October 1967). The banking practices adopted after 1971, described above, make the approach to credit creation via asset ratios misleading.

6
Other financial institutions and financial intermediaries

Above all, the maintenance in the primary market generally and by the clearing banks of long-established arrangements on interest rates, following a rigid pattern, left wide open opportunities which the new markets, with their uninhibited flexibility, were not slow to fill.
Midland Bank Review, August 1966.

In this chapter financial institutions other than the commercial banks (discussed in the previous chapter) are looked at. First, we deal with the parallel money markets: those markets concerned with local authority debt, with Euro-dollars, with inter-bank deposits and with certificates of deposit.

Next we look at acceptance houses and overseas banks. The important growth in these institutions has largely taken place since the Radcliffe Report of 1959; it coincided with the granting of convertibility to external holders of currently earned sterling in 1958, and has benefited from the general relaxation of monetary restrictions which has taken place since. Then we look at a group of institutions performing various functions which usually go under the title of 'financial intermediaries'. After a brief description of these, their implications for monetary policy are taken up, as well as their impact on liquidity and, finally, their influence on financial markets.

Parallel money markets

The term 'parallel money markets' is given to a number of markets which have grown up since 1955. These markets are not geographically centred, as is the case with the stock exchange, but are essentially a system of telephone and telex links of dealers and organisations who form the markets.

LOCAL AUTHORITIES

Local authorities have not been included as financial intermediaries, although a case can be made for doing so. Local authorities are large borrowers on the market, especially in the short term, and in considering financial flows they rank large in the picture. To the extent that local authorities re-lend for house purchase and house improvements, they act in a similar way to other financial intermediaries, but their borrowing is linked to their own needs for finance and not directly to their lending activities.

Until 1955 local authorities had to meet their needs for borrowing by going to the Public Works Loan Board (PWLB). In 1955 a change of government policy occurred and local authorities were required to meet their needs in the market if they could. Access to government funds through the PWLB was to be available only if funds could not be raised from the market. They were so successful in this policy that at times they embarrassed the monetary authorities, who found that their efforts to reduce liquidity in the economy were being nullified by the increase in short-term borrowing by the local authorities. In recent years this policy has been eased and local authorities now have easier access to the PWLB.

Table 6.1 shows the growth of local authority temporary borrowing. From a figure of £169 million in 1955, it had grown to nearly £1,000 million six years later, had doubled again by 1970, and almost reached £4,000 million by 1976. Over half of this money was recallable by the lender within seven days, as the breakdown shows. These funds were drawn from a wide market including the commercial banks, acceptance houses, overseas banks, other financial intermediaries, individuals and overseas.

Table 6.1

Local authority temporary debt by terms of repayment 1st quarter figures (£m.)

Year	Up to 7 days	7 days to 3 months	3 months to 12 months	Total*
1955	–	–	–	169
1961	558	229	146	933
1965	1,239	315	293	1,847
1970	1,437	240	323	2,000
1976	2,019	921	969	3,909

*Total includes inter-authority borrowing. In 1976 this amounted to £380 million.
Source: Financial Statistics, *HMSO, London.*

In addition to temporary borrowing, local authorities also borrow on a smaller scale by way of mortgages for periods of one or more years, by the issue of stocks and more recently by the issue of bonds.

The period since 1955 has therefore seen the rapid growth of a local authority short-term money market. Local authorities have to pay rates marginally higher than the Government for equivalent-dated securities. They also pay 0.5 per cent more than nationalised industries (with Treasury guarantee) for bank loans.

The fact that local authorities have to pay rather more when borrowing on their own account has long been a matter of dispute between them and the Government. The Radcliffe Committee gave this and the difficulties it created for monetary control as the chief reasons why the local authorities should be given freer access to the PWLB. The National Board for Prices and Incomes (in the *Bank Charges Report*, 1967, paras 90–2) has come out in substantial agreement with the Radcliffe recommendations. As an alternative suggestion, they put up the idea that a new co-operative financial institution, guaranteed by the Treasury, be set up for local authority borrowing. Our interest here, however, is that a sophisticated short-term money market has grown up. Local authority borrowing has almost the same market standing as government debt, and rates obtainable in this market exercise a powerful effect on the rates which financial intermediaries need to give in order to attract deposits.

THE EURO-CURRENCY MARKET

The Euro-currency market started in US dollars, which still form the largest currency. As sterling was the currency in which most international trade was conducted in the inter-war period, so the dollar has become the currency since. The Euro-dollar market refers to dollar-denominated deposit liabilities in banks outside the USA in which much of this international business is conducted. There are a number of reasons why the market has grown up outside the USA, besides the convenience of customers. One of the most frequently cited is the presence of regulations in various countries, particularly in the USA. The most important is Regulation Q in the USA which sets limits on rates which the banks may pay on domestic deposits. Another factor was that interest rates were in general higher outside the USA; thus the Euro-dollar market started when holders of dollar deposits in the USA transferred the title to that deposit to some bank outside the USA. Markets in many other currencies have also grown up on the same principle.

London-held foreign currencies amounted to some £75,767 million in

June 1976, and represent an important marshalling of funds. However, it is difficult to assess their relative importance since funds may be passed around many banks and inflate the level of holdings, and the totals fluctuate sharply over time. (A succinct account of the Euro-currency market can be found in Revell (1973) with greater detail given in Einzig (1970).)

THE INTER-BANK MARKET

The inter-bank market refers to the arrangements by which banks lend to other banks when they have surplus funds, or borrow when they are short. Deposits may also be placed in the market by outsiders through deposit brokers. This market was mostly confined to banks outside the clearing system until 1971. In July 1976, £7,553 million was outstanding in sterling and £21,119 million in other currency assets.

CERTIFICATES OF DEPOSIT

Certificates of deposit (CDs) are an American innovation. They are, as we have seen, a process by which term deposits at banks can be made more liquid for the holder. If the holder requires funds before the terms of his deposit matures, he can sell his claim on the market. The banks can shade the terms which they offer on certificates of deposit, but of more importance they increase the willingness of depositors to commit themselves for longer terms. The depositor is no longer locked into the institution until his deposit matures, or faced with the usually harsh penalty clauses for earlier retrieval of his balance. The depositor in need can sell his claim on the market, although what his claim will fetch will depend on market conditions. Certificates of deposit may be designated in sterling or in some other currency. In July 1976 they amounted to £2,031 million in sterling and £1,954 million in other currencies.

OTHER MARKETS

The market for finance house deposits is now comparatively small since six of the biggest houses obtained recognition as banks after 1971. Liabilities totalled a little over £1,100 million in 1976.

Since 1968 a small market in inter-company loans has developed. (See Revell (1973, pp. 282–4), on which this section draws.) The markets developed with the need to finance the exports deposit scheme. For a period of six months in 1968, 50 per cent of the value of imported goods had to be deposited with the authorities. Import deposit receipts were recognised as equivalent to government bonds and a market grew up to finance them. Although some lending does take place between companies, banks have always provided the bulk of the finance to this market. The market developed as a source of finance for companies, particularly after the change in bank regulations in 1971.

Acceptance houses, other overseas banks and consortium banks in the United Kingdom, and other deposit-taking institutions

The distinction has already been drawn between clearing banks with their extensive branch networks and other banks. The first category is easy to delimit but 'other banks' covers a range of institutions.

Acceptance houses clearly fall in the category of banks. So, too, do the wide range of foreign banks who have set up in the United Kingdom, mainly in London. Beyond these institutions are others, to some of which the term 'fringe banks' was applied in the 1970s.

There is in Britain no general statute defining a bank, but a number of restrictions are imposed on a company wishing to gain this status. (The following account draws on Crockett (1973, pp. 128-31).) To use the word 'bank', 'bankers', or 'banking', in its title a company must satisfy certain conditions. This safeguard to unwary depositors is, however, virtually nullified since this restriction only relates to the registered title of a company, not to a description of how the company describes its activities in advertisements. The accolade of a registered banking name is reserved for companies with an established reputation as a bank in the financial community, although branches of overseas banks are able to use their own name.

The most important way a company can carry out banking activities and not fall foul of the Moneylenders Acts is to apply for a Section 123 certificate from the Department of Trade and Industry to the effect that it is 'bona fide carrying on the business of banking'. A certificate will normally be issued if a company has capital of at least £100,000, a significant current-account business, competent management and satisfactory banking experience. It is among Section 123 companies that the term 'fringe banks' has come to be used, although the term may also cover companies not so registered.

After these preliminaries, we will look at acceptance houses, other banks, overseas banks and other deposit-taking institutions in that order.

A wide variety of City institutions are known as 'merchant banks'. This name reflects their origin in the trading of goods. Today they undertake a wide variety of financial services. Since 1972 seventeen of them belong to the Accepting Houses Committee, to which the term 'acceptance house' can properly be applied. They contain such well-known names as Rothschilds, Hambros and Barings. The acceptance of bills of exchange (for a commission) is an important part of their business, amounting to some £1,000 million at any one time during 1975–6. They have always had close associations with the Bank of England, and at one time a merchant banking background was necessary to obtain a Governorship at the Bank of England.

The Radcliffe Committee in its Report stated (1959, para. 186):

> A Bill of exchange accepted by a British bank or by one of the eighteen accepting houses is, if it has one other British name on it, 'eligible paper' at the Bank of England, and has therefore the highest degree of liquidity, shared only by Treasury Bills and short-dated Government bonds. Having this maximum of liquidity and the complete assurance of payment (on which of course the liquidity depends), it commands the lowest rate of discount available for any non-Government paper. An acceptance house thus, when accepting a bill, confers on the drawer of the bill (and on anyone who discounts it for him) the certainty of being able to get sterling in exchange for it from a bank or discount house in London, at the least possible sacrifice in discount.

Besides acceptance, these houses carry out a wide range of other services: in raising loans, dealing in foreign exchange, managing new issues of securities, managing portfolios, financial advice (which includes advice to firms contemplating takeover bids, or are themselves the subject of takeover offers), and a wide range of other activities.

Table 6.2 shows the main liabilities and assets of the acceptance houses as at July 1976. Reserve assets comprise balances at the Bank of England, money at call, and mostly British Government bills and short-dated stocks. From this table it will be seen that the acceptance houses have an ordinary banking function in taking deposits; but these will generally be large accounts, including deposits from banks. The funds are used in a wide variety of ways: lending to the inter-bank market, to local authorities, and advances to both the public and private sectors. Over half of their business at this time was in foreign currencies.

OTHER UK BANKS

Other UK banks are those banks outside the clearing system with majority UK ownership.

A comparison of Tables 6.2 and 6.3 will show that the category 'other UK banks' is considerably larger in size of deposits than acceptance houses, and they have substantially more business in foreign currencies. Their

Table 6.2

Acceptance houses' liabilities and assets (£m., July 1976)

	Sterling	Other currencies
Liabilities (deposits by)		
UK banks	522	930
Other UK	1,655	266
Overseas	179	1,942
Certificates of deposit	149	105
	2,505	3,243
Assets		
Balances at Bank of England	1	–
Money at call	177	–
Treasury and other bills	79	–
Special Deposits	50	–
Inter-bank lending	675	734
Certificates of deposit	227	204
Local authorities	397	–
Advances and loans		
UK	1,002	449
Overseas	64	1,729
British Government stocks	14	–
Other	320	439
	3,006	3,555
Acceptances	1,001	

Source: **Bank of England Quarterly Bulletin**, *vol. 16, no. 3, September 1976.*

assets show the same spread as those of the discount houses, as would be expected from institutions doing much the same kind of business.

OVERSEAS BANKS IN THE UNITED KINGDOM

Statistics of overseas banks now cover over 200 institutions. Since 1975 the Bank of England has classified them as American 58, Japanese 19, other overseas 108, and consortium 28, with the first having the biggest business. The number of banks in each category relate to the position in October 1976.

The category 'overseas banks' therefore covers diverse institutions. Some are head-offices of banking concerns operating mostly overseas, most of them formed in the last century to provide banking services for the colonies. The majority of the rest will be branch-offices of banks whose head-offices are overseas. The category of consortium banks are

Table 6.3

Deposits of other UK banks (£m., July 1976)

	Sterling	Other currencies
Liabilities (deposits only)		
UK banks	3,242	2,635
Other UK	3,820	378
Overseas	985	6,752
Certificates of deposit	910	857
	8,957	10,622
Assets		
Balances at Bank of England	3	–
Money at call	324	–
Treasury and other bills	661	47
Special Deposits	164	–
Inter-bank lending	2,704	2,175
Certificates of deposit	692	206
Local authorities	912	–
Advances and loans		
UK	4,032	1,636
Overseas	138	6,659
British Government stocks	296	–
Other	632	1,163
	10,558	11,886
Acceptances	310	

Source: Bank of England Quarterly Bulletin, *vol. 16, no. 3, September 1976.*

banks which are owned by other banks but in which no one bank has more than 50 per cent ownership, and in which at least one shareholder is an overseas bank.

The very rapid growth both in numbers and importance of these banks since 1969 can largely be traced back to the growth of international companies and companies operating abroad. London was one of the main centres of the Euro-currency markets and provided an obvious place for a bank to establish itself if it wished to serve its industrial clients with business in Europe.

These banks: operate as exchange dealers, particularly on the Eurodollar market; finance the movement of goods between countries, which will include acceptance credits, thus giving rise to bills of exchange which can be negotiated in the discount market; and accept and deploy funds moving to London from abroad.

Regarding their activities in the United Kingdom, the Radcliffe Committee (1969, para. 201) was able to say that 'This domestic business is negligible in comparison with the activity of the clearing banks. It is as holders of Government bonds and as operators in the discount market that the overseas banks have their main relevance to the liquidity structure of the economy.'

Since the publication of the Radcliffe Report this situation has been transformed. While still important in the fields quoted, these banks have greatly extended 'domestic business'.

Table 6.4 shows the predominance of American banks in the overseas banking sector; they have 56 per cent of the sterling deposits and 46 per cent of other currency deposits. By way of comparison, the London clearing banks at this time had sterling deposits of £23,785 million and other currency deposits of £4,534 million, so the overwhelming importance of the overseas banks in the foreign currency sector is clear.

The importance of inter-bank lending stands out, with UK banks being the largest sector making sterling deposits and the second largest making other currency deposits.

OTHER DEPOSIT-TAKING INSTITUTIONS

At the beginning of this section attention was drawn to the confusion that exists over the use of the title 'bank'. A White Paper was issued in August 1976 called *The Licensing and Supervision of Deposit-Taking Institutions.* This set out the Government's intentions in this area which would satisfy its obligations under the prospective EEC directive on the commencement and carrying on of business by banks and other credit institutions.

Table 6.4

Liabilities and assets of overseas banks (£m., July 1976)

	Sterling				Other currencies			
	American banks	Japanese banks	Other banks	Consortium	American banks	Japanese banks	Other banks	Consortium
Liabilities (deposits by)								
UK banks	1,795	274	879	197	5,929	3,855	4,470	2,250
Other UK	1,392	84	860	140	1,214	86	620	43
Overseas	385	15	638	53	26,574	10,106	16,707	3,594
Certificates of deposit	864	1	249	37	4,519	687	1,655	138
	4,436	374	2,626	427	38,236	14,734	23,452	6,025
Assets								
Balances at Bank of England	1	–	1	–	–	–	–	–
Money at call	191	33	198	9	–	–	–	–
Treasury and other bills	237	10	96	19	–	–	–	–
Special Deposits	88	8	52	5	–	–	–	–
Inter-bank lending	931	57	742	221	8,035	1,691	6,216	959
Certificates of deposit	415	–	95	71	453	12	797	222
Local authorities	322	–	224	74	–	–	–	–

Advances and loans								
UK	2,129	220	1,078	191	2,888	657	1,861	405
Overseas	51	56	94	8	26,705	12,298	14,419	4,622
British Government stocks	77	–	30	19	–	–	–	–
Other	112	17	117	43	–	–	–	–
	4,554	401	2,727	660	38,081	14,658	23,293	6,208
*Acceptances**	246	187	377	40				

*Acceptances may be in sterling or other currencies.

Source: Bank of England Quarterly Bulletin, *vol. 16, no. 3, September 1976.*

The control is intended to cover those institutions that have been loosely referred to as 'fringe banks'. Clearing and other major banks, building societies, trustee savings banks, the National Savings Bank, the National Giro and Friendly Societies are already satisfactorily regulated.

Under the new system institutions will be allowed to carry on the business of taking deposits only if they hold a licence granted by the Bank of England, unless they are recognised as a bank or come into the category where supervision is already adequately carried out.

The Bank will be empowered to grant a new statutory recognition as a bank to certain deposit-taking institutions which will exempt them from the licensing provisions of the proposed Act. It is expected that most of the institutions in the present primary banking sector will qualify for such recognition.

In order to obtain and hold a licence, institutions will be required to comply with certain general conditions as to capital, reserves and general competence. The precise nature of the criteria is being worked out.

Institutions which receive a licence will thereafter have to satisfy the Bank that they continue to meet those criteria and will be subject to examination by the Bank. A licence may be revoked or suspended by the Bank, in which case there will be a right of appeal to the Treasury.

As a further safeguard of the public a compulsory deposit protection scheme is to be implemented to provide protection for sterling deposits up to £10,000, or the first £10,000 of larger deposits.

Financial intermediaries

One characteristic of a developed economy is the pressure of a wide variety of financial intermediaries. This is in contrast to the situation in many underdeveloped countries, where an individual who does not wish to spend the whole of his income has little choice but to hold currency or precious metals, deposit the money in a bank, or lend the money directly to an individual or to a business. A developed country has a great variety of institutions interposed between the owner of funds and the user of funds. Lending can still take place directly, but usually it takes place by means of the intermediaries. The intermediaries receive money from a variety of sources and employ or invest it in a variety of ways.

Financial intermediaries should be clearly distinguished from brokers, who merely act on behalf of their client to arrange a transaction and then drop out of the picture. Financial intermediaries accept claims on other people and in exchange offer their liabilities, i.e. claims against themselves.

If their claims were widely accepted in payment of debts, as bank deposits are, they would be on the same basis as banks. They are inferior in this respect, for example a deposit with a building society must first be turned into money to pay off a debt whereas a bank deposit can be transferred directly. However, these claims do act as a store of value (which can economise in the use of money) and the intermediaries are a source of credit.

Table 6.5 lists most of the main financial intermediaries in order of size of their assets at the end of 1975. This is not necessarily the same as their economic importance. The figures for stocks at the end of 1975 are a mixture of book and market values; for assets acquired in the year the figures show the value at cost. Other financial intermediaries not included in the table are hire-purchase finance houses, with assets of over £1,000 million, property unit trusts and special finance agencies.

These intermediaries differ widely from one another. In particular,

Table 6.5

Main financial intermediaries (£m.)

	Stock of assets at end of 1975	Assets acquired in 1975 (cash value)
Insurance companies	27,891bv	2,524
Building societies	24,365bv	4,075
Superannuation funds		
Public sector	4,433mv	860
Local authorities	1,644mv*	355
Private sector	7,706mv	993
Investment trusts	5,651mv	39
Unit trusts	2,537mv	210
Trustee Savings Banks	2,011mv	169
National Savings Bank	515mv	37

*As at 31 March 1975.

bv = book value.

mv = market value.

Source: Financial Statistics, *no. 172, August 1976.*

insurance company life funds, which form the bulk of the assets of insurance companies, and superannuation funds are on a different footing to the other intermediaries. Both are collectors of long-term contractual savings, which have shown an upward trend in recent years. In general their liabilities to the public are less liquid than those of many of the other intermediaries. Funds in superannuation schemes are not usually available to the beneficiary before retirement. Insurance policies are in an intermediate category from a holder's viewpoint; cashing in before the policy matures usually involves financial loss, particularly in the earlier years of the policy. However, a policy can frequently be used as collateral for a loan from the insurance company concerned, a bank or other lender. Insurance companies have long-term obligations, often fixed in money terms; they will be relatively impervious to short-term economic fluctuations as their funds are largely invested in long-term securities. Superannuation funds find it more difficult to adopt the matching principles of insurance life funds since many of their obligations are related to the final salaries of the superannuated persons; for this reason they are likely to be more heavily invested in equity shares.

Assets of building societies have grown rapidly in recent years; some 80 per cent is invested in house loans on mortgages, which is about three-quarters of private debt for house purchase. They lend for a fixed term, commonly twenty-five years, at a rate of interest which moves in line with market rates of interest, but the rate is changed relatively infrequently, so that building society rates lag behind most other market rates. Building society deposits are highly liquid from the depositor's viewpoint: he is usually able to obtain up to £2,000 on demand from the large societies, and to obtain a greater sum than this at short notice.

Building societies are able to offer this facility, in spite of lending long term, because they have built up with the public a general confidence in the way they are run. They are regulated by the Registrar of Friendly Societies and have to keep reserves to meet normal withdrawals, but more importantly their lending is less long than it seems.

Most mortgages are being repaid over the course of the loan so that a continual flow of capital is coming into building society hands; together with early redemptions this results in a fairly liquid position.

Building societies are also, to some extent, able to influence the flow of deposits into and out of their accounts by changing the rate of interest they are offering. Here we are not considering the general level of interest rates prevailing in the economy, which will be taken up in a later chapter, but the differential effect of particular interest rates. We have seen that building societies do not follow other rates up or down immediately. However, if rates change for a considerable length of time they are forced to follow suit. In the case of an increase in MLR they may find funds flowing from them to institutions who have raised rates, for example from local authorities and finance companies; also existing deposits may be withdrawn for the same purpose. In this circumstance building societies are forced to increase their rates in order to protect themselves. In a similar way societies reduce their rates, after a decrease in MLR, when their reserves are built up sufficiently.

Investment trusts and unit trusts both specialise in investing in companies; the difference lies in the nature of liability to the purchaser. Investment trusts are ordinary companies who happen to specialise in investing in other companies. In this case a saver can purchase shares in such a company and the price of these shares will fluctuate according to market views of the performance of that company. The purchaser of a unit in a unit trust is buying a fraction of the underlying portfolio that the trust has purchased. The value of his units is directly calculated from the value of these securities. It follows that these types of asset are some way along the spectrum of liquidity: money can be obtained quickly by sale of the investment shares or unit trusts but their monetary value varies from day to day.

The Trustee Savings Banks (TSBs), most of which were established in the early nineteenth century as savings institutions, have at last emerged as banks. They reorganised themselves after the report of the Committee to Review National Savings (1973), called the Page Committee after its Chairman. Instead of seventy-two groups their numbers are now reduced to seventeen and they were given the right to make loans to their customers in 1977. They are managed by non-paid trustees under close government supervision, although it is expected that this will cease some time in the 1980s and that they will then be subject to the same regulations as other banks. At present the first £70 of interest on an ordinary account is tax free, though that privilege should cease in three years. Page (1977) regrets that the TSBs did not follow the advice to scrap the ordinary and savings accounts in favour of a single account. The TSBs collectively represent a considerable addition to the banking scene and competition for the traditional banking sector. The possibility of a unitary organisation in the future is not ruled out.

The National Savings Bank (called the Post Office Savings Bank before 1969) is a Government-run service operating through post offices. Like the Trustee Savings Banks it runs an ordinary department and investment account and through the National Giro system operates a current-account service. Its funds are invested by the National Debt Commissioners and invested in public-sector securities.

Of the financial intermediaries not listed in Table 6.5, the finance houses are the most important. There were nine finance houses listed as outside the banking system in October 1976. Finance houses traditionally specialise in hire-purchase and instalment credit. Increasingly they rely on deposits as opposed to bank advances as a source of funds. They have been subjected to control by the monetary authorities since 1965. With the change in money control in 1971 a number of the larger houses applied for, and obtained, banking status. Car, central heating and double-glazing are important sectors of their business, and in recent years industrial financing by hire purchase and leasing of equipment has gained in importance.

Property unit trusts are specialist trusts which invest in commercial property for pension funds and charities. They came into existence to fill a need which became evident after the 1965 Finance Act. Tax-exempt pension funds and charities could obtain a larger return by investing in property direct rather than buying shares of property companies, since the latter were subject to corporation tax on profits and capital gains. Many pension funds and charities lacked the resources and expertise to invest direct so the property unit trusts were set up. They are therefore similar to unit trusts but can only raise funds from approved pension funds and charities. The bulk of the money comes from the former.

Special finance agencies include the following institutions: the Agricultural Mortgage Corporation, the National Film Finance Corporation, Finance for Industry Ltd, and the Commonwealth Development Finance Company (CDFC). In general the capital of these institutions comes from the Bank of England and the commercial banks, with, in the case of the CDFC, some being subscribed by a number of overseas (ex-Commonwealth) central banks. Generally, these agencies are not concerned to raise funds from the public, rather they are Government-inspired to meet the needs of agriculture and business for medium- and long-term funds, and in particular to meet legitimate needs where the enterprises find difficulty in raising funds from normal market sources.

Finance for Industry Ltd was formed in December 1973 from the merging of the Finance Corporation for Industry (FCI) and the Industrial and Commercial Finance Corporation (ICFC). These companies had been formed in 1945 to help companies re-equip after the war; their activities still continue, with the FCI side of the operations being concerned with large-scale borrowing and the ICFC side with medium and small firms. ICFC continues to operate as a holding company for a number of subsidiary companies specialising in particular finance. These are: Technical Development Capital Ltd (TDC), formed in 1962 to help finance new technical developments; Industrial Mergers Ltd (IML), formed in 1967 to facilitate mergers, especially between smaller companies; Scottish Industrial Finance Ltd, formed in 1964 to provide merchant banking services in Scotland; ICFC Leasing Ltd, to facilitate industrial leasing and renting; Ship Mortgage Finance Company Ltd (SMFC), formed in 1951 to help finance the construction of British-built ships; and, finally, Estate Duties Investment Trust Ltd (EDITH), formed to help family-owned businesses to meet the tax payable on the death of a major shareholder and to continue in business.

Power to create credit

From a monetary management point of view, one of the major questions is: Supposing the commercial banks are controlled, will the presence of financial intermediaries thwart their attempts at credit control?

The answer to this question is quite clearly 'yes'. In the case of overseas banks operating in this country this is obvious; if they have any sizeable sterling business, then monetary control, to be effective, must attempt to regulate this part of their business. The need for regulating the other financial intermedaries is as follows. Most of the payments in the economy take the form not of exchange of notes and coin (primary money) but of bank deposits (secondary money). This means a large part of initial deposits can be reloaned subject to the need to keep adequate liquidity. There was a theoretical stalemate at this point for about 100 years, i.e. *on whether banks created credit or just loaned out part of existing deposits.* This has been sorted out by considering the flow of income. So long as deposits do not leave the banking system, the process of lending by the banks, or of the banks buying securities, can repeat itself many times. The process comes to an end because of the need to keep a proportion in reserve at each 'round' of lending and because of leakages from the banking system.

An analogous picture can be drawn for financial intermediaries. A building society can be used as an example: it will find that a certain proportion of money that it lends out will be redeposited with it. This money can be re-lent, subject to the need to keep a reserve for that proportion of depositors who demand the return of their money. If we postulate the same sort of closed system of circulation of money, as was done for the banking system, for example a house-builder who receives the sum of money loaned by the society deposits this sum back in the building society, then it is clear that the building society can re-loan this money leaving a certain proportion of it to build up its reserves.

The difference between banks and financial intermediaries is thus only one of degree, not a difference in kind. Because financial intermediaries' liabilities are not counted as money, they are likely to have to keep a greater proportion of money as a reserve, or, as we have seen, by ensuring an adequate flow of repayments over time and influencing new deposits. More importantly, the flow of funds back to the building societies is likely to be much less than the flow of funds back to the banking system.

As was the case when considering the banking system, it is necessary to distinguish between a single financial intermediary and financial intermediaries considered as a whole. Although lending by, say, a building society may not lead to very much money being deposited back in the building society, collectively financial intermediaries may be taking in each other's loans and so be able to expand collectively in a way analogous to the banking system considered as a whole.

Credit creation need not be at the expense of the banking system

It is important to realise that the ability of the financial intermediaries to create credit does not necessarily affect the commercial banks, unlike, for example, the purchase of government securities.

Let us take the case where £1,000 is withdrawn from a bank and is deposited in a building society. From the point of view of the banking system, all that has happened at this stage is that an individual's account is debited by £1,000, while the building societies' account is credited by a corresponding amount. The total of bank deposits is unchanged but the total of financial claims has increased by £1,000, i.e. the increase in the deposit at the building society (a liability of the building society to repay this sum).

Whether, and to what extent, the banks are affected at the next stage depends on the use to which the building society and subsequent holders put this money. Let us assume for simplicity that the whole of this £1,000 is lent by the building society to a borrower who pays it over to a builder for a house. If the builder deposits the money back in the banking system once again, all that has happened from the banks' point of view is that the ownership of deposits has changed once more. It is clear that the banks will only be affected if there is a 'leakage' in the flow of income; from *their* point of view a cheque drawn in favour of a financial intermediary is no different from a cheque drawn in favour of an individual. This is so because financial intermediaries bank with the banking system. As we have seen, commercial banks are affected if the money is deposited with an acceptance house or an overseas bank.

Implications for monetary policy

From the point of view of the monetary authorities, a transaction as outlined above is not neutral. The transfer of £1,000 to a building society did not alter the total of bank deposits; it did, however, enable the building society to lend more. We see why the presence of financial intermediaries is so essential to a developed economy and at the same time poses problems for monetary management. The financial intermediaries provide a channel for finance to get to ultimate borrowers. Individuals are not likely to lend substantial sums directly for house purchase but *are* likely to lend to a building society, which in turn lends for house purchase. This aspect will be taken up in the next section. The problem comes if the monetary authorities are trying to control the amount of credit in the economy by limiting the banks' power to lend. If deposits flow to the financial intermediaries (merely a change of ownership of deposits from the banks' point of view), the financial intermediaries can extend the credit instead of the banking system.

The Radcliffe Report (1959, para. 511) went to some length to spell out the implications touched on in this section and came to the following conclusion:

> Since we envisage the use of monetary measures as not in ordinary times playing other than a subordinate part in guiding the development of the economy, we do not consider such an elaborate extension of compulsory powers to be justified in the conditions immediately before us. In times of emergency we believe that the rough justice of the blunter measures we propose in paragraphs 524 and 528 would be appropriate. But it is not impossible that there may be longer periods, not amounting to emergencies, in which excessive liquidity persistently embarrasses the authorities in their conduct of economic policy. In such circumstances an extension of direct control over credit-giving to cover other groups of financial institutions besides the banks would reinforce the efficacy of the restraints imposed on the banks, as well as having the appeal of equity, and it might therefore be necessary to accept the degree of interference with business, and to overcome the practical difficulties, which such a wide-ranging scheme of registration and direction would entail.

In practice, control by the Bank of England was found necessary and has been gradually extended. In 1965 a request to limit advances was extended from the clearing banks to the acceptance houses and overseas banks in respect of their sterling advances. The London Discount Market Association and the leading associations of hire-purchase finance houses were asked to observe a comparable degree of restraint: and members of the British Insurance Association, the National Association of Pension Funds and the Building Societies Association were also requested to co-operate in maintaining restraint – in particular in relation to the finance of building and property development, other than housing for the owner-occupier.

In 1968 the Bank announced that a 'new, and to some extent experimental' form of control had been agreed with overseas and foreign banks to be known as the Cash Deposits Scheme. This was analogous to the system of Special Deposits that already applied to clearing banks, but the scheme was not implemented before the change to 'Competition and Credit Control'.

In 1971 the Bank of England ushered in, as we have seen, a new era of 'Competition and Credit Control'. From 1971, therefore, control over financial institutions has been rather more uniform, although there are variations to take account of the special circumstances of particular types of institution. The general requirement is to keep a minimum ratio of reserve assets to liabilities of 12½ per cent. In addition, Special Deposits may be called for as under the old system, which in effect makes the 12½ per cent ratio variable.

The period from 1971 to 1975 was a time of exceptional strain. It saw a large growth in fringe banking activities, a boom and subsequent slump in property and stock market values, the collapse of a number of fringe banks with severe strain on the rest of the financial system. Inflation was a world-wide problem, exceeding 25 per cent in 1974–5 in the United Kingdom. As a result, since 1975 the Bank has further extended its control over the financial system by collecting additional information on which it can act, and by instituting prudential examinations, details of which have already been given in Chapter 3.

Increase in liquidity

In a previous section we dealt with the ability of the financial intermediaries to create credit. Another aspect of a well-developed sector of this kind was touched on: the increase in liquid assets which they bring about. In general the financial intermediaries enable long- and medium-term investments to be financed, although the securities which they issue in exchange for deposits are often liquid, i.e. quickly convertible into a known amount of cash. One result of this is that medium- and long-term interest rates are lower than they would otherwise be. This is one of the reasons why interest rates are likely to be higher in underdeveloped countries.[1]

The ability to lend money for a longer period of time than the funds borrowed is an important function in a modern economy. Banks have of course long cultivated this art. At the root of this process lies the confidence which must be built up between depositor and the institution accepting the deposit. The early history of banking, and the bank failures that have occurred in some countries in recent times, together with the secondary bank failures in 1973, are evidence of this. The problem of a country trying to establish a financial sector is not merely that of duplicating the institutions of a developed economy but of engendering confidence in them once they have been set up. In Britain confidence in the financial sector, and the financial intermediaries in particular, is achieved in numerous ways. The various parts are linked together in many ways as a result of formal and informal ties, many of the institutions are subject to legal restrictions governing their reserves and other matters, and most are subject to regulation from their own professional associations.

Impact on financial markets

The final aspect of financial intermediaries that we wish to stress is their impact on financial markets. This impact can come about in two ways: first, from the existing flow of funds; and second, from switching of existing assets. The financial intermediaries shown in Table 6.5 above acquired assets in excess of £9,000 million during 1975. Of this sum roughly 41 per cent went into government or local authority stocks, 21 per cent in company shares or stocks, 30 per cent was used for loans and mortgages, and the remaining 8 per cent for land property and ground-rents.

The size of the financial intermediaries and the size of the flow of funds to them make these institutions of prime importance. We do not know at present how much of this money is channelled into buying old assets and how much into new assets, but the impact on both markets is likely to be very considerable. The Bank of England estimated that the institutional share of turnover in UK equities in 1963 was about a quarter of the whole and that they accounted for rather more than three-fifths of the turnover in fixed-interest stocks.

It is clear that if the authorities can keep these institutional investors happy, these financial markets are likely to be orderly.

Summary

The clearing banks, and associated money markets operating through the discount houses, are still important but in recent years new money markets have come into existence and the growth of other financial intermediaries has been very fast. The parallel money markets concerned with local authority debt, with Euro-dollars, with inter-bank deposits and with certificates of deposit were outlined. An account of acceptance houses, other banks, overseas and consortium banks was given followed by information on other financial intermediaries.

These institutions are important because, like clearing banks, they create credit, and also because they increase liquidity and have a marked impact on financial markets.

Control by the Bank of England has been gradually extended over this wider sector and in spite of its very diverse elements it now presents a more homogeneous whole.

Note

1 It is sometimes asserted that the movement of funds into institutional hands means that the institutions, as opposed to individuals, are less inclined to invest in newer and riskier projects. The special finance agencies must be exempted from this conjecture as they were set up expressly to provide finance in this field. A counter-argument used is that we might expect institutions to exercise their responsibilities of share ownership more effectively. Either of these conjectures could be important but there is little satisfactory evidence on either side and it is easy to exaggerate both points of view.

7
Monetary expansion and contraction

We conclude that the proper spirit of approach to control of the money supply is a decent humility in the face of a highly complex task. Both old-orthodox and new-orthodox arguments are inadequate. The only policy for influencing the money supply on which practical reliance could be placed would be based on control, not of bank cash or of liquid assets, but of security sales to the non-bank public. If the authorities are to be criticised it is because of their timidity in experimenting with methods of controlling the gilt-edged market.
A. B. CRAMP (June 1966), 'Control of the Money Supply', *Economic Journal.*

The previous chapters have outlined briefly the financial sector of the British economy. A picture of the Bank of England and its relations with the Government, the commercial banks, the discount market, other financial institutions and financial intermediaries has been built up. Also, some of the interrelations of these institutions with each other have been indicated.

We now turn to the question: 'What determines the amount of money and liquidity in the economy?' This will be tackled by looking first at what determines the amount of primary money and secondary money and then considering the broader issues introduced when acceptance houses, overseas banks and financial intermediaries are brought into the picture.

We should not make a common mistake and forget that money has a *demand* as well as a *supply* aspect. Thus the question 'What is the potential power of the commercial banks to create money?' may not be the same as 'How much do they actually create?' The former question takes us over the whole field of government policy, while the latter question brings in bankers' prudence and aspects which they take into account before granting loans and overdrafts. Again, the monetary authorities can attempt to diminish the supply of money or they may be able to achieve the same ends by strengthening the demand for money or for government securities.

In looking at these questions it will be found that the net flows of money to or from the Exchequer, *vis-à-vis* the rest of the economy, are the crucial factors, together with the way in which the authorities and the commercial banks are able to deal with these flows. Much of this chapter is taken up in detailing these matters. One section is taken up with a discussion of how a government deficit in a particular year is financed. The next section goes into more detail about the factors affecting the size of a government deficit or surplus in a year. This is followed by a brief look at how the market is managed day to day. These factors are then drawn together to see how they influence the amount of money and liquidity in the economy.

Amount of primary and secondary money

Primary money has been defined as 'coin, notes and Bankers' Deposits at the Bank of England'.

Coin and notes need not detain us long. In Britain they are issued by the Bank subject to the formal consent of Parliament. They are kept at the level demanded by the public so that issues reach a peak just before summer holidays start and before Christmas. (For details of the mechanism of the note issue the reader is referred to the *Bank of England Quarterly Bulletin* (March 1965).)

The practical effect of an increase in the note issue is to lessen the Exchequer's need to borrow on other forms of debt. However, this is merely a by-product of the issue of a token currency. The Government *does not* make an issue of notes to finance its expenditure; it does so because there is a demand for notes. Coin and bank notes are, in a Radcliffe phrase, 'the small change of the monetary system'. We should expect to find in normal times that coin and notes bear a relatively stable relationship to national income, or to consumers' disposable income, after allowance has been made for seasonal factors referred to above.

So Bankers' Deposits at the Bank of England is the main item we should have in mind when we think of primary money. Transactions between the Government and the rest of the economy will (except for sums that take place in coin and notes and in addition are not paid into the banking system) be reflected initially in a change in Bankers' Deposits. For example, to make a payment to the Government an individual will write a cheque on his account in favour of the Inland Revenue, or to another appropriate department. The end-result is that besides the individual's account being debited, Bankers' Deposits at the Bank will be debited and the Government's account credited.

We know that commercial bankers have to maintain their reserves at a minimum of 12½ per cent of eligible liabilities. Thus when implying that Bankers' Deposits are increased or decreased, we are implying that commercial bankers either have to alter their structure of assets and liabilities so as to maintain the ratio at its old level (in a manner which has been outlined in Chapter 5), or if the ratio is above the minimum they have to acquiesce in a lower ratio.

Payments from the Government that take place by way of cheques reverse the process; as well as an individual's account being credited, Bankers' Deposits at the Bank are increased, while the Government's account is decreased.

What is relevant to this situation is the net flow of payments between the Government and the rest of the economy and the way in which this flow is financed. To this we now turn.

The financing of a government deficit

Let us suppose that the budget in a particular year, taking both above and below the line items,[1] shows a deficit, that is the Government will be spending more than it receives, assuming no tax changes are made. The issue of notes and the direct borrowing from the Bank of England have both been ruled out as a means of financing the deficit. *It will be met by the issue of securities, and it makes a considerable difference whether these are long-term or short-term securities and to whom they are sold.*

We have two streams of payments to consider: on the one hand, payments from the government to the non-government sector in excess of payments the other way, so that individual and company accounts at commercial banks will be increased and, as we have seen, a consequence of this is that Bankers' Deposits will be increased; and on the other hand, we have the consequences following on from the issue of securities – the first effect is a potential increase in purchasing power, while the second may be a potential decrease in purchasing power.

Let us first assume that the Government attempts to finance the deficit by the issue of long- or medium-term securities (here a decision has to be made on what rate of interest they will be offered to the market, a point that will not be taken up at this stage). This issue may be taken up by either the public, or the commercial banks.

It is clear that if the public takes up the whole of the issue they will draw cheques in favour of the Government, and Bankers' Deposits will be reduced. The increase in deposits brought about by the budget deficit has been matched by a decrease because the public have been induced to exchange cash for bonds.

Sales by the Government to the banks have the effect of increasing the money supply. There is an increase in deposits to the public brought about by the government deficit. The banks' liabilities are unchanged in total: there are smaller Bankers' Deposits and more government securities.

Failure to sell long- or medium-term debt will result in the need to issue short-term securities, i.e. Treasury Bills. In Chapter 4 it was seen that the discount houses undertake to cover the tender; they can do this because they can always get accommodation at the Bank of England. In so far as the discount houses take up the securities rather than the public, there is no offset to the government deficit. Sales to outside tenderers will reduce Bankers' Deposits by a like amount and reduce their liquid assets ratio. However, Treasury Bills represent potential spending power since they are very liquid and their holders will, in any case, have money in three months.

We can summarise so far and say that notes and coin come into circulation because the public desire more or less of them. They are not of operational significance. Bankers' Deposits and the amount of secondary money depend on the acquisition of debts by the commercial banks and the public, and is the result of the whole fiscal and budgetary process, that is, it depends on the stream of payments to and from the Government and public and the method of financing any deficit.

Determinants of the Government's annual surplus or deficit

The preceding section presented a static picture of how a deficit could be financed. We now examine more closely the factors that in any one year will determine the size of the Government's surplus or deficit and then go on to examine day-to-day management.

Table 7.1 presents a fuller picture of changes that occur in a year. The top part of the table presents the items that require financing in a year, while the lower section shows how the finance was provided. The bottom is the inverse of the top; thus 'Net balance' is either a deficit (and a figure will appear in the top half showing the amount that requires financing), or a surplus (in which case a figure will appear in the bottom half showing the amount of finance provided).

Item 1. This shows the over-all deficit in the year. This was the only item considered in the previous section: it is the Central Government's borrowing requirement, and is a measure of the net expenditure (including lending) of the Central Government resulting broadly from decisions of a budgeting nature.

Item 2. It may seem strange that foreign currency borrowing and an increase in reserves appears under the heading of items requiring finance and that a fall provides finance. The explanation is that when holdings of gold or foreign currencies increase (i.e. foreigners exchange their currencies for pounds), the Exchange Equalisation Account (EEA) draws on its reserves to provide these pounds. These reserves are mainly held in the form of tap Treasury Bills, so that the Exchequer is obliged to replace these bills by borrowing from another source.

Likewise a fall in reserves (foreigners exchanging pounds for gold or other currencies) means that the EEA has more of its assets in pounds. As we have seen, these are held mainly in the form of Treasury Bills.

Item 3. The change in overseas holdings refers to changes in amounts of government securities held by foreigners. Many of these changes will be accompanied by opposite changes in the EEA. For example, when foreign currencies are converted into sterling with the EEA (with the result, as we saw under item 2, of increasing the Exchequer requirements) and then invested in government debt, the Exchequer requirements will be unaffected; the EEA will hold less debt, foreigners more. In the same way government borrowing from abroad usually results in opposite changes in the EEA so that it has no effect on the amount of Exchequer financing.

In addition to these movements, balances held in sterling may be put into, or taken out of, government securities with no attempts made to change into other currencies.[2]

Items 4 and 5 are straightforward. Movements in these will directly affect Exchequer requirements. A reduction in the public's holding of any of these items has to be financed in some other way. These items are 'passive' savings in the sense that the Government is always ready to issue tax reserve certificates, savings certificates, premium bonds, and the like, on demand. The more of these that people are willing to take up, the less need there is to sell other securities and vice versa.

From time to time these issues are made more attractive, but this is usually when the interest on them has fallen behind other rates.

Items 6 and 7. Again, a reduction in the public's holding of these requires financing. The contrast between Treasury Bills and stocks compared with National Savings is that the monetary authorities may actively be trying to alter the composition of the former, in particular they may

Table 7.1

Exchequer financing (£m.)

	1971–2	1972–3	1973–4	1974–5	1975–6	1976–7
Items requiring finance						
(1) Net balance or over-all deficit	584	1,981	2,164	5,087	8,799	5,845
(2) Foreign currency borrowing and increase in reserves	2,312	–	123	–	–	496
(3) Decrease in overseas holdings of British debt	–	28	100	–	660	72
(4) Reduction in notes and coin	–	–	–	–	–	–
(5) Withdrawal of National Savings and tax certificates	–	–	155	–	–	–
(6) Reduction in Treasury Bills	–	4	164	–	–	798
(7) Decrease in stocks	–	461	–	–	–	–
(8) Miscellaneous	181	–	–	391	–	362
	3,077	2,474	2,706	5,478	9,459	7,573

	1971–2	1972–3	1973–4	1974–5	1975–6	1976–7
Items providing finance						
(1) Net balance or over-all surplus	–	–	–	–	–	–
(2) Foreign currency lending and decrease in reserves	–	1,250	–	787	1,199	–
(3) Increase in overseas holdings of British debt	260	–	–	990	–	–
(4) Increase in notes and coin	170	448	454	921	619	733
(5) Increase in National Savings and tax certificates	478	222	–	79	494	893
(6) Increase in Treasury Bills	121	–	–	486	2,683	–
(7) Increase in stocks	2,048	–	1,485	2,215	4,218	5,947
(8) Miscellaneous	–	554	767	–	246	–
	3,077	2,474	2,706	5,478	9,459	7,573

Source: Bank of England Quarterly Bulletin, *vol. 17, no. 2, June 1977, table 7.*

be trying to fund, that is sell long-term securities instead of Treasury Bills.

Item 8. The 'Miscellaneous' category covers debt changes with the Northern Ireland Government, changes in borrowing from the Bank of England, changes in debt holding of the Issue Department of the Bank and changes in Government-guaranteed stock.

Table 7.1 presents us with a picture of actual changes that took place in the economy during the years in question. The top of the table shows the way changes in the items increased the financial requirements of the Exchequer, the bottom half how changes in the items provided finance. The question of what determines the amount of money and liquidity in the system cannot therefore be separated from consideration of the whole economic system. In particular it is possible to imagine adverse circumstances for the authorities. Suppose, for example, the aim is to reduce the amount of money and liquidity in the economy, then adverse circumstances might be as follows: (i) a budget deficit, i.e. a stream of expenditure being injected into the economy, and the need to increase debt as a result; (ii) an inability to fund because of unwillingness of the public and the banks to buy bonds; and (iii) a large amount of government debt maturing which, because of (i) and (ii) above, will mean that short-term debt must be issued to replace it.

In the post-war period these adverse circumstances have been present and have coloured a great deal of monetary policy, this being a period in general of over-all deficits, of large amounts of debt maturing, and of the cult of the equity share rather than fixed-interest stock.

The authorities had little choice but to increase short-term debt to provide the necessary finance. In these circumstances it is not surprising that the monetary authorities should feel that control of the banking system – of secondary money – by the traditional means of controlling primary money and liquid assets left something to be desired, and thus they sought to supplement control by other means.

The over-all deficit shown in the top line of the table has increased rapidly since 1970–1 and has caused increasing concern. As we shall see in Part II on public finance, it is not necessarily correct to identify the health of an economy with the size of deficit or surplus at any particular time. For example, government expenditure may be on consumption or investment goods, on transfer payments or on loans to other sectors of the economy. An evaluation of a surplus or deficit needs to take account of the underlying reasons for that state of affairs. Having said this, however, it remains true that the rapid increase in the deficit has eroded the confidence of some people, and more especially some foreign investors and holders of sterling, in the management of the British economy. Such loss of confidence, if it results in an unwillingness to invest in government stock, or even to a withdrawal of funds, obviously compounds the country's problems.

Day-to-day management of money

So far we have seen that imbalance in the flow of payments out of, and receipts into, the Exchequer in a particular year results in the issue of some sort of security. Within the context of a deficit or surplus expected in a year, the flow of payments from day to day, which may be distinctly uneven, and from one time of the year to another, has to be evened out. The Bank, working closely with the Treasury, has the job of ensuring, if a deficit on the day is forecast, that finance is available, or, alternatively, if a surplus is forecast, that these surpluses are used to buy back Treasury Bills from the market, thus minimising the net cost of the National Debt.

From our point of view the second, connected task, that of managing the London money market, is more important. A new flow of payments to the Government has the effect of reducing Bankers' Deposits. As a result the banks are likely to be drawing upon money lent at call to the discount market (*Bank of England Quarterly Bulletin*, March 1963):

> The discount houses find themselves short of funds in consequence, and unless the Bank take steps to relieve the shortage – usually by buying Treasury Bills either from them (the so-called 'direct' method of giving help) or from the banks (the 'indirect' method) – they may be forced to borrow from the Bank at Bank Rate or over. The enforcement of such borrowing increases the average cost of the houses' total borrowings and is one of the main ways (short of a change in Bank Rate) in which the Bank of England exert an influence on short-term interest rates and particularly on the rate at which the discount houses may be expected to bid for Treasury Bills at the following Friday's tender.

The monetary authorities are thus faced with a choice either of maintaining the existing structure of short-term rates, with the consequence that they relieve the shortage of money, or of maintaining the shortage and allowing short-term rates to rise. In practice, the authorities normally try and create a shortage, to give themselves this option, by issuing Treasury Bills slightly in excess of the Exchequer's estimated needs. At this point the issues become more controversial (see Cramp, June 1966, and references therein).

In considering how effective control by means of a money shortage can be, the controversy turns on whether or not the discount houses are able to escape from the penal rate imposed if they borrow from the Bank, either by reducing their share of Treasury Bills, or by borrowing from elsewhere. Either way of escape is unlikely to be effective in current conditions, because the discount houses undertake to 'cover the tender' and because the sources of outside finance are limited.

The reasoning of this section leads to the conclusion that the authorities would find it very difficult to control the commercial banks by controlling cash. Since the authorities are concerned with the level of short-term rates, they are prevented from provoking a severe and long-lasting shortage of money because of the effect this would have on short-term (and eventually long-term) interest rates. The authorities have to be concerned with the level of short-term rates for a number of reasons. A powerful one is the need to keep rates in line with foreign monetary centres so as to avoid destabilising monetary flows. Related to this are the effects of servicing the debt and the effects on the balance of payments if the debt is held abroad. Domestically they may also wish to keep interest rates from rising for a number of social and economic reasons.

The previous assertion that the amount of secondary money in the economy depends in a complex way on a number of factors, in particular on the fiscal and budgetary policy of the Government, the public's attitude to government debt, and the reactions of the commercial banks, has now been justified and spelt out at some length.

Other financial institutions and financial intermediaries

The presence of a large financial sector apart from the commercial banks means that wider issues of credit and liquidity have to be considered. It has been argued that a number of factors have to be taken into account in considering the operations of the banks, and it is clear that these factors will also apply to these other financial institutions, for example the public's choice between holding deposits with the commercial banks or holding them with the acceptance houses, overseas banks or building societies. The monetary authorities have also to take the amount and composition of government paper into account, not only because it affects the commercial banks but because it is also important to these other institutions.

Previous chapters have traced the gradual unification of control over the financial sector and this will not be repeated here. What emerges from recent financial history is how quickly in a developed economy new money markets can spring up, how quickly new institutions come into being to meet new needs and how quickly existing institutions adapt to changing conditions. These may be highly desirable but they pose difficult problems for the management of money and credit.

Summary

This chapter set out to examine the forces that determine the amount of money (in the narrow sense of coin, notes and bank deposits) and the amount of liquidity in the economy and whether the amount of money and liquidity is under the control of the monetary authorities. Not surprisingly, no simple answer emerges. Monetary control is never likely to be a precise instrument, since it depends on so many things, in particular the whole fiscal and budgetary process and the attitudes of the public to saving and holding government debt.

The adaptability of existing institutions and the ease with which new institutions spring up is an added factor that makes control even more difficult.

Notes

1 The distinction between above and below the line items is historical. Items above the line were intended to cover expenditures met out of taxation and revenue derived from taxation. Below the line items, expenditures and revenue derived from borrowing. The distinction has little economic merit. For a discussion of alternative ways to present Exchequer accounts, see Peacock (January 1964).

2 These balances could, for example, be invested in local authority securities, in equities or left on deposit with commercial banks. A full analysis would try and take into account the secondary effects of foreign funds being invested in one type of security rather than another. The most important of these would be the effects on the commercial banks, interest rates and on the lending, borrowing and spending of the private sector. (For further details, see *Bank of England Quarterly Bulletin* (June 1962).) The tentative conclusion reached in the article cited was: 'It may be said that, in a period of restrictive credit policy such as 1960 and 1961, a substantial part of an inflow or outflow is likely to occur in ways that directly cause no change in bank deposits and domestic spending. Nevertheless some parts are likely to be in forms that do cause changes in the liquidity of banks and other credit-giving institutions.'

Part II
Public finance

8
Introduction to public finance

We cannot therefore settle on abstract grounds, but must handle on its merits in detail what Burke termed 'one of the finest problems in legislation, namely, to determine what the State ought to take upon itself to direct by the public wisdom, and what it ought to leave, with as little interference as possible, to individual exertion.
J. M. KEYNES, *The End of Laissez-Faire.*

The economic welfare of an individual is his command over goods and services. This command comes from a number of sources. It is derived from work, from accumulated wealth, from inheritance and gifts, and from government provision and legislation.

This book will not be concerned with the return from work as such. It is sufficient for our purpose to note that returns from different kinds of work are altered by society in various ways. For example, the beginning of the twentieth century saw the start of minimum-wage legislation, and in the 1970s we see efforts to have a more extensive incomes policy. Of more practical importance has been the extension of the provision of education out of general taxation so that entry to work requiring formal training is no longer confined to those able to afford the training. Within the existing framework of the returns from work this part of the book examines how the individual and the corporation are influenced by taxation of income, wealth, inheritance and gifts and the effects of government provision and legislation.

Public finance is about the revenue, expenditure and debt operations of the Government and the impact of these measures. The need for government spending (and therefore the need to raise revenue or debt) is argued on a number of grounds. A start can be made by considering the imperfections of the competitive pricing system.

Imperfections of competitive market prices

The model of a perfectly competitive pricing system has often been held up as an ideal: prices act as a guide to producers as to the things and quantities that they should produce and, assuming certain assumptions are met, output will be optimised. The usefulness of prices in this respect, in invisibly (but not costlessly) planning the immensely complex assortment of goods and services found in a modern developed economy, should not be underestimated. It is, however, the imperfections of the pricing system which give much of the interest to a study of public finance.

One drawback of a pricing system in allocating goods is that it only takes account of effective demand (i.e. demand backed by money). If income and wealth are spread unevenly deficiencies in allocation will occur. This deficiency in allocation provides one reason for state intervention, either to redistribute income and/or wealth to some extent, or to ensure in other ways some standard for its citizens. This point will be developed later in this chapter.

Another important modification to the optimality of the competitive pricing system has long been recognised: it is usually discussed under the heading of collective goods, externalities, or neighbourhood effects. These terms are used to draw attention to the fact that some goods confer large benefits not only on the purchaser but on other people too. The opposite may also be true: disadvantages may be imposed on other people, for example noise, dirt and pollution. In the former case where benefits are apparent this may result in the demand for this type of good being lower than the optimum level. We have a 'free-rider' problem, people hope to benefit from the provision made by other people without providing any themselves. In the case of harmful externalities, private demand is likely to exceed the socially optimum level. Minimum provision for sewerage disposal can be left to the individual in a sparsely populated area, but concentration of population in towns makes it essential to ensure that sewerage disposal is adequate. It is no accident that serious plagues have been eliminated from developed countries. Services of this type usually result in 'natural' monopolies. The waste in having more than one company digging up the same street to lay sewage pipes is obvious. The principle applies to other services such as gas, electricity, water supply, telephones, and so on. This conclusion leaves open the question of whether in cases such as this the Government should itself undertake the provision of the service and, if so, how the cost should be met, or whether the Government should merely supervise, and, if necessary, subsidise the private provision of the service. Also, where a good imposes a cost on the community (usually termed a 'social cost'), there are alternatives. The Government may just forbid the nuisance, say the disposal of waste in rivers, and thereby leave the cost of alternative means of disposal on those causing it (or on their customers); it may assist those concerned financially to make other arrangements, or the Government itself may make the alternative arrangements and decide how the cost shall be met.

In extreme cases any provision of a service means provision for everybody. These services are indivisible. Defence against external aggression and police protection are obvious examples. These are sometimes called 'pure public goods'. In cases such as these, the pricing system cannot operate, and provision of these services if left in private hands is likely to result in zero supply. In other words, the pricing system requires 'exclusion' – the ability to exclude those not paying from enjoyment of the product. Private consumption is described as rival: consumption by *A* excludes consumption by *B*.

The smooth working of a market system may also be upset by groups exercising some degree of monopoly power. Such power may be exercised by producers, workers, or, more rarely, consumers. Monopoly power may be exercised through some legal right, by the large size of the unit in relation to the total market or from collusion between smaller groups in the market.

Further distortions may occur because of the lack of markets (Joan Robinson, 1962, p. 124):

> There is a still more fundamental bias in our economy in favour of products and services for which it is easy to collect payments. Goods that can be sold in packets to individual customers, or services that can be charged for at so much per head, provide a field for profitable enterprise. Investments in, say, the layout of cities, cannot be enjoyed except collectively and are not easy to make any money out of; while negative goods, such as dirt and noise, can be dispensed without any compensation being required. When you come to think of it, what can easily be charged for and what cannot, is just a technical accident.

Finally, we may note that the market system can fail to establish an equilibrium. If left to itself the system may be subject to periodic boom and slump. Intervention in the market system in this case may take various forms, such as the establishment of future markets or markets for risk-taking, and planning by the Government. The intention is to reduce the uncertainty of a free-market system and thereby to reduce the fluctuations to which such a system is exposed.

It has been established that the free-market system has drawbacks; it must also be borne in mind that intervention by the Government to correct for these deficiencies also has a cost, and if carried too far can be self-defeating. The cost of intervention makes itself felt in the resources of manpower and materials that have to be devoted to this correction. As with so many economic activities, there is a trade-off situation in this case between correcting the deficiencies and the growth of bureaucracy, with the friction and frustration which this can engender.

The government sector

The above account of the inadequacies of the private pricing system helps to put a discussion of the public sector in perspective. Three questions are frequently posed:

1 How big should the government sector be?
2 How to determine how much to produce when the price system is inoperative, either through necessity, or a deliberate choice to meet the cost out of general taxation?
3 How to ensure that expenditures are efficiently, not wastefully, applied?

1 On the first question the writer believes that the economist, *qua* economist, has no unique answer. Indeed the question implies incorrectly that a level of activity can be specified which will be valid over time, valid under varying conditions, and which admits of a unique solution. 'Public goods', where externalities are large, are not constant over time. The growth, and particularly the concentration, of population means that problems of health and amenities (open spaces, clean air, water supply, communications, and so on) have more externalities. Again, if size is measured by the amount of government expenditure, it is worth emphasising that different decisions on the way to achieve a particular object will involve different levels of government expenditure. For example, a decision to maintain employment in the shipbuilding sector of the economy can be achieved by subsidies to shipbuilders or by providing cheap loans to purchasers, which will raise expenditure, or by tariffs, which will not. The conclusion to which this section tends is that the level of government activity at any one time is, in a democracy, essentially decided by political means.

2 The question of how much to produce, say of defence or public health, where the price system is inoperative, is an important one that admits of no easy solution. The principle of achieving equal marginal benefits

from various expenditures needs to be borne in mind; it may avoid crude waste of expenditure. For example, the argument is sometimes heard that 'if only one life is saved the expenditure (on, say, a road modification, or a particular safety device) is worth while'. If the objective is to save life the question that should be considered is 'In what way can this particular sum of money be spent so as to save the most lives?' However, as a practical guide for day-to-day decision-making, knowing whether £1 million spent on hospitals would yield more benefit than £1 million spent on defence or roads is more a matter of judgment than fact. This principle is likely to be more fruitful in allocating expenditure within a particular field, for example whether to spend £1 million on operating-theatres in hospitals, or on the provision of more hospital beds.

One possible way out of the difficulty of weighing up expenditure in disparate activities is to set up minimum standards of service,[1] say a policeman for every 1,000 of the population, the elimination of serious epidemics, maximum size of school classes of 25, maximum permitted levels of pollution, and so on. Provided these standards are based on the cost and benefits that flow from reaching them, they should aid decision-making. The standards will not be obtainable overnight but quantification of the costs and benefits and listing of the non-quantifiable advantages and disadvantages should enable more rational decision-making.

On the question of deciding how much of a particular good should be produced in the absence of price guide-lines, no economist would claim that, with existing knowledge and techniques, he can do more than assist in decision-making. Intuition, judgment and flair have their part, perhaps the major part, to play.

3 The question of ensuring economy in public affairs, in the sense that after expenditure decisions have been made the money is used efficiently and not wastefully, is important. However, the process whereby the Government attempts to secure economy in this sense, the weaknesses of present methods and hopes of improvement by new statistical and other techniques must be considered outside the scope of this book.

It may be noted in passing that 'extravagance' may be an indication of too little rather than too much administrative expenditure, in the sense that the misallocation of resources might have been avoided wholly or in part if there had been more, or better-trained, government officials. Aircraft development costs since the end of the Second World War seem an apt illustration.

The minimum level of government activity

The above outline enables us to discuss the minimum level of government activity – the level on which all reasonable people can agree.

Nearly all societies give some help to those who are incapable of helping themselves (mainly the young, the old, the sick and the disabled) and have no one on whom they can depend.

Collective goods such as the administration of justice and defence of the realm will form part of government activity for the reasons given in this chapter. (There may be deep divisions of opinion about the nature and extent of defence, about whether it is necessary at all, but if the need is granted nobody seriously suggests that private armies be formed.) The nature of collective goods is that they are non-rival: consumption by A does not preclude consumption by B.

Again, it is generally agreed that where an operation must, by its nature, be monopolistic in order to be efficient, for example sewerage and the supply of electricity, then the State should either control, or itself run, the service at the central or local government level.

General agreement occurs that where there are strong externalities government action is needed. Difficulties occur over those goods which have both a benefit to the individual and externalities: education is an example. Elementary education is recognised as having strong externalities: our present society would not be able to function without a certain level of education of the population. Not everybody agrees that, as yet, higher education has sufficiently strong externalities to justify meeting the cost out of general taxation.

This, then, is the minimum scope of state activity: some form of aid for the unfortunate, justice, defence, the regulation of natural monopolies and of those goods which have strong externalities, and expenditures necessary to regulate the economy. Public opinion in most societies would recognise this as the lowest common denominator of government action. Even at this level disagreements can creep in. If government action is admitted as necessary in a certain area, say education, it leaves open the question of whether the Government should itself undertake the provision of the service, or merely supervise its provision, and, if necessary, subsidise the private provision of the service.

Government activity, even at this minimum level, involves some redistribution of resources from the 'better off' to the 'worse off'. The questions raised by redistribution will now be tackled.

Redistribution of income and wealth

Redistribution in a community can take place by provision of services above the minimum levels just discussed, provided these are met out of taxes paid by the 'better off', or alternatively by direct money transfers from the 'better off' to the 'worse off'.

In talking about redistribution of income and/or wealth, three strands of thought are apparent. These will be discussed in turn. One is unavoidable if it is granted that help should be given to the unfortunate. The second strand of thought aims at deliberate redistribution above the level required to supplement the lowest incomes. The third strand is directed at changing the conditions which help create and foster the inequalities. In practice, these ideas may be interwoven, but conceptually much confusion can be avoided if they are kept separate.

If it is granted that a society should assist those who are incapable of helping themselves, then this implies that society has already made a decision that some redistribution of income and/or wealth is desirable. This conclusion is inescapable. In these circumstances the Government cannot be neutral in its attitude to the redistribution of income and/or wealth since a decision to help a needy section of the population entails redistribution from a 'better-off' to a 'worse-off' section.

Leaving to one side humanitarian arguments, the core of the case of those who advocate government provision, or alternatively argue for some redistribution of income and/or wealth above the minimum level just discussed, is that, as we have seen, needs are not satisfied equally if income is spread unequally, i.e. that economic welfare can be increased by government provision or redistribution. This case was well put by Dalton (1959, p. 10):

> Income consists of the means of economic welfare, and great inequality in incomes in any community implies great inequality in the economic welfare attained by different individuals. But this is not all. For it implies also considerable waste of potential economic welfare. Put broadly, and in the language of common sense, the case against large inequalities of income is that the less urgent needs of the rich are satisfied, while the more urgent needs of the poor are left unsatisfied. The rich are more than amply fed, while the poor go hungry. This is merely an application of the economists' law of diminishing marginal utility, which states that, other things being equal, as the quantity of any commodity or, more generally, of purchasing power, increases, its total utility increases, but its marginal utility diminishes.

This quotation contains two ideas. One that the economic welfare of different individuals can be compared. However reasonable such an idea may seem, particularly when we compare extreme positions such as giving a loaf of bread to a man who already has plenty with giving a loaf to a man who is hungry, there are those who hold that we have no objective measure by which we can compare needs of different individuals. We need not enter into this controversy because the second idea contained in this quotation is that the community should judge relative needs. Such judgment will not be to any absolute standard but will change as ethical, political, social, economic and other conditions change in the community. Much of the study of public finance can be taken up with a consideration of how these changes in community standards have affected ideas about government spending and revenue. Chapters 9 and 10 look briefly at the changes in Britain since 1900.

The more fundamental problem is to change the conditions of society which create and foster the inequalities and paradoxically this seems to receive less practical attention. It is perhaps inherent in most of us to regard as 'normal and just' whatever framework of society exists at the time. Even Plato carried forward the conditions of slavery into his *Republic*. We shall examine an important example of this tendency in Chapter 13 ('The criterion of ability to pay'), which is concerned with the extremely narrow definition of income which has grown up for income-tax purposes. A great deal of discussion that takes place is confined to rates at which taxes shall be applied within the current legislative mould. As we shall see in later chapters, questions about the nature of wealth and income are at least as important in discussing a tax system as the rates which happen to be applied at any particular time.

It should not be thought from the above discussion that redistribution is always and necessarily an act forced on individuals. The existence of charities is a contrary indication that voluntary transfers take place. Redistribution may have a number of aims. It may indeed be a forced redistribution, a reflection of existing political power. It may reflect a social preference for security against drastic income fluctuations, for example a willingness to be taxed now to ensure a right to payments if sick or unemployed in the future. Some redistribution may be welcomed as a hoped-for protection against disease, riots and civil disorders emanating from the poor. More widely, if individual utility functions are interdependent, it is possible that some redistribution will increase everyone's welfare, in the same sense that a transfer of pocket-money from parents to children can increase the welfare of both. The recognition that man is a social animal that can gain welfare from seeing a transfer to a less fortunate person enables redistribution to be analysed in terms of Pareto optimality, which seeks in this context to establish transfers that can take place with nobody being worse off. People may voluntarily consent to be taxed for these purposes to rule out the 'free-rider' problem, that is people may be willing to be taxed provided they know persons in similar positions will also be taxed. (For a seminal article analysing voluntary redistributions, see Hockman and Rodgers (1969).)

Horizontal and vertical equity

Underlying much of the discussion of public-finance matters is treatment of persons relative to each other. One of the few generalisations in public finance that commands wide acceptance is the idea that persons in equal positions shall be treated equally, termed 'horizontal equity'. It follows logically from this that persons in unequal positions shall be treated differently, termed 'vertical equity'.

Equal treatment is usually regarded in terms of equal sacrifice, or equal welfare loss. The rationalisation behind the rule is the assumption that welfare between individuals can be compared, that welfare is a function of income and/or wealth, and that the marginal utility of income is the same for all taxpayers. Given these assumptions, it follows that people in equal positions should be called upon to pay equal taxes (and receive equal benefits) and that people in unequal positions should pay different taxes (and receive unequal benefits).

It will be seen how fragile is the underpinning for tax and benefit discussion on these grounds. We have already referred in the previous section to the difficulties of making interpersonal comparisons. The assumption that welfare is a function of income may be regarded by many as a sufficiently close approximation to the truth, but the assumption that the marginal utility of income is the same for all taxpayers will leave many unsatisfied. As well as disagreements over these assumptions, the criteria on which equal positions are to be judged need to be reached. Should it be some abstract definition of income, or wealth, or both; or income, or wealth, or both as defined for tax purposes; or consumption? More contentious is how people in unequal positions shall be treated. Regressive, proportional and progressive taxes have all been advocated at different times. There is probably widespread agreement now that taxes that fall on the 'better off' rather than the 'worse off', and are progressive rather than proportional, are to be preferred.[2] These questions will be examined further in Chapter 13.

In the previous discussion on the redistribution of income and wealth we in effect postulated a social-welfare function, i.e. we inferred that society does make decisions of an interpersonal nature and that these decisions imply a set of preferences for social welfare at a particular time. These preferences may change over time, may indeed be inconsistent at any time. Part of the task of a study of public finance is to try and understand the reason for the changes and point out the consequences of the inconsistencies and the consequences of the particular social-welfare function that is being applied. In particular, there may be a trade-off between horizontal equity and vertical redistribution,[3] i.e. we may be willing to accept some horizontal inequality as the price of redistributing income from the rich to the poor. Thus a higher rate of value-added tax on goods such as luxury yachts which are purchased by the rich, but only some of the rich, violates horizontal equity but may be accepted by society in general as a means of obtaining revenue to achieve some vertical redistribution of income.

Dissatisfaction with welfare theories of public finance that rely on interpersonal comparisons or invoke a social welfare function has led some economists to try and ground a theory in the standard economic ideas of maximisation. See Downs (1956), Buchanan and Tullock (1962), Tullock (1976) and Buchanan (1977). They hypothesise that democratically elected governments seek to maximise their chances of re-election and voters seek to maximise their real incomes. While such forces may in the long run mould the fiscal system – the extension of the franchise with subsequent laws in favour of the enfranchised group is an example – the theory seems, at least at present, to be too restricted to provide a very adequate explanation, and will not be developed here.

Summary

By the economic welfare of an individual is meant his command over goods and services. This command comes to the individual from a number of sources. It is derived from work, from wealth, from inheritance and gifts, and from government provision and legislation.

Imperfections in the competitive marketing price system leave a vacuum for the community to fill. These are due to the uneven spread of income and wealth, leading to deficiencies in allocation, the presence of public goods and goods which have strong externalities, the natural bias of the private sector of the economy towards goods for which it is easy to collect payment, monopoly elements and failure of the market system to establish an equilibrium.

It has been suggested that there is no unique solution to the question about what is the correct level of government activity. The level itself is likely to change with time, with changes in population, and in the complexity of society. Also, changes in political ideals are likely to change ideas about goods which could be produced by the private sector, but which the State (for economic or other reasons) decides to control.

In deciding the quantities of goods to be produced, where no pricing system acts as a guide, the economist has a useful, if limited, role to play.

Government provision and legislation form the back-drop of a public-finance study. Government provision out of general taxation, or transfer payments such as pensions, are an obvious way of supplementing income deficiencies. Society judges the extent to which redistribution above this level is desirable. The economic justification for such provision is that command over goods and services is spread unevenly and a democratic society, in no very exact fashion, judges the relative needs of its members and deems that some minimum needs must be met for all; that is, some redistribution of command over goods and services shall take place.

Notes

1 Suggested by Drees jr (1967). This book was devoted to the *Papers and Proceedings of the Twenty-Second Session of the International Institute of Public Finance*. Many of the ideas touched on here are dealt with more fully in this volume.

2 In view of the tax on national insurance that is proportional only up to a level of income of £125 a week, and the increased emphasis on indirect taxes, this view is perhaps too sanguine.

3 I am indebted to Professor A. B. Atkinson for this point.

9

The pattern of government expenditure since 1900

Crying wolf at the drop of an index.
E. J. MISHAN (1967), *The Costs of Economic Growth.*

Conceptual difficulties

Government spending and taxation affect every individual. It is not therefore surprising to find that in public finance there are perhaps more attempts made by sectional interests to present biased information than in other economic fields. It is not uncommon to find people asserting opposite things, for example one will claim that public expenditure has gone up, another that it has gone down. Ignoring deliberate attempts to mislead by, for example, choosing a base period when prices were either particularly high or particularly low, or deliberately picking on the item which 'proves' the point in question and ignoring all the evidence to the contrary, there are still a number of difficulties to be overcome, which we shall look at briefly. After this the evolution of government spending during this century can be tackled.

First, figures of money expenditure, although useful in showing how expenditures on different sub-categories have changed relative to each other, tell us little about the share of government expenditure in relation to total resources. In order to measure the latter it is necessary to make allowances in some way for changes in the value of money. This can be done by some form of price index which can be used to represent the money figures in 'real' terms, i.e. in terms of command over goods and services, or by expressing government expenditure as a percentage of Gross National Product (GNP). Unfortunately, all ways of allowing for price changes have limitations, which means, not that the results are useless, but that we must use them with care.

Second, items should be related to population. The longer the period under consideration, the more misleading it can be to ignore this factor; for example, double expenditure in real terms does not imply double the amount of government activity if population has changed significantly in composition, or absolute numbers, or both.[1]

Third, we need to take account of the nature of government expenditure and draw a clear distinction between transfer payments on the one hand and direct government expenditure on goods and services on the other. Transfer payments are, as the name implies, payments made by the Government, such as pensions, family allowances and interest payments on the National Debt.

Transfer payments do not involve the Government in direct use of the nation's goods and services. Transfers may be classified in different ways: for example, transfers between persons, as between rich and poor; transfers over time, as with the provision of pensions; and transfers to meet contingencies such as sickness or unemployment. The use of the term 'fund' in National Insurance Fund can be misleading. It does not represent a transfer over time, in the sense that individuals pay now to build up a fund to pay for their future pensions and other benefits. Current payments are used to pay existing benefits. Pensions, for example, are largely a transfer from the working population, because they pay contributions, to the pensionable group. Existing workers in their turn, on the current method of financing, will have their pensions paid by the population working at the time they retire.

Finally, a great deal of confusion is caused because different concepts of 'government' are selected. Should government spending include spending by local authorities? Should it include spending by the nationalised industries? Fortunately, there is no need to seek a non-existing 'right' definition. Sometimes one definition, sometimes another, is useful; what we must avoid is misleading conclusions from figures drawn up on different bases.

Expenditure since 1900

Table 9.1 shows government expenditure for selected years since 1900. The definition of 'government' adopted will, throughout this book, include local government but exclude the nationalised industries, unless the contrary is stated. Nationalised industries have been excluded because they are not, as a rule, on the same footing as other government activities. Neither the nationalised industries' investment nor their charges form part

Table 9.1

Expenditure of central and local government on current and capital account, at current and at 1900 prices per head of population for selected years 1900–76 (£m. at current prices)

£m. at current prices

Year	Central government	Local government	Total	%*	Gross National Product (£m.)	Total spending as % of GNP
1900	182	99	281	35	1,944	14
1910	142	130	272	48	2,143	13
1920	1,275	317	1,592	20	6,070	26
1928	695	399	1,094	36	4,523	24
1933	676	390	1,066	37	4,141	26
1938	1,056	531	1,587	33	5,294	30
1950	3,479	1,060	4,539	23	11,636	39
1955	4,607	1,536	6,143	25	16,784	37
1955	4,683	1,622	6,305	26	16,974	37
1960	6,234	2,251	8,485	27	22,790	37
1965	8,649	4,112	12,761	32	31,310	41
1970	14,112	6,322	20,434	31	43,924	47
1974	26,366	12,300	38,666	32	74,958	52
1975	34,850	15,908	50,758	31	93,978	54
1976	40,278	17,408	57,686	30	110,259	52

1900 price deflated by population growth

Year	Price† index	Population index	Central government	Local government	Total
1900	100	100	182	99	281
1910	103	109	118	123	241
1920	282	106	432	101	533
1928	197	111	316	184	500
1933	173	113	344	201	545
1938	186	115	494	246	740
1950	380	122	765	215	980
1955	469	124	808	248	1,056
1955	469	124	805	279	1,084
1960	537	127	914	330	1,244
1965	632	132	1,037	493	1,530
1970	799	133	1,328	594	1,922
1974	1,220	133	1,625	758	2,383
1975	1,525	133	1,718	784	2,502
1976	1,761	133	1,720	743	2,463

Because of rounding, figures may not add up to the totals shown.

*Total local government expenditure at current prices as percentage of total government expenditure (i.e. that for central *and* local government).

†1900 prices for the years 1900–55 were arrived at by breaking down government expenditure into various parts, e.g. capital formation and goods and services, and appropriate price indices were applied to each component part. The 'price' index shown gives a rough average of these price indices. The index for the years 1955 onwards, shown beneath the line, is that for 'All final goods and services sold on the home market' from *National Income and Expenditure* tables adjusted to base year 1900.

Sources: for price index, population index and GNP up to 1955, Peacock and Wiseman (1961), table A.20, pp. 201–2, and table A.2, pp. 153–4; 1955 and after National Income and Expenditure *tables.*

of the budget process in quite the same way as other government activities. This will be taken up at the beginning of the next chapter. Table 9.1 shows expenditures for central and local government separately and a 'Total' column with them combined. The figures are given in £ million, first at current prices, that is at prices in the year in question, then in 1900 prices after allowance has been made for growth of population. For the sake of completeness a price index and a population index are given. Attention to the footnote to this table will make it clear that the price index is intended only as a rough guide. In practice, expenditure in the period 1900–55 was broken down into various parts, for example capital formation and goods and services, and appropriate price indices were applied to each component part. The 'price' index shown gives a rough average of these price indexes. The index after 1955 is that for 'all goods and services sold on the home market' from the *National Income and Expenditure* tables – adjusted to the base year of 1900.

The source of these figures, the price and population indices up to 1955 are from Peacock and Wiseman (1961). No attempt has been made to match the sophistication of Peacock and Wiseman's price index. The adjustment for price and population changes after 1955 are only intended to serve as a rough approximation. For this reason a line has been drawn across the table and figures for the year 1955 appear from both sources.

Table 9.1 shows very clearly that government expenditure has increased markedly in this century. The rather meaningless comparison in money terms is an increase from £281 million in the year 1900 to £57,686 million in 1976 or a 205-fold increase. However, prices increased over seventeen-fold in this period and population increased by 33 per cent. When allowance is made for these changes we get nearly a ninefold increase in expenditure in real terms per head (either a staggering increase or a revelation of the fantastic underspending in earlier years, according to one's viewpoint!). The changes in expenditure have not occurred at a steady rate, a point which will be considered later. Central government expenditure has increased more rapidly than local government expenditure. As a proportion of the total, local government expenditure decreased from 35 per cent or higher at the beginning of the century to around 25 per cent after 1945, but in recent years it has shown a tendency to increase once more. The effect of two world wars on centralising expenditure can be seen, expenditure in real terms by local government being lower after the wars than it was before. Part of the explanation of the change in local government expenditure is the transfer after the Second World War of gas and electricity services to nationalised industries.

Table 9.1 also shows Gross National Product (GNP) in current prices and total government spending in current prices as a percentage of GNP. The results, using a general index to deflate prices and GNP, do not differ very greatly from those using current prices, so the latter only have been shown in the table.

As a whole government spending rose from 15 per cent of GNP in 1900 to 52 per cent in 1976. In 1900 most of this expenditure was on goods and services and on capital account. By 1976 spending on transfer payments accounted for 39 per cent of this total.

These facts can be expressed rather differently. The money increase in GNP of about 57 times between 1900 and 1976 has the effect, when allowance is made for price and population changes, of increasing real GNP per head some 2.4 times. Against this increase over seventy-six years, government expenditure in real terms has increased nearly nine times; however, government spending on goods, services and capital account increased rather less than this at 6.1 times, the difference being made up by the bigger increase in spending on transfers and subsidies.

Table 9.2 splits the total figures of Table 9.1 into expenditure on goods and services, and expenditure on transfers and subsidies. The importance of this distinction has already been commented on. Together these expenditures equal the current-account transactions. If to the current-account expenditures we add expenditure on capital account, we reach the figures of total expenditure which agree with Table 9.1.

Tables 9.2 to 9.4 use figures at current prices but this does not matter as we are here interested in how the proportions spent on various services have changed, and deflating by a price index is not likely to alter these in any significant way.

The bottom part of Table 9.2 expresses these expenditures as a percentage. Taking the current-account transactions, we see that transfers and subsidies run at much higher levels in the later period. Subsidies are mainly to agriculture; transfers are either payment of interest on the National Debt or various social services payments. Fluctuations in social services payments will also cover very interesting variations, reflecting, for example, high amounts on unemployment pay during the slump of the 1930s, more on education, health and housing in the later years. Interest payments exhibit interesting variations during this period. Greater detail is available in Tables 9.3 and 9.4.

Expenditure on capital account exhibits wide variation. This is not unexpected since capital expenditures create durable assets. Neither the creation of the original assets nor their replacement is likely to be spread

Table 9.2

Expenditure of central and local government: on current account (goods and services, and transfers and subsidies) and on capital account for selected years 1900–76 (£m. at current prices)

Year	Goods and services	Transfers and subsidies	Current account	Capital account	Total expenditure	Capital expenditure as % of current account
	(1)	(2)	(3) = (1)+(2)	(4)	(5) = (3)+(4)	
1900	194.2	36.2	230.4	50.4	281	21.9
1910	171.8	55.1	226.9	45.1	272	19.9
1920	887.7	602.5	1,490.2	101.9	1,592	6.8
1928	451.9	534.1	986.0	108.7	1,094	11.0
1933	438.9	538.6	977.5	88.5	1,066	9.1
1938	822.7	545.6	1,368.3	218.7	1,587	16.0
1950	2,071	2,031	4,102	437	4,539	10.7
1955	3,192	2,333	5,525	618	6,143	11.2
1955*	3,171	2,305	5,476	829	6,305	18.2
1960*	4,163	3,260	7,423	1,062	8,485	21.2
1965*	5,919	4,822	10,741	2,020	12,761	25.0
1970	8,692	7,413	16,105	4,329	20,434	26.8
1974	15,981	14,746	30,727	7,939	38,666	25.8
1975	22,094	18,638	40,732	10,026	50,758	24.6
1976	25,742	22,523	48,265	9,421	57,686	19.5

Expenditure as a percentage of the total

Year	Goods and services	Transfers and subsidies	Capital account	Total
1900	69	13	18	100
1910	63	20	17	100
1920	56	38	6	100
1928	41	49	10	100
1933	41	51	8	100
1938	52	34	14	100
1950	45	45	10	100
1955	52	38	10	100
1955	50	37	13	100
1960	49	38	13	100
1965	46	38	16	100
1970	43	36	21	100
1974	41	38	21	100
1975	43	37	20	100
1976	45	39	16	100

Because of rounding, figures may not add up to the totals shown.

*In these years nationalised industries' figures were included in the analysis; these sums have been netted out, and assumed to relate to the capital account.

Sources: for 1900–55 Peacock and Wiseman (1961), table 5, p. 71, and table 6, p. 78; for 1955 and after National Income and Expenditure *tables.*

Table 9.3

Expenditure of central and local government on current and capital account by function for selected years 1900–67 (£m. at current prices)

Year	Administration and other	National Debt	Law and order	Overseas services	Military defence	Social services	Economic and environmental services	Total
1900	17	20	10	1	135	51	48	281
1910	22	20	13	1	74	89	53	272
1920	72	325	33	3	520	412	228	1,592
1928	49	305	31	1	125	434	149	1,094
1933	44	228	31	2	112	497	151	1,066
1938	61	213	39	3	473	596	202	1,587
1950	175	507	79	179	836	1,932	831	4,539
1955	182	707	115	80	1,606	2,692	761	6,143
1955	145	770	118	135	1,567	2,732	838	6,305
1960	194	1,025	174	213	1,612	3,877	1,390	8,485
1965	228	1,349	295	301	2,131	6,420	2,037	12,761
1970	414	2,026	521	333	2,465	10,176	4,499	20,434
1974	756	3,570	1,060	650	4,145	20,329	8,156	38,666
1975	1,067	4,231	1,386	677	5,225	26,297	11,875	50,758
1976	1,193	5,446	1,704	1,045	6,205	31,527	10,566	57,686

Current prices expressed as percentage of total government expenditure

1900	6	7	4	0.4	48	18	17	100
1910	8	7	5	0.4	27	33	19	100
1920	5	20	2	0.2	33	26	15	100
1928	5	28	3	0.1	11	40	14	100
1933	4	21	3	0.2	11	47	15	100
1938	4	13	2	0.2	30	38	13	100
1950	4	11	2	4.0	19	43	18	100
1955	3	12	2	2.0	26	44	12	100
1955	2	12	2	2	26	43	13	100
1960	2	12	2	3	19	46	16	100
1965	2	11	2	2	17	50	16	100
1970	2	10	2	2	12	50	22	100
1974	2	9	3	2	11	52	21	100
1975	2	8	3	2	10	52	23	100
1976	2	9	3	2	11	55	18	100

Because of rounding, figures may not add up to the totals shown.

Sources: for 1900–55 Peacock and Wiseman (1961), table A15, pp. 186–7 and table A16, pp. 188–9; for 1955 and after National Income and Expenditure *tables.*

evenly over time. The mistake should not be made of equating capital expenditures with 'useful' expenditures, and current expenditures with 'wasteful' expenditures. Both statements may be true, but both may be false. The tendency which regards expenditure on bricks and mortar as somehow 'better' than expenditure on training and pay of the staff to run the schools or hospitals or institutions once they have been built is all too apparent.

The period since the 1930s reflects the growth of Keynesian ideas that government spending can be used to take up the unemployment in the economy. In present-day conditions these ideas have been re-examined. The first crude idea of government expenditure acting as a regulator of the economy – expanding when the private sector contracts and vice versa – looks odd when the nature of much government expenditure is considered. Do we really wish to put off spending on roads, education or hospitals until such time as there is a danger of recession?

In the post-war period the authorities have been groping in a new direction. Fiscal and monetary policy is seen as a means whereby the private sector of the economy can be regulated. If the economy is slack, the private sector can be encouraged to undertake more capital investment by, for example, tax incentives, or attempts can be made to influence private expenditure on goods and services by reducing tax or by other changes. This can be in addition to, or in place of, changes in government spending. In a like manner, in times of inflation the private sector can be discouraged by tax increases from trying to undertake too much investment or consumption; the full brunt of the adjustment need no longer be borne by the government sector.

There is probably wide agreement on the principle involved in trying to regulate the economy in the way outlined in the preceding paragraph. Disagreements occur on the ability of the Government to undertake the regulation, and on the advantages and disadvantages of various monetary and fiscal weapons as means to achieve the regulation. Value-judgments enter when regulatory measures are at variance with equity aspects. These matters will be taken up in Part III.

Table 9.3 sets out information on government spending in the same two ways. The first part of the table gives figures in £ million. The second part expresses expenditure on each service as a percentage of the whole.

The following brief notes on the headings should make clear the nature of expenditure referred to and the main changes which have occurred.

ADMINISTRATION AND OTHER

This is a heterogeneous category covering the cost of tax collection, government buildings and maintenance. While these have, of course, increased in money terms, they have not done so in percentage terms. Not surprisingly, they take a smaller proportion of the budget.

NATIONAL DEBT

This is simply interest paid to sectors other than the government sector, that is the so-called 'net' debt which excludes inter-government transactions.

The National Debt interest payments show interesting variations. In the 1920s they amounted to well over a quarter of government expenditure, falling in the 1930s after the conversion operations in 1932 and 1934. The contrast in the proportion of the budget going in debt payments after the two world wars is very striking, and reflects the very different ideas of paying for these wars held at the respective times. A great deal of the credit must go to the ideas of Keynes (in particular see Keynes, 1940). The difference between the two war periods reflects the greater use of taxation in the Second World War compared with the greater use of debt policy in the First World War. The Second World War also introduced a special war-time tax known as 'post-war credits'. Sums paid in this form of taxation remain to the credit of the individual, returnable at the discretion of the Government. At present these are paid back to a woman on reaching the age of 55, to a man on reaching the age of 60. Since 1959 interest at the rate of 2½ per cent has been paid on sums still retained.

LAW AND ORDER

This includes the police, prisons, law courts and judges' salaries. In view of the current emphasis on crime it may seem surprising that a smaller proportion is spent on law and order in 1976 than in 1900. This relative change in emphasis poses interesting questions which cannot be pursued here. It might be argued that we are spending too little on this service, that, for example, our prison system is largely a relic from the nineteenth century. On the other hand, it may be that increased expenditure on other services has redressed the balance and reduced the relative needs of this sector.

OVERSEAS SERVICES

This is expenditure of the Foreign Office, colonial administration, the British Council and overseas broadcasting.

From very small absolute and relative amounts prior to the Second World War overseas services account for 2 per cent of total government expenditure after 1955. Part of the difference is explained by loans to overseas governments and net lending abroad for private industry, etc., which were excluded from the figures above the line, but included in the figures from 1955.

MILITARY DEFENCE

This includes civil defence. Military defence has always occupied a significant slice of expenditure in this period. From around a third of expenditure before 1920, a significant drop in the 1920s and 1930s to around a quarter of the budget in the 1950s, the 1960–76 period shows the proportion declining to 11 per cent.

SOCIAL SERVICES

These comprise education, child care, health, National Insurance (unemployment, sickness benefits, retirement pensions, etc.), supplementary benefit, housing (subsidies and capital expenditure), school meals, milk and welfare foods.

The importance of social services expenditure from the 1930s is evident from Table 9.3 and now accounts for 55 per cent of expenditure. The figures hide important changes in the nature of the expenditure which can be seen from Table 9.4.

ECONOMIC AND ENVIRONMENTAL SERVICES

These comprise services to agriculture, forestry and fishing, and include food subsidies and expenditure on industry and commerce – also the provision of basic services: roads and public lighting, fire, water, sewage, refuse, land drainage, coast protection, town planning, parks, libraries, museums and the arts.

These expenditures fluctuate a good deal, and accounted for 18 per cent of the total in 1976.

Table 9.4 presents the main items of social services expenditure. Differences in classification at this more detailed level mean that the proportions shown for the period 1920 to 1955 are not strictly comparable with those after 1955, but the broad trends are evident. While the proportion spent on education has accounted for nearly a quarter of expenditure during this period, expenditure on health, which includes some amounts for local welfare services and child care, has increased from around 12 per cent to around 23 per cent. The most important category, 'Social insurance and assistance', shows considerable variation and the figures do not bring out

Table 9.4

Expenditure of central and local government on current and capital account, on social services at current prices and as a percentage (£m. at current prices)

Year	Education	Health	Social insurance and assistance	Housing	Total
1920	97	49	213	53	412
1928	105	66	202	61	434
1933	107	75	269	46	497
1938	139	99	278	80	596
1950	440	478	674	340	1,932
1955	675	582	1,015	420	2,692
1955	549	619	1,075	489	2,732
1960	916	919	1,574	468	3,877
1965	1,588	1,375	2,537	920	6,420
1970	2,532	2,237	4,092	1,315	10,176
1974	4,601	4,515	7,103	4,110	20,329
1975	6,561	6,122	9,292	4,322	26,297
1976	7,340	7,310	11,687	5,190	31,527
Expenditure as a percentage of the total					
1920	24	12	51	13	100
1928	24	15	47	14	100
1933	22	15	54	9	100
1938	23	17	47	13	100
1950	23	25	35	17	100
1955	25	23	38	15	100
1955	20	23	39	18	100
1960	24	24	40	12	100
1965	25	21	40	14	100
1970	25	22	40	13	100
1974	23	22	35	20	100
1975	25	23	35	17	100
1976	23	23	37	17	100

Note: Because of rounding, figures may not add up to the totals shown.

Sources: for 1900–55 Peacock and Wiseman (1961), table 10, p. 92; for 1955 and after National Income and Expenditure *tables.*

the different nature of the expenditure in particular periods. The high proportion shown for 1933 reflects the high level of unemployment and hence unemployment payments of this period, while the later figures reflect the growth of social insurance. The fluctuations in housing reflect to some extent the different political emphases put on municipal housing by the respective Conservative and Labour parties.

Summary

Government expenditure has increased since 1900 in money and real terms per head of population. Of this expenditure the central government has increased its importance relative to local government. Although in recent years the trend has been for the local government share to increase, it has not reached pre-war proportions.

Of the broad categories of government spending we selected, the increasing importance of the social services showed up clearly, and within the social services the largest increase in expenditure was on health. Military defence fluctuated, as we would expect, and it still accounts for a sizeable amount of spending. Finally, the interest payments on the net National Debt showed interesting variations.

The rate of growth of the Government's claim on the national product (as measured by expenditure on goods and services) is impressive, if somewhat less than the rate of increase in government expenditure as a whole. Put the other way, expenditure on transfers and subsidies has increased faster than expenditure on goods and services.

Note

1 Looked at from a different viewpoint, if the Government undertakes exactly the same functions over a time period, it does not follow that expenditure, when allowance is made for price changes and population growth, will also be static. Age changes in the population will mean that different amounts need to be spent on, for example, education and old-age pensions. The figures have not been adjusted for this factor.

10

The pattern of government revenue since 1900

It has been maintained – and the assertion is scarcely an exaggeration that the theorems of Euclid would be bitterly controverted if financial or political interests were involved.
I. FISHER (1911), *The Purchasing Power of Money.*

Introduction

First of all this chapter takes a factual look at the pattern of government revenue since 1900. It then goes on to consider the aims of a tax system and the principles of taxation.

In looking at the pattern of government expenditure in the previous chapter it was possible to treat as a whole the expenditures of central and local government on both current and capital account. In presenting figures of revenue a similar procedure will be adopted whereby the items of tax revenue of central and local government will be presented. It is not the intention to present a complete revenue account, and some items such as trading income and income from rents, interest and dividends are not included.

The decision to exclude trading income is in line with the general treatment throughout this book. If, however, a government-run service is operated primarily as a tax device, this decision would clearly be incorrect. For example, some countries have a tobacco monopoly so that 'profits' from this service are no different from the large amounts raised in tax from tobacco in Great Britain. In a similar way services run at a loss represent a subsidy to the users of the service, met out of general taxation. In Great Britain lip-service at least is paid to nationalised concerns breaking even, taking one year with another. Three industries do not fit very well into this formula. For many years the postal services made a profit and contributed sums to the Exchequer, but on the other hand the National

Coal Board and the railways have made much larger losses. Arguments are put forward from time to time that some parts of a nationalised service will always have to be run at a money loss, the social or neighbourhood effects of these losses being held to justify the subsidy involved. In the absence of separation in the accounts of nationalised concerns of that part of the service run for social purposes as opposed to that part run on more commercial lines, taking account of the 'tax' or 'subsidy' involved is bound to be an arbitrary process. Therefore trading profits or losses are omitted. Our concern will be with the items of taxation which are regarded as variable in the budget to suit the revenue needs of the government.

Revenue since 1900

Table 10.1 presents the information on revenue, first in current money prices and then in percentage form. Since our interest is in the amount of revenue drawn from various kinds of tax, we can work in current prices without worrying that price and population changes will seriously distort the picture (see the opening remarks in the previous chapter). One should be warned that in looking at changes in the amounts yielded by different types of taxes the aggregate figures conceal changes in the rates of tax and of the income or goods which are subject to tax. The details of customs and excise taxes will be looked at in this chapter, while details of the other taxes will be taken up in later chapters.

Income tax has accounted for a quarter or more of total revenue since the 1930s, and, in much of the post-war period, for around 31 per cent. For 1975 and 1976 the percentage increased to 37 per cent, a small part of this increase being due to the amalgamation of surtax with income tax from 1973, but mainly the increase reflects the fact that tax rates were not fully adjusted to take account of the level of inflation in that period. Inflation results in more people being drawn into the income-tax system and increased numbers subject to the higher tax brackets. Income tax is subject to almost annual changes, either as to the rates applied, or to tax concessions granted. The impression that we have a steeply progressive marginal tax system is frequently obtained because income tax has steeply progressive marginal tax rates. However, income tax (and surtax when it was in operation) accounts for less than 40 per cent of total revenue, and when all taxes are taken into account the picture is rather different, as will be seen in Chapter 20 when we look at the incidence of taxes and benefits.[1]

The percentage yield from surtax (amalgamated with income tax from

1973–4) shows a diminishing trend from a high of 6 per cent before 1939 to 1 per cent in the post-war period.[2] It cannot be concluded from these figures that high incomes have diminished significantly in this period. Changes in rates and in the level of income subject to surtax, already mentioned, have to be taken into account, as well as the extent of legal avoidance. Faced with high marginal tax on money incomes, employers and employees have taken advantage of the fact that many tax-free benefits can be given: free meals, generous expenses, top-hat pension schemes, and so on. These benefit those concerned to the detriment of the Inland Revenue and other taxpayers, whose taxes are correspondingly higher. It may also be possible to convert incomes into a capital gain, which until recently was untaxed. For example, instead of a salary increase an executive may be offered share options or better pension prospects. Estate duties, incorporated into a capital transfer tax in 1974–5 have also been eroded by avoidance to a much greater extent. Estate duty accounted for 12 per cent of revenue in 1900, about 6 per cent in the 1930s and 1 per cent in the 1970s. Since taxes on estates are now much higher than they were before the war, amounting to 80 per cent on large estates as opposed to 40 per cent, it might be supposed that wealth is now more equally distributed. As we shall see, very little of the change in yield can be explained by redistribution effects. Rather, the explanation is to be sought in the fact that death duties were to a great extent a discretionary tax which could be legally avoided.[3]

Stamp duties cover miscellaneous items of revenue, of which the bulk is from *ad valorem* duties on the sale of houses, land and shares. Also included are the fixed duties once payable on cheques and other deeds. A not insignificant source of revenue in the early years of the century, these items now account for less than 1 per cent of revenue.

Taxes on companies were introduced to gather some of the excess profits which some companies were able to make in time of war. The high percentage figure shown in 1920 for profits tax was a reflection of the abnormal conditions still being felt as a result of the First World War. The corporate form of business has been growing in importance throughout this century and in interpreting these figures this fact must be borne in mind. The yield has increased in recent years and in 1974 was 10 per cent of total revenue. Because of special provisions for inflation and low profits, however, the yield for company tax is lower for 1975 and 1976. Whether companies should be taxed as companies, as opposed to taxing only the owners of the companies, together with the structure of tax and allowances, will be discussed in Chapter 15 ('Company taxation').

Table 10.1

Sources of UK tax revenue (£m.)

Year	Income tax (land and property)[1]	Surtax	Estate duties	Stamp duties	Profits tax[2]	National Insurance and health[3]	Customs and Excise	Motor vehicles[4]	Rates	Capital gains tax	Other	Total
1900	21	–	19	9	–	–	61	–	45	–	3	158
1909	37	–	18	8	–	–	63	–	68	–	4	197
1920	320	42	41	23	290	29	283	–	119	–	297[6]	1,443
1928	251	61	77	27	2	80	251	25	188	–	86	1,048
1933	252	61	77	19	2	88	288	28	165	–	30	1,010
1939	336	63	77	21	22	104[5]	341	36	214	–	23	1,236
1939	346	65	77	19	28	104[5]	382	34	214	–	23	1,292
1950	1,404	114	190	53	277	440	1,583	59	338	–	16	4,474
1955	1,964	132	184	75	223	594	1,990	85	475	–	17	5,739
1960	2,285	178	236	94	262	913	2,366	123	771	–	28	7,256
1965	3,374	184	287	76	466	1,685	3,425	189	1,228	3	41	10,958
1970	5,520	266	378	124	1,634	2,654	5,129	426	1,824	264	940[7]	19,159
1974	9,400	308	379	179	2,840	5,000	7,571	485	3,057	478	145	29,842
1975	14,154	124	307	266	2,260	6,835	9,064	662	3,983	520	173	38,348
1976	16,582	87	359	276	2,055	8,426	10,802	768	4,540	525[8]	275	44,695

Year	Income tax (land and property)[1]	Surtax	Estate duties	Stamp duties	Profits tax[2]	National Insurance and health[3]	Customs and Excise	Motor vehicles[4]	Rates	Capital gains tax	Other	Total
Percentages												
1900	13	–	12	6	–	–	39	–	28	–	2	100
1909	19	–	9	4	–	–	32	–	34	–	2	100
1920	22	3	3	2	20	2	20	–	8	–	20	100
1928	24	6	7	3	–	8	24	2	18	–	8	100
1933	25	6	7	2	–	9	28	3	16	–	4	100
1939	27	5	6	2	2	8	28	3	17	–	2	100
1939	27	5	6	1	2	8	29	3	17	–	2	100
1950	31	3	4	1	6	10	36	1	8	–	–	100
1955	34	2	3	1	4	11	35	2	8	–	–	100
1960	31	2	3	1	4	13	33	2	11	–	–	100
1965	31	2	3	1	4	15	31	2	11	–	–	100
1970	29	1	2	–	9	14	27	2	10	1	5	100
1974	31	1	1	1	10	17	25	2	10	2	–	100
1975	37	–	1	1	6	18	24	2	10	1	–	100
1976	37	–	1	1	4	19	24	2	10	1	1	100

Note: Because of rounding, figures may not add up to the totals shown.

[1] Land and assessed taxes were about £2.5 million until 1924 and thereafter declined in amount.
[2] Profits tax, called at various times excess profits tax, corporation profits tax, national defence contributions (profits), etc., and known in 1978 as corporation tax.
[3] From 1965 redundancy fund contributions are included.
[4] Prior to 1921 motor licences were included under Excise. From 1965 export rebates were introduced; these have been excluded from the figures.
[5] Refers to year 1937.
[6] Mainly receipts from the sale of war property.
[7] Includes £850 million from Selective Employment Tax, a tax which yielded revenue from 1966–73.
[8] Includes £31 million on lifetime transfers and distributions from trusts under the capital transfer tax.

Sources: for 1900–39 Financial Accounts of the United Kingdom *and* Statistical Abstracts of the United Kingdom; *for 1939 and after* National Income and Expenditure *tables.*

National Insurance and health contributions show the biggest percentage change of any tax in the table and in 1976 accounted for 19 per cent of total revenue. These contributions are now a proportionate tax up to a level of income of £120 a week, payable in part by the employer and in part by the individual.

The social services at the present time represent a not very happy mixture of services which are intended to be self-financed, some of which are intended to be partly met by way of contributions and partly met out of general taxation, and some met solely out of general taxation. Chapter 12 gives details of the financing of National Insurance and the health services. In current conditions the idea of earmarked taxes is a polite fiction that bears little relation to government accounting, a fact which has long been recognised in the case of the 'Road Fund'.

The broad category of taxes labelled 'Customs and Excise' has always represented a sizeable portion of revenue. From the 1920s up to the 1970s they accounted for roughly the same proportion of revenue as income tax. Table 10.2 gives the breakdown of customs and excise duty in 1976.

Table 10.2

Customs and Excise duty in 1976

	£m.	%
Alcohol	1,889	17
Tobacco	1,808	17
Hydrocarbon oils	1,941	18
Value-added tax	3,982	37
Protective duties	659	6
Car tax	224	2
Betting and gaming	285	3
Other	14	–
	10,802	100

Source: National Income and Expenditure 1966–76, *HMSO, London, 1977.*

From Table 10.2 it can be seen that the three stand-bys of the Exchequer are alcohol, tobacco and hydrocarbon oils, which accounted for 52 per cent of Customs and Excise revenue in 1976. Value-added tax brought in 37 per cent, details of which will be found in Chapter 16. The remainder of Customs and Excise revenue comes chiefly from protective duties, with betting and gaming contributing a small amount.

The revenue shown under motor vehicles in Table 10.1 covers the annual licence duty, which for private motor-cars was raised to £50 per annum in 1977.[4] Commercial vehicles are charged at a higher rate and goods vehicles are subject to a rising scale of charges based on the unladen weight of the vehicle. Cars are also subject to a car wholesale tax and fuel is taxed; the receipts for these appear under the heading 'Customs and Excise'.

In view of the annual outcry that is made against rates, it is perhaps surprising to find that as a percentage of revenue rates show a sharp decline from nearly a third of revenue in 1900 to 10 per cent in 1976. Rates are a local authority's only major source of revenue that is independent of the central government. They are levied by local authorities at so much in the pound on the rateable value of premises. One reason for the unpopularity of rates could be laid on the local authorities themselves. Rates are levied in two annual instalments so that the householder or ratepayer is faced with two payments to make of quite large magnitude, whereas most income tax is deducted by the employer under 'Pay As You Earn' (PAYE), and indirect taxes are included in the price of the article subject to the tax. Local authorities are now required to allow payment of rates by instalments. One reason for the decline in the share of revenue from rates is due to *derating*; this is the exemption, whole or in part, from rates for certain kinds of property. These first occurred in the depression of the 1930s and have continued with modifications ever since. At the present time buildings of charities are 50 per cent derated and agricultural land and buildings are wholly exempt. Manufacturing premises were 50 per cent derated, but were brought back into the rating system in 1963. Legislation in 1966 takes the amount due for rates into account in assessing the needs of applicants for pensions or other assistance.

Comment

Income tax and Customs and Excise duties have been the two most substantial sources of revenue in most years of this century. The impact of inflation in the 1970s has, however, tended to increase the proportion raised by income tax and decrease the proportion due to Customs and Excise. There are significant decreases in the percentages obtained from surtax, death duties and rates and a significant increase in sums raised by way of National Insurance and health contributions.

The tabulation of the existing sources of revenue that has been carried out in this chapter hides a curious feature. This could be brought out more clearly by having many more headings which until recent years would have shown nil returns. The majority of taxes shown in the table fall on current income; wealth as such was virtually untouched, apart from the small amounts raised by death duties and a portion of stamp duty that can be attributed to wealth movements. An outsider looking at this tax system might well conclude that our society despised and generally tried to discourage earned income while it looked up to and tried to encourage inherited wealth. A deeper probe of the system, to be found in Chapter 13 ('The criterion of ability to pay') will reveal that it is only income very narrowly defined which is heavily taxed. Spending power that comes in the form of gambling winnings, capital gains or gifts was virtually untaxed for most of the period covered by Table 10.1.

Table 10.1 does not bring out important changes that have been made in recent years, as these have as yet made little impact on the revenue received. Details of the taxation of petroleum and gas from the North Sea are given later in this chapter. A capital gains tax of a very restricted kind was introduced in 1962; a more thorough-going tax was introduced in 1965 and subsequent changes have been made. Chapter 14 ('Personal income taxation') gives details. Chapter 17 ('Wealth') looks at the major changes that have been brought in with the capital transfer tax.

International comparisons of tax

Meaningful international comparisons are notoriously difficult to make, and this is certainly true in the tax field. For example, different definitions of taxes, differences in the proportions of social security which are financed out of general taxation, and different treatment of small businesses, complicate the picture. The economic effects of the proportion raised in tax will also depend on the nature of public expenditure, particularly the proportion which goes to grants and subsidies.

The comparisons made in this section draw on *Tax Statistics 1970–1975* (1976); these are drawn up by the Statistical Office of the European Communities and present figures for the member countries on a consistent basis. Since we are closely allied with these countries, a comparison is not without interest. A rather wider coverage of OECD countries will be found in *Revenue Statistics 1970–1975* (1976).

Figure 10.1 shows the countries of the European Community ranked in order of the size of their total tax receipts and actual social contributions expressed as a percentage of their GNP at market prices. The United

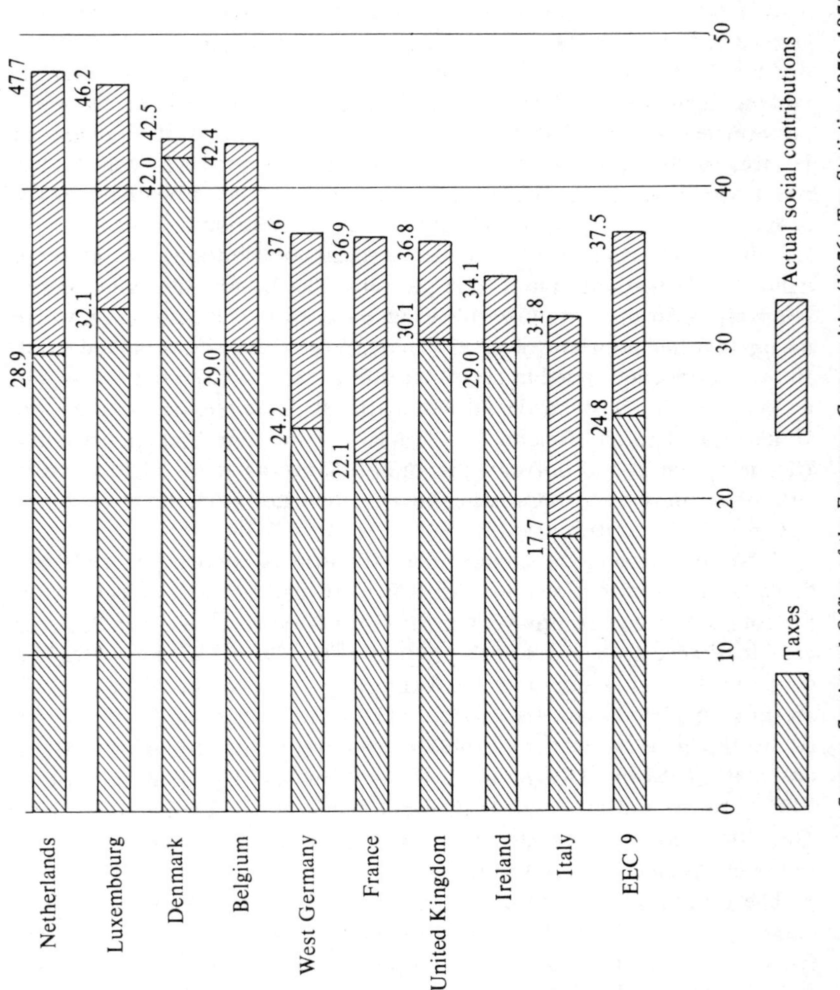

Figure 10.1 *Total tax receipts and actual social contributions in 1975 as a percentage of GNP at market prices*

Kingdom comes well down the list, being ranked seventh out of nine. West Germany, France and the United Kingdom come very close together in the middle of the tax table. Comparisons taken back to 1970 do not alter the ranking significantly. Attempts, therefore, to relate the poor economic performance of the United Kingdom, compared with West Germany or France, to the high over-all level of taxes in the United Kingdom do not stand up to scrutiny. The figure shows the marked differences in the proportions raised by taxes and by social contributions. Denmark raises less than 1 per cent of her revenue by social contributions; on the other hand, the Netherlands raises 18.8 per cent. The United Kingdom raises a relatively small proportion in this way: she is again ranked seventh, which means that her position for taxes is much higher and she is ranked third. But the proportion raised in taxes, excluding social contributions, is within a close band in five countries: the Netherlands, Luxembourg, Belgium, the United Kingdom and Ireland. The average for the nine Community countries is shown at the bottom; the United Kingdom raises slightly less in total than the average but a rather higher proportion from direct taxes and less from social contributions.

Table 10.3 shows the comparative structure of total tax receipts and actual social contributions in 1975. There are marked differences between the countries. General-turnover taxes, e.g. VAT, varies from a high 23.4 per cent in France to a low of 8.7 per cent in the United Kingdom. On the other hand, when excise duties and consumption taxes are added to VAT receipts, differences are less marked. The United Kingdom is one of five countries where receipts from these two sources cluster around the 20 per cent mark. The United Kingdom has a low rate of VAT compared with other EEC countries but taxes, in particular, tobacco and alcohol more heavily. The United Kingdom's high proportion shown under 'Other taxes' is due to the inclusion of local authority rates.

The significant difference in the table is the proportions raised from current taxes on income and wealth and from social contributions. The two extreme countries are France with 18.4 and 39.9 per cent respectively, and Denmark with 60.9 and 1.4 per cent respectively. The United Kingdom is closer to the Danish pattern, with 45.2 per cent raised from income and wealth taxes and 18.2 per cent from social contributions. Since both sets of taxes fall on income, can any significance be attached to these differences?

The financing of social security exhibits many differences in detail, but except for Denmark, where the overwhelming bulk of finance comes from general taxation, the broad pattern is the same. A proportion of the cost is met out of general taxation, some is met by specific charges for services

Table 10.3

Comparative structure of total tax receipts and actual social contributions in 1975

	West Germany	France	Italy	Netherlands	Belgium	Luxembourg	United Kingdom	Ireland	Denmark
General-turnover taxes	14.0	23.4	14.4	14.1	15.7	11.9	8.7	14.6	17.4
Excise and consumption taxes	8.4	6.2	13.5	6.0	6.5	7.4	12.4	25.7	13.4
Sub-total	22.4	29.6	27.9	20.1	22.2	19.3	21.1	40.3	30.8
Other taxes*	10.1	11.3	3.8	5.0	5.5	10.5	14.7	12.0	6.6
Total taxes linked to production and imports	32.5	40.9	31.7	25.1	27.7	29.8	35.8	52.3	37.4
Current taxes on income and wealth	31.6	18.4	23.7	35.1	40.0	39.4	45.2	31.6	60.9
Capital taxes	0.1	0.7	0.2	0.4	0.7	0.3	0.8	1.1	0.3
Actual social contributions	35.7	39.9	44.4	39.4	31.5	30.5	18.2	15.0	1.4
Total	100	100	100	100	100	100	100	100	100

*Other taxes comprise import duties and agricultural levies, taxes on services, taxes on land and buildings, stamp registration and similar duties, and other taxes linked to production and imports.
Note: because of rounding, columns may not total 100.
Source: Statistical Office of the European Communities (1976), Tax Statistics 1970–1975.

and some from social contributions which come from a levy on employers and employees. That part of the levy that falls on firms is thus in the nature of a general employment tax which can be expected to raise prices proportionately. The employees' tax is either flat rate or, like the UK contribution, graduated up to some level of income. The social contribution is not in general assessed on unearned income, e.g. retirement income, so that the working population's combined income-tax and social contributions will be considerably more than those not in work with the same income. There is clearly a value-judgment involved in the more desirable tax structure to aim for. In this book the judgment has been made that social contributions and income tax could be combined, a move towards the Danish model, but not without considerable modification of the income-tax structure.

Table 10.4 looks at maximum percentage marginal rates of income tax in 1976.

Table 10.4

Maximum percentage marginal rates of income tax, 1976

	%	Approximate sterling figure of taxable income above which highest rate is payable (£)
United Kingdom	83	21,000
Ireland	77	not available
Italy	72	not available
The Netherlands	72	34,000
Denmark	*	*
France	60	not available
Belgium	60	64,000
Luxembourg	57	13,700
West Germany	56	32,000

*The state income tax is at a top rate of 39.6 per cent, which is payable on income levels above, approximately, £8,000. To this must be added county and municipal income taxes and certain other social contributions. It is therefore difficult to state a maximum marginal rate. Average rates are such that if a person's combined state, county and local income tax, and old-age pension contribution exceeds 66⅔ of taxable income, relief is given by reducing the national income tax. Similarly, if national and local income taxes, the national pension contribution and net wealth tax exceed 70 per cent of taxable income, the national income tax is reduced.

Source: Commission of the European Community (1977), Inventory of Taxes 1976, *Edition Directorate of Taxation, EEC, Brussels.*

Table 10.4 goes a long way to explain why it is generally thought that the United Kingdom is a high-tax nation, in spite of the fact that she was ranked seventh out of nine when tax and social contributions are expressed as a percentage of GNP. Table 10.4 shows that the United Kingdom ranks first when looking at marginal rates of tax on earned income. The comparison with unearned income is even more unfavourable. With the exception of the United Kingdom, the Netherlands and Denmark, the rates of tax do not distinguish between earned and unearned income. In the United Kingdom the top rate on unearned income reaches 98 per cent. The second column of this table shows very approximately the taxable income levels above which the highest rates of tax are payable. The United Kingdom again appears in an unfavourable light. A full-scale study of tax comparisons would have to take the peculiarities of each tax structure into account, for example the steepness of the progression, and the nature of the income-tax base. Such a study would be unlikely to reverse the conclusion that the maximum marginal rate reached in the United Kingdom is too high and likely to be counter-productive. (For a provocative account on these lines, see Bracewell-Milnes (1976; 1977). Also, Messere (1975) analyses trends in a number of countries over the period 1965–72.

Petroleum and gas taxation

A substantial source of revenue until at least the 1990s should be provided by the revenues obtained from the extraction of North Sea oil and gas. The system of taxation is rather complicated as it tries to accommodate the sometimes conflicting aims of ensuring exploration of the resources and at the same time that the Exchequer benefits adequately from the discoveries. (Early muddle was disclosed by the North Sea Oil and Gas Committee of Public Accounts (1972-3).)

The system of taxation now consists of a royalty, petroleum revenue tax (PRT) and corporation tax, levied in that order.

ROYALTY

Royalty in 1978 was 12.5 per cent of gross revenues, with the latter assessed as the value of production if the oil were to be sold in the open market to an independent purchaser. In the first four rounds licensees were allowed relief on their transportation costs from well-head to shore. The Secretary of State for Energy is empowered, with the consent of the Treasury, to refund royalties in whole or in part in order to provide an incentive to a licensee to develop or continue production from a field which would not otherwise satisfy normal commercial criteria. Royalties are allowed as a deduction against PRT and corporation tax.

PETROLEUM REVENUE TAX

PRT is chargeable on each field separately, and the liability shared among the licensees in proportion to their stakes. It is 45 per cent of the net income from the field.[5] Net income is defined as the gross revenue, minus royalties and operating costs (excluding interest payments). The tax came into force on 13 November 1974, although capital expenditure incurred earlier is allowed against it. Gas sold under long-term contracts signed not later than 30 June 1975 to the British Gas Corporation is exempt as these contracts were negotiated without taking account of PRT liability.

There are substantial allowances which lessen the impact of PRT. No PRT need be payable until the net revenue received exceeds the capital expended on exploration and development, together with an 'uplift' of 75 per cent on most of this expenditure. The latter provision aims to partly compensate for the fact that interest payments are not allowed against PRT, and so help companies to recover their capital early in the life of a field. A group may also set off, against its profits on an operative field, abortive exploration expenditure or a loss incurred on an abandoned field elsewhere in the North Sea.

An oil allowance which is equivalent in money terms to 500,000 tons of production each six-month tax period is allowed up to a cumulative maximum of 10 million tons per field. This can be set against PRT liability after account has been taken of all other deductions. The allowance cannot be carried forward or backward to any other tax period.

There is a safeguard provision that restricts the total PRT charge to no more than 80 per cent of the amount (if any) by which net income exceeds 30 per cent of the accumulative capital expenditure on the field to date. If the net income is less than this proportion of capital expenditure, no PRT is payable. This provision was designed to offer protection to the licensees against a fall in the price of oil relative to other prices.

CORPORATION TAX

In calculating profits for corporation tax, operating costs, royalties and PRT are deducted. To protect the revenue a so-called 'ring fence' system was put in operation in July 1974. This was designed to ensure that losses and capital allowances from other activities and associates are not offset against oil revenues.

REVENUE

The Treasury forecasts made in 1977 estimate that the revenue from oil and gas will total some £5 billion in the five years from 1976 to 1980, and will be some £3.5 billion a year by the mid-1980s. These estimates use 1976 prices. Revenue of £3.5 billion represents about 9 per cent of total government revenue for 1975, so this will provide a substantial, though temporary, source of finance.

EFFECTS OF NORTH SEA OIL AND GAS

The latest estimates for North Sea oil envisage output rising to a peak in the late 1980s and thereafter falling away as the reserves are used up. This is likely to make it necessary for Britain, assuming the present make-up of energy sources, to again have to import substantial amounts of oil some time in the 1990s. Current estimates point to there being a world energy shortage in the 1990s and this has coloured most comments on how Britain should use this windfall.

There are two major effects flowing from the North Sea discoveries. One is the temporary release from the balance-of-payments deficit which has constrained economic policy very tightly since the Second World War. This improvement comes from oil imports that we no longer have to buy at a cost to our currency reserves and also from expected receipts from oil exports. In the absence of sensible action this balance-of-payments constraint would reappear in the 1990s as oil and gas reserves run down. The second effect is that the expected revenue from the discoveries would, if used rightly, avoid the difficulties foreseen for the 1990s.

The worst situation would be one in which the improvement in the balance of payments due to oil takes place at the expense of manufacturing industry. If Britain does not adopt a sufficiently vigorous energy policy and if she allows her exports to be priced out of foreign markets, by allowing excessive appreciation of sterling, paying herself too large wage benefits and not modernising her industry, then the difficulties of the early 1970s are likely to appear in worse form in the 1990s.

In contrast the revenues provide an opportunity for the economy to be revitalised, and for some of the resources to be devoted to alternative energy sources and energy-saving. The inquiry into the proposed extension for nuclear processing at Windscale in 1977 sharply focused attention on the latter issues. There are those who see the solution to the expected energy gap in the extension and development of nuclear power. Many others, of whom the author is one, prefer to put off the extension of nuclear power, particularly the fast-breeder reactor. The radiation and other dangers are seen as so great, extending over so long a time span, and irreversible, that these should be put off as long as possible.

The Department of Energy (1976-7) produced a series of discussion documents on alternative energy sources which could bear fruit if acted upon. It could lead to more balanced expenditure on research and development than that shown in 1976-7, when £95 million went in nuclear fission compared with £9 million for all other energy sources. In a similar manner, using existing materials to insulate buildings has been estimated to bring substantial cuts in energy demands. In terms of future capital needs for energy this represents a large saving and a very cost-effective use of funds.

Aims and principles of taxation

A fiscal system serves various purposes besides the obvious one of providing revenue. Following Musgrave (1959, p. 5) these will be collected under the three headings of allocation of resources, distribution of resources, and stabilisation of the economy.

ALLOCATION OF RESOURCES

This aspect of taxation is concerned with the allocation of resources between, for example, private and public goods and between investment and consumption goods. It is also concerned with correcting deficiencies in the pricing mechanism due, for example, to monopoly elements, the existence of external economies or diseconomies, and cases where social costs diverge sharply from private costs.

DISTRIBUTION OF RESOURCES

Chapter 8 has already indicated that the distribution of income and wealth depends on a number of factors including work, educational opportunities, inheritance, gifts, government fiscal policy and legislation. The distribution heading is concerned with the adjustments that society decides to make in order to correct for deficiencies in the distribution of income and wealth.

STABILISATION OF THE ECONOMY IN TERMS OF CURRENT OBJECTIVES

Current objectives usually include: obtaining and maintaining a satisfactory level of growth, maintaining full employment, ensuring stability in the value of money and maintaining a satisfactory balance of payments.

It should be noted that, until recently, only the 'allocation of resources' has been considered as a part of public finance. After about 1900 the 'distribution of resources' began to be considered. Interest in the 'stabilisation of the economy' is due to the ideas of Keynes in the 1930s.

Within the aims selected by society as relevant, persons have been looking for centuries for a general principle that could be used as a guide to apportion taxes in an equitable manner. Two principles have long been canvassed and we shall now discuss these.

The 'benefit principle' and 'ability to pay'

These have mainly been discussed in relation to the allocation of resources.

When the aims of public finance are drawn more widely to take in the distribution and stabilisation aims, neither will be found without fault, but both can contribute to our understanding of the problems involved. (A detailed discussion of these principles will be found in Musgrave (1959, chs 4 and 5).)

The benefit approach dictates that taxes are apportioned to individuals according to the benefits they derive from government activity and spending. Taxes are treated as a payment for the goods and services provided by the Government. The provision of government goods and services will, like the provision of private goods and services, be dictated by market demand. In a society where the aims of the Government are conceived in minimum terms of defence against external aggression and in the administration of justice, as during eighteenth-century England, this approach is understandable. The existing structure of wealth and income was taken as given, and the economy was conceived as self-regulating. These ideas have given ground on all fronts. It is generally conceded that private provision in the absence of government intervention will be seriously deficient where there are strong positive externalities, and will be over-supplied where there are negative externalities. Some redistribution of income and wealth is granted as necessary in all developed countries and stabilisation of the economy has been taken for granted since the 1930s. With these wider aims the benefit rule is clearly inadmissible as a principle of general application. The more the Government did to help the needy, the more the needy would have to pay. The whole transfer process which has been seen taking place, particularly in this century, would be frustrated. Again the allocation of some benefits, for example defence, would be an arbitrary process; and the aims of stabilisation would not necessarily be carried out by following the benefit principle of taxation. Nevertheless, the benefit principle may have application in limited areas where a close relationship between outlay and benefit can be established. Thus where the Government undertakes the provision of a service, which could equally well be undertaken privately and there are no strong externalities, the danger of not charging according to the benefit principle is that demand for that service is likely to be stimulated at the expense of services where costs are allocated to users. This may represent an uneconomic use of the nation's resources. For some services, for example health and education, this extension of demand is deliberately aimed for: neighbourhood effects apply. In others, for example government provision of some forms of transport, or some forms of fuel, failure to charge users with the costs of the services or commodity is likely to have the effect of distorting the use of the nation's resources in an undesirable way. No general solution emerges. It is necessary in each case to weigh the social benefits and costs involved in charging users for the full costs of the service and in meeting these costs out of general taxation, or of some compromise between these two methods.

The ability-to-pay approach is concerned with the equitable distribution of taxes according to the stated taxable capacity, or ability to pay, of an individual or group. It leaves the correct contribution that government provision should make to be decided on political grounds. This rule, in terms of the objectives stated at the beginning of this section, enables the distribution and stabilisation objectives to be carried out in an equitable manner. Its disadvantage, that the allocation objective has to be decided by other means, has just been stressed. With the ability-to-pay principle, the criterion on which ability is to be judged has to be set out – i.e. whether it is to be income, wealth, income and wealth, or spending power. This will form the main concern of Chapter 13. In their usual formulation these criteria do not take into account benefits from government expenditure that accrue to the individual. However, it is possible to define the criteria to include these benefits. This partial synthesis of the two approaches will be developed further in Chapter 23.

Summary

Taxes on income account for roughly a third of government revenue and excise duties for about a quarter over much of the period considered. In 1976 excise duties received almost equal revenue from tobacco, hydrocarbon oils and alcohol, with value-added tax accounting for most of the balance. National Insurance and health contributions show the largest increase and now account for 19 per cent of total revenue. The proportions raised from surtax, estate duties and rates show a sharp decline. It is not correct to conclude from this that high incomes have diminished dramatically or that the distribution of wealth has altered radically.

Recent years have seen the introduction of a number of important taxes: on capital gains, on betting and gambling, and on capital transfers, to be outlined in future chapters.

An international comparison of taxes in the EEC countries was given. The United Kingdom ranks low in the list for the total amount of taxes and social contributions as a percentage of GNP, but ranks first in having the highest marginal rate of income tax.

The important and complicated system of North Sea oil and gas taxation was examined and the implications of the substantial, but temporary, revenues looked at.

A fiscal system is aimed at providing revenue and also serves other purposes. These were collected under three headings: allocation of resources, distribution of resources, and stabilisation of the economy. Within the aims selected by society as relevant, two principles of taxation have been put forward: the 'benefit principle', and 'ability to pay'. Neither of these principles, in present-day conditions, is without fault, but an understanding of them is useful in trying to formulate a satisfactory fiscal system.

Notes

1 This fallacy of taking income tax as representing the tax system and thereby concluding that 'governments have generally striven to spread the burden of taxation as fairly as possible having regard to ability to pay, taking account of family circumstances as well as income and wealth' was enshrined in the 1977 Central Office of Information Pamphlet No. 112, *The British System of Taxation*, p. 1.

2 Sums shown in Table 10.1 for surtax in 1975 and 1976 represent residual payments from past years.

3 Those who regard this statement as a wild exaggeration might ponder the advertisements that appear in newspapers. For example, the *Financial Times* on 16 December 1967 carried two advertisements on this theme. The largest, spaced over two columns, read: 'ESTATE DUTY IS ALMOST A VOLUNTARY TAX! If you have an estate duty problem and love someone more than the Exchequer – we can assist you. We have specialised in designing original schemes for Top People for over 20 years.'

4 The Government announced in November 1978 its intention to change from the system of vehicle licensing duty to one where an additional tax was placed on petrol. Such a change should benefit the low mileage motorist and encourage the sale of cars with high miles-per-gallon.

5 A field is defined by Act as 'any area which the appropriate authority may determine to be an oil field', the appropriate authority being the Secretary of State.

11
Government expenditure and revenue concluded

They [politicians and experts] have to say whether it is better to try for a surplus or to acquiesce in a deficit. They both have to consider economic and political consequences. But, so far as taxpayers are concerned, all such questions are subsidiary to the critical issue of distribution. . . . It is usually assumed that other problems may be best resolved by shifting the burdens elsewhere. And there is no lack of ingenuity in providing the necessary rationalizations for the desired results.
L. EISENSTEIN (1961), *The Ideologies of Taxation.*

To explain adequately the changes in expenditure and revenue would require a full-scale social and economic history of the post-1945 period. Similar trends to the ones observed in this country can be seen in most developed countries over the same period. In this chapter the main pressures that have helped to mould the system are outlined.

Pressures on government spending

Adolph Wagner (1890) was predicting that public expenditure would increase (at least for a time) at a faster rate than national output. We get a law of 'growing public expenditure'. He based his observations on the results of a study of developed Western countries and on the grounds that state activity would need to increase as a result of social progress. To date, Wagner's prediction has proved to be accurate. The extent to which it will continue to hold good in the future is more problematical. The fact of adult male suffrage in 1887 and the start of female suffrage in 1918 is likely to have played a very important (though largely unquantifiable) part. With adult suffrage Parliament is likely in its spending and revenue to reflect the needs of the community as a whole more closely than before, because Members of Parliament depend on the goodwill of the majority of the community for their seats.

Not always stressed as much as it deserves to be is the pressure on public spending caused by the *growth* of population and the *concentration* of population. Services which can be safely left to the individual in a sparsely populated country have to be undertaken by the community in a more populated country, sewage and water supply being obvious examples. The process is still at work today. Government spending or regulation on smoke abatement in large urban areas is beginning to take on the nature of a social necessity and we can expect expenditures under this head to increase in the future; the motor-car is creating its obvious pressures on the public purse; and so on.

It is sometimes possible to distinguish two trends under this general heading. One which has been called 'externalities' refers to the benefit which the whole community derives from the service. Leaving the provision of such a service to the goodwill of the individual who is likely to take only his private benefit into account would result in serious deficiencies, and would be to the general detriment of all. The basic services referred to in the previous paragraph come into this category.

We can also distinguish cases where technical considerations apply, i.e. where, in order to obtain a better use of resources, collective provision is needed. Thus the generation of electricity could be left to the individual, but each building with its own generator is a very inefficient way, at the present time, of obtaining electricity. The State usually steps in at the local or central level to run the service, or to supervise the provision of the service, if monopoly powers are granted to a private concern. New processes and inventions change these technical considerations in no very predictable manner. We have already reached the stage where it is technically an extremely inefficient use of resources for each building to supply its own needs for heat and hot water. Centralised provision of hot water to houses and other buildings in selected areas could yield large economies in the use of fuel, as well as yielding benefits in terms of cleaner air and better living conditions.

In contrast to the neighbourhood and technical effects stressed above, social reasons for public spending, i.e. the wish to spread benefits to the community at large, have played an important (but once again hard to determine) part. This is particularly noticeable in the extension of education, health and the social services generally. The desire to spread income and wealth more evenly has also helped to shape the expenditure and the revenue sides of public finance. Finally, since the depression of the 1930s most Governments accept that they have a positive role to play in keeping the economy in balance, avoiding both the extremes of slump and of severe inflation. This compensatory aspect will lead to a larger rather than a smaller government sector.

Pressures on government revenue

To pick out some of the pressures that have shaped public expenditure is analogous to explaining price by looking at demand and ignoring supply. If we look at public expenditure and revenue over time, we find that they are uneven. In particular we can single out wars as causing large jumps in government expenditure. By itself this is not a surprising feature. What is interesting is that government expenditure does not go back to its former level after the war. This observation is apparent even when allowance is made for price changes and when war-related expenditures are excluded.

Peacock and Wiseman (1961) use the term 'displacement effect' to cover this phenomenon. Once again we find that many strands knit together to cause this effect. Peacock and Wiseman develop the idea that in normal times there is a dichotomy between the desire for public goods and services and the level of taxation which is considered tolerable. A large-scale disturbance, such as a war, may create an upward displacement of the level of taxation considered tolerable, so that new levels of public spending can afterwards be maintained.

In time of war new methods of raising revenue or new methods of collecting existing revenue may be accepted; there is some release from the 'bonds of the revenue'. The introduction of purchase tax was an example of the former, PAYE is an example of the latter. War also focuses attention on social ills: 'It has taken the catastrophe of war to bring home to those in power that economic progress does not automatically disseminate the benefits of education and health' (Peacock and Wiseman, 1961, p. 93). Such a period may also see an acceleration in the reorganisation of government accounts, statistical information and in civil service procedures. Thus periods of crisis such as war and the severe slump in the earlier 1930s seem to act as catalysts. We do not know what would have happened in the absence of these disasters, but in the light of hindsight they appear to break the 'cake of custom'.

Recasting the system of revenue

In the 1960s and 1970s there have been a number of major changes on the revenue side. On indirect taxes we have moved from a system of purchase tax on selected goods to a broadly based value-added tax (VAT) on most goods and services. Some of the inequalities of income taxation have been tackled indirectly by subjecting some of the spending power which escaped taxation to other forms of tax. The most notable change has been the capital gains tax and taxes on betting and gambling. Wealth taxes have been the latest to receive attention with the old inequitable system of death duties swept away and replaced by a capital transfer tax that includes a tax on gifts. This period also saw the rise and fall of Selective Employment Tax (SET). This tax and details of the tax on betting and gambling will be outlined in the rest of this chapter. Details of other changes will be found in following chapters.

SELECTIVE EMPLOYMENT TAX

Although Selective Employment Tax (SET) was phased out in 1973, it had a number of interesting features. The tax was introduced in September 1966 with the intention of taxing labour in the service, distribution and construction industries.

Two justifications were given in the White Paper *Selective Employment Tax* (1966) for this tax. The first, and generally agreed, aim was that service and distributive trades should bear a portion of the tax bill since purchase tax was only payable on certain goods. This has the important advantage of allowing the Government to restrict consumer demand without causing the whole impact to fall on those industries subject to purchase tax and excise duties. The second, more controversial aim, was that it would in the longer term encourage the redeployment of labour from the service, distribution and construction trades to industry. The tax also had the effect of acting as a mild stimulus to exports, since wage costs in manufacturing industries were lowered.

On the first aim, if a system of indirect taxes is in operation the only economic arguments for taxing a small range of goods and services is the ease of collection. On social grounds it may be desired to tax goods consumed mainly by the rich, but such goods are not easy to discover. On economic grounds the case for taxing all goods and services, rather than taxing fewer items more heavily, is that consumer prices will reflect more closely their relative costs. In turn this is likely to lead to a more efficient allocation of resources. In the past relative prices of services and manufactured goods were distorted because the former were untaxed while the latter were subject to various rates of tax. Under any system of tax some items, such as alcohol and tobacco, will probably be taxed more heavily for social reasons; but here the deliberate intention, as well as to raise revenue, is to choke off some of the demand for these products.

The second aim of encouraging redistribution of labour by giving what is in effect a subsidy to manufacturing establishments is more open to criticism. Manufacturing as well as other concerns may be guilty of hoarding labour, and SET did nothing to encourage the manufacturing sector to use its labour wisely, rather the reverse.

The method used to collect the tax was by way of surcharge on employers' National Insurance contributions. Since these contributions do not draw any distinction between employers in different industries, all were subject to the tax at different rates for men, women, boys and girls. Manufacturing industry received back after six months the contributions paid plus an addition which was originally 37.5p per week in respect of each male employee, with lesser amounts for the other categories. A number of other sectors received back just the sum paid, with service, distribution and construction trades receiving no rebate.

Changes were made in rates of SET from time to time and in its operation, for example, to remove the discrimination against the employment of part-time workers. A major alteration came into operation in September 1967 when the tax was seen as a method of increasing employment in the development areas. Since January 1966, development areas are defined to include, except for small areas deemed to be sufficiently developed, Scotland, Northern England (i.e. the four northern-most counties of England plus the North Riding of Yorkshire), Wales, Merseyside and the South-western area which takes in much of Devon and Cornwall. Premiums to manufacturing industries in these areas were to be paid out for not less than seven years and then planned to be phased out over another two or so years. These premiums were in addition to the refunds already received, and amounted to £1.50 for men, 75p for women and boys, 37.5p for girls, with half the premium in each case being paid in respect of part-time employees. The premiums at these rates were estimated to be worth about £100 million a year to the development areas.

The aim of these premiums was to reduce the disparity in unemployment levels between the development areas and the rest of Britain. It was argued that, if successful, this would have the effect of helping Britain's growth without adding to inflationary pressure or leading to any worsening in the balance of payments, and could be done without the need to increase taxation. These desirable effects would be brought about, it was believed, because any increase in demand for imports would be offset by increased exports, and the competitive loss by manufacturing industry in the rest of the country would offset the extra demand deriving from the higher levels of income and output in development areas. Therefore, higher levels of tax would not be required to release resources for the subsidy. The White Paper discounted the idea that the premiums would only result in increases in wages, and that firms would use them to increase profits and not reduce prices.

The extra rebate to industry was subsequently withdrawn from manufacturing industry outside the development areas and the rates of SET increased.

SET was abandoned in 1973: the coming of VAT achieved the purpose of a broader tax base. The regional employment premium, however, continued to be applied to manufacturing industry in development areas. It was ended at the end of 1976 in favour of more flexible measures to help these areas.

SET was never a popular tax but it proved an extremely flexible tool. In its short life it was used to discriminate between different regions of the country, different sectors of the economy, and by age, sex and time worked. It was relatively simple to administer. Although abandoned and unlikely to be resurrected in its old form, the idea of a tax on labour, or a payroll tax, must appeal to Chancellors of the Exchequer when hard pressed for funds.[1]

BETTING AND GAMBLING

To the future historian the most surprising thing about betting and gambling may well be the length of time that elapsed before they were taxed. This was so in spite of the example, from a number of other countries, that large sums could be raised from this source. The reasons for this immunity have been partly objections on moral grounds and partly difficulties of collection. Winston Churchill's betting levy between 1926 and 1929 was a failure, and may have acted as a deterrent.

A pool betting tax was introduced in 1947. This was a tax virtually confined to football pools which were taxed at 33⅓ per cent on weekly turnover. A 10 per cent totalisator tax on dog races was also imposed at the same time. In 1963 on-course bookmakers at dog tracks were required to have an excise licence; this was abolished in 1966. A football fixed-odds betting tax was introduced at 25 per cent in 1964 and football pool tax reduced to this level. The totalisator tax on dog races was reduced to 5 per cent at the same time.

It was not until the Finance Act of 1966 that an attempt was made to tax gambling and betting more comprehensively. This act introduced 2½ per cent tax on the amount staked with a bookmaker or on a totalisator, so that the tax on dog races was again reduced. The tax on football pools remained at 25 per cent. In addition, gaming was taxed by requiring premises where gaming was carried on to have an annual gaming licence.

The Budget of 1968 increased the betting tax from 2½ to 5 per cent, and raised the pool betting duty to 33⅓ per cent. Fees for gaming licences were also raised. Currently, in 1978, the betting tax is 8.1 per cent, except for on-course bets, where it is 4 per cent, with pool betting 40 per cent unless the proceeds benefit a society established for charitable, athletic or cultural activities when it is 33⅓ per cent. The lower tax on 'on-course' betting is supposed to encourage the racing industry by encouraging attendance at meetings. A uniform betting tax with an agreed proportion returned to the industry for selected uses might be a preferred alternative.

Collection of the betting tax

The betting tax, on the amount staked on any bet with a bookmaker, is now therefore standardised at the rate of 8.1 per cent for off-course betting and 4 per cent for on-course betting, regardless of the type of event or contingency which is the subject of the bet.

The bookmaker, or operator of a totalisator, is responsible for payment of the duty, which is due when the bet is made and *not* when the account is settled. The collection of the tax is administratively straightforward. The operator of the totalisator normally pays the tax weekly. The most usual method for a bookmaker is to purchase betting duty sheets, in advance of the duty becoming due, on which summarised details of the bets have to be recorded. The sheets are available in various denominations from £5 to £9,995. The alternative method of paying the tax applies only to off-course bookmakers who may apply to make monthly returns. Approval is subject to the bookmaker satisfying minimum security arrangements in order to safeguard the revenue.

Incidence of the betting tax

There is no standardised procedure for passing on the betting tax. Some bookmakers put a loading on the bet staked, some make a deduction from winning bets. Off-course bookmakers commonly make a levy of some 8 to 8½ per cent to recoup their overheads and payment of the betting levy.

GAMING

Gaming was first brought into the tax net in 1966 by requiring premises where gaming was carried on to have an annual gaming licence. The cost of this licence varied with the rateable value of the premises and according to whether bingo only or other gambling games were played. In 1969 the system was changed in respect of places where bingo only is played. These are now subject to a duty of 5 per cent of the stakes in each week plus one-nineteenth of any amount by which the value of the prizes won in a week exceeds the total of the money taken after the deduction of the duty payable. Premises where other gambling games are played are still subject to duty by a licence valid for six months. The licence is now for each gaming table, not for the premises, and the cost varies with the rateable value of the premises, as shown in Table 11.1.

Table 11.1

Rateable value of premises	Duty per table per half year (£)
Not exceeding £1,500 (or no rateable value)	500
Between £1,500 and £3,000	750
Between £3,000 and £4,500	1,250
Between £4,500 and £6,000	2,500
Between £6,000 and £7,500	3,750
Between £7,500 and £9,000	5,000
Between £9,000 and £10,500	6,250
Between £10,500 and £12,000	8,750
Exceeding £12,000	11,250

Gaming-machine duty

A licence is normally required for any machine provided for gaming, the most common type of machine being the so-called 'one-armed bandit'. The amount of duty depends on: (i) the number of machines; (ii) whether they cost more than 1.25p to play once – 'higher rate' machines – or 1.25p or less, in which case they are 'lower-rate' machines; (iii) whether the premises have local authority approval under the Gaming Acts; and (iv) whether the licence is for a whole year or a half year. The half-year licences cost eleven-twentieths of a full-year licence.

Table 11.2 sets out the main details. As Table 11.2 shows, the cost of having gaming machines in premises which are not licenced under the Gaming Acts is considerably higher than having them in licenced premises.

Table 11.2

Gaming-machine duty annual rates in 1978

	No. of machines	Premises with local authority approval	Premises without local authority approval
Lower rate	1	£12.50	£50
	2 or more	£12.50 plus £50 per machine in excess of one	£50 plus £100 per machine in excess of one
Higher rate	1	£25	£100
	2 or more	£25 plus £100 per machine in excess of one	£100 plus £200 per machine in excess of one

In both cases the cost of two machines is considerably in excess of twice the rate of a single machine.

A holiday season licence, valid between 1 March and 31 October, may be taken out at a cost of £7.50 per machine provided the machines can be played once for a penny or less and certain other conditions are met. Charitable entertainments and pleasure fairs are exempt, subject to conditions on stakes, prize money, etc. being met.

LOTTERIES

A lottery has been canvassed for a long time by a number of people as a way of raising revenue. The amount of money raised in a number of overseas countries is cited in support of the idea. Since lotteries, unlike taxes, are entered into voluntarily they have attractions to the revenue-raiser whether at local or national level.

Lotteries in England were limited to a turnover of £5,000 with a maximum prize of £1,000, but from 1 May 1977 local authorities and charitable, sporting and cultural societies have been empowered to run lotteries on a slightly more ambitious scale. The biggest lottery, which must not be held more than four times a year, is restricted to a turnover of £40,000 and single prizes of £2,000. Total prize money can be up to 50 per cent of the take. Tickets must not be more than 25p and expenses in general limited to actual expenses, with a limit of 15 per cent of turnover. There are limits on where the tickets may be sold, for example they may not be sold on the street or in betting offices, bingo halls or amusement arcades.

While the moral arguments against allowing betting, gambling and lotteries can be appreciated, the moral twist that allows only private enterprise, such as football-pool promoters, to give large prizes is harder to follow.

CONCLUSIONS

The taxation of betting and gambling, perhaps inevitably, presents a complicated picture. From Tables 10.1 and 10.2 we see that in 1976 it raised £285 million compared with £768 million from vehicle licence fees, £359 million from estate duty and £525 million from capital gains tax.

The fact that now, with two exemptions, the rate of tax is uniform, regardless of the type of event or contingency which is the subject of the bet, is to be welcomed. The exemptions are curious. One is the lower rate of tax on on-course betting, a roundabout method of assisting the racing industry. The other is the rate of tax of 40 per cent on football pools which, if we take net expenditures, i.e. expenditure less the amount returned to punters as winnings, is markedly higher than other betting and gambling taxation. The rates of tax on these other forms look low when compared with the high rates of income tax.

The argument is sometimes put forward that betting and gambling reflects a circular flow of income with most of the stake money being returned to the winners and being restaked, and so on, and that to tax at higher rates would kill the industry. Since all economic activity can be represented as a circular flow, this argument hardly provides a case for lower taxes on betting and gambling.

The device of taxing gambling by rateable values of the premises is obviously an extremely crude procedure. This is not the place to examine alternatives, but examples from a number of foreign countries show that there are feasible and better alternatives.

In July 1978 the Royal Commission on Gambling (1978) made a highly critical Final Report. It found the situation it had unearthed as scandalous. 'There is wholesale disregard of the law (which is inadequate and confused), commercial exploitation to a totally unacceptable degree, gross lack of security and, we strongly suspect, a good deal of plain dishonesty.' Amongst its more than 300 recommendations was the proposal to have a national lottery with a top prize of £500,000, the proceeds to be used for deserving causes. Football pool top prizes should be restricted to £500,000 and the two biggest operators' profits should be limited to 2.5

per cent of the money staked. Football pool betting duty should be reduced from 40 per cent to 37 per cent. Horse racing should be reorganised and revision made of the rules governing bingo and jackpot machines. The management of local authority lotteries was severely criticised. Tax rates on casinos should in general be raised by a factor of eight, and a new 3 per cent levy on the cash drop (money exchanged for gambling tokens or chips) made where the drop exceeds £10 million annually. The Commission estimated that in 1977 casino tax receipts would have risen from £5.5 million to £54.4 million had this been in force.

Summary

Britain, in common with other developed countries, shows a marked increase this century in government expenditure and hence in taxation. Political pressures, growth and concentration of population, the wish of the community to spread benefits to the population as a whole, and the desire to spread income and wealth more evenly, can all be identified as major forces that have helped to shape expenditure and revenue. From the revenue side two world wars, as well as focusing attention on social ills, has enabled fiscal innovation to take place and given Governments larger tax resources to continue a higher rate of expenditure.

Two taxes were examined: SET, introduced in 1966; and the new taxes on betting and gambling. This latter area of taxation still exhibits illogicalities with pool betting being taxed at a much higher rate. In general gambling is taxed by the crude method of taxing the rateable value of premises where the activity takes place. It is still the case that a person who has spending power from earning will be likely to pay a great deal more in tax than a person who has the same sum as a result of a bet.

Note

1 As the National Insurance surcharge referred to on pp. 166–7 indicates. So that Britain has now moved from a system where labour was subsidised under certain circumstances in the period 1966–73 to one where since 1977 there is a general tax on labour. The matter is further complicated by employment subsidies of various kinds which are available in selected areas.

12
The social services

> The ideal towards which we would like to see policies directed would be a world in which large social groups, such as pensioners, the disabled and students, whose needs are in total reasonably predictable, rarely have to rely on a last-resort means-tested, labour-intensive service for their incomes. Households of average size should rarely have to turn to supplementary benefit when drawing contributory unemployment and sickness benefits. Now that a more generous pension scheme is slowly taking shape, the adequacy of family benefits in general, and the new child benefits in particular, seems to us to be the most urgent concern of the whole field of social security.
>
> Supplementary Benefits Commission, *Annual Report, 1975* (1976), Cmnd 6615, HMSO, London, September 1976, para. 2.34.

A list of the major public social services is given in Table 12.1. Finance comes from diverse sources. These are contributions from local authorities, contributions from employed persons and from employers, part payment from the users of some of the services and contributions from the State out of general taxation.

With the exception of National Insurance, these services are financed in the main out of general taxation of the central government with the lesser part being financed by local authorities. Attention will be confined to discussing the financing of National Insurance and looking at the differences between the National Insurance and social security schemes.

National Insurance

The basic ideas of Beveridge (1944) which provided the basis for the National Insurance system after 1946 was that the system would 'guarantee the income needed for subsistence in all normal cases'. Social security supplementary benefit (formerly 'national assistance') is a system of

Table 12.1

Social security
National Insurance
pensions
unemployment and sickness benefit
maternity benefits
industrial injuries
Family allowances
Social security supplementary benefits (old title 'national assistance')
Public health
National Health Service
hospital and general practitioner services
Environmental health services
sewage, home refuse, water supply, etc.
Education
Housing
Other services, such as
employment exchanges, retraining, town and country planning, highways, administration of justice, child-care, parks, the arts

means-tested benefits designed to catch what was thought would be a small number of people who 'fell through the meshes' of the insurance system. The National Insurance scheme pays benefits as of right, but with some benefits for limited periods, to those who have paid sufficient contributions.

From the start the implementation of the scheme has fallen short of these ideals. The basic flat-rate insurance benefits are still insufficient to raise a person with no other income above the poverty line, so that individuals and families with few other resources have to seek supplementation. Also, Beveridge's proposals that payments should 'continue' so long as needs last was never implemented for unemployment benefits; these now cease after twelve months and the earnings-related supplement is not paid after six months.

Whether the term 'National Insurance' is a good one to use has been debated since its inception. There are two basic principles of private insurance, the less important one being that the premium to be paid should be based on an assessment of the risks involved. Thus a thatched house pays a higher premium against fire risk than a similar house with a tiled roof, motor insurance premiums may vary with the age of the insured, his accident record and occupation, type of car, etc. A person in chronic poor health, or over a certain age, is unlikely to be accepted at all in a private medical-care scheme. In contrast, state insurance was instituted on the principle of collective risk and flat-rate contributions and benefits.

The more important principle of private insurance is the actuarial aim that premiums should more than cover the claims paid out. There has been disagreement from the start whether state insurance should operate on similar lines. The idea that the State should build up a fund to meet future contingencies was not contemplated. The issue is between those who wish to see a 'pay as you go' system, and those who wish to see the whole, or part, of the expenditure met out of general taxation. Lord Beveridge, whose report formed the basis of the extension of the National Insurance scheme after the war, envisaged the scheme as being financed on a tripartite basis: from employers, employees and the State. It was envisaged that employers' and employees' flat-rate contributions would provide the bulk of the necessary revenue. However, it was foreseen that the State would need to contribute a large amount for many years towards the provision of pensions since people nearing retirement age at the start of the scheme would not be able to contribute much towards the scheme.

The flat-rate personal contribution was assessed as the rate of contribution at the minimum age of entry to the scheme which, say, a male would have to pay over his working lifetime to ensure the benefits on an actuarial basis. This rate, less the employers' and state contributions, was the flat-rate contribution for all males. In any one year such a scheme will leave the State with a larger, or smaller, contribution to make, depending on many factors, such as the age structure of the population and the degree of sickness and unemployment.

Many commentators have pointed out the weakness of this idea. Financing the bulk of the service by flat-rate contributions sets a limit to the amount that can be collected without imposing undue hardship on the poorest in the community. The amount so raised may bear little relation to the needs of the community. This fact, and the general inflation which has occurred since 1945, has eroded to some extent the concept of self-financing outlined. These ideas of self-financing on the one hand, and of meeting expenditures out of general taxation on the other, continue to be debated.

The departure from the flat-rate system has been very gradual, a fact all the more surprising given the regressive nature of such contributions. In 1961 a proportionate element was introduced into the pensions part of the insurance contributions. Those employees not contracted out (i.e. other than those whose employers' pension scheme met certain standards) paid an additional 4¼ per cent of earnings between certain limits in return for graduated pension rights. Employers paid a similar contribution. The scheme had a certain element of redistribution in it since the element of graduated pension was tapered off at the top end of the scale. In 1966 a similar type of levy was imposed at the rate of 0.5 per cent of earnings between certain limits to meet the cost of earnings-related benefits.

This rather cumbersome system combining flat-rate and graduated contributions was largely replaced on 6 April 1975 by a mainly proportional system of wholly earnings-related contributions, payable by both employers and employees. The contributions are collected through PAYE income-tax arrangements for employed people. In April 1978 rates were differentiated according to whether a person was or was not contracted out of the new pension arrangements. There are four classes of rates which from 6 April 1978 are payable by working men under 65 and women under 60 if they continue to work; contributions cease, even if working, at 70 for men and 65 for women.[1]

Class 1 rates[2,3]

Employer: 12 per cent on earnings up to £120.00 a week if employee is not contracted out. If employee has contracted out, 12 per cent on earnings up to £17.50 a week and 7.5 per cent on earnings between £17.50 and £120.00 a week

Employee not contracted out: 6.5 per cent on earnings up to £120.00 a week

Employee contracted out: 6.5 per cent on earnings up to £17.50 a week and 4 per cent on earnings between £17.50 and £120.00 a week

Reduced rate for certain married women and widows: 2 per cent on earnings up to £120.00 a week.

If an employee earns less than £17.50 a week no contribution is paid either by himself or his employer.

At £17.50 a week the employee pays about £1.14 and his employer £2.10 a week. At the top end employees earning £120 a week or more if not contracted out pay £7.80, if contracted out £4.10, while their employers pay £14.40 and £9.79 respectively.

Class 2 and class 4 self-employed rates[3]

Class 2 flat-rate contributions

£1.90 a week

(Application may be made not to pay if earnings are below £950 a year.)

Class 4 contributions[3]

5 per cent of profits or gains between £2,000 and £6,250 a year, so that the maximum payment is £212.50.

Class 3 voluntary rates[3]

£1.80 a week

Class 1 rates will be paid by the bulk of the employed population. Employees not contracted out pay higher contributions and will be entitled to an earnings-related pension. Employees who are contracted out must be in a private pension scheme which is at least as good as the state scheme.

The reduced rate applies to married women and widows if they have elected to forgo certain benefits; the employer's rate is not affected by this choice. This right is being phased out as part of the pension scheme introduced in April 1978, although married women who have opted, before this date, for the reduced rate may continue with it.

All self-employed persons with profits or gains over £950 pay the flat-rate class 2 contribution of £1.90 a week; in addition if profits or gains are between £2,000 and £6,250 an additional 5 per cent is payable. This means that the self-employed will pay just the flat rate of £1.90 a week if earnings are between £950 and £2,000, and at the top end £5.98 a week if earnings reach or exceed £6,250. The flat rate is paid, like the old system, by sticking stamps on a National Insurance card or, if preferred, by direct debit from a bank or National Giro account. Class 4 contributions will normally be collected by the Inland Revenue along with Schedule D income tax. For these higher contributions the self-employed get fewer benefits as they are not entitled to unemployment benefit or to earnings-related benefits.

The voluntary contributions of class 3 are only payable if it is desired to qualify for certain benefits and not enough class 1 or class 2 contributions have been made. They are paid by stamps or direct debit.

A person who has two jobs, one as an employee and the other in self-employment, has to pay both class 1 and self-employed class 2 contributions and is liable to class 4 if profits or gains are sufficiently large. There is, however, an upper limit to the amount of contributions that need to be paid in this case.

Two simultaneous systems of income tax

Britain has now moved very closely to a system of dual income tax. The tax called 'income tax' is a tax on income with allowances giving a starting-point well above the first pound of income with rates beginning at 25 per cent and going up to 83 per cent on earned and 98 per cent on unearned income. The other income tax, called 'National Insurance', is on income earned before retirement. It taxes all earned income without any exemptions (provided income is above £17.50 a week) at rates which for employees are proportional to earnings up to £120 a week; thereafter the percentage declines as earnings above this are not subject to any contribution.

Amalgamation of income tax and National Insurance contributions is, fairly obviously, a strong candidate for consideration on several grounds as well as administrative simplicity. It would provide an opportunity to look at several unsatisfactory features of both systems. Examples under income tax include the system of tax allowances, the high starting rate of tax, the degree of progression and the top rates of tax. On the National Insurance side, examples include the regressive nature of the contributions since contributions are only proportional up to a level of £120 a week of earnings, the unsatisfactory distinction between the self-employed and others and the curious vindictiveness to those who have dual employed/self-employed status. If, as seems reasonable, it is desired to exempt retirement incomes from National Insurance contributions, this could be achieved by a change in tax coding for the retired. The position of the unemployed and the sick who are exempt from National Insurance contributions would not be very different if amalgamation with income tax took place, since less tax would be payable if income drops as a result of these misfortunes, and it can be argued that if income is maintained in sickness by an employer there is no reason for exempting such a person from levy.

The arguments against amalgamation tend to cluster round the idea of benefit taxation: that certain services should be paid for by the user. For example, an increase in pensions should be met by an increase in the pension component of the National Insurance contribution and not from some other source. It has already been shown that the connection between charges and benefits is very tenuous, the State contributing varying amounts out of general taxation to all these services. In particular, there is no funded pension scheme, current pensions being largely paid by current National Insurance contributions with the hope that future contributors will in their turn provide pensions for existing payers when their turn for retirement comes. Amalgamation would not stop the Government announcing that so much of a change in income tax was due to the change in National Insurance benefits. It need not stop the separate parliamentary accountability of the accounts of the National Insurance Fund if it desired to retain this feature.

The argument is sometimes put forward that people would not be willing to pay in increased taxes what they are currently paying in National Insurance contributions (*National Superannuation and Social Insurance Proposals for Earnings-Related Social Security*, 1969). This argument cannot be rejected out of hand if it is simply meant that the straight combination of National Insurance and income tax would be unacceptable. What is provided, it has been suggested above, by combining the two types of tax is an opportunity to amend the gross anomalies present in both these taxes. The argument that people regard National Insurance contributions and taxes as somehow being less onerous than the same amount deducted by way of income tax (with a portion of income tax earmarked for insurance) is not very convincing, particularly now that for most people both are deducted by way of PAYE.

Another argument put forward to the House of Commons in 1975 by the Secretary of State for Social Services and quoted in Lister (1975) was:

> there has been an enduring feeling in this country, particularly among the trade unions, that there is a kind of guarantee about a contributory system – a guarantee that would not obtain in the same way if the scheme were financed entirely out of taxation. It gives some assurance that Governments will not use the lack of a contributory principle as an excuse to economise in the important matter of pensions.

The argument seems to be that the system cannot be changed because people are under the illusion that guarantees exist within the present system; an alternative is to educate people to the true facts. The sentiment of the last sentence of the quotation is clearly contradicted by the facts: pensions have been economised on from the start; and they were never implemented on a higher-than-subsistence level. In December 1975 nearly a fifth of all pensioners were having to seek financial help in spite of the majority of them having National Insurance pensions.

National Insurance benefits

A number of benefits are given at a flat rate but the most important benefits, i.e. pensions, unemployment and sickness, maternity, and industrial injury, are now earnings-related, some for limited periods.

The basic National Insurance pension is paid at 65 for men who have retired, and 60 for women who have retired, provided they have paid the requisite number of contributions over their working lifetimes. Married, widowed or divorced women are entitled, by virtue of their husbands' contributions, to a reduced-rate pension when they are 60 provided their husbands have reached the age of 65. Those who do not qualify for a pension under National Insurance, the very old who retired before the present scheme and those whose contribution record is insufficient to give them a pension above the old person's rate, receive the non-contributory old person's pension, which is in 1978 some 60 per cent of the flat-rate insurance pension. Graduated pensions are paid to those who have qualified: an increase of 2½p per week for every unit of £7.50 contributed by a man and of every £9 contributed by a woman. The higher rate for women reflects the earlier pensionable age of women and their greater life expectancy.

For unemployment the flat rate is payable after three days and ceases after twelve months when recourse has to be made to social security. For sickness benefit the basic rate is paid after three days' sickness and continues for 168 days (excluding Sundays), when those still incapable of work move on to invalidity benefit. In the case of both unemployment and sickness benefit an earnings-related supplement is payable to those who qualify starting on the thirteenth day and ceasing after 156 days (not counting Sundays).

Supplementation is calculated according to average weekly earnings arrived at by dividing annual earnings by 50. A curious piece of vindictiveness is the rule that where annual earnings are lower than normal, due, for example, to a spell of sickness or unemployment, no allowance can be made for periods for which earnings were not received.[4]

Changes

Two important pieces of legislation are now on the statute book and have important implications for the National Insurance and supplementary benefits systems.

PENSIONS

The Social Security Pensions Bill was enacted in 1975 and came into operation in April 1978. In return for higher contributions, it aims to provide income-related pensions, although these will not be paid in full until twenty years' contributions have been paid.

The existing flat-rate retirement, widows' and invalidity pensions and widowed mothers' allowance will be gradually replaced by a system of earnings-related pensions made up of a basic and an additional component. The effect of the scheme will be to give the lower paid a higher percentage of their earnings than that of the higher paid.

An important provision is the protection against inflation to be provided by linking the basic component of the pension with the index of national average earnings and the earnings-related part with movements in the retail price index.

The question of pensions is a highly complex one. Britain has a mixed system in which a considerable proportion of its population is entitled to private pensions. The quality of these private pensions varies considerably. The state pension provisions, as we have seen, make a sharp divide between those who are retired or near retirement age and those who will be able to make contributions for twenty years. The equity of this division is rather hard to see in the context of a pay as you go scheme; it seems to amount to a hope by the existing working population that when the time comes for their retirement they will be treated rather more generously than they themselves treated the retired. (For a recent discussion of a number of these issues, see Fogarty (1976) and Field (1975).)

CHILD BENEFITS

The Child Benefit Bill was passed in 1975 and was intended to replace the existing dual system of family allowances payable to mothers and income-tax allowances normally received by fathers as a tax-free benefit. The benefit would be received as of right and normally payable wholly to the mother. This scheme was intended to be put into effect from April 1977 but was deferred because the Government thought that there would be adverse trade-union reaction to the apparent cut in pay of workers (as they lost the benefit of child tax allowances). No provision is made in the Act for automatic increases in line with the cost-of-living index, as proposed for pensions. The scheme was partly implemented in April 1977 and details will be found in Chapter 14.

Social security supplementary benefits

When National Insurance benefits cease, or are inadequate to meet needs, social security supplementary benefits take over. These are part of a system of discretionary payments independent of prior contributions. It is therefore a complex labour-intensive service, as the means and circumstances of claimants have to be investigated before payments are made. On 3 December 1975, there were about 2.8 million claimants of supplementary benefit. With their dependants they numbered about 4.5 million people, or 8 per cent of the population of Britain (data obtained from the Supplementary Benefits Commission *Annual Report,*

1975). It is also known that a large number of persons, in the region of one million, are eligible to claim but do not do so. Some idea of the complexity can be gained by looking at Leaflet N.I. 146, *Catalogue of Social Security Leaflets*. This lists 124 leaflets which are available to the public to explain various aspects of the National Insurance and supplementary benefits schemes.

Table 12.2 lists the main categories of those receiving supplementation. It will be seen from Table 12.2 that pensioners form the major category of those needing to seek supplementation, with the unemployed forming the next largest category, followed by one-parent families and the sick and disabled. As the Supplementary Benefits Commission says (*Annual Report, 1975*, 1976, para. 2.12):

> But this system also poses characteristic problems: there are few urban industrial societies in which old age pensioners, the unemployed, the disabled, one-parent families and other large and predictably vulnerable groups are so likely to have to seek the help of a means-tested service originally devised as a last-resort safety net for the poor.

The official definition defines those in poverty as those whose incomes fall below the levels set for claimants dependent on supplementary benefits. To some extent this scale reflects the concept of 'relative deprivation', owing to the manner in which supplementary benefits are upgraded.

The concept of 'relative deprivation', as opposed to one of setting up

Table 12.2

Those in receipt of supplementary benefit in December 1975

Category	Approximate percentage of total
Pensioners	60
Unemployed	19
One-parent families	10
Sick and disabled	9
Other	2
	100

Source: Supplementary Benefits Commission (1976), Annual Report, 1975, *HMSO, London.*

minimum standards below which individuals should not be allowed to fall, was expressed concisely by Townsend (1974):

> Poverty can be defined objectively and applied only in terms of the concept of relative deprivation. . . . Individuals, families and groups in the population can be said to be in poverty when . . . their resources are so seriously below those commanded by the average individual or family that they are, in effect, excluded from ordinary living patterns, customs and activities.

Supplementary benefits are payable at two main rates: the ordinary rate applies to non-retired, short-term claimants; and a higher 'long-term' rate of benefit is payable to those over retirement age, and to those who have received supplementary benefit for two years without having to sign on for work. A slightly higher rate than the long-term rate is payable to those over the age of 80. The scales are linked to National Insurance benefits and to some extent to the average earnings of manual workers. From 1972 it was the practice to increase the main, adult-scale rates by the same amounts as the corresponding National Insurance benefit rates. After the Social Security Act of 1975, long-term National Insurance rates were uprated by reference to movements in earnings unless movements in prices were more favourable, with the result that long-term supplementary benefits are also uprated in the same way. Ordinary rates are still linked to movements in prices. The result was to increase the differential in favour of long-term rates as earnings were increasing faster than prices.

Since 1971 Family Income Supplement (FIS) has been payable to those men in full-time work who have at least one child and whose total income is below certain levels. In 1978 the level was £43.80 a week for those with one child, rising to £55.80 for those with four children. For each additional child a sum of £4.00 was added.

FIS consists of half the difference between the family income and the qualifying income, with an upper limit of £9.50 where there is one child, going up by £1 for each additional child. The following example sets out the position for a couple with two children:

Couple with two children

Qualifying income level	£47.80
Man's earnings before deductions	£39.00
Difference	£ 8.80
Family Income Supplement (half of £8.80)	£ 4.40

In the case of a couple it is the man who must be in full-time work. A single-parent family and a self-employed person are entitled to claim if they meet the other conditions.

Overlap of social security benefits and the tax system

A particular difficulty caused by the overlap between social security benefits and the tax system has received considerable attention (see *Financing Strikes*, 1974; and Howell, 1976).

Because social security benefits are untaxed, a person in receipt of means-tested benefits may be better off than a person in work who receives the same gross income which is liable to tax. Since these benefits are given on a needs' basis it makes no sense to subject them to tax. Raising tax thresholds would help with this problem but there is bound to be some area of overlap.

Part of the difficulty is caused by the fact that income tax is assessed on annual earnings, and benefits such as unemployment pay do not count as earnings. By way of illustration, if we take a married man with two children under 11, in the tax year 1978–9, his tax allowances are £1,735. Assume that he is unemployed for twelve weeks and receives social benefits of £35 a week and then finds work at £50 a week:

12 weeks at £35	=	£ 420
40 weeks at £50	=	£2,000
Total income	=	£2,420

His taxable income is £2,000 less allowance of £1,735, which equals £265. His tax payable is 25 per cent of £265, which equals £66.25. If the whole of his income of £2,420 had been earned, his taxable income would be £2,420 less £1,735, which equals £685. His tax, 25 per cent of £685, equals £171.25, an increase in tax of £105. In addition, the unemployed person is exempt from National Insurance contributions during his period of unemployment.

Changes in the supplementary benefits system

In their *Annual Report, 1975*, the Supplementary Benefits Commission detail five closely related problem areas. The first is the growing reliance on discretionary powers: by the end of 1975, 39 per cent of claimants were in receipt of discretionary payments, of which the bulk were for heating. They list as undesirable the moral judgments which this forces officials to make, the uncertainty of claimants as to their rights, and disputes that result as a consequence of this, as well as the calls it makes on experienced staff. In the end they say 'we cannot be sure that it gets help to all those in the greatest need'.

The complexity of the system was the second problem. The Government's desire for uniform treatment over the country has resulted in local offices being encouraged to (*Annual Report, 1975*, 1976, para. 2.19):

refer each new exception to Regional offices or headquarters for decision, and volumes of instructions have been assembled to provide guidance to every kind of case. Those instructions are so long, so complex, and so frequently amended, that officials themselves often find them very difficult to understand.

Apart from radical simplifications which would require significant changes in policy, the Commission make two suggestions that could be adopted fairly speedily: one is to reduce the number of special benefit rates, and perhaps of more importance they suggest that a vast amount of work would be saved if upratings of benefits, the revision of rates and council rents, together with the rebates on both, all took place once a year on the same date.

The third problem is one of frontiers, i.e. areas where the services of supplementary benefit overlap with other services. In recent years they have become involved in helping claimants find jobs, in running re-establishment centres, in providing massive subsidies for housing costs, in providing temporary shelter in reception centres and with students who may be claiming support for out-of-term time. The Commission say (*Annual Report, 1975*, 1976, para. 2.32):

we must beware of taking on tasks for which we are not well equipped. We should instead do our best, in collaboration with other services, to ensure that our claimants receive the help of the appropriate organisations and professions as soon as that can be arranged, and receive it on terms which do not stigmatise them or distinguish them unnecessarily from their fellow citizens.

The fourth area is the reappraising of the system for dealing with appeals against supplementary benefit decisions (see the work done by Bell, 1975).

The final problem discussed is the increased demands on staff which current policies impose.

As the opening quotation to this chapter indicates, the Commission, in answer to these problems, would like to see a movement to a system in which large social groups such as pensioners, the disabled and students rarely have to rely on a last-resort, means-tested, labour-intensive service for their incomes. They recognise clearly the difficult decision that this poses for the community in terms of increased costs.

Summary

This chapter has looked at National Insurance benefits, which are paid as of right to those who have sufficient contributions, and at the complex system of means-tested benefits. The hope of Beveridge, whose work was the basis for the system, that most needs would be met by National Insurance have not been realised. Some 8 per cent of the population of Britain in 1975 were in receipt of supplementary benefit – adding in those who were eligible, but did not claim, the figure rises to about 10 per cent. The new pension proposals which were outlined should in time relieve many pensioners from the need to seek supplementary benefit, but the proposals will take twenty years to mature fully. The new proposals for paying child benefit to the mother and not through a tax allowance to the father should again assist a number on low incomes if the proposals are in fact implemented fully.

Payment for National Insurance benefits is for most employed persons at a proportionate rate up to a level of earnings of £120 a week. It is collected in the same way as income tax and may be contrasted with the elaborate provisions of that tax to ensure a progressive average rate of tax tailored via tax allowances to meet different circumstances of taxpayers. Some of the difficulties and advantages in merging the two taxes were examined, and will be taken up again in Chapter 23.

The system of supplementary benefits was outlined and the main categories of those receiving benefit given. The problems of the present system and some suggestions for change as seen by the Supplementary Benefits Commission were outlined.

Notes

1 In April 1977 a 2 per cent surcharge to the employers' Class 1 rates was imposed. The revenue accrues for general use of the Exchequer, not the National Insurance Account. The stated intention was to use the revenue to reduce the Public Sector Borrowing Requirement. The rates quoted include the surcharge.

2 In October 1978 the surcharge was increased by 1½ per cent so that the employer pays 13.5 per cent if the employee is not contracted out. If

the employee is contracted out the employer pays 13.5 per cent on earnings up to £17.50 a week and 9 per cent on earnings between £17.50 and £120.00 a week.

3 From April 1979 the following limits and rates are proposed:
Class 1 rates limits will be £19.50 and £135.00 instead of £17.50 and £120.00.
Class 2 rates raised to £2.10 from £1.90.
Class 3 rates raised to £2.00 from £1.80.
Class 4 limits £2,250 to £7,000 instead of £2,000 to £6,250.
Those paying Class 1 rates and earning less than £120 a week will pay the same as at present if they are not contracted out of the State Pension scheme and a few pence more a week if contracted out.

4 Civil servants, in common with many professional groups, get full pay at least during the early months of sickness and often have job security. If this had not been the case, one wonders if this provision would have still been incorporated. This is not to impute deliberate malice to the legislators but merely to point out that provisions can quite unintentionally have a sharp impact on different sections of the community. In this case the distinction is largely between salary-earners and wage-earners, particularly low wage-earners. For example, an inquiry found that one in five men who had been earning less than the national assistance level had been unemployed in the previous twelve months compared with one in twenty-five of all men in the sample (*Circumstances of Families*, 1967). Likewise, sickness is higher amongst the low paid (Atkinson, 1973).

13 The criterion of 'ability to pay'

The last comprehensive review of the basis of taxation as a whole was undertaken by the Royal Commission on the Taxation of Profits and Income, which sat between 1951 and 1955. We think that circumstances have changed so significantly in the last 20 years that a further review would now be justified.
Report of the Sandilands Inflation Accounting Committee (September 1975, para. 697).

From the discussion in Chapter 10 of the benefit and ability to pay approaches it was clear that, given the current objectives of society, the benefit principle by itself cannot serve as an adequate guide to taxation policy. Some form of criterion based on ability to pay is needed and this is now examined.

Ability to pay

In the search for a criterion to judge ability to pay, in order to achieve horizontal equity, claims are put forward for income, wealth and expenditure.

By wealth is meant the accumulated assets of a person or institution; by income is meant receipts that accrue per period of time. Wealth taxation may mean the taxation of any income that wealth earns in a period but it should strictly refer to a tax on the underlying assets. Taxing the stock of wealth will not provide sufficient revenue by itself: the issues raised by wealth taxation will be examined in Chapter 17.

Expenditure as a base for taxation was advocated by Kaldor (1955), and more recently by the Meade Committee (1977). An expenditure tax makes the distinction between income and wealth irrelevant: both are taxed, not as they accrue, but when they are spent. However, the difference in principle between expenditure- and income-based taxes is not as wide as it might appear at first glance. The issue is not, it should be stressed, one of progressiveness. It is possible to build into a tax system on either base whatever degree of progressiveness is required. An expenditure-based tax does not have to entail the detailed recording of expenditures. These can be computed as the difference between certain money incomings and outgoings. Forms to compute expenditures in this way would be somewhat more complicated than the current income-tax form, but not unduly so. The real difference between taxes on these different bases lies in the exemption from tax of savings under an expenditure tax. In a general way, using consumption (i.e. expenditure) as a base is taxing according to what a person takes out of the common pool, and income with what he puts into the common pool.

There are a number of reasons for not developing the idea of an expenditure-based tax here, besides the necessity to keep this book within limits. One is that an expenditure tax has been brilliantly elaborated by Kaldor (1955) and examined more recently by the Meade Committee (1977). Another that has just been noted is that the only major theoretical difference between an expenditure tax and the tax on total accretion lines that is developed here lies in the different treatment of savings, and in practice this difference is more apparent than real. On the one hand, a progressive tax on expenditures mitigates to some extent for not taxing saving; it can be equivalent to a lower tax on expenditures and a tax on savings. On the other hand, the treatment of savings under the present income-tax system is frequently favourable. For example, savings through pension schemes and life insurance receive tax concessions and the interest on National Savings Certificates is tax free, together with the first £70 of interest from National Savings Bank or Trustee Savings Bank deposits. Likewise, with free depreciation for plant and machinery savings by businesses for this purpose have very favourable treatment. The present system of income tax, therefore, because of its favourable treatment of many forms of saving, comes close to an expenditure base. It is also true that because expenditures are basically calculated as the difference between income and savings, the problems of what is the correct definition of income is still embedded in an expenditure-tax base.

Finally, the important problems this chapter deals with – valuation, inflation and deflation, fluctuating income and the taxpaying unit – are common to whatever tax base is selected. We choose to discuss them in the context of an income base since most countries use such a base and the concept has been elaborated over many years.

Definition of income

One concept of income has gained wide acceptance and is termed *total accretion*. Income is defined to equal consumption during a given period, plus the increase in net worth valued at market prices for the beginning and the end of the period. Income is thus defined to include consumption, savings and changes in wealth. The principle is uncompromising: all accretions to wealth are included, in whatever form they are received or from whatever source they accrue. In practice, the principle may have to be modified, but if it is accepted as a principle it gives a basis from which to judge our present tax system and any proposed changes. The principle accepts that a change in net worth may be negative; in other words gains and losses should be allowed for.

The Memorandum of Dissent to the Royal Commission on the Taxation of Profits and Income's *Final Report* (1955, para. 5) sets out very clearly the rationale behind this definition:

> In our view the taxable capacity of an individual consists in his power to satisfy his own material needs, i.e., to attain a particular living standard. We know of no alternative definition that is capable of satisfying society's prevailing sense of fairness and equity. Thus the ruling test to be applied in deciding whether any particular receipt should or should not be reckoned as taxable income is whether it contributes or not, or how far it contributes, to an individual's 'spending power' during a period. When set beside this standard, most of the principles that have been applied at one time or another, to determine whether particular types of receipt constitute income (whether the receipts are regularly recurrent or casual, or whether they proceed from a separate and identifiable source, or whether they are payments for services rendered, or whether they constitute profit 'on sound accountancy principles', or whether, in the words of the Majority they fall 'within the limited class of receipts that are identified as income by their own nature') appear to us to be irrelevant. In fact no concept of income can be really equitable that stops short of the comprehensive definition which embraces all receipts which increase an individual's command over the use of society's scarce resources – in other words his 'net accretion of economic power between two points of time'.

It cannot be emphasised too strongly that the consequence of adopting this definition of income would be that current rates of income tax could be reduced without a loss in revenue, or indirect taxes could be reduced, or some downward reduction made in both. In other words, at present, income, in the narrow sense, bears a disproportionate share of tax precisely because spending power other than income is taxed less or not at all. For example, capital gains are taxed at a maximum rate of 30 per cent. Betting and gambling is, on the whole, taxed at flat rates. Earned income is taxed more favourably than unearned income. Inherited wealth is not taxed according to the position of the recipient but according to the wealth of the donor. The present system is the result of the haphazard growth of the tax and benefit system over the years.

Is the principle workable?

It is one thing to talk about a principle, but is it workable in practice? As a preliminary we shall deal briefly with the drawbacks of the present system, and then go on to deal with the difficulties of implementing the accretion principle. These difficulties are present in our existing system, and some would be emphasised in the system of accretion.

Possibly the main drawback of the present system has already been mentioned. It is curious that it has not received more attention. That is, by the present very narrow definition of income, any receipt unfortunate enough to fall in this category is liable to steeply progressive marginal tax rates. Widening the base would give the authorities room to manoeuvre: a greater range of small incomes could be exempt from tax, or rates throughout the range could be reduced, or indirect taxes could be reduced, or some compromise made between these possibilities.

From this advantage it would follow that there would be no gain in reshuffling assets (from, say, income to capital gains) because both would be income and subject to the same tax. The so-called 'blight' of modern times, the amount of time, money and effort which goes into tax avoidance, would be lessened. (Avoidance is used here to mean legal means to reduce tax.) Tax avoidance has always, and probably always will be, a profitable occupation, but the great reductions in taxation that can be achieved under the present system has made it into a thriving industry. It is not the purpose of this book to specify the means of avoidance at length but the subject is important enough to merit mention.

Numerous devices have been thought up to reduce tax on income. Some of the practices mentioned have now been stopped, or modified to limit abuse, but efforts to find new loopholes may be expected to continue unabated given the present very diverse rates of tax on different receipts. Employers, instead of a salary increase to their top executives, may offer generous non-contributory pensions, a wide range of 'fringe benefits' and lavish entertainment expenses. An old favourite is to turn income into capital gains, which formerly went untaxed and are now taxed at a maximum rate of 30 per cent. Share options to employees and various forms of 'dividend stripping' were the best known among these devices. It will be pointed out in Chapter 14 ('Personal income taxation') that advantages may accrue to the person who is able to arrange his affairs under the mantel of company status. Titmuss (1962, p. 72) has pointed out that:

> The British system of taxation is almost unique in the world in recognizing a payment voluntarily undertaken by the taxpayer as a charge on his income, provided that payment (a) is made under a promise backed by a deed of covenant extending to a period of more than six years; (b) is not made in favour of an unmarried infant of the covenantor; (c) is not in exchange for value received from (or goods or services rendered by) the recipient . . . [and he adds in a footnote] Covenants by men in favour of their mistresses can only be regarded as ineligible for tax relief if the Inland Revenue can establish that they are given 'for services rendered' (see Monroe, J. G., 'Annual and Other Periodical Payments', *British Tax Review*, December 1956, p. 289).

Avoidance devices on capital are looked at briefly in Chapter 17.

Implementation of the total accretion principle

The total accretion principle is defined as accretion to wealth, which is equal to consumption plus increases in net worth valued at market prices for the beginning and the end of the period. The chief problems are presented by valuation, inflation or deflation, fluctuating income, and the taxpaying unit. These are now discussed in turn.

VALUATION

As anybody who has had something to do with valuation for purposes of probate will know, valuation can cause a great deal of work and involve a great deal of arbitrariness. There is little problem with items which are standardised and traded regularly, such as quoted company shares. Unquoted shares, unique items such as original paintings, plots of land, and so on, are much more difficult to value, short of actual sale in the marketplace. On the grounds of practicality it seems that annual valuation is ruled out. An alternative is to bring the item into the tax net on sale, or on death of the owner, when valuation has to take place in any case. It is argued against this that such a process discriminates in favour of people who enjoy unrealised accretion. This is true but it seems to have little weight against the bigger distortions that have been mentioned caused by not taxing some items at all. Similar considerations apply to the argument that treating sales proceeds as income will interfere with the market process of buying and selling. Once again it is necessary to weigh any loss likely to be caused in this way with the undoubted losses and distortions caused by the present system.

INFLATION AND DEFLATION

Should the valuation of assets and liabilities allow for changes in the value of money, that is for inflation or deflation? It is argued that a gain of, say, £100 on selling shares is a gain in money terms only, that what should be relevant is the gain in real terms, i.e. the gain in command over goods and services. In inflationary conditions this gain will clearly be less than £100 and vice versa.

Most commentators agree that, in principle, changes due to changes in the value of money should be allowed *for all receipts*, whether income, capital gains or anything else; that is, in principle, it should be in real terms. However, most also agree that in practical terms money values will have to be used. The difficulties of finding a correct index, or indices, with which to obtain real values are a serious deterrent to working with deflated values, and allowing for inflation would be administratively complex. Because of these difficulties, it is by no means clear that a system which attempts to take account of inflation and deflation would be more equitable than one that does not.

To argue for compensation for changes in the value of money for all receipts is not, however, a good argument for compensation for some of these receipts – a point that is frequently overlooked.

At the moment a money wage increase which restores the real purchasing power of wages to the level of the previous year nevertheless results in more tax being paid if tax rates are unaltered. The claim that one particular slice of income should be protected from changes in the value of money thus begins to look like special pleading on behalf of interested parties.

If the principle is good for one, it is good for all, but of course adjustment for all loses much of its point. The Government starts out with clear ideas of the amount of revenue it wants from the economy; if adjustments were made on the income side for price changes, adjustments would have to be made on the revenue side to tax rates to ensure that the tax revenue target was reached. The only change from the present system is that the Government obtains more revenue[1] from inflation at the moment if it keeps tax rates the same. If adjustments were made automatically to income, then the present hidden increase in tax revenue would not occur.

In other words, if the Government wanted more revenue it would have to increase rates rather than relying on the automatic increase brought about by inflation.

A similar argument is used when it is asserted that since capital gains can accrue over a long period of time, it is unjust to tax them at income rates. The valid point in this argument is that the realisation of capital gains will, under a progressive tax structure, raise the tax liability in the year in which the gains are realised over and above the liability which would have been incurred if the gain had been realised evenly over time. The remedy for this is some form of averaging income for tax purposes, a measure which is desirable under any form of progressive tax. This will be touched on later. The assertion that capital gains are different from other income cannot be sustained under the total accretion concept. This concept seeks the 'taxable capacity' of a person; it is irrelevant whether one person has a higher taxable capacity than another due to higher earnings, receipt of a legacy, receipt of a capital gain or in some other way. A person who invests money in shares which show a gain in money terms is better off than a person whose shares show no gain or a loss. The degree of inflation or deflation cannot alter this conclusion.

It is also argued that a capital gain is illusory if the proceeds are to be reinvested in a similar asset. Thus in the case of a house purchased for £10,000 and sold for £15,000, it is probable that the whole of the proceeds will be needed to reinvest in a similar type of property. This is easily seen as a case of special pleading, that house-owners should be protected against inflation as opposed to other groups. The person who invests £10,000 in a house in the above example gains over the person who invests the £10,000 in securities and makes the same gain. The latter person will pay tax on his gain and be at a disadvantage in entering the housing market in competition with the former householder. The fact that owner-occupied houses are exempt from capital gains for social and political reasons should not be allowed to obscure the fact that once an owner obtains a house (on the assumption that his property moves in line with the general market trend in house prices), he is largely indifferent to the subsequent trend in house prices. A wedge is driven between those who have houses, and are largely protected from subsequent inflation in house prices, and those who subsequently enter the market.[2]

Although housing was selected as an example, the principles involved apply to any asset: exemption from tax confers benefit on the existing owners of the asset *vis-à-vis* the rest of the population. It is not suggested that no case can be made for the exemption of certain assets but that the nature of the privilege being conferred needs careful examination. No presumptive economic argument can be set up that particular assets merit exemption.

Pro or con?

In the mass of words on the subject of inflation and capital gains the assumptions of the protagonists are seldom made explicit.

Those who argue that capital gains should take inflation into account presumably have in mind some concept akin to 'keeping capital intact'. If this is the correct premise, it is clear that taxing a paper gain is unjust.

Those who argue against this view take as their starting-point that what is relevant for taxation and equity purposes 'is the relative income positions of taxpayers'. If this is the correct premise, a person who has a capital gain in money terms is better off than a person who has no such gain or loss, and should be taxed. On this assumption not to tax a paper gain is unjust, *or* alternatively everything should be adjusted for price changes.

This argument seems particularly protracted because the principle of 'keeping capital intact' is both a sound accounting principle and an unsound principle for public finance. The point has been investigated by successive Royal Commissions in relation to depreciation allowances for companies and whether these allowances should be based on historic or replacement cost. Allowances based on the latter would, of course, allow for price changes. Such a change had been decisively rejected until the Sandilands Inflation Accounting Report (1975).

The Sandilands Committee was concerned with inflation accounting; it was not primarily concerned with the tax system, but rather with the implications of inflation on companies. On taxation it was requested to consider 'any implications for the taxation of the profits and capital gains of companies'. The Sandilands Committee came out in favour of a system of 'current cost profit', which it believed should form the basis for company accounts and be used for tax purposes. If adopted such a system would substantially afford companies protection against inflation. However, the Committee strongly emphasised that such a change should not be made until a major review of taxation was undertaken (1975, para. 656):

> In practice, such an important change [to current cost profit] in the basis of tax assessment of companies could not be introduced in isolation without consideration being given for other sectors of the economy. Such

consideration falls outside our terms of reference and in our opinion requires a major review of the basis of the taxation of profit and income such as that undertaken by the Royal Commission under the chairmanship of Lord Radcliffe, which presented its Final Report in 1955. Pending such a review we have concluded that, with one exception, we should not put forward proposals which would result in the permanent exclusion from taxation of any part of the taxable profits of companies as at present computed.

This paragraph seems to offer substantial support to the conclusion reached above that either all should be compensated for inflation, or none, at least until the matter has been investigated fully. These questions will be discussed in some detail in Chapter 15. The viewpoint adopted here is that, however desirable it may be for the individual to maintain his wealth position, it is no part of the fiscal system to do this for him. The aim of the fiscal system is not to maintain the status of those who happen to have wealth or to make gains. On the contrary, at any one time society aims for a certain degree of progression and a certain redistribution of income and wealth. The argument adopted here for the rejection of compensation for inflation is clear: inflationary and deflationary conditions affect all sectors of the community in different degrees, and compensation for one sector results in less equity, not more.

FLUCTUATING INCOME

The difficulty posed by any progressive tax is the inequity between those persons whose income fluctuates from year to year and those who receive their incomes in regular equal amounts. Authors, artists, sportsmen, farmers, fishermen and a number of people in professional occupations who rely on fees are likely to be in the former category.

As an illustration of inequity, an unmarried actor on rates of tax applicable in 1976–7 who receives £50,000 for a film and nothing for the next four years will pay about £35,790 in tax. On the other hand, a single man who receives a salary of £10,000 a year for five years will pay approximately £3,909 in tax a year, or £19,545 in tax over the five years (assuming 1976–7 tax rates hold the same over this period).[3]

The only provisions for spreading or averaging income at the moment apply to authors, to patent royalties, and since 1969, to painters and sculptors and since 1978 to farmers. The author of a literary, dramatic, musical or artistic work who sells the copyright or an interest in it for a lump-sum payment, or is in receipt of royalties from such a work, can sometimes spread his tax payments. This applies if he was engaged on the making of the work for more than twelve months. He can spread the payment over two years if the period of production does not exceed two years, over three years if the period was longer. A person who is chargeable to tax in respect of a capital sum received on the sale of patent rights is entitled to spread the sum in equal amounts over the year of receipt and the five succeeding years. There is a further provision for spreading royalties received as consideration for more than two years' use of a patent. In this case the payment is spread back in equal annual instalments subject to a limiting number of six. Since 1969 painters and sculptors can spread the receipt for a work over the period during which it was made. The budget in 1978 allowed farmers to average their incomes when the profits for two consecutive years differ by 30 per cent or more of the higher of the profits for the two years. The profits can then be aggregated and one-half of the sum treated as profits for each year. Thus if profits chargeable in one year are £10,000 and those in the subsequent year £6,000, the farmer can average and pay tax on £8,000 for each of the two years. The profits of the third year would then be compared with the average of £8,000 for averaging purposes. Marginal relief is available where the difference in profits is between 25 and 30 per cent.

It needs to be stressed that the problem of fluctuating incomes occurs under the present tax system. The Royal Commission on the Taxation of Profits and Income in its *Final Report* was of the opinion that 'It was quite impossible to regard as satisfactory the present position of fluctuating incomes' (1955, para. 197). The problem becomes more acute under the accretion principle of income because more income will be volatile. Legacies and gifts are examples of receipts which cannot be expected regularly.

The seemingly straightforward solution of aggregating income over, say, a five-year period or a lifetime falls to the ground because if a person has a drop in income in any year, his tax bill in that year will be based on his average income over the relevant period – which may be higher than his current income. The fact that a rising income gives a correspondingly lower tax bill does not compensate for the hardship which is likely to be involved in meeting high tax payments during periods of reduced income.

The usual assumption of averaging is that the total sum of taxes paid over the averaging period should be the same as if the income had been received in equal amounts in each year of the averaging period. With a five-year plan, tax could be computed by finding the average income over this period (i.e. total income for the five years divided by five) and reworking the tax liability for each of the past years on the basis of this average. Not surprisingly, the Royal Commission (1955, para. 189) rejected proposals on these lines 'since the administrative burden of operating it cannot be contemplated'. However, the assumption of the Commission that, to achieve averaging, tax for past years must be reworked is not a feature of all schemes of averaging. The *Report of the Canadian Royal Commission on Taxation* (1966) suggested the use of special averaging schedules which would mean that only one computation of tax would be necessary, instead of a new computation for each year averaged. An alternative, using the current year's cumulative average income and subtracting from this the amount of taxes already paid for earlier years of the averaging period, is outlined by Vickrey (1947, pp. 172–95, 417–27).

Conclusion

Failure to adopt some form of averaging is unfair to those who have fluctuations in income. Any form of averaging will result in some complication of the tax system compared with a similar system without averaging, but not necessarily compared with a modified tax and benefit system. The amount of difficulty that would result from averaging was greatly overstressed by the Royal Commission in 1955 because it worked on the assumption that tax in past years of the averaging period would have to be recalculated.

The taxpaying unit

The problem of the taxpaying unit has been described as the most neglected problem in public taxation. If the structure of society is such that the composition of all taxpaying units is the same, say a husband, wife and two children, we have little difficulty. But taxpayers differ greatly: from those who are single with no dependants to look after, to married persons with large families and many dependants.

The Royal Commission on the Taxation of Profits and Income reported as follows (1954, para. 119):

> We have come to the conclusion that the taxation of the combined incomes of husband and wife as one unit is to be preferred to their separate taxation as separate units because the aggregate income provides a unit of taxation that is fairer to those concerned. That is why we do not recommend a departure from the present system. The combined incomes of married persons are sometimes described as a joint purse. We do not think that so wide a generalisation can safely be made on such a question of social habit: but it does appear to us, on the one hand, that marriage

creates a social unit which is not truly analogous with other associations involving some measure of joint living expenses and that to tax the incomes of two married people living together as if each were equivalent to the income of a single individual would give a less satisfactory distribution than that which results from the present rule. Such a method of taxation would mean that one married couple bore a greater or less burden of tax than another according to what must surely be an irrelevant distinction for this purpose, namely, the proportion in which the combined income was divided between the partners.

The Commission was sensitive to the abuses that can arise with separate assessment for husband and wife by the transfer of income from the spouse with the highest income (and therefore under a progressive tax system the higher tax) to the partner with the lowest income. This abuse is most likely in the case of unearned income, as it is much more difficult to transfer earned income to another before tax is paid. The exception to this is provided by some private companies where the husband or wife can be paid a director's remuneration though he or she has had little or nothing to do with the running of the business.

On the other hand, aggregation is hard on those married couples who both have high incomes. The extreme is found where the spouses earn equal amounts. For example, if we just take the single person's allowance in 1978–9 of £985 and the married person's allowance of £1,535 into account we get the following situation. A single person can earn up to £7,985 before being subject to higher tax rates; on such an income £2,312 tax is payable. So two single persons each with an income of this figure pay a total of £4,625 in tax. If such a couple marry, their joint income of £15,970 will attract £6,205 in tax, an increase of £1,580. To meet this criticism, since the tax year 1972–3 it has been possible for a husband and wife jointly to elect to have the wife's earned income assessed as if she were a single person. The husband is then assessed on his earned income, and, as before, the whole of any unearned income is aggregated to his income for tax purposes. The husband, where such an election takes place, loses the benefit of a married person's allowance and reverts to a single person's allowance. It will be seen that this change is of great benefit to a married couple in which both earn substantial incomes since each pays only at the basic rate of tax on the first £7,000 of his or her taxable income, and the wife is subject to higher rates of tax only on her income in excess of this.

Whether it pays to opt for separate taxation depends on the level of income of each marriage partner and the allowances they can claim. Each case needs to be worked out and the onus is on the couple to make the claim for separate taxation, or, having made the election, to revoke it when circumstances change. The Inland Revenue does not assess the couple to the system which gives them the most favourable treatment.

In Britain children's earned income is not aggregated with the parents' income; they are taxed in their own right. A child is an unmarried person under 18 years of age. However, if the child's income (either his earned or investment income) comes to more than £115, the parents normally lose £1 of their child allowance for each £1 of the child's income over £115.

The treatment of children's investment income has tended to change with the change in political power. It has sometimes been aggregated with the parents' income and sometimes not. During the years from April 1969 to March 1972 it was aggregated. Since that time it has not been aggregated, although the Labour Government of the 1970s said that it would revert to the previous system. Settlements and arrangements made by the parents whereby the child receives investment income are, for obvious tax-avoidance reasons, normally aggregated (if the amount is £5 or more) with the parents' income.

We have reached one of the many conflicts in public finance whereby it is very difficult to find a simple way to do justice both to single persons and to married couples in different circumstances. To go over completely to a system whereby the individual is the unit of taxation may seem unjust to a single person who is not in a position to spread any of his income to a wife or family. Aggregation of income of husband and wife, or by families, may impose a heavy tax penalty on them.

This problem is one that is inherent in any system of progressive taxation. It is particularly acute in Britain because of the many tax allowances which can be claimed which reduce one's marginal rate of tax, because of the high starting rate of tax, and because of the high levels reached by the top rates of tax. In Chapter 23 these matters will be examined at greater length.

The taxation mix

It should be clear from what has already been said that the total accretion principle is an attempt to achieve horizontal equity. The assumption is made that the source of income is a matter of indifference: whatever the source, it represents purchasing power, and should therefore be included in income. On reflection it should also be clear that other types of tax do more or less violence to the principle of horizontal equity. Taxes on consumption goods will fall unequally on persons in equal positions if they have different consumption patterns. Most noticeably, if tobacco and alcohol are to retain their present very high rates of tax for social reasons, then two individuals in equal positions, except that one smokes and drinks and the other does not, will pay very different amounts of tax.

In Chapter 9 the benefit principle of tax, and the social-cost argument, were examined. It is clear that the application of either is likely to violate the ability-to-pay approach of the accretion principle.

The impossibility of laying down a universal principle of tax, which will be valid under all conditions, is that the extent of government activity varies widely. In a mixed economy the Government may be providing services which would not be provided at all, or provided on an insufficient scale, if left in private hands. In such cases as this the benefit principle is not applicable, and defining ability to pay is essential if equity is to be achieved. At the other extreme the Government may be providing goods and services which could equally well be provided by private enterprise (albeit under some form of monopoly regulation). Steel, telephones, railways and power are cases in point. Here, failure to charge on the benefit principle is likely to cause a misuse of the nation's resources.

A division on these lines is, in a rough and ready manner, apparent in our society. The nationalised industries are expected to pay their way – although at any one time this instruction may fail to be realised. It has already been argued that if these industries are to be expected to pay their way, and this is desirable on allocation grounds, then it is essential that social functions that they are expected to perform should be clearly separated from their strictly commercial activities. Then the commercial side can be expected to pay its way, and the activities that are continued for social reasons, because the social benefits outweigh the money cost involved, should be subsidised out of general taxation based on ability to pay.

Thus the following conclusions are drawn: many government services, such as defence and justice, either cannot be charged to individuals, or should not be charged because of neighbourhood and social effects, e.g. transfer payments, education and health; for these services, taxation according to ability to pay is necessary; the accretion principle has been set out as a method of judging ability to pay; commercial activities should be charged on the benefit principle.

These conclusions do not still controversy. However, general agreement is likely over a wide range of services which can be classified unambiguously in one category or the other. Some areas remain controversial, for example some people argue that higher education should be financed by loans on a benefit basis rather than by grants. Here it is necessary to weigh the advantages and disadvantages that flow from the alternative ways of financing. Charging the beneficiary is likely to deter the use of the good or service and this needs to be weighed against the social loss involved.

Company taxation is rather more controversial. It can be argued that companies belong to individuals and that company income (both distributed profits and undistributed profits) should be allocated to individuals as part of their income. Imputing undistributed profits to shareholders is not difficult administratively, but is impractical for incentive reasons. A case can be made for taxing companies as well as individuals. This will be further considered in Chapter 15.

Whether wealth taxes should be imposed in addition to taxes on income is once again a wider issue that a democratic country has to decide through the polls. The accretion principle would, as we have seen, include bequests and gifts, along with other additions, as income. The issue is whether some sort of wealth tax should be imposed as well. The issues will be examined in Chapter 17.

In concluding this brief section on the coexistence of different types of tax we again come up with the problem that not all the considerations involved are economic ones. In trying to establish horizontal equity between taxpayers we find that other taxes usually breech this principle. However, principles of taxation are set up as a guide to policy, not as inflexible rules. There may well be social and other reasons for deliberately departing from a principle in particular cases. This does not make the principle invalid. On the contrary, it illustrates the use of the concept very well: instead of taxing in the present haphazard way it forces particular taxes to be justified and it makes it that much harder for particular groups to indulge in special pleading.

Summary

Horizontal equity – that people in equal positions shall be treated equally – presents few problems in principle. The correct treatment of people in unequal positions, or vertical equity, is more difficult. Even when, as in all developed economies, progressive taxation is generally agreed upon, the question of the precise degree of progression is an open one that has to be decided by political consensus.

Even in setting aside questions of progression as a political decision, the important point remains as to the criterion on which equal and unequal positions shall be judged; that is, what shall be the taxation base? Two claims have been put forward and generally acknowledged. One is that taxation should be based on expenditure. On this criterion the source of spending power, whether it comes from income, or wealth, or exceptional receipts, is irrelevant: taxation accrues as spending takes place, not as accumulation proceeds. The other base broadens the definition of income so as to take in changes in wealth and other receipts. These concepts, at first sight so very different from each other, turn out to have only one major difference in principle, that expenditure as a base exempts savings from taxation while the other does not. The problems posed by valuation, inflation and deflation, fluctuating incomes and the taxpaying unit, which were detailed in this chapter, are common to both and indeed to any system of taxation. Finally, some of the problems associated with the fact that we have a system of mixed taxes, rather than a single tax, were looked at.

Notes

1 Whether the Government gets more revenue in real terms with inflation depends on the degree to which its expenditures are affected by inflation, the people who obtain an increase in income and the degree of progression of tax to which these people are subject.

2 This aspect of protection must also increase the demand for houses and so be responsible in some degree for the rise in house prices.

3 The matter is not quite so simple as this example suggests. The actor will pay tax in arrears under Schedule D, while the salary-earner will pay as he earns under Schedule E. Claims for expenses are usually treated more leniently under Schedule D. This point will be taken up in Chapter 14.

14
Personal income taxation

Albert Einstein once admitted that working out his income tax was beyond him – he had to go to a tax consultant. 'This is too difficult for a mathematician,' said Einstein. 'It takes a philosopher.'
Time.

In this chapter an outline will be given of the main taxes on personal income. However, as will be shown, it is impossible to treat personal tax entirely separately from tax on businesses. It is necessary to distinguish between the individual, the incorporated business, usually termed a company, which has a separate legal entity, and what will be termed unincorporated businesses. The most common form of unincorporated business is the partnership. Income of the unincorporated business is treated as the income of the persons concerned, but, as we shall see, treatment for tax differs in important respects from the tax treatment of the individual. Incorporated company tax will be treated in the next chapter.

This chapter deals first with income tax. Income tax was introduced by Pitt in 1797, as a temporary tax, to help finance the Napoleonic wars. It ended in 1816. It was reintroduced by Gladstone in 1842, again as a 'temporary measure', and has continued ever since. In the course of looking at income tax the position of unincorporated businesses will be taken up. Consideration is then given to the tax on capital gains.

The structure of income tax

From 1909 up to 1973 a dual system of income tax and surtax operated. The latter was a progressive tax applied to high incomes. Surtax was abolished in 1973 and income tax has operated with a progressive scale of rates applied to successive slices of income. This change was mainly of an administrative nature representing a considerable simplification of the tax structure. The amounts paid in tax under the two tax structures were substantially the same for any individual.

Income tax is imposed by a Finance Act, introduced every year, which determines the rates of tax and other details which are to apply to the next year beginning 6 April. The tax is chargeable under a number of schedules.

Schedule A	income from rents, and other receipts from unfurnished property.
Schedule B	applies to woodlands managed on a commercial basis.
Schedule C	covers interest on public loans.
Schedule D	covers income of a professional and business nature, namely trades, including farms, and professions and vocations; and in addition income from a variety of sources, for example interest not taxed at source, e.g. bank interest, foreign securities, foreign possessions, miscellaneous profits, e.g. from letting furnished accommodation.
Schedule E	covers income from employment, i.e. wages, salaries, pensions, and the like. The tax is collected by the employer under the system known as 'Pay As You Earn' so that the employee receives his remuneration net of tax.
Schedule F	covers assessments on companies in respect of tax deducted by them from interest and dividends.

The individual is allowed to make certain deductions from his income before tax is charged. The main deductions ruling in the tax year 1978–9 are:

1 For a married man £1,535; for a single person £985. If a wife is working she is also, in effect, allowed an allowance equal to that of a single person if her earnings are sufficient; otherwise she gets a proportion of the allowance.
2 Further deductions are made in respect of children. For details see the next section.
3 Deductions are also allowed to cover a variety of circumstances: for a widow or widower who has to employ a housekeeper; for dependent relatives; in respect of age and blindness; for single-parent families; and

on life-assurance premiums and interest payments on house purchase. The latter has been subject to a limit on borrowing of £25,000 since 1974.

4 Certain expenses incurred in obtaining the income are deductible before tax is charged.

The allowances outlined in 1 to 3 above apply to all individuals. As we shall see, the treatment of expenses, 4 above, differs according to whether tax is paid under Schedule D or Schedule E.

In passing the Finance Bill in 1977 sections were inserted to the effect that personal allowances for 1978–9 and subsequent years shall be changed by not less than the percentage movement in the retail price index, unless the Chancellor gets an Order approved by the House for some level below this. Indexation will be discussed at the end of this chapter.

After deducting the appropriate allowances, the individual paying tax under Schedule E is left with his taxable income which, for earned income, is subject to the rates of tax shown in Table 14.1.

For unearned income above a certain level a surcharge on the marginal rate of tax shown in Table 14.1 is made. The income level is higher for

Table 14.1

Rates of tax for 1978–9

Taxable income (£)	Marginal rate of tax	Total tax at top of income bracket (£)	Average rate of tax (%)
0– 750*	25	187.5	25.0
750– 8,000	33	2,580	32.3
8,000– 9,000	40	2,980	33.1
9,000–10,000	45	3,430	34.3
10,000–11,000	50	3,930	35.7
11,000–12,500	55	4,755	38.1
12,500–14,000	60	5,655	40.4
14,000–16,000	65	6,955	43.5
16,000–18,500	70	8,705	47.1
18,500–24,000	75	12,830	53.5
Over 24,000			

*A reduced rate band introduced in 1978.

persons 65 years of age and more. Table 14.2 gives details. The individual under 65, therefore, with more than £21,750 of taxable earned income and £2,250 of unearned income (which will give him a taxable income in excess of £24,000) will be paying tax at 83 + 15 = 98 per cent on the slice of his investment income over £2,250.

Table 14.2

Investment income surcharge

Persons less than 65 years of age		Persons 65 years of age or more	
Investment income (£)	Surcharge (%)	Investment income (£)	Surcharge (%)
Between 1,700-2,250	10	Between 2,500-3,000	10
Over 2,250	15	Over 3,000	15

In looking at the figures in Tables 14.1 and 14.2 it should be borne in mind that the rates given are for taxable income, that is after allowances have been deducted. Thus from Table 14.1 an individual's gross income will be considerably in excess of £8,000 before he comes into the higher tax brackets, which start at taxable income over £8,000 and reaches 83 per cent on taxable incomes over £24,000. The 'marginal rate of tax' column shows the tax payable on the top slice of income as income rises. The 'average rate of tax' column gives the total tax paid at each income level divided by that income. Thus, for example, at a taxable income of £18,500 the top slice of income of £2,500 is taxed at 70 per cent, the total tax paid on a taxable income of this level is £8,705, or 47.1 per cent of total income.

TREATMENT OF CHILDREN

In the period 1946 up to April 1979 a parent received family allowances as well as tax allowances. Family allowances were introduced in 1946 at the rate of 25p a week per child for all children except the first. This was raised to 40p in 1952 and has been raised again from time to time to the level of £1.50 per week in 1977. Although family allowances were paid irrespective of income, the increased benefit above 40p (the 1952 level of allowance) was confined to small-income families, as tax allowances were changed so as to recoup the increase from those who pay income tax.

Child tax allowances are sums that are deducted from a person's gross income before arriving at taxable income. The rates for the tax year 1976–7 were £300 for each child under 11, £335 for each child over 11 but not over 16, and £365 for each child over 16.

In April 1977 a start was made on scrapping the system of child tax allowances and replacing it by a system of weekly payments. These child benefits, as they are called, replace the old system of family allowances. They are paid at the rate of £1 a week for the first child (who received nothing under the old system of family allowances)[1] and £1.50 for other children. Child tax allowances are being reduced as child benefits are increased. The tax allowances for 1978–9 are given in Table 14.3.

Table 14.3

Tax allowances

	For each child (£)
Not over 11	100
Over 11 but not over 16	135
Aged 16 or over, if receiving full-time instruction at a university, college or school or is being trained for not less than two years for a trade, etc.	165

The stated intention of the Government is to phase out child tax allowances entirely and replace them by increased child benefits. It hopes to achieve this for children under 11 by April 1979. Child benefit is paid tax free. The rate in April 1978 was £2.30 per week for all children including the first with an announced intention to increase this by 70p to £3 in November 1978 and a further increase of £1, making it £4, in April 1979. Single-parent families receive an additional sum of £1 for the first child, increased to £2 in November 1978.

The initial overall effect of the changes was to make a family who paid no tax better off by the sum paid for the first child. A standard-rate tax-payer's family gained slightly as the child allowance was a little more than the loss due to the change in the tax allowance.

The old system of family allowances was introduced at a figure well below the estimate of Beveridge of the average cost of subsistence of children and remained so. The changes have resulted as indicated above in some improvement for less well off families, but at this level of child benefit many will still have to seek supplementary benefit.

EARNED AND UNEARNED INCOME

Under both the accretion principle of tax, and the expenditure base for taxation, the source of the income or expenditure is irrelevant.[2] Tax systems frequently distinguish between earned and unearned income and tax the latter receipts more heavily. Differential treatment was introduced in Britain in 1907 when unearned income was taxed more heavily. From 1920 up to 1973 this was achieved by allowing an earned-income deduction. As an illustration, earned income in 1973 up to a figure of £4,005 was given a two-ninths allowance, with smaller relief on earned income above this figure. The effect was that the tax rate of 38.75 per cent then in force was reduced to a rate of about 30 per cent for earned income below £4,005. The system was changed to an unearned-income surcharge from 1973, as part of the simplifying measures then introduced. One reason for the change was that there appeared to be wide misunderstanding of the marginal rate of tax under the old system; the current rate of tax, before allowing for the earned-income relief, was frequently quoted as the rate of tax even on those with only low earned incomes.

At present, earned income is defined as wages and salaries, income from a trade or profession, a pension or retirement annuity paid under an Inland Revenue-approved scheme, family allowances, old-age pensions and widows' pensions paid under the National Insurance Acts, income from a patent or copyright if the person actually created the subject-matter and amounts received from the employer after leaving employment. Unearned income is then the category into which other receipts fall. The main items under this head will be dividends, interest and rents.

Many and varied reasons have been given for taxing unearned income at a higher rate. The Royal Commission on the Taxation of Profits and Income (1955) laid some emphasis on the precarious nature of earned as opposed to unearned income. The word 'precarious' is subject to different interpretations: it may refer to the fact that earned income depends on the receiver being able to give services in a way that unearned income does not; unearned income is not affected by age, sickness or other disability. It is easy, however, to overstate the certainty of unearned income, unless one is considering the interest from a government security: most other unearned income is subject to uncertainty which can involve the complete loss of such income when, for example, a company fails and there are insufficient funds to pay ordinary-shareholders.

Also, some stress has been laid on the fact that expenses are incurred in obtaining earned income of a kind that does not occur with unearned income.

Another argument used relies more on redistributive ideas. Studies show that unearned income, as one would expect, is heavily concentrated at the upper-income levels, and taxing unearned income more heavily is seen as a redistributive device. Before the advent of a capital gains tax it was also suggested that higher taxes on unearned income was a rough and ready way of compensating for the non-taxation of certain receipts. Allied to this is the argument that the possession of capital conveys psychic advantages over and above any money return obtainable from it, and that this advantage should be taxed.

On allocative grounds there is a conflict. The converse of the argument that lower taxes on earned incomes is likely to stimulate work effort is that a higher tax on investment income is likely to diminish savings and investment.

The practical issue of higher tax on unearned income cannot be separated from the nature of the current tax system. If the desired amount of redistribution of income can be achieved without a differential tax, then the distorting effects of such a differential can also be avoided. If the tax base for income is drawn very narrowly and in particular much unearned income escapes taxation, then the case of those who argue for discrimination in tax rates is strengthened.

The taxpaying unit

Chapter 13 looked at the problem of the taxpaying unit. In Great Britain the general rule is that income of husbands and wives is aggregated for tax purposes, though important exceptions have been made in recent years. It is now possible to have a wife's earned income taxed separately from her husband's, but her investment income will continue to be aggregated. If such an election takes place, each spouse gets a single person's tax allowance – the husband thus loses the larger married person's allowance. For married couples where both have substantial earned incomes, the higher tax paid because of the loss of the married person's allowance is more than offset by the fact that they escape the higher brackets of tax or reach them much later than would be the case if their joint incomes were aggregated.

The position of children's income depends on the source of that income and whether it is earned or unearned. For many years investment income of a child has been aggregated with that of the parents for tax purposes. A change in the rule that income from a gift from anyone other than the parents should not be aggregated was introduced in 1972, although the Labour Government announced it would repeal this. The rule that the income from property settled by the parents on a child is nevertheless counted as part of the income of the parents is an obvious one to stop tax avoidance.

If a child has earned income in its own right, this is not aggregated with the income of the parent and the child receives a single person's allowance and any other allowance he or she may qualify for. However, for income, earned or unearned, in excess of £115 (the old figure of tax allowance for a child) the parents lose £1 of allowance for every £1 by which the child's income exceeds £115.

Schedule D and Schedule E

The most important categories falling under Schedule D are shopkeepers, professional persons working on their own account and other unincorporated businesses. Wages, salaries and pensions are covered by Schedule E.

In the case of wages, salaries and pensions the matter is straightforward, as we have just seen. Income as defined by current law (not to be confused with the definition of income under the total accretion principle) is, using standard-tax terminology, called 'gross income'. From this gross income the appropriate personal allowances are deducted in order to arrive at 'taxable income', which is charged under Schedule E through the system known as 'Pay As You Earn' (PAYE).

In the case of income from trades, farms and professions, it is necessary to ascertain the total statutory income; from this sum adjustments are made to cover the using up of capital involved in the business in order to arrive at the figure of taxable income. If more than one person is involved, the taxable income is allocated to the partners in whatever proportions the partnership has agreed on. This portion of the profits is then the 'gross income' of the person concerned, and after the personal allowances have been deducted we arrive at the taxable income of the individual as before.

First- and second-class citizens?

The growth of unincorporated and incorporated businesses in this century, and the increase in tax rates, brings up some of the most contentious problems in taxation. Incorporated businesses are taxed separately from individuals; the method of tax will be treated in the next chapter on company taxation. A problem in equity arises if the incorporated company is in effect a 'one-man business' or partnership rather than a company owned by a large number of shareholders. Profits retained in the business do not count as income of the owner and are not therefore subject to progressive rates of personal income tax. This problem has long been recognised, and provision is made for a closely controlled company which makes inadequate distributions to be charged income tax on the shortfall, except to the extent that it can show that retention of profits is necessary or advisable for the maintenance and development of its business. In the past this provision appears to have been used only rarely, and some income must have been subject to lower tax as a result.

A not dissimilar problem is the achievement of equity between taxpayers who receive their income by way of wages and salaries and are therefore taxed under Schedule E, and those who receive income from unincorporated businesses and pay under Schedule D. The latter are able to make deductions for the using up of capital before arriving at a figure of taxable profit.[3] Expenses are dealt with more leniently under Schedule D and since 1975 stock relief provisions apply of a kind which is explained in the next chapter. Both the Majority and Minority Reports of the Royal Commission on the Taxation of Profits and Income (1955) had much to say on capital allowances and expenses. The following quotations are from the Minority Report (pp. 360–1; the paragraph references therein refer to the Majority Report):

The other main respect in which the present legal definition of taxable income causes inequality of treatment between classes of taxpayers concerns not receipts, but outlays. As the Majority point out one particular source of these differences consists in the allowances given for the wastage of capital. The original theory which ignored the wastage of capital altogether 'has been profoundly modified in the course of time, but not to the same extent or in the same way in respect of all the different sources of income'. (Para. 38). While incomes derived from trades, vocations or professions 'now receive a full allowance out of taxable income to make good money expended in acquiring assets that are used up in the production of the income' (Para. 39) no allowances are given with respect to the capital expenditure incurred in vocational and educational training or for the expenditure which a man incurs 'in developing and improving his expert knowledge' (Para. 41). Another and, in our view, even more important cause of such inequality arises out of the difference in the legal definition of deductible expenses in respect of income from a trade, profession or vocation assessed under Schedule D, and in respect of income from an office, employment or pension assessed under Schedule E.

Both the Majority and Minority Reports of the Commission were agreed that it would be impracticable to extend the scheme of capital allowances to expenditure incurred on investment by the individual in the human person. The Minority Report adds: 'we believe therefore that short of withdrawing capital allowances altogether – a course that, on grounds of expediency, we should not favour – the difference in treatment cannot in this respect be avoided and ought therefore to be recognised and compensated for' (1955, p. 361). Compensation could be achieved by taxing individuals at a lower rate or by imposing an annual charge, perhaps graduated to the size of the business, for the privilege of company status whether of unincorporated or incorporated form.

On the 'even more important' point of deductible expenses no obviously best solution emerges (1955, paras 113–14):

> Advertising and entertaining are typical examples of expenses incurred for building up the goodwill of a business, which though fully chargeable against the current year's receipts, are frequently linked with receipts, if at all, only through the enhancement of future rather than current earnings. Nothing similar to this would be a deductible expense under Schedule E. The wage or salary earner cannot charge as expenses the cost of entertaining his present or his potential employers even though the expense might be 'wholly and exclusively' incurred with a view to securing for himself a better job. Nor could he charge the cost of training or education (whether in the form of a capital allowance or as current expenses) or the annual wear-and-tear to his physical earning powers. For all these reasons 'income' under Schedule E is not analogous to the net profit under Schedule D; it is more analogous to some conception of a 'gross profit' of trade, before the deduction either of depreciation or of all those other expenses which are not directly associated with the current receipt from trading activity.

The Minority Report goes on to point out the economic distortion that can result from these expense provisions. It refers to the 'very considerable subsidy from the Exchequer on outlays of doubtful value, which it might not have been worth the trader's while to incur at all in the absence of taxation'. The argument against extending these expense provisions to taxpayers under Schedule E is that these 'outlays of doubtful value' would be extended rather than curtailed. The argument against stopping these provisions is the difficulty of separating legitimate business expenses from other outlays, and the handicap which exporters would face if their overseas competitors continued to receive tax advantages.

Since the Report of the Royal Commission, action has been taken on two fronts. Deductible expenses under Schedule D have been tightened up and a slight relaxation of allowable expenses has occurred under Schedule E. The position, perhaps inevitably, still leaves many loopholes, and further changes are likely in the future.

Evaluation of current income tax

A number of criticisms have been made in previous chapters. The prime one is not the nature of income tax itself but the definition of income which is subject to this tax. In this chapter attention has been drawn to some of the advantages which many individuals can obtain by forming themselves into unincorporated or incorporated companies.

Another criticism can be made: that reliefs given by way of tax concessions do not help the most needy. The present tax system, as we have seen, makes fairly elaborate provision for differences in taxpayers' circumstances. To recapitulate: single person's allowance of £985, married person's allowance of £1,535, allowances in respect of the taxpayer's age, dependent children and some other dependent relatives, and for certain interest payments, e.g. house mortgage payments and life-insurance premiums, and special allowances are also given to the blind. Thus a single man does not start paying tax until his income is at least over £985, while the corresponding figure for the married man is £1,535. Thus the additional reliefs that a person might be entitled to are of no value to a single man whose income is below £985, and a married man whose income is below £1,535. To take an example, a married man with income of £1,535 obtains no benefit from the children's allowances even though he has children.

In a similar way, if we take children's allowances into account, a couple with one child under 11 do not start paying tax until their income is £1,635, with two children under 11 £1,735, with three children under 11 £1,835. Thus families in these circumstances with incomes below their respective levels obtain no benefit from other allowances, for example on insurance premiums.[4]

The tax system thus helps those who are relatively well off without assisting the really poor. The high taxpayer gains most from the system of reliefs, since these allowances have the effect of reducing the amount of income subject to the higher marginal rates of tax; the poorest members get nothing. This paradox of the tax system is inseparable from the present system of giving reliefs via income tax.[5]

It has been suggested that tax concessions should be confined to relief at the standard rate of tax and that they be extended to all citizens. Married couples, for example, who have income below the tax allowance of £1,535 should receive a supplement to bring their income up to this level. The child-benefit scheme proposes to take child allowances out of the tax system, and the present housing option mortgage scheme was also designed to overcome the drawback noted above that only those above a certain income level benefit by tax allowances. Under the housing scheme, a person has been able since 1968 either to pay the market rate of interest and claim a deduction from his assessable income, or to take a loan at a reduced rate of interest. The basis of the social services and social provision is undergoing a reappraisal and it can be questioned whether the child benefit and housing scheme does more than partly patch up a system which needs more drastic remodelling. An alternative approach is to scrap some, or all, of the tax allowances and substitute other payments, as is being done with child allowances. For example, it has been suggested by Lister (1975, p. 5) that the married man's tax allowance should be abolished and, instead, a cash payment made to those who stay at home to care for dependent children, graded in favour of parents with children under 5:

> The shift of resources from the married man's tax allowance to some form of home responsibility allowance, where one parent stays at home to care for children, would help concentrate resources on families with young children and would end the anachronistic assumption, underlying the married man's tax allowance, that married women are their husbands' dependants.

These matters will be re-examined in Chapter 23.

A look at the tax rates in force (Table 14.1) shows that marginal rates (tax paid on the last increment of income) do not impinge on successively higher income levels in a smooth progression.

Figure 14.1 shows the marginal and average tax rates for a married man with two children under 11 taking into account just his married person's and children's allowances. Tax starts at an income of £1,735. A small band of income over this figure of £750 is then subject to a rate of 25 per cent. Next comes a very broad band of £7,250 where the marginal rate is 33 per cent; after this, higher marginal tax rates come into force. On the diagram the long band near the beginning where the marginal rate is constant at

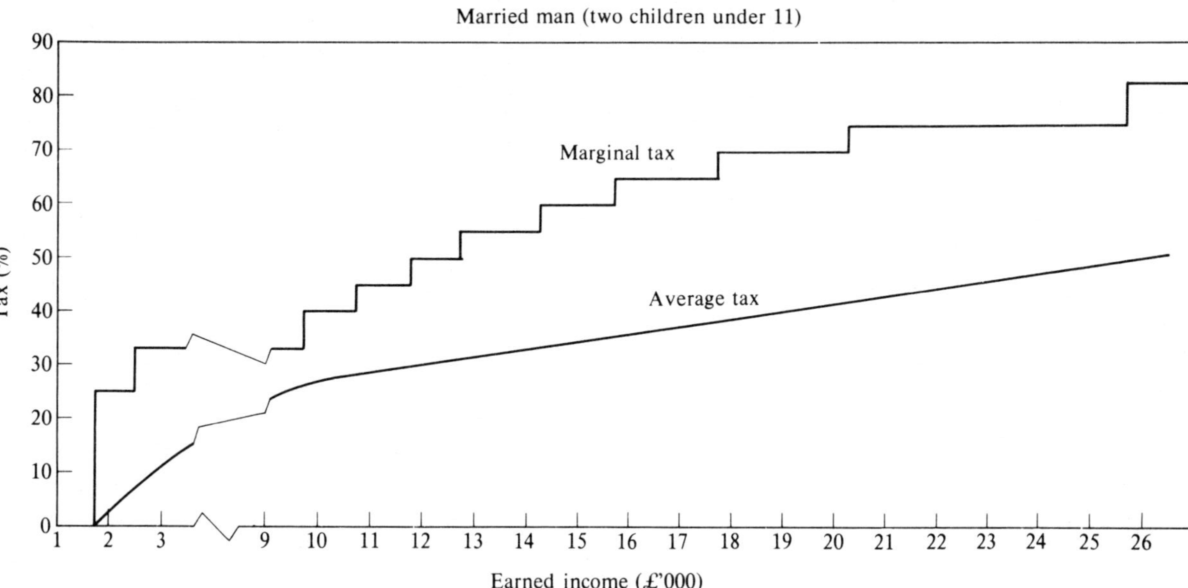

Figure 14.1 *Average and marginal rates of tax on earned income of married man (two children under 11).*

34 per cent has been truncated so that the upper-income levels can be shown. The system of allowances reduces a person's marginal rate of tax since it shifts the whole marginal tax curve to the right – the higher tax bands are not reached until a greater income is earned. Presumably we have such a system because originally income tax was a low flat rate – not until tax is made progressive does the form in which allowances are given take on importance. An alternative form of allowances which will be elaborated in Chapter 23 is a system of tax grants. Basically all income is subject to tax, but a uniform system of allowances is used to offset or partly offset the tax bill. This would result in the same money benefit to all above a minimum level of income. The high rates of tax on very high incomes have frequently been said to act as a disincentive to effort, or to drive high-rate taxpayers to take up residence abroad, although definitive empirical evidence on this matter is lacking. Taking the latter point first, it has already been shown that these high rates are to some extent a sham because of the way income is defined at present. If the definition of income is reworked on the lines of the total accretion principle, then it may well be that the degree of progression in the system and the levels reached by the highest rates will have to be looked at again. The present levels may well be tolerated because people reason that rough justice is being done: high rates on some parts of income being offset by low or nil rates on other parts of income. The waste that this causes by the reshuffling of income and assets has already been noted. If income is redrawn on total accretion lines and comes to form the main source of revenue, then also the problem of jumps in the degree of progression takes on a more serious aspect.

A glance at Table 10.1 on sources of UK tax revenue will reveal a common error. There seems to be an almost universal tendency to take a particular tax in isolation from the rest of the tax system and to make judgments about the regressiveness or unfairness of that particular tax. A particularly blatant form of this error is to assume that, because income tax is highly progressive, we therefore have a highly progressive tax system as a whole. However, as the revenue table shows, income tax accounts for roughly 37 per cent of government revenue. Some of the other sources of revenue are regressive in their impact – for example, many of the Customs and Excise taxes and National Insurance contributions.

The Chancellor of the Exchequer (Denis Healey) introduced a unique step into his April Budget of 1976. He announced tax changes conditional on the voluntary acceptance by the Trades Union Council of pay-increase limits. Subject to a pay limit of about 3 per cent, a single person's allowance would be increased by £60 to £735, a married person's by £130 to £1,085; in addition, the allowance for one-parent families would be increased by £70 to £350 and the starting-point for tax rates above the standard rate of 35 per cent would be £5,000 instead of £4,500. In the event a voluntary pay limit was worked out and these allowances became effective from 6 April 1976. The Chancellor took a similar step in the Budget of March 1977 when he announced that he proposed to reduce the basic rate of income tax from 35 to 33 per cent, conditional upon a satisfactory agreement on a new pay policy. In the end guidelines on pay were announced, the basic rate of income tax was cut to 34 per cent, and rather bigger increases in tax allowances were made.

The announcement of the first package in 1976 was met with extreme reaction. It was seemingly a measure designed to get over the escalation in recent years of money wages on the one hand and tax on the other, the latter being considered necessary to claw back the increase in purchasing power. It was condemned by the opposition Conservative Party as 'taxation without representation' whereby the income-tax burden on the majority was being handed over to the TUC. The real income-tax burden, which is what matters, is of course the result of the interaction of the level of income with the level of taxes and the price level, and this Budget provided for the first time an explicit policy that recognised this linkage. Far from an abdication of parliamentary power it can be seen as a strengthening of the power of Parliament over the level of incomes. Control of incomes has been attempted by voluntary and compulsory means on many occasions in the post-1945 period with, at best, only limited success. This new coupling of tax measures with wage conditions is potentially a powerful device which we are likely to see used further. It forces the wage-negotiating parties to consider the links between wages and prices as well as the tax link between wages and take-home pay.

Self-assessment of income tax

For most persons the PAYE system, which works on a cumulative basis over the tax year and is administered by the Inland Revenue and employers, obviates the need for an annual tax return. Suggestions are made from time to time, most recently by Barr, James and Prest (1977), that we should adopt the practice of many other countries and have a self-assessed system of income tax. The major reason cited by the above authors appears to be the saving in administrative costs which such a system would bring.

They do point out, however, that the saving in real resources may be nil since, while public costs of administration will fall, private costs of citizens will increase with the need to understand and complete tax forms. Unemployed tax inspectors will presumably set up private tax offices to help citizens with their returns. Other positive reasons given for self-assessment were the flexibility this would give to changing marginal tax rates and the help this would give to bringing in a system of tax credits and a local or regional income tax. The period of transition would present formidable problems, and the interested reader is referred to the book cited for further details.

Capital gains tax

Any taxpayer, including an individual, a company, trust, partnership, etc., is liable to capital gains tax. Sufficient has already been said to make it clear that the position before capital gains tax was introduced was far from satisfactory.

The Finance Act of 1962 (passed by a Conservative Government) was the first attempt at taxing capital gains. The importance lies not so much in the Act itself as in introducing the principle of taxing capital gains. The debate that preceded and followed the Act did much to blow fresh air into this corner of taxation, and made the passage of later changes easier.

A number of substantial changes have been made in capital gains taxation since its introduction. The following is a brief outline of the position in 1978.

ASSETS CHARGEABLE

The general presumption is that all forms of property are chargeable other than those specifically excluded, whether situated inside or outside the United Kingdom, except that disposals of assets liable to capital gains tax up to £1,000 in value can be made in any one year without incurring the tax. For this purpose husbands' and wives' disposals are aggregated.

The following assets are exempted from capital gains tax:

1 Owner-occupied houses.
2 Personal chattels (i.e. tangible moveable property) such as furniture, antiques and jewellery, provided the value of each chattel at the time of disposal is £2,000 or less.
3 Gifts of taxable assets of £100 or less to any individual during the tax year.

4 Animals, boats and other wasting assets, defined as having a predicted life of fifty years or less. Business assets will, however, normally be liable.
5 Life-insurance policies and deferred annuities.
6 British government stocks if held for a year or more, or inherited. National Savings Certificates, British Savings Bonds, 'Save As You Earn' contracts.
7 Gifts, of any value, to charity.
8 Gifts of important works of art, scientific collections, etc. – provided they remain in the United Kingdom.
9 Gifts of land or buildings 'for the public benefit', for example gifts to the National Trust.
10 Compensation or damages for any wrong or injury suffered to the person, or in connection with a person's profession or vocation.
11 British money. Foreign currency obtained for personal or family expenditure.
12 Betting winnings and premium-bond prizes.
13 Private motor-cars.
14 Any decoration for gallantry (unless purchased).

DISPOSAL OF AN ASSET

An asset becomes chargeable on disposal. Disposal is deemed to occur when the asset is sold, given away, exchanged, lost, destroyed or made worthless, and also if rights to the asset are sold, such as the granting of a lease. Compensation for damage counts as disposal if the compensation is not spent on restoring the damage. A transfer of an asset between husband and wife living together is not counted as a disposal. A substantial concession is that although death is deemed to lead to disposal of the deceased's assets, capital gains tax is not payable. The inheritor receives the assets at their market value at the time of death.

THE RATE OF CAPITAL GAINS TAX

Any loss on disposal of a chargeable asset can be offset against a capital gains tax but not any other type of tax. Capital losses can be carried forward without any time limit against future capital gains.

The chargeable gain is ascertained for assets acquired after 6 April 1965 as the amount obtained when disposing of it, or its market value 'if given away' less the cost or its market value when obtained if it was inherited or received as a gift.

For assets acquired before 6 April 1965 only the proportion of the gain attributable to the period after 6 April will be taxable. The tax is not retrospective. The gain can be ascertained in one of two ways: first, the difference between the amount actually received on sale and its market value of 6 April 1965 – this method must be used for quoted shares and securities and land sold with development value; the second method of ascertaining the taxable gain is a straight time-apportionment formula limited to twenty years prior to 6 April 1965. Thus an asset acquired before 6 April 1945 is nevertheless deemed to have been acquired in 1945. The formula for working out the amount of gain can be expressed as follows. If the gain is G and the asset was held for x months prior to 6 April 1965 and y months after that date, the taxable gain is $Gy/(x+y)$. Thus if we suppose that an asset was acquired 24 months before 6 April 1965 at a cost of £10,000 and it is sold 144 months later for £30,000, the gain is £20,000, and 20,000 × 144/168 = £17,142, which is the amount of that gain subject to tax. Expenses incurred in acquiring and disposing of the assets can be deducted from the gain or added to the loss.

For the individual the maximum rate is 30 per cent but a rule whereby he could elect to have one-half of his marginal rate of tax payable on the whole net capital gains, where gains are below £5,000, or pay half his marginal rate of tax on the gains less £2,500 where the net gain is over £5,000, meant that for most persons the rate of tax was substantially below 30 per cent. The rate of capital gains tax varied, therefore, between 17 per cent (half the standard rate of 34 per cent) and 30 per cent. The rate was increased above the level of 17 per cent for those persons paying more than the standard rate of income tax and those making capital gains in any year in excess of £5,000. In passing the Finance Act 1977 an undertaking was made that consideration would be given to some form of indexing of the capital gains tax. The April Budget in 1978 introduced a reduced rate of tax of 15 per cent on gains between £1,000 and £5,000. Marginal relief will mean that only gains of £9,500 or more in a year will bear the full rate of 30 per cent.

For companies, fifteen-twenty-sixths of any chargeable gains are added to the assessable profit of the company and charged to corporation tax at 52 per cent, making an effective tax rate of 30 per cent, except for unit and investment trusts where the rate since 1978 is 10 per cent. However, substantial concessions have been introduced for family businesses. If a person is over 65 and disposes of the whole or part of a business which he has owned for the past ten years that person is exempt from capital gains tax on the first £50,000 of any gain arising in respect of the 'chargeable business assets' of the business. Disposals between the ages of 60 and 65 get reduced relief. A wife is also eligible for the relief if she works in the business and owns part of it. In order to assist this type of business the Budget in 1978 also allowed the tax on gifts of business assets either within a family or to employees to be deferred until the assets are sold. Also losses on loans and guarantees were allowed to qualify for capital gains tax relief.

EVALUATION OF THE CAPITAL GAINS TAX

How does the capital gains tax stand up to the standard of the 'total accretion of income'?

The revenue from this tax is likely to be quite modest for many years to come. An asset acquired many years ago may have appreciated several hundred times in value but the change in value from 6 April 1965 is on the valuation basis, all that matters for the purpose of the tax. If the asset in question depreciates in value from this date, then a loss is available which can be offset against other gains in spite of the fact that the asset may have appreciated many times in value over its purchase price. This criticism does not apply if the time-apportionment formula is used. There is a general presumption against retrospective legislation, and in particular retrospective *tax* legislation. There may be very good grounds for circumscribing the Government's power in this direction, but at the same time it must be pointed out that it gives an excellent weapon to vested interests to resist changes that are not in their interest but could conceivably be in the nation's interest. In view of the sharp rise that has taken place in many capital values since 1945, and in view of the general agreement that the old system was inequitable, a case can be made that the tax should have been backdated for a number of years, or at least that where the value of the assets was known at 6 April 1965 the over-all gain should be taken into account before allowing offsetting of loss.

Although the revenue gain is likely to take many years to build up, in principle the tax represents a major breakthrough – one of the few major changes in the fiscal system that has come about in peace-time conditions. Some of the criticisms that can be made of the tax result from the inevitable conflict that results from putting principles into practice. Of this kind is the exemption from tax of gifts of chargeable assets provided that their value does not in total exceed £1,000 each year, and the exclusion of chattels disposed of for £2,000 or less. Because of the ease of evasion and the cost of trying to collect tax on small sums, it is almost inevitable that such exemption should be given.

It is much more difficult to justify the taxation of long-term gains at a maximum rate of 30 per cent. The principle of progressive taxation of 'income' (narrowly defined) has long been accepted and it seems illogical to charge a lower-rate tax on part of income when this is more widely drawn. It seems little justification to argue, as some commentators have done, that current income-tax rates are too high. Income-tax rates are to some extent as high as they are because income is so badly defined, and one of the benefits to be expected from widening the scope of income is that tax rates and the progression of the tax can be looked at anew.

The only valid case that it seems possible to make, on total accretion lines, for the more lenient treatment of capital gains is the present inability to spread fluctuating income over a number of years. In Chapter 13 on the criterion of ability to pay it was argued that some form of averaging was desirable under any form of progressive taxation. The argument against taxing that part of the gain which is due to inflation was dismissed on the grounds that there is no case for protecting one section of income from inflation.

Since capital gains on a significant scale are likely to accrue to a very small section of the population, the case for a flat rate of 30 per cent appears even more inequitable. A single man with a taxable income of £10,000 will pay £3,430 in tax. A taxable gain of £10,000 will be liable for much less tax than this regardless of how much or how little income and wealth the owner already possesses. The peculiar ethic that it is only income, narrowly defined, which should be taxed at highly progressive rates has still to be exorcised from the system.[6]

In view of the very unequal distribution of wealth in this country, already commented on, the exclusion of net gains at death seems indefensible in a country where all political parties pay lip-service to the need for some redistribution of wealth. Redistribution at death is the least painful way of achieving this end, and the one likely to cause least economic disturbance.

It was argued in Chapter 13 on the criterion of ability to pay that the total exclusion of owner-occupied houses from the capital gains tax confers a benefit on house-owners as compared with those who rent property, and is, in addition, likely to inflate the demand for houses. In the USA, where capital gains have been taxed for many years (Schultz and Harris, 1965, p. 249):

> Gain on the sale of a residence is taxable as a capital gain but a loss is not deductible. Since 1954, for the federal tax, the capital basis of a residence sold may be transferred to a new one acquired within 18 months if

the cost of the new is the same or higher than the sale price of the old, and pro rata if the cost is less, so that capital gains is in effect postponed for such 'paired' transactions. In 1964 Congress allowed additional exemption for gains on homes sold by persons over age 65.

Amendment on these lines would appear desirable. Owner-occupied houses would then be liable for capital gains, either when the proceeds were used for other purposes, or at death.[7]

Finally, some word should be added on the cost of administering this tax. It should be noted that – in so far as it is now less profitable to switch assets around for a pure tax advantage – in time it could lead to a more productive use of manpower even though the Inland Revenue staff may have to be increased. The costs of tax collection do not form a large percentage of the amount of revenue collected, but there is no doubt that the capital gains tax will increase costs for some time to come. In the author's opinion, the serious distortions present in the old system justify this increase in cost. The 'cake of custom' has been broken. It can be hoped that a fruitful period of public discussion can now take place on the kind of modifications still needed.

Development gains

There is a tax on development gains on land and buildings which was brought in after 17 December 1973. This subjects such gains to income tax under Schedule D. This tax is to be replaced by a more comprehensive development land tax at a flat rate of 80 per cent, so only a few brief details will be given here.

The tax is payable when property which is liable for capital gains is sold for more than £10,000. The tax does not therefore apply to owner-occupied houses since these are exempt from capital gains tax.

In these cases the development gain is taxed as income and not as a capital gain. However, if the property has been owned for more than a year, the gain can be averaged over the time it has been owned subject to a maximum averaging over four years.

Indexing

Indexing is, as we have seen, now incorporated for personal tax allowances from 1978–9 and is being considered for capital gains. The choice of the retail price index for indexing allowances is, it is suggested below, a bad one.

In evaluating the likely effects of indexing, the first question that has to be settled is whether most or only some contracts are to be covered. Should it cover wages, fiscal policy such as tax rates, and monetary contracts such as borrowing and lending, or should it be confined to one or more of these sectors?

A number of people have considered the question of indexing (see, for example, Friedman, 1974a; Jackman and Klappholz, 1975; Leisner and King, 1975; and Morgan, 1977). A number of claims are put forward for indexing, notably that it would help to reduce the rate of inflation and that it would remove the redistribution effects of inflation.

Equity is only fully dealt with by complete indexation, but partial indexation may be used to deal with some of the more important anomalies. The necessity on equity grounds for indexing contracts which are frequently renegotiated, such as wages, is less than in the case of long-term contracts since the renegotiations are likely to take inflation into account. State pensions and some social security benefits are the most important items that have been indexed. Mortgage borrowing and lending is perhaps the next most important area where indexation would help achieve equity, although the administrative costs would be considerable. Indexation in Britain has been adopted only on a very limited scale for savings. One scheme is for contractual savings over a period of five years with a maximum monthly payment of £20. Another is the provision for retired persons to have up to £700 indexed. In both cases it is the capital which is indexed: interest is not paid on the capital sum. Suggestions for indexation to be applied to company accounts have also been made, and details are given in the next chapter.

The argument that indexing would help to reduce the level of inflation is usually put in terms of indexing government securities.

By itself indexation is compatible with any rate of inflation. Arguments that it would help to reduce the rate of inflation rely on two main points: one is the effect that this would have on people's expectations about inflation; the second is the terms on which an indexed security could be issued compared with an unindexed security. Indexation of securities may take the form of indexing the capital, or the rate of interest, or both. We have seen that the Government has been able to offer a zero rate of interest on contracts which have the capital sum indexed. Under certain circumstances this will be more inflationary than with no indexation; in other circumstances it will be less inflationary. If nominal rates of interest are below the rate of inflation, the general situation in recent years, then real rates of interest are negative. In this case indexation of the capital will return more to the lender and, other things being equal, will therefore be more inflationary. If the presence of indexation induces a higher level of saving, by providing a more secure refuge than money or goods, then this may be sufficient to outweigh this factor.

Adjusting tax rates or tax allowances for changes in the value of money reduces fiscal drag and the built-in flexibility of the economy. Without indexation the Government automatically gets an increase in revenue (without changing taxes) when there is inflation. If we take the case of income tax, as incomes increase so more persons are pushed past the tax threshold, and more people are pulled into higher tax brackets. If government expenditure is not increased, this acts as a deflationary factor in the economy; hence the term 'fiscal drag'.[8] With indexation this extra revenue is not forthcoming: extra revenue must be budgeted for. Since personal tax allowances are to be adjusted but not the rates of value-added tax (the absolute amount of which increases as prices subject to value-added tax increase), we have a further distortion; in the absence of compensation direct tax will become a smaller proportion of revenue during an inflationary period and indirect tax will become a greater proportion of revenue, the opposite of the case without indexing when direct taxes increase as a proportion of total revenue.

The most obvious choice of an index would appear to be the retail price index, which is published monthly. A little reflection will show that this index, if unmodified, is far from ideal. An increase in indirect taxes pushes up the retail price index, but the purpose of indexing is not to isolate the community against indirect tax increases by adjusting direct taxes. Likewise, it is not sensible to compensate for price increases due to increased import prices. Increased import prices mean a reduction in living standards; indexing may shift the loss but it cannot prevent it. The retail price index could be modified to exclude these factors, or some other index could be used which omits these items, such as, for example, the index of Gross Domestic Product at factor cost. It follows that a general index for all is required and not, as some have argued, different indices for different sectors. The purpose of indexing is to insulate contracts against average changes in the price level, *not* relative price movements.

On equity grounds, then, the case for general indexation is strong but likely to be costly in terms of administration. Partial indexation produces distortions in the economy which have to be weighed against the benefits to be expected from indexation. Also, the argument that indexing would help to cure inflation is uncertain; in certain circumstances it could even make matters worse. And the proposal to index tax allowances using the retail price index has the paradoxical effect that a change in indirect taxes, since these affect retail prices, will change tax allowances.

Summary

Past attempts to allow for differences in individual and family circumstances have resulted in a complex code of personal income taxation which nevertheless fails to help the most needy in the community. Details of the tax structure were given.

In recent years differences between citizens who obtain their incomes from an employer and those who obtain their income from a business have been accentuated, and have led many, who are able to do so, to arrange their affairs in this form. The latter are able to deduct for the using up of capital before arriving at a figure for tax; profit retained in the business is not, generally speaking, subject to the progressive rates of tax of personal income; and finally they are able to claim more generous expenses. Suggestions have been put forward that individuals should be taxed at a lower rate to compensate for these advantages, or that an annual charge should be imposed on businesses for these privileges. Both suggestions are not without their difficulties.

The capital gains tax, in spite of the small amount of revenue received at present, represents a major shift in principle. The maximum rate of this tax at 30 per cent does not appear to be based on any valid grounds except the present inability to spread fluctuating income over a number of years. If a scheme of income averaging is adopted, the case for counting all gains as income would be very much strengthened.

Finally, some of the pros and cons of indexing were examined. The conclusion reached was that the system of partial indexation which is present in the current system is likely to produce distortions in the economy and the choice of the retail price index to adjust tax allowances will create an undesirable link between indirect and direct taxation.

Notes

1 Except that single-parent families in the tax year 1976–7 were paid £1 a week for the first child; these families in 1977–8 received £1.50 a week for the first and subsequent children.

2 Income tax (or corporation tax for companies) is, broadly speaking, charged on all income, wherever it originates, that accrues to a person resident in the United Kingdom. Residence is somewhat complicated but anyone living in the United Kingdom for six months or more in a

tax year is defined as a resident, and a person may be resident even if present for less than six months. A company is deemed resident if its central management and control is exercised in the United Kingdom.

Income that arises in the United Kingdom is subject to tax regardless of the residence or nationality of the person who receives the income.

In order to avoid double taxation in the above cases, a series of agreements have been made with many other countries. The general principle of relief is the same for persons and companies, and details as these affect companies will be given in the next chapter.

3 The taxable sum may be more or less than the profits shown in the books of the company. For example, if capital items have been charged to revenue, this will be disallowed, as will purely personal expenditure of the proprietor, i.e. these sums will be added back to arrive at a figure of taxable profit. Certain types of capital investment attract allowances, but the details of these will be left to Chapter 15.

4 Proposals have been made to allow policy-holders to deduct an appropriate amount from each eligible premium, instead of having a tax allowance.

5 In recent years the term 'Tax Expenditures' has been given to the loss of revenue as a result of tax allowances. The sums of money involved are large. For a recent estimate for the United Kingdom see Willis and Hardwick (1978).

6 It may be argued that the man may have less 'real capital' after realising his gain of £10,000 than when he made the original investment and that he is paying tax on a non-existent real gain. The pros and cons of this argument were dealt with in the previous chapter at some length. It was there concluded that public finance should be concerned with a person's relative tax position; changes in the value of money affect all sectors of the community in different degrees, and compensation for one sector results in less equity, not more.

The fact that many tax concessions have now been capitalised in the selling prices of houses makes large and abrupt changes of tax allowances undesirable on equity grounds but it should not stop a gradual movement to a more rational system.

7 The exclusion of capital gains completely from tax in the case of owner-occupied houses serves to further entangle what has been for many years an illogical, absurd and unjust situation. The only people who do not receive a subsidy from public funds are the occupants of privately rented houses. About half of these private tenants are 'subsidised' by their landlords because their premises are subject to rent control. All tenants, both private and council, pay rents out of taxed income, but most council tenants receive subsidies. A much larger element of subsidy usually accrues to the owner-occupier while he is buying his house because of tax relief allowed on interest payments. Since the change of Schedule A tax, no income is imputed to the owner for the value of the services of his property, so that this tax relief results in a direct reduction in tax. Always an unpopular tax we are unlikely for political reasons to see the reintroduction of imputed rent, however desirable this would be on grounds of equity. An alternative

way is to allow private tenants to offset the part of his rent that goes towards interest payment on the capital sum invested in his house against tax, in the same way that an owner can offset his mortgage payments. This proposal, while it would go some way to achieving equity between persons, suffers from administrative complexities and the drawback noted previously that the poorest section of the community derives no benefit from income-tax concessions. More drastic remodelling of the system is required if we are to break out of the present tragic situation. For a discussion of this and other aspects of housing, see Hemming and Duffy (August 1964) and Stafford (November 1976). A spirited defence of the *status quo* is provided by *Housing Policy: A Consultative Document* (1973), which was prepared after nearly three years' work by the Department of the Environment and the Welsh Office. The preface sets the tone: the reader is warned not to pursue theoretical or academic dogma. While it is recognised that 'The present basis of pricing and general assistance can be criticised as tending to encourage excessive consumption of housing', we are told that 'the decisions and family budgets of millions of households have been shaped by the expectations that existing arrangements will continue in broadly their present form'. Possible links between changes in relief and compensatory changes in taxes are not investigated.

8 The opposite tendency is known as 'fiscal boost', e.g. most of the tax on tobacco and alcohol is related to weight or volume respectively. Inflation then reduces the effective tax rate.

15
Company taxation

This indirect benefit of incorporation [retained profits on which surtax is not payable] cannot fairly be ignored in framing the tax system applicable to corporation profits. It is a fiscal matter and bears upon the proper distribution of the burden of tax upon different kinds of income. The difficulty remains, however, that the saving achieved is achieved on behalf of the shareholders as a whole; the money is in most cases outside the control of any one individual shareholder and is certainly not directly at his disposal as free personal income.
Royal Commission on the Taxation of Profits and Income (1955, para. 54).

Company taxation is a complex matter in which the public-finance, accounting and legal aspects twist and are interwoven. This chapter attempts to give a broad description of company taxation, concentrating on important issues. It starts with a factual description of changes in company taxation. This leads to a discussion of the principles of company taxation and to a discussion of the value or otherwise of tax discrimination against distributed profits. The next section then treats important, and even more controversial, matters relating to the concept of profit which is subject to tax. Finally, it looks at the important system of investment allowances and grants which has grown up since 1945.

Company taxation in this context is used to cover the ordinary meaning of taxes levied directly on company profits. It will be clear from previous chapters that a number of other taxes affect companies and may be paid in whole or in part by them. VAT will be considered in Chapter 16. As a general rule it is probably correct to treat VAT as a tax on consumers, but changes in VAT may have repercussions on industry in altering demand for the products concerned; this will be taken up in Part III. Capital gains tax and social security contributions were looked at in previous chapters and will not be developed further.

Changes in company taxation

During the years immediately following the First World War a special tax was levied on the profits of companies to absorb some of the excess profits they were able to make as a result of the war. In 1937 a national defence contribution was imposed; this continued until 1947, when a profits tax (paid on profits above a certain amount) was levied. This differentiated according to whether the profits were retained in the business or distributed to shareholders. Table 15.1 lists the changes made in company tax.

The column under income tax merely reflects the changes in the standard rate of income tax to which taxable profits of the preceding accounting year were subject. The next two columns show the additional profits tax

Table 15.1

	Income tax	Net profits tax	
Year	(%)	On undistributed profits (%)	On distributed profits (%)
1947	45.0	5.4	13.8
1949	45.0	5.4	16.5
1951	47.5	5.2	26.3
1952	47.5	2.5	22.5
1953	45.0	2.5	22.5
Apr 1955	42.5	2.5	22.5
Nov 1955	42.5	2.5	27.5
1956	42.5	3.0	30.0
1958	42.5	10.0	10.0
1959	38.8	10.0	10.0
1960	38.8	12.5	12.5
1961–66	38.8	15.0	15.0
1966–73	Change to corporation tax: initially at 40%, 42½% from April 1968 and 45% from April 1969. Shareholders liable to tax on dividends.		
1973–	Corporation tax at 52% but shareholders credited with tax at the standard rate on dividends. Lower rate for companies with small profits.		

Source: For figures up to 1960 Rubner (June 1964).

which were levied on profits of the current year if these were above £12,000, with reduced rates for profits between £2,000 and £12,000. Except for the period 1958–66, a heavier, sometimes a much heavier tax, was levied on that part of profit which was distributed to shareholders than on that part which was retained in the business. From 1961 to 1966 the amount of tax was not affected by the amount of dividend paid out. In 1966 the system of company taxation was changed to corporation tax and this was introduced in a way that effectively discriminated against dividend payments. A change in the way corporation tax was administered in 1973 reverted to the previous system whereby the amount of tax was not affected by the amount of dividend. Discrimination seems to be based on no clear logical principle.

The principles of company taxation

The erratic gyrations of company taxation lead to the question of whether or not it is possible to find any principles on which it should be based. On referring back to the section on total accretion of income (p. 170) it will be found that if we are adhering strictly to this principle and if we are trying to treat people in equal positions equivalently, then it is the shareholders, as owners of companies, that should be taxed rather than the companies themselves. It is only in the case of profits retained in the business that a problem of reallocation arises.

It is sometimes suggested that company taxation should be reduced or abolished and that the whole of company profits should be allocated to the owners. In the case of public companies, shareholders would receive with their dividend warrants a statement of their portion of the profits which the company had decided to retain in the business. The shareholder would be liable for tax on both sums.

This solution has weighty objections. It is usually rejected on the grounds that a person should not be liable for more tax than the sum he receives. This could occur under this scheme, for example where a top-rate taxpayer is a shareholder in a company that retains most of the profit in the business. Even if this argument is accepted in principle, it is one which is likely to carry less weight under the total accretion principle, since the adoption of this would enable a revision of tax rates to be made. The argument that this would stop the flow of funds to companies, from high-taxpayers, even allowing for the adjustments of tax rates under the accretion principle, is more serious. However, just on grounds of equity it seems unlikely, for this reason, to be a practical proposition.

The adoption of the accretion principle of income would greatly reduce the problem of inequity. Distributed profits would be part of the income of the recipient, as at present. Retained profits, to the extent that they enhance the value of the business, would also be taxed as income when the gains are realised. This solution favours the investor, both because he has a deferred liability for tax, and also because he has a tax cushion if retained profits do not enhance the value of the business. This degree of inequity may be thought tolerable because of the incentive it is likely to give to investment.

The solution outlined above leaves open the question of whether companies should be taxed as entities in their own right, apart from taxing shareholders: on the one hand, there are those who hold that the only problem is to achieve a system that will tax shareholders as closely as possible to the position that would be reached if all profits were distributed; on the other hand, there are those who argue that, in effect, companies can be considered as entities or personalities in their own right who reap considerable benefits from government expenditure and should be taxed accordingly. Incorporation as a limited liability company is seen as an important privilege which on the benefit principle of taxation should be taxed. Before definite answers can be given it is necessary to know the incidence of company taxation, whether, that is, this ultimately falls on the shareholder, the workers or the consumer. Incidence is taken up in the next chapter and looked at in more detail in Chapter 23. The importance of this question also tends to merge with that of tax incentives to business investment, which is taken up at the end of this chapter.

The system of tax before the Finance Act of 1965

A company's taxable profits of the preceding year was liable to tax at the standard rate of income tax, and in addition the taxable profit of the current year, if large enough, was subject to profits tax. From 1961 profits tax was an additional 15 per cent if profits exceeded £12,000 per year. The rate was scaled down for profits between £2,000 and £12,000; below £2,000 profits were only taxed at the standard rate of income tax. Under this system it was thus a matter of indifference (from a tax viewpoint) to a company whether it paid out profits in the form of dividends or whether it retained these in the business. (The recipient of the dividend was credited with the standard rate of tax paid by the company so that he had no more to pay if he was himself a standard-rate income-taxpayer. If he paid at lower or higher rates he was entitled respectively either to a rebate of tax or indebted to the Inland Revenue for the difference.) The system before 1956 was, as we have seen, one where distributed profits were taxed more heavily than retained profits.

One reason why it is very difficult to link changes in tax on companies with changes in their investment behaviour is that both their current-year profits and preceding-year profits were liable to tax because the liability to income tax was lagged by one year. Since companies are under no obligation to keep standard accounting dates for making up their accounts, tax changes affected companies were spread over two or more years.

The Finance Act of 1965

The Finance Act of 1965 introduced a *corporation tax* in place of the two-tier system just described. Corporation tax separated the taxation of companies from that of individuals. Companies became liable to this tax on their taxable profit, including capital gains, but were not liable to income tax. Payment of interest (e.g. on debenture stock) was treated as a charge against profits and was not therefore subject to corporation tax. The initial rate of the tax was 40 per cent, increased to 42½ per cent from April 1968 and to 45 per cent from April 1969. However, shareholders were liable to income tax and surtax, where appropriate, on dividends and other distributions. As a matter of machinery, companies were required to deduce income tax, as the standard rate, from payments to shareholders and hand the sums over to the Inland Revenue. In essence companies paid a flat rate of tax of 45 per cent and split dividend payments into two, one part of which they sent to the shareholders, and the balance to the Inland Revenue. This is back to the position that operated before 1958 of effective discrimination against dividends, the rationale of which will be discussed later.

Corporation tax made other changes which had far-reaching results – now considered.

BASIS OF ASSESSMENT

The old system of tax was concerned, as has been shown, with two years' profit. The new tax fixed the rate of corporation tax each financial year and that rate was applicable to the profits of that year. Normally the tax was payable nine months after the end of the company's accounting year, or for the majority of existing companies on 1 January. The financial year referred to above starts on 1 April and ends the following 31 March.

If a company's accounting year coincided with the dates of the financial year, no problem arose as to the rate of tax that was applicable to those profits. If, however, the two did not coincide, then a time-apportionment basis would be used. Thus a company whose accounting year ended on 31 December 1968 would have one-quarter of its taxable profits charged at the rate fixed for the financial year ending 31 March 1968, and the remaining three-quarters at the rate for the financial year ending 31 March 1969. (Obviously, if the tax rate remained unchanged, no problem of time apportionment arose.)

General opinion seemed to be that this method of assessment, once the complications of the changeover had been assimilated, was a welcome simplification of the tax structure, companies being subject to an assessment on one year's profits, rather than two.

The Finance Act of 1973

A Green Paper in March 1971 (*Reform of Corporation Tax*, Cmnd 4630) set out proposals for company taxation. The House of Commons appointed a Select Committee to consider it and it reported in October 1971. The Committee came out in favour of the imputation system of company taxation. The system came into operation from April 1973. In essence the new system is as follows:

1 The company with profits in excess of £35,000 pays corporation tax at a single rate (now 52 per cent) on all its profits, whether distributed or not.
2 A company distributing profits in the form of dividends, etc. will be required to make to the Inland Revenue an advance payment of corporation tax now at the rate of 34/66ths of the dividend paid, known as *franked investment income*.
3 Advance payments under 2 will be set off against its corporation tax bill on its profits for that accounting period, known as *mainstream tax bill*, which is normally payable nine months after the end of the accounting period.
4 The recipient of a distribution under 2 will be entitled to a *tax credit*. This means that a standard-rate taxpayer will not have any further tax liability. A shareholder who is not liable for tax can claim back a rebate and a higher-rate taxpayer will have to pay extra.

For a UK company with all profits earned in this country, this merely means that corporation tax is paid by instalments: when the dividends are paid and when corporation tax is settled. At the other extreme in the case of a company where no tax is payable, because of a tax credit for foreign tax paid, the company will be acting as an agent for collecting tax on the dividends. The system of franked investment income referred to in 2 above ensures that dividends received by a UK company are not subject again to corporation tax.

Small companies (those in the 1978–9 tax year with taxable profits below £85,000!) get a reduction in corporation tax. Profits up to £50,000 get a 10 per cent reduction, so their tax is now 42 per cent, with tapering provisions for profits from £50,000 to £85,000. The argument for this is that small companies find it more difficult to raise capital than large ones and therefore need to retain more of their profits. A special rate, now 40 per cent, applies to building societies and co-operative societies which do not make distributions in the same way as other companies. The new corporation tax is assessed on the profits of accounting periods in the same way as the previous corporation tax. Profits are defined to include a fraction of capital gains.

Does tax discrimination against distributed profits help investment?

Since 1945, the UK Government has been concerned to increase capital investment; the changes in tax on distributed profits, as opposed to undistributed profits, reflects to some extent a conflict on ways of achieving this. The rationale behind sharp discrimination against distributed profits is that this should encourage capital investment by the ploughing back of profits.[1]

Considerable controversy has grown up over the success or failure of this policy. A concise survey is given by Whittington (1974) but see also Sumner (1975). There are very serious statistical difficulties in trying to relate company investment to tax changes where companies' accounting years need not coincide with the fiscal years. In addition, the very frequent changes that have been made in taxes mean that the number of observations is very limited. Besides these technical problems, a number of other factors have to be weighed in order to evaluate the claims made: there is the extent to which discrimination actually influences retentions; the extent to which retentions result in real investment, and whether this investment is efficient compared with what would have taken place without the tax discrimination. It can be said that discrimination against paying dividends by itself causes no incentive to material investment in the firms concerned, since they may merely acquire liquid assets. The number of takeover bids that took place after dividend discrimination had been in force for some years is often quoted as evidence that this is so, since in a number of these takeovers the excessive liquid position of the company being taken over was an attraction. As many factors enter into the decision to take over another company, this evidence is hard to quantify.

More serious is the question of how important different sources of finance are to companies. Relying on ploughing back profits limits a company to a growth that is compatible with its profits. A company wanting to expand faster than this must seek funds from outside. Borrowing on fixed interest by way of debentures or preference shares has its limitations. Too high a 'gearing', that is the level of its fixed-interest payments compared with its ordinary or equity shares, leaves a company very vulnerable if profits should fall. In a bad year equity dividends can be reduced or passed over altogether but fixed-interest payments must be met, or, as a rule, the debenture or preference holders have a right to supersede the management by appointing a receiver or other person to look after their interests. An equity issue means that the market for the shares needs to be a good one, and one of the most important means of ensuring this is to have a liberal dividend policy. We thus come to a direct conflict. If dividends are deliberately discriminated against in order to encourage investment, the effect may be to hamper those companies which want very fast growth and need to go to the equity market in order to make this possible.

A further point sometimes made against the discrimination of distributed profits is that such a policy favours the *status quo*: companies making large profits have the ability to grow but these may not be dynamic companies. Distributing the profits to shareholders leaves them free to invest in any company. The extent to which dividends are used directly or indirectly to finance new investments is once again a field where little empirical evidence is available.[2]

What emerges from this mass of contradictory opinion? It would appear that many factors influence the real investment of companies. These factors are not likely to be stable over time for one company, nor in aggregate to lead at one particular time to a predominance of one or more factors. This negative conclusion has policy implications. Simple-minded theories that investment will be increased or decreased by this or that amount of dividend discrimination seem incorrect; such discrimination is unlikely to make any substantial difference one way or the other to investment.

'Close' companies

As has long been the case special provisions apply to 'close companies', which are, broadly, companies which are under the control of five or fewer persons, or are under the control of their directors.

If the *relevant income* of a close company – roughly its distributable income after tax and after providing for business requirements – exceeds its actual distributions, the amount of that excess may be apportioned among the members of the company, normally in proportion to their respective interests. For a trading company the need to retain profits for the maintenance or development of the business is taken into account in arriving at the figure of relevant income.

Taxation of company profits earned overseas

The essence of the problem can be quite simply stated: should companies which earn profits overseas and pay taxes to overseas governments be given any allowance against taxes that they are liable for in their home country?

Over the years a general principle has been established that income so earned should be subject to home taxation, with various concessions granted. Britain has made agreements with many countries whereby she agrees to forgo her right to tax at full rates in return for concessions of a like nature. Unilateral relief provisions are given in other cases.

The distinction must now be made between a company that has a subsidiary company which is *located, managed and controlled* abroad, and other companies. The general rule is that no UK tax is payable by subsidiary companies in the first group on profits *retained abroad*. Profits that are remitted to the United Kingdom and *all profits* of other subsidiary companies are subject to UK tax, but allowance is given for tax paid abroad.

The allowance takes the form, not of a deduction from gross profits to arrive at taxable profit, but as a direct offset to UK tax liability. Therefore, if foreign tax is no higher than UK tax, a company pays no more tax than would be the case if the profits were earned in the United Kingdom.

FAIR OR UNFAIR TO COMPANIES TRADING OVERSEAS?

The changes in tax on companies, in particular the change in 1966 to corporation tax, caused a major discontinuity in the tax position of companies trading overseas, for which special relief provisions were made. This arose because prior to 1966 companies could offset foreign tax against the standard rate of income tax to which they were subjected and for profits tax if they were liable to this. So that in 1965, for example, so long as overseas tax was below 53¾ per cent, it was offset against UK tax. After 1966 relief was extended only in respect of corporation tax, originally brought in at a rate of 40 per cent and not allowed to be offset against income tax charged to the individual on dividends (but collected by the companies). The effect on companies who were subject to overseas taxation in excess of 40 per cent was that they lost the relief they had been previously getting up to a figure of 53¾ per cent. Indeed, one argument put forward for changing the system was that companies had little incentive to take overseas tax rates into consideration when setting up overseas, since in general UK direct company taxation was higher than most overseas rates. As a result UK revenue suffered.

The 1973 corporation tax continued the broad provision for tax relief that had been built up, as follows. In general a company resident in the United Kingdom is entitled to claim credit for foreign tax paid on income or capital gains against the UK corporation tax payable on the same income or gains. This relief may be due to a double taxation agreement with the country concerned or to unilateral relief provisions.

In the most important case of dividends received from abroad, all companies can claim credit against the UK corporation tax charged on those dividends for any tax *directly* charged on the dividends abroad. Whether a company is further entitled to claim credit for *underlying* taxes, i.e. foreign tax on the profits out of which the dividend is paid, depends on a number of factors. For cases covered by double taxation agreements, such relief is normally applicable. In other cases relief for underlying taxes is given if the UK company controls or is a subsidiary of a company which controls, directly or indirectly, 10 per cent or more of the voting power in the foreign company. There is a provision that where voting control is reduced below 10 per cent for reasons beyond the control of the UK company, and if reasonable endeavours on its part could not restore 10 per cent control, then this relief will nevertheless continue.

The concept of 'taxable profit'

So far in this chapter it has been assumed that the 'taxable profit' of a company is a just and equitable one and we have been looking at ways of taxing this sum. It is now necessary to look at this assumption and find out how taxable profits are determined. It should be stated at the outset that this question is even more controversial than the matters of company tax just discussed. It is just as fundamental: a correct method of taxing companies would give incorrect results if the tax was applied to an incorrect figure of company profit. The divisions on this subject are sometimes between accountants and economists, but not infrequently there are wide differences within each group. The subject is a complex one and no more is attempted in this book than an outline of some of the most important features.

Profit and taxable profit

A company incurs costs in making a commodity or in providing a service and receives a revenue when the product or service is sold. The difference between costs and revenue (which can be positive or negative) during a specified period of time is profit or loss. Profit or loss, being a residual figure, depends on what the tax authorities allow to be called 'costs' and what they allow to be called 'revenue'.

A convenient division of costs is into *fixed* and *variable* costs. 'Fixed' refers to items which are necessary to carry on business, but are not completely used up in the process, for example buildings and machinery. The problem arises of how the costs of these fixed items are to be apportioned to each year's output. 'Variable' refers to costs which cease if output ceases, for example labour and raw-material costs. These variable costs are more easily apportioned to annual output, but even here doubt can arise. Should advertising, which is aimed partly at selling current output and partly at building up the long-term goodwill of the firm, be allocated to the one, or the other, or both? If both, how is it possible to separate the one kind of expenditure from the other? These, and a large number of other definitional points, must be decided, but will not be our main concern. In what follows we shall try and concentrate on the most important aspects. Depreciation will be discussed first. Investment allowances will be treated separately, although perhaps the two should be regarded together. A case can be made for separate treatment on the grounds that depreciation allowances take care of the equity aspect, while investment allowances are primarily concerned to increase the level of real investment, even though the practical use of these measures may not accord with this simple division.

Depreciation

It is not generally realised how recent is the relief for the using up of assets in the course of business. To quote from the Royal Commission on the Taxation of Profits and Income (1955, para. 325):

The conception of depreciation allowances for fixed assets to which the first Tucker Committee gave their support illustrates how far expert views on the tax system had moved since 1920. In that year the Royal Commission were able to assert that income for purposes of taxation should in general be computed without regard to the amortisation of wasting assets. In contrast, in 1951 the Report of the expert committee accepted as a guiding principle . . . 'the general proposition that the Income Tax system should give relief in respect of the wastage of all assets that are used up or consumed in the course of carrying on a business'. (Para. 322) . . . [and] One thing must be said in this connection. The practical result of the changes since 1920 has been to afford a scheme of protection to 'material' capital that is not available to 'personal' capital. Our predecessors were apprehensive about this possibility when they wrote of the risk of creating 'grave inequalities between different classes of income'; and we have seen that it was on this ground, amongst others, that they rejected proposals for a general allowance for the amortisation of wasting assets.

The precise details of current depreciation allowances is the concern of the accountant, rather than the economist. The broad system is to lay down the method of depreciation: the amount or the percentage of the cost of the asset which can be written off, and the number of years over which it is to be written off. These agreed sums may be deducted from gross profit before tax liability is calculated. The agreed system of depreciation varies for different assets, the main categories being:

1 Industrial buildings and structures, now 54 per cent initial allowance, 4 per cent per year subsequently.
2 Plant and machinery other than cars now allowed free depreciation.
3 Exploration, development and construction work in connection with mines, oil-wells and other mineral sources.
4 Agricultural buildings and works.
5 Patent rights.
6 Expenditure on scientific research.

A business may adopt any system of depreciation that it wishes, but it is only allowed to offset against tax on the agreed scale.

Free depreciation means that a company is allowed to write off the cost of plant and machinery when it chooses and can do so completely in the year of purchase if it wishes. The effect of depreciation can be illustrated by considering the case of a 100 per cent write-off in the first year. If we suppose a company invests £10,000 on plant and makes gross profits of £100,000, then taxable profits will be £90,000 for that year. With corporation tax at the rate of 52 per cent the cost to the company of the £10,000 investment is £4,800 since £5,200 less is paid in taxation.[3]

Almost every aspect of the depreciation allowances is subject to some amount of controversy. Does depreciation cover the right items? Should more flexibility be allowed to companies to write off assets against tax as they wish, or should more uniformity be imposed? What is the correct treatment for an asset that is sold before it is fully depreciated? And so on. (The reader is referred to the Royal Commission on the Taxation of Profits and Income (1955) for a discussion on these matters.) Below a brief look is given to the principle of depreciation and to depreciation and inflation.

The principle of depreciation

On the question of whether or not depreciation should be deductible from profits before tax, no clear principle seems to emerge. The Majority Report of the Royal Commission fell back on the argument (1955, para. 328):

> Whatever be the right rationalisation, it is clear to us that they [capital allowances] have come to stay and they must be taken as an integral part of our system of taxing business profits. We are content to accept them on this basis.

The Minority Report of the Royal Commission was more positive. It granted that an anomalous position was created because allowances are not given in respect of the wastage of human capital, but thought it would be impractical to try and introduce human capital into the system of depreciation allowances. The Minority Report put more weight on the anomaly that 'allowance is given for capital wastage, whilst no charge is imposed on capital gains'.

As the Minority rather than the Majority Report was followed in respect of capital gains, and we now have such a tax, this particular anomaly is taken care of. It seems that the general consensus of opinion now is that depreciation provisions should be allowed, the distortions that would be caused by their omission being greater than that due to the omission of human capital from the provisions.

Depreciation and inflation

The present system of depreciation allowances is based on the historic cost (i.e. the original money cost) of the asset. In times of rising prices the replacement cost of an asset may well be higher, and sometimes considerably higher, than the historic cost. Companies and their accountants frequently urge that allowance should be made for the change in the price level by basing depreciation either on replacement cost, or some alternative measure. It should be noted in this connection that while replacement costs may increase, so also may the receipts from current output of the capital asset, so that a firm is in a position to protect itself from inflation if it can raise prices.

The argument that depreciation should make some allowance for inflation, on which so much has been written, was rejected by successive governments until a limited breach was made in 1973–4. The grounds for rejection may be summarised as being that such protection for inflation represents a case of special pleading: the case was put by the 1955 Royal Commission, quoting with approval the findings of the 1951 Tucker Committee on the Taxation of Trading Profits: 'one objection common to all schemes, namely that they involve giving preferential treatment to all owners of businesses as against other classes of taxpayers' (para. 330).

The 1955 Royal Commission summed up its position as follows (para. 368):

(1) We do not accept that as a matter of principle a trader's profits in times of inflation must be computed with allowance for the cost of replacement of fixed assets or the fall in the purchasing power of money.
(2) We think that for the purposes of taxation a system of computing his profits that does not make allowance for these factors is preferable to one that does.

The grounds for the rejection of depreciation which allows for inflation is thus clear: inflationary and deflationary conditions affect all sectors of the community in different degrees, and there is no case on equity grounds for trying to compensate one sector. As will be seen later in the section on investment incentives, these have the effect of making investment cheaper and so can be considered as making some allowance for inflation. It seems better in principle to regard these allowances not as attempts to allow for changes in the value of money but as devices whereby the Government can attempt to influence investment. They violate equity between different classes of taxpayers but are accepted on grounds of investment criteria.

Stocks and inflation

The principle of not allowing for inflation received its first limited breach in 1973–4 with a system which allowed tax deferment on increases in the value of stocks.

The old system was one where to ascertain profit we take:

Sales *less* purchases
minus value of opening stocks } at cost of acquisition
plus value of closing stocks }

If the physical volume of stocks remains the same, inflation nevertheless causes the money value of closing stocks to be higher and therefore profits and tax to be higher. This caused many firms a liquidity problem. To assist it was decided that for tax purposes companies should have the right to reduce the closing value of their stocks and work in progress for the accounting period which ended in the financial year 1973–4 by an amount which the increase in the book value of stocks and work in progress exceeds 10 per cent of the trading profits of the business in the same accounting year (i.e. tax on stocks and work in progress is limited to 10 per cent of trading profit). The sums involved are not insignificant. Sandilands estimated that in 1974 nearly half the declared profits of companies were due to stock appreciation (Sandilands, 1975, p. 5).

The Sandilands Committee objected to this form of stock relief other than as a temporary measure, since it pays no regard to changes in the volume of stocks. Relief is based on the difference between closing and opening stock valuations: a company which allows stocks to run up to inefficient levels before the end of the accounting period might nevertheless get substantial tax relief.

This system is one of tax deferment since a fall in stocks could result in a claw-back of the tax. To end companies' uncertainty of their tax liabilities the Budget in 1978 announced that a six-year limit would be put on this liability and that relief outstanding for the tax years 1973–4 and 1974–5 would be written off by the Inland Revenue. Under the six-year rule, relief given in the year 1975–6 which is still outstanding can be written off in 1981–2. This measure was seen as temporary until more permanent inflation provisions could be agreed.

Inflation accounting[4]

So far we have dealt with questions of fact. We now turn to what might be. The Sandilands Report on inflation accounting led to the Accounting Standards Committee issuing a draft standard of current-cost accounting in November 1976. This was known as Exposure Draft 18 and is sometimes referred to as the Morpeth Proposals after its Chairman. Comments on the document were requested within six months and the Committee hoped to publish as a result of this a Statement of Standard Accounting Practice in January 1978. However, in July 1977 a meeting of English chartered accountants rejected by ballot Exposure Draft 18 and talks continue. The Hyde Committee (December 1977) issued interim recommendations intended as guideance in the preparation of profit and loss accounts of companies. The document covered three areas. One was that an adjustment should be made for the difference between depreciation at current and historic cost. A similar adjustment was also recommended in respect of stocks. Finally it recommended what was termed a 'gearing' adjustment to cover the effects of inflation on monetary items. These adjustments would be shown as a separate statement to the accounts.

The Sandilands Committee and subsequent discussion cover a very wide field. Accounts of companies serve many purposes: the needs of management, shareholders, employees and the Government to name a few. Their proposals have tax implications but they were not primarily concerned with tax issues. The following presents a brief outline of the main factors that are germane to our previous discussion.

The Sandilands Committee distinguishes three types of gain or loss:

1 *A holding gain or loss* is the difference between the 'value to a company' of an asset at any point in time and the original cost of purchase. Such gains may be realised or unrealised.
2 *Operating gains* (profits), which are the excess of sale proceeds over replacement cost at the time of sale.
3 *Extraordinary gains*, the difference between the amounts realised for items which do not form part of a company's normal output and their 'value to the company' at the time of disposal.

The Committee says that, during inflation, holding gains may be high and an important part of company affairs but they are different in character and should be shown separately in the accounts.

The basis of the Committee's recommendations is a system of *current-cost accounting*, the principal features being:

1 The accounts will continue as at present to be drawn up in terms of monetary units (pounds) – cf. indexing.
2 The accounts should show the 'value to the business' of the company's assets at the balance-sheet date.
3 Profit for the year should consist of the company's operating gains, and should exclude all holding gains. Extraordinary gains may be shown as profit but should be distinguished from operating gains.
4 Accounts drawn up in this way should become the basic published accounts of companies. In addition, the net book value of assets and

depreciation for the year on a historic-cost basis should be shown in notes to the accounts.

Depreciation should be a proportion of the figure of the 'value to the business' of assets shown in the balance-sheet, rather than a proportion of their historic cost.

Stock appreciation should be taken to revaluation reserve by making a cost-of-sales adjustment in the profit and loss account if it is required to maintain the 'substance of the business'. The government statistical service should make available a series of price indices for stocks purchased by specific industries.

The provision that separate price indices should be used for specific industries is a particularly dangerous one if such adjustment is brought into a company's tax position. It amounts to insulating a company from *relative* price changes rather than insulating them from movements in *average* prices. Movements in relative prices occur independently of the level of inflation or deflation and it is economically desirable that firms should take account of relative price movements. Thus when the price of an input is increased (say oil) the increase in price can be expected to lead to desirable adjustments that will economise in oil use. To partially isolate a firm via a tax adjustment for this change would be highly damaging to the economy.

Almost every aspect of the Sandilands, Morpeth and Hyde proposals has come in for critical debate by the accounting profession and other interested parties and, at the time of writing, it is by no means certain what proposals will be put into effect and what time scale will be adopted. (For a concise critique see Scott (1976).) It is clear from what has already been outlined that the proposals extend far beyond the tax field, although they have important implications for the tax position. We finish with details of the proposed interim tax measures.

THE TAX POSITION

The Sandilands Committee believes that a fundamental change to current-cost accounting should not be introduced without a fundamental review of taxation (pp. 198–211). This should extend beyond the corporate sector. Pending such a review the Committee recommends:

1 Tax relief on stock appreciation should continue as a deferral of, not an exemption from, tax.
2 100 per cent first-year allowances should continue to be given on qualifying capital expenditure.
3 Commercial building should in future qualify for capital allowances.

4 Roll-over relief on capital gains should be continued and consideration should be given to extending the relief to other classes of assets and to investment companies. Roll-over relief means that tax is deferred if the proceeds are reinvested in the same type of assets, and applies to land, building and fixed plant, ships, aircraft, goodwill and hovercraft.
5 Recognition of the effects of changing prices in assessing liability to capital gains should be considered.
6 No change should be made in the treatment of interest for tax purposes.
7 Further study should be given to the practical effects of the advance corporation tax.
8 Provision should be made for deferred tax on any gain arising on asset revaluation.

Investment incentives

During the post-war period the Government has had an overriding aim of increasing capital investment in industry. This has been interspersed with the aim of encouraging particular types of investment and especially investment in particular areas to improve their employment prospects. Not perhaps surprisingly we will see a number of inconsistencies in the various policies.

INITIAL ALLOWANCES

Initial allowances were introduced with effect from April 1946 as part of a new scheme of taxation designed to encourage the re-equipment and modernisation of productive industry. The scheme was one of accelerated depreciation. In addition to the allowance for depreciation that could be offset against profit before tax, a further allowance was granted in the year of purchase. However, over the remaining period allowed for depreciation, lower depreciation was given, so that over the whole period the same benefit was received. These allowances can be looked upon as a device to defer tax liability, or the same thing as a tax-free loan from the Government.

The rates at the beginning were 20 per cent for plant and machinery, 10 per cent for industrial buildings and 10 per cent for mining works. In 1949 the rate for plant and machinery was raised to 40 per cent. They were suspended from April 1952 because it was thought that the heavy calls which the defence programme would make on the engineering industry made it desirable to reduce the pressure of civilian demand for plant and machinery. In 1953 they were restored for the purpose of increasing investment in the assets selected: 20 per cent was given for plant and machinery, 10 per cent for industrial buildings and 40 per cent for mining works. In 1954 they were largely changed to investment allowances.

As an inducement to invest, the initial allowance made only a small impact. Dow (1964, p. 205) has estimated that it was equivalent to 'something like a reduction in the rate of interest by ½%'. Its importance lay in providing an internal source of finance for the firm undertaking investment, providing the firm was paying taxes.

INVESTMENT ALLOWANCES

In 1954 investment allowances were given on a range of assets, but initial allowances were not discontinued for those assets that formerly received them and were not given the new allowance. The allowances were given in the year of purchase in a similar manner to the initial allowances, but unlike them they were not recouped in later years. Industrial and agricultural buildings and works were given a 10 per cent investment allowance, machinery and plant, mining works and scientific research assets 20 per cent.

The system of initial and investment allowances continued with several switches and changes until 1966, when they were largely superseded by a system of grants.

ASSESSMENT OF INITIAL AND INVESTMENT ALLOWANCES

The Royal Commission on Taxation in 1955 expressed strongly the opinion that these allowances violate the principle that persons with equal incomes should bear an equal burden of tax. The Commission continues (1955, para. 421):

> For these reasons we think that instruments of this kind will require to be justified in due course by convincing evidence that they are not only effective in achieving the results anticipated but also worth-while in the value of the results contrasted with the revenue foregone.

The evidence as given in a White Paper on *Investment Incentives* (1966), is that these measures have largely failed in their objectives:

> The National Plan makes it plain that the overriding need during the next few years is to give priority to those sectors of industry which can make the greatest contribution to strengthening the balance of payments. The benefits of the present system are too widely dispersed to be fully effective. Investment allowances are given for some items which have little or no relation to productive investment. For example, purchases of furniture, curtains and carpets in offices or cutlery in dining rooms or canteens

qualify for investment allowances. Television sets rented by the public do so too, since the purchase of the set by the rental firm qualifies.

The White Paper goes on to list other defects: the fact that the allowances take on average eighteen months to be felt, that they are spread over a long period and uncertain because of the uncertainty about future tax rates, and that firms with small profits get little benefit.

A more fundamental criticism is mentioned as a result of a survey (Investment Incentives Survey, 1965) carried out by the Confederation of British Industry (CBI). It appears that a substantial number of firms still do not take tax allowances fully into account in investment decisions. In many cases firms seem to have no rational policy of making investment decisions but proceed 'by God and by guess'.

The remedy carried out to meet these criticisms was not to stop the incentives, or to confine them to firms which could present a reasoned case for the allowances, but to convert them into cash grants. No mention was made in the White Paper of the equity aspects that had troubled the Royal Commission; the whole emphasis was on the need to provide an effective investment incentive.

INVESTMENT GRANTS

From 17 January 1966 the system of investment allowances was swept away and replaced by a system of grants. Initial allowances continued on some assets.

The system of grants applies in respect of expenditure on new plant and machinery used in manufacturing or extractive industries but excluding furniture and similar items mentioned above which were criticised as making no contribution to productive investment. 'Manufacturing' covers all the processes of making articles, including the intermediate stages of processing materials. 'Extraction' covers quarrying, mining, etc. of natural deposits. Excluded from the grants are service and construction industries. Special arrangements were made in respect of ships, hovercraft and computers. In addition, the new legislation swept aside the old development district (areas of the country that were deemed to need special measures) and introduced 'development areas'.

The development areas covered much wider tracts of the country. In these areas investment grants were given on a more generous scale. The most usual grant was 20–25 per cent in a non-development area and 40–45 per cent in a development area.

The country is now divided into special development areas, development areas, intermediate areas, Northern Ireland and the rest of the country. Northern Ireland receives the range of incentives applicable to special development areas, with higher rates in some cases or extra assistance being available in certain other cases, and will not be detailed separately. (See Table 15.2.) These grants were still in force in 1978.

Table 15.2

Incentives for industry, 1975

	Special development areas	Development areas	Intermediate areas
Grants			
New machinery, plant and mining works	22%	20%	Nil
Buildings and works	22%	20%	20%

In any part of the country 100 per cent first-year allowances are given on plant and machinery (other than cars) and industrial buildings may have 54 per cent of construction costs written off in the first year, with a write off of 4 per cent per year subsequently.

Grants are not treated as reducing the capital expenditure in computing tax allowances. A wide variety of other types of assistance is also provided, for example loans on favourable terms or at reduced interest rates, removal grants and periods of rent-free factory occupation. The grants are paid both to firms entering the area and for expansion of existing firms.

EVALUATION OF INVESTMENT INCENTIVES

The post-1945 period has seen a variety of fiscal measures used to try and influence investment. The instruments used have been frequently changed, and the rates of grant or allowance applied to each instrument have been changed even more frequently. Policies have tried to encourage investment generally and to encourage investment in particular areas.

A basic inconsistency of the measures, except the abandoned regional employment premium, has been that the incentives designed to stimulate employment in development areas have been capital incentives. Thus large capital-intensive projects like oil refineries, which on completion employ few workers, have been encouraged to set up in areas with high unemployment.

Also, in London the Government pays its own employees a 'London allowance', which is commonly adopted by private firms, while at the same time encouraging firms to move out of London.

A House of Commons Expenditure Committee gave a devastating critique of regional policy as follows (Second Report from the Expenditure Committee Session 1973–4, *Regional Development Incentives. Report and Minutes of Evidence*, paras 170, 172):

> Much has been spent and much may well have been wasted. Regional policy has been empiricism run mad, a game of hit-and-miss, played with more enthusiasm than success. We do not doubt the good intentions, the devotion even, of many of those who have struggled over the years to relieve the human consequences of regional disparities. We regret that their efforts have not been better sustained by the proper evaluation of the costs and benefits of policies pursued. . . . Everything in this enquiry pointed to the need for Government to create a more rational and systematic basis for the formulation and execution of regional policy.

The Report just quoted draws attention to ten particular areas of uncertainty (para. 172):

1 The effectiveness of regional policy over the last ten to fifteen years, in terms of increased employment and investment in assisted areas compared with what would have occurred otherwise.
2 The resource costs of regional financial incentives, allowing for changes in revenue and expenditure estimated to result from changes in employment.
3 The amount and nature of secondary employment (the 'multiplier' effect) created by regional development policy in assisted areas, both in industries serving the incoming firms and in service industries benefiting from increased purchasing power.
4 The effects on employment, wages, prices and profits of regional employment premiums and of alternative aids towards labour costs.
5 The incentive effect of expenditure incurred on different kinds of infrastructure, compared with more direct financial incentives.
6 The cost effectiveness of alternative transport systems as a regional incentive.
7 The economic and social costs of 'over-heating' and congestion in labour, housing, transport and other fields.
8 The likely cost effectiveness of giving a measure of financial assistance through a regional public purchasing scheme, compared with equivalent expenditure on direct incentives.

9 The measurable costs to industrial firms of locating a project in an assisted area through refusal of an Industrial Development Certificate (IDC).
10 The resource costs to the country of IDC policy.

What has happened in response to this rather devastating critique? The Government's reply in a White Paper, *Regional Development Incentives* (1975), contains a number of platitudes and some attempts at reply.

The Government stated its intention to maintain and develop the existing system of incentives to maintain continuity. It continued and strengthened the system of regional employment premiums (but these have since been abandoned) and IDC control was strengthened.

A White Paper, on the *Regeneration of British Industry* (1974), proposed the setting up of a National Enterprise Board and planning agreements to assist regional development. In addition, Scottish and Welsh development agencies have been set up and selective assistance is to be extended. More information was promised.

Taken together with the depreciation allowances, there is no doubt that in manufacturing and extractive industries firms have been placed on a favourable footing, *vis-à-vis* other firms and individuals. In time the benefits are likely to be fairly widely spread over the community in the form of better goods, or goods cheaper than they would have been in the absence of grants, and in a better export performance or higher employment. In the short run it should not be forgotten that these grants create an opportunity for the owners of these businesses to take most of the gain to themselves (by not passing on the benefits to the consumer). Time alone will show which path has been taken.

There are strong arguments for modernising sectors of British industry, and the arguments as to whether the present mixture of incentives is right is likely to continue. One possibility is that discretionary powers could be given and exercised to ensure a more rigorous selection among firms. The granting of allowances to all firms will undoubtedly help the progressive firm to keep in the forefront of developments, but it will also have the effect of propping up the inefficient firm for a period of time. If minimum requirements were drawn up for each industry, on criteria to be taken into account when making investment decisions, the receipt of an investment grant could be made conditional on these requirements being met. The working out of these criteria would be likely to stimulate fruitful discussion in the industries concerned, as well as spreading existing knowledge, a process that can do little but good.

Summary

The taxation of companies raises many contentious problems and conflicts between the aims of equity and of giving incentives to investment. Brief details of company taxation changes since 1945 were given, together with details of the current system of corporation tax.

If, on the grounds that it will act as a disincentive to invest, the owners of companies are not to have the whole of business profits attributable to them, the taxation of capital gains at income-tax rates, with allowance for averaging the gains, would go a long way to achieving equity between shareholders and other taxpayers without seriously weakening investment in businesses.

On the general question of tax discrimination against distributed profits, it was concluded that there is no clear evidence that this is likely to have marked effects on over-all investment. While such discrimination is likely to help the company relying on ploughing back profits for investment capital, it hinders rather than helps the company which relies on raising new equity capital.

The impact of taxes on companies trading overseas was examined.

The evidence of previous Royal Commissions on Taxation is unanimous that the granting of depreciation allowances puts companies in a privileged tax position *vis-à-vis* the individual taxpayer. The system of initial allowances and of investment grants further substantially favours companies, as do the recent provisions for stock relief. The Sandilands Committee's recommendations on inflation accounting discussed such far-reaching changes that they considered a Royal Commission should be set up before they were implemented. These tax privileges are generally accepted as desirable in order to achieve investment and growth in the economy, and it is likely that at least some of the benefits will in time be spread more evenly through the economy in the form of prices lower than they would be in the absence of these privileges.

The system of investment allowances and grants has been criticised on a number of grounds. One is the frequency of the changes and the absence of any evaluation of the effect of the allowances. A further inconsistency is the use of capital incentives, rather than employment incentives, in development regions.

Notes

1 It is sometimes suggested that discrimination against distributed profits

is in effect discrimination against consumption by shareholders. In view of the facilities for consumption, given by capital appreciation in the post-1945 period, this argument is not very sound.

2 This argument is important on 'welfare' grounds. If it is a good thing that capital should be mobile and the rate of return should tend to equality in different use, it would seem desirable to distribute profits and let the recipients reinvest (or consume) them as they think fit. equality in different uses, it would seem desirable to distribute profits and let the recipients reinvest (or consume) them as they think fit.

3 First year allowances can in fact be offset against the profits of the three previous years, and they may be carried forward against future profits for an indefinite period.

4 I am indebted to Mr H. Mellett of the Accountancy Department of University College, Cardiff, for comment on this section.

16
Value-added tax

Reactions to new taxes conform to a clear pattern: shock, opposition, understanding, acceptance.
From *The Times* editorial, 7 May 1966.

From 1940 up to 1973 the major indirect tax in the United Kingdom, apart from Customs and Excise duties, was purchase tax. This was a tax levied at various rates on certain goods, whether home-produced or imported. No services were charged in this way. The tax was comparatively simple to collect as it was imposed at the relatively small wholesale stage: the good being passed on to the retailer or final buyer with the value of tax added on. The tax attempted to achieve some degree of equity by exempting items such as food and subjecting 'luxury' goods to the highest rate. Purchase tax attracted a good deal of criticism, partly because of the bias in exempting services from the levy and the narrow range of goods included, but chiefly because the Government used the tax as one of their main means of trying to regulate the economy. The frequent changes in rates, and the resulting changes in the pattern of demand, made planning in those industries affected by the changes very difficult.

Whatever the merits or otherwise of switching from purchase tax to a value-added tax (VAT), and we shall look at some of the arguments later in this chapter, the decision to change was more or less forced by the decision to join the European Economic Community (EEC). The EEC had already decided to adopt a single type of turnover tax based on the French TVA (*taxe sur la valeur ajoutée*) system. At present the tax in the various countries of the Community differs both in respect of the tax base and the tax rates. The intention is to finance part of the EEC budget, from 1 January 1978, from the equivalent of up to 1 per cent of VAT levies in the member countries. In December 1976 agreement in principle was reached by the EEC Ministers on providing a roughly uniform base over a five-year period ending in 1983. Harmonisation of rates is the ultimate intention but no time-table for this has yet been agreed. In the case of items on which Britain zero rates, her VAT contribution will be assessed as if these items were rated; it does not mean that items such as food and children's clothing will have to be taxed.

The current operation of VAT

The tax at the appropriate rate, in 1978 at 8 per cent and 12½ per cent, is levied at each stage of production, but is levied only on the value added at that particular stage. This is achieved administratively by allowing each stage to deduct the tax paid by previous stages as shown on the invoices of their suppliers. Since the sum of values added at successive stages is equal to the final price of the product, the amount of tax paid will be the same as if the tax was charged once on this final value. The tax has an element of self-policing in it since it is to the advantage of each business in the chain to ensure that the correct amount of VAT is shown on the invoices of its suppliers in order that the business may in turn receive credit for this amount.

Firms must normally send in returns to the Customs and Excise every three months showing the amount of goods and services supplied and purchased. VAT is payable one month after the end of the return period.

In August 1977 the Government announced that the Commissioners of Customs and Excise were inviting interested trade and professional bodies and others concerned with the administration of VAT to put forward suggestions for improving any aspect of the VAT system. In particular they wanted to hear 'any views concerning a proposal for a scheme of annual accounting for VAT'.

An example of a value-added tax

Suppose we assume a manufacturer of a product requires materials, fuel and containers (but nothing else) to be brought in from outside suppliers, and VAT is applicable at a rate of 8 per cent on the tax-exclusive price. The transactions take place during the three-month period covered by a VAT return (see Table 16.1).

Here the manufacturer purchases materials, fuel and containers which cost him £189, of which £14 is tax. He adds £100 to the value (his wages,

Table 16.1

	Tax-exclusive price (£)	Tax (£)	Tax-inclusive price (£)
Purchases			
Materials	100	8	108
Fuel	50	4	54
Containers	25	2	27
	175	14	189
Value added by the manufacturer by way of salaries, wages, profit, etc.	100	8	108
Final price	275	22	297

profit, etc.) and pays a further £8 in tax, so that the final price invoiced is £297.

The manufacturer will show on his tax return:

Total outputs	£297	
VAT chargeable		£22
Total inputs	£175	
VAT paid		£14
Balance of tax due		£ 8

This example makes clear that, subject to reservations in a later section, the business does not itself bear the tax. The manufacturer pays the previous suppliers for the tax they have incurred, and pays Customs and Excise for the value added by his concern, but both elements of tax are invoiced either on to the next stage in the distributive chain, or on to the final consumer (as the case may be).

It is also clear that one advantage of this type of tax is that the tax is the same regardless of how many stages a good or service passes through. Each distinct stage, say from sub-component firm, to manufacturer, to wholesaler, to retailer, pays on the value added and receives a credit for accumulated tax that has been paid. The amount of tax is invariant whether the same value has been added by one vertically integrated organisation or by a dozen different concerns.

VAT was originally introduced at a single rate of 10 per cent but this quickly became a two-tier rate of 10 per cent and 25 per cent. The current rates are 8 per cent and 12½ per cent. The more important items bearing the higher rate are: domestic appliances, radio and television sets, pleasure boats and aircraft, towing caravans, photographic equipment, furs, jewellery and petrol.

VAT is, as already shown, basically a tax on sales *less* purchases. The figures can be arrived at directly by an inspection of the sales and purchases figures or by adding up the money spent on wages and salaries, depreciation, interest and profit. Stocks present an accounting problem but no problem of principle. With capital equipment the decision has to be made if this is to be subject to the tax or not. The practice followed, on the grounds that investment should be encouraged, is that net capital expenditure should not be taxed, so that a firm is assessed for tax on value added, calculated either: (i) upon the difference between the total of its sales and the total of its purchases, including purchases of capital equipment; or (ii) upon the sum of its wages and salaries, depreciation, trading profits and interest payments *minus* its purchases of capital equipment. In both cases goods which are exported receive a rebate of tax, and imports are subject to the tax, so that the tax is one based on final expenditure.[1]

Zero-rating and exemption

So far it has been assumed that all inputs and outputs of a firm are taxable. In practice, these may be zero-rated or exempt.

It may seem perverse to say that certain output is taxed at a zero rate, but this turns out to be the most favourable position under VAT. It means that outputs that are zero-rated bear no tax but that the supplier may claim for any tax paid on his inputs. The following are some of the more important items that are zero-rated: most items of food for human consumption except alcoholic drinks, ice-cream, chocolate, soft drinks and potato crisps; water, fuel, power and passenger transport except petrol, derv, taxi journeys and the cost of hired cars; drugs, medicines and medical and surgical applicances on a doctor's prescription; books, newspapers, magazines, music, maps – however, diaries and stationery are taxed; construction, alteration and demolition of buildings, but not repairs; clothing and footwear for young children, industrial protective clothing and motor cyclists' crash-helmets.

Exemption means that, as with zero-rating, no tax is imposed on the output, but in this case no credit is allowed for the tax on inputs. This is therefore an intermediary position between the other two. On the assumption that VAT is passed on fully to the consumer, the product will be raised in price only by the VAT imposed on non-exempt stages.

The following are the main goods that are exempt: sales, leases and hiring out of land and buildings – but hotels, holiday accommodation, camping, parking, timber, mooring and sporting rights are taxed; insurance; postal services except telegrams, telephones and telex; betting, gaming and lotteries; banking, buying and selling of stocks and shares; education and health services; and burial and cremation. Firms with an annual turnover of less than £10,000 may also claim exemption from VAT registration.

Is the value-added tax a tax on costs or a tax on the consumer?

It is worth looking briefly at the incidence of a profits tax. It is frequently asserted that, at least in the short run, a tax on profits does not affect prices. The theoretical case is that if a firm is already charging prices that are maximising profits, an increase in profits tax will not alter the optimum price and output decisions of the firm. There may be exceptions to this rule if a firm is in a monopolistic or oligopolistic position. If an industry's pricing structure is maintained by a firm, or small number of firms, acting as a price leader, or if the firms in an industry act together on pricing, and if they look to a level of return on capital *calculated after taxation is taken into account*, then a change in profits tax could be reflected fairly quickly in a change in prices. The consumer is in this case bearing all or part of the tax. In the long run it is generally accepted that a profits tax is more likely to be passed on to the consumer through adjustments in output and the size of the industry (for a selection of articles on incidence, see Musgrave and Shoup, 1959).

The case of VAT seems rather more straightforward: the procedure of invoicing that has been outlined leads to the expectation that the amount of tax will be carried through each stage of processing to the retail level.

On these assumptions VAT is primarily a tax on consumption, although it can be conceded that some firms faced with inelastic demand for their products may be forced to bear part of the cost themselves, at least in the short run.

VAT is the more likely to be passed on to the consumer since any firm in a particular industry will know that if the rate of VAT is increased, costs will increase for all firms, and this is likely to result in a general increased price level which will leave its relative share of output unchanged.

Is the value-added tax an incentive to exports?

The significance of the change to VAT for exports is that (like the more narrowly based purchase tax) it can be imposed on imports and rebated on exports. This can lead to difficulties if one country uses some of its VAT receipts to cover part of the cost of social services and the other country does not. The exports of the second country will have to bear the VAT of the first country to which it is exporting, part of which we have assumed is used for social service payments. On the other hand, imports to the country do not bear this social service tax. The question is complicated, since many countries do not earmark taxes for particular purposes, and is one that is likely to lead to international retaliation if international agreement cannot be reached. A US Congressional Foreign Trade Committee has voiced criticism on these lines and has called for an international review of all non-tariff barriers. And the US Administration has said it may impose retaliatory 'border taxes' to offset the effect of the European Economic Community's use of VAT.

Is the value-added tax an incentive to efficiency?

If VAT is, by and large, a tax on consumers, can it at the same time be claimed that it is a spur to business efficiency? The grounds for arguing that this can be the case run on the following lines. A firm will find that its tax bill will be higher than its competitors' if its costs are higher than theirs. Attempts to pass on this tax in excess of the amount the most efficient firm in the industry passes on will therefore result in loss of sales, and act as a direct incentive to the firm to reduce its costs by increasing its efficiency. This argument will now be examined.

THE TAX POSITION IN THE COMPETITIVE CASE

Let us take two firms producing for a competitive market, so that the pricing policy of the firms is the same (see Table 16.2). Firm *A* is assumed to be the more efficient, its labour costs are lower and trading profits higher than firm *B*, while other costs are assumed to be the same.

In this situation, despite the fact that firm *B* has a lower profit, each firm would pay the same amount of VAT. The amount of VAT can be

Table 16.2

	Firm *A* (£)	Firm *B* (£)
Wages and salaries	400,000	500,000
Depreciation	200,000	200,000
Materials	100,000	100,000
Interest	100,000	100,000
Trading profit	200,000	100,000
Total sales	1,000,000	1,000,000

calculated either as sales *less* purchases of materials (£1,000,000 *less* £100,000), or as the sum of its wages and salaries, depreciation, interest and trading profit. In both cases, for both firms, this leaves £900,000 as the sum subject to VAT. It is not correct to say therefore that because firm *A* has lower costs than firm *B* that it will pay less tax. This is so because the tax base includes not only costs but also trading profit, since profit forms part of the value added by the firm.

The 'incentive' to investment comes about because firm *B* will have the same amount of VAT to pay as firm *A*. In the competitive situation outlined, firm *B* cannot increase its prices to improve its profits; it needs to reduce costs to improve its position.

THE IMPERFECTLY COMPETITIVE SITUATION

If the case is now taken where the firms are working in a market which is less than perfect, the situation changes a little. If firm *B* is able to maintain its profits by charging a higher price, the situation shown in Table 16.3 emerges.

Firm *B*'s sales are higher, because its final prices are higher. Firm *B* will pay tax on £1,000,000, as opposed to firm *A* paying tax on £900,000. If firm *B* passes the tax on to the consumer, its prices and tax bill will diverge even further from firm *A*. The inducement to firm *B* to reduce its costs thus depends on two things: first, the amount of tax paid itself compared with the most efficient firm in the industry; and second on the degree of monopoly power it can exercise. While the tax, in these circumstances, is an inducement to reduce prices and improve efficiency, it seems easy to overstate the benefits that can be expected from it.

Table 16.3

	Firm *A* (£)	Firm *B* (£)
Wages and salaries	400,000	500,000
Depreciation	200,000	200,000
Materials	100,000	100,000
Interest	100,000	100,000
Trading profit	200,000	200,000
Total Sales	1,000,000	1,100,000

Value-added tax and equity

Generally speaking, it is very difficult to devise a tax which is borne by companies. The reason, as we have seen, is that companies are often in a position to alter their price and output policies and shift all or part of the tax on to the consumer.[2]

Adopting the position that VAT is a tax on consumers collected by companies, an equity problem arises. It is concerned with the regressive nature of indirect tax. Although (assuming a comprehensive tax) the actual amount of tax paid will increase with the amount of expenditure, the tax is regressive because as a rule expenditure represents a decreasing proportion of income as income levels rise, for example with a uniform rate of VAT at 10 per cent a person earning £30 a week will probably have to spend the whole of his income – in this case he will pay £3 in tax, or 10 per cent of his income. If a man earning £100 a week can save £20, he will pay tax on his purchases of £80, or 8 per cent of his income.[3] This question will be taken up in Chapter 23.

Summary

The adoption of VAT removed some of the bias in the old system of purchase tax whereby only a narrow range of goods and no services were subject to tax. One of the costs of this widening of the tax base has been a considerable increase in both the Government's administration costs and particularly in the compliance costs of business. The latter are likely to be particularly high where business is concerned with inputs and outputs subject to different rates of tax and to cases where zero-rating and exemption apply to some parts of the business and not to others.

Since VAT is rebated on exports and imposed on imports, it raises complicated and difficult problems as third countries may feel that their own goods are, in effect, being handicapped.

As VAT is administered currently it offers some incentive for a less efficient firm to try and match its competitors.

Notes

1 If in (i) purchases of capital equipment are excluded and depreciation charges are deducted from sales, and in (ii) capital equipment is excluded and profits taken net of depreciation, the tax becomes one on final expenditure and investment.

2 Part of the tax may, in effect, be shifted on to the employees if the employer is able to use the tax as a counter to resist wage claims.

3 Some of these expenditures are likely to be in ways that do not attract the tax, such as the payment of rates, but this does not alter the principle.

17
Wealth

Thus, for example, the proportion of sons leaving £100,000 and over and having fathers who had left more than £50,000 was 58% both in 1956/7 and in 1965. The fact that between a half and two-thirds of those who left £100,000 or more in the 1950s and 1960s were preceded by fathers leaving at least £25,000 illustrates the importance of having had a moderately wealthy father. If there were no connection between wealth of fathers and sons, one would expect less than 1% of the population of sons to have had fathers with this size fortune. . . . This has important policy implications for wealth taxation, in so far as it means that many wealth transfers have simply been of a kind which redistribute wealth between different generations of the same family.
C. D. HARBURY and P. C. McMAHON, 'Inheritance and the Characteristics of Top Wealth Leavers in Britain', *Economic Journal*, September 1973.

Anybody that's got money can hire somebody who's smart to make them money, it's a son of a bitch that hasn't got any money that has to be smart.
R. Hibbard, a self-made multi-millionaire quoted by J. BAINBRIDGE, *The Super-Americans.*

Apart from minor stamp duties, which may fall on wealth transfers, and legacy and successive duties that were abolished in 1949, the only tax on wealth in Great Britain until recently was estate duty.

The 1970s saw both of the main political parties putting forward proposals for wealth taxation. A number of strands contributed to this interest besides the obvious liking for a new source of revenue. At bottom was the growing awareness that estate duty had become a mockery, with high progressive rates on the one hand, and enormous loopholes on the other. Increasingly the tax was seen as arbitrary in operation and a more effective taxation of wealth was envisaged as a way of not increasing, or even reducing, the burdens on income and other taxes. These matters will be looked at in more detail in this chapter before outlining the change to capital transfer tax and some of the proposals for wealth taxation. First, we give an outline of present wealth ownership in Britain.

Distribution of wealth

PROBLEMS OF ESTIMATION

The latest information on the distribution of income and wealth for Britain is provided by the Royal Commission on the Distribution of Income and Wealth (1975), on which this section draws, and Atkinson and Harrison (1977). There are many problems in trying to present a picture of wealth ownership, not least because, as the Commission says, there is 'a serious shortage of reliable statistical information' (para. 175), and 'the dearth of reliable statistical information is a central theme of our discussion of evidence on the distribution of wealth' (para. 177).

A basic problem is concerned with the definition of wealth: which items should be included? To take a particular case, should the concept of wealth be confined to assets which can be realised by the owner, or should the concept include non-transferable rights such as pensions? Inland Revenue data, on which most of the wealth estimates are based, cover about half of the population aged 18 and over. The 'excluded' population will in general be the less rich, and different assumptions can be made about their average wealth holdings. The extreme assumption would be that they have zero wealth.

There are two other basic problems. First, should we be seeking a definition of wealth on an individual or family basis? The surprising fact about the Commission's work in this area is the low range of variation it obtains under different assumptions. The Commission produced figures adjusted for marriage on the assumptions that: (i) all married wealth holders have spouses with no wealth, to produce the lower extreme of concentration; (ii) the wealthiest married men are married to the wealthiest married women regardless of age, to produce the upper extreme of concentration; and (iii) within each age group the wealthiest married men are married to the wealthiest married women, and this produces figures close to, but slightly below, those of assumption (ii).

Comparing extreme assumption (i) above, that married wealth holders have spouses with no wealth, with wealth on an individual basis, the Commission found that this assumption about marriage reduces the share of wealth of the top 1 and the top 5 per cent of wealth holders by some 5 percentage points and of the top 10 and top 20 per cent by some 11 percentage points. The other assumptions about marriage produced figures that were very close to those found on an individual basis.

The second basic problem is that wealth figures present a picture of wealth holding at a particular moment in time. Individuals, however, are likely to have a different wealth pattern over their lifetimes. Therefore, even where individuals of the same age have the same wealth, the figures will show some degree of inequality due to different ages of the population.

Assumption (i), in Table 17.1, is the most rigorous as it assumes that individuals are identical in terms of life expectancy, lifetime earnings and tastes. Each individual is assumed to work for forty years and to have ten years in retirement, and earnings and the pattern of savings are the same with the rate of interest assumed to be zero. This absurd degree of 'equality' still produces the degree of concentration of wealth shown in the table due to differences in the ages of the population. On this basic model more realistic assumptions can be tested to see what increase in concentration takes place (see Atkinson, July 1971).

Table 17.1

Percentage of total wealth

	Assumption (i)	Assumption (ii)
Top 1%	1.99	5.5
Top 5%	9.75	16.5

Source: Royal Commission on the Distribution of Income and Wealth (July 1975), Report No. 1.

The figures shown under assumption (ii) relax the equal-earnings rule and assume earnings for each percentile group are those actually found in practice. Thus the top 1 per cent of income recipients had, in the mid-1960s, post-tax incomes 5.4 times the mean income. Using these data, the share of our top 1 per cent in this model goes up to 5.5 per cent and of the top 5 per cent to 16.5 per cent.

This type of model-building can be used in two ways. It may be used as a bench-mark by which an actual distribution of wealth can, to some extent, be evaluated. How close does the distribution of wealth come to that predicted by the model? This method could also be used to indicate to those who wish to achieve a more equal distribution of wealth the likely gain to be expected from different measures. The model illustrated above does not take inherited wealth into account – which we know is an important factor in causing differences in wealth (see Harbury and McMahon, September 1973). A model that incorporated both differential earnings and different inheritance patterns would enable some prediction to be made about the likely change in the distribution of wealth if, say, earning differentials were changed or inheritance taxed at different rates.

METHODS OF ESTIMATING WEALTH

The common method of estimating wealth is to use the estate multiplier. The estates of persons who die in a year are treated as a random sample of the wealth of the living. The chances of dying at any particular age are known, so that the estates of the deceased can be multiplied by the reciprocal of the appropriate mortality rates for each sex and age group to give an estimate of total personal wealth. There are well-known drawbacks with this method, not least where there are only a few deaths in each category, and because for more than half the deaths in a year the estates left are so small that they are not recorded in the estate figures. The recent change from estate duty to a capital transfer tax may cause a discontinuity in the figures.

A different method of estimating wealth is the investment-income approach. Here the data on investment are used to determine underlying asset values that generate the investment income (for a recent study on these lines see Atkinson and Harrison, June 1974). The chief difficulty with this method is that investment-income returns do not cover the whole of the wealth-owning population. Adjustment has also to be made for important categories of wealth, such as owner-occupied houses, which do not yield a money income to their owners. There is also no clear-cut distinction in the tax returns between earned and unearned income since, where allowable interest payments exceed the value of investment income, the residual is offset against earned income. It is also the case that the estimates of wealth calculated in this way are highly sensitive to the particular asset yields assumed. However, this method does provide information on the joint wealth of husband and wife, which in many cases is the most appropriate base for studying the distribution of wealth. It also provides a means of linking data on the distributions of income and wealth, and also of serving as a cross-check on the estate-multiplier method of estimating wealth. It is likely to be of most use in estimating the upper wealth ranges.

A third possibility is to collect information on wealth by sample surveys. Although potentially of great use, surveys suffer from the high incidence of non-response, particularly among the most wealthy. Even amongst those willing to co-operate, the value of the response may be limited as people are not usually in the habit of keeping a running account of the value of their assets and considerable guess-work may be involved. In spite of these drawbacks, surveys may be of use in providing evidence of particular categories of wealth such as the ownership of consumer durables. It can also be of use in relating wealth to other factors such as age, sex, occupation, or education.

THE DISTRIBUTION OF WEALTH

It will be clear from what has been said that no single statistic can adequately summarise the many dimensions of the distribution of wealth even if the data sources are adequate. In Table 17.2 we give two views.

Table 17.2

*Estimates of the distribution of personal wealth in Great Britain, 1972**

Quantile group	Probable range (%)	Estimate when occupational and state pension rights included (%)
Top 1 per cent	27–29	17.4
Top 5 per cent	51–55	34.9
Top 10 per cent	64–69	45.7
Top 20 per cent	79–84	59.3
Bottom 80 per cent	16–21	40.7

*Percentage share of total personal wealth owned by given quantile groups of the population aged 18 and over; Inland Revenue estimate, assuming that the 'excluded' population have no wealth, and when pension rights are included.

Source: Royal Commission on the Distribution of Income and Wealth (July 1975), Report No. 1.

The column headed 'Probable range' gives the figures that come closest to the idea of 'disposable' wealth. The persons not covered in the Inland Revenue data have been assumed here to have no wealth. The figures give a range of values rather than a best single estimate. The final column gives information on a wider definition of wealth where occupational and state pension rights are included. The estimates of state pension rights are subject to a very large margin of error. Since nearly all persons have rights to a state pension the share attributed to the bottom 80 per cent of the population almost doubles to 40.7 per cent, while the share of the top 1 per cent falls to an estimated 17.4 per cent.

Table 17.3 gives the trend in the distribution of wealth since 1960. The definition of wealth and treatment of excluded persons is the same as in the column headed 'Probable range' in Table 17.2. The figures differ from those in Table 17.2 because that table adjusted the Inland Revenue estimates on the basis of personal-sector, balance-sheet asset totals. These corrections have not been applied to the time-series data.

Table 17.3

*Trends in the distribution of personal wealth in Great Britain (selected years)**

Quantile group	1960 (%)	1963 (%)	1966 (%)	1969 (%)	1970 (%)	1971 (%)	1972 (%)	1973 (%)
Top 1 per cent	38.2	35.7	31.8	29.0	29.0	27.6	29.9	27.6
Top 5 per cent	64.3	62.2	56.7	54.0	56.3	52.1	56.3	51.3
Top 10 per cent	76.7	75.4	71.8	69.4	70.1	67.4	71.9	67.2
Top 20 per cent	89.8	89.2	87.8	86.8	89.0	85.7	89.2	86.4
Bottom 80 per cent	10.2	10.8	12.2	13.2	11.0	14.3	10.8	13.6

*Percentage share of estimated personal wealth owned by given quantile groups of the population aged 18 and over; Inland Revenue estimate, assuming that the 'excluded' population have no wealth.

Source: Royal Commission on the Distribution of Income and Wealth (July 1975), Report No. 1.

These estimates of the distribution of wealth by the Inland Revenue are produced as far as possible on a consistent basis. It would be foolish to attach too much importance to the percentage of wealth ascribed to each quantile group because other definitions of wealth can be used and the figures can be corrected in various ways. It is plausible, however, that over time the trend will give a fair indication of the movements in the way wealth in general is redistributed. Short-term changes in capital values, particularly in stock market prices, mean that too much should not be read into year-to-year changes: established trends are more likely to appear if, say, we compare the distribution in 1973 with the distribution in 1963. Using Table 17.3 in this way there seems to have been a marked movement of wealth away from the wealthiest, with most of the change taking place in the 1960s. Until new data are available this interpretation of these trends must remain largely conjectural. In particular data for wealth holding by families would help in determining how much of this redistribution from the wealthiest has been a shifting of assets to other family members as opposed to redistribution outside the family.

Wealth taxation

LEGACY AND SUCCESSIVE DUTIES

Legacy and successive duties were minor duties, complementary to estate duties. The rate at which duties were charged was determined solely by the relationship of the beneficiary to the donor. They varied according to whether: (i) the beneficiary was the husband, wife or lineal issue or ancestor of the donor;(ii) the beneficiary was a brother or sister, or a descendant of a brother or sister; (iii) all other cases. The lowest duty was payable in case (i), the highest in case (iii).

The duties were based on the idea that a person who comes into an inheritance may justly be asked for a special contribution to the needs of the State, and that, if the inheritance has in it something of the nature of a windfall, the contribution should on that account be at a higher rate. These duties were abolished in 1949 when estate duty was increased.

OUTLINE OF ESTATE DUTIES

Estate or death duties were introduced in 1894. Before 1969 the system was to subject an estate to duty at a rate which progressed (in 1969) in twenty-four steps from 1 per cent on an estate between £5,000–6,000 to 80 per cent on an estate exceeding £1,000,000. Marginal relief was given to an estate which just came into a higher-duty category. In 1969 the size of estate on which duty was payable was raised to £10,000 and a *tranche*, or slice, system of duty was adopted. Under this system each slice of estate was subject to its own rate of duty. Thus the first £10,000 was tax free, the next £7,000 paid at a rate of 25 per cent, the next £13,000 at 30 per cent, and so on up to a rate of 85 per cent on an estate over £750,000, with, however, a ceiling provision of 80 per cent over all. This was not primarily a revenue change but a change to avoid the difficulty of working out marginal relief. It resulted in some estates paying a little more duty than under the old system and some a little less, but the difference was not very great in either case.

These rates, if they had been effective, might be considered unduly harsh. As Chapter 10 pointed out, the yield from this source is comparatively small, accounting for 1 per cent of government revenue since 1974. The system of high but ineffective rates has been described by Simons (1938, p. 11), when commenting on surtaxes, as:

a subtle kind of moral and intellectual dishonesty . . . a grand scheme of deception, whereby enormous surtaxes are voted in exchange for promises that they will not be made effective. Thus, the politicians may point with pride to the rates, while quietly reminding their wealthy constituents of the loopholes.

That the rates were nominal, rather than effective, was due to two main causes: one the extensive concessions that the legislature granted over time; and two the ease of avoidance.

The simplest way to avoid or lessen estate duty was to give one's wealth, or part of it, away. There was in Britain no gifts tax as such, although gifts within seven years of death were aggregated and taxed with the deceased person's estate. However, even in this case reduced rates were payable if the donor lived for five years.

The device of the trust, particularly the discretionary trust, had become an increasingly important means of avoidance. A discretionary trust enabled the trustee to distribute income or capital to a specified list of beneficiaries. When a beneficiary dies, no property is deemed to pass, so long as at least two beneficiaries are left. An estate could in favourable circumstances be isolated from the Inland Revenue for up to 100 years, and duty could be minimised at the close of the trust by suitable distributions.

A significant and curious provision was the relief granted to agricultural land and appropriate property thereon. Relief was first granted in 1925 and subsequently took the form of abatement of the duty of 45 per cent, a particularly inept way of assisting farming since this concession took no account of when the land was acquired, so that a death-bed purchase qualified for relief. In 1954 a reduction of duty of 45 per cent was given to industrial premises, plant and machinery used by the deceased or by a company under his control where there was no stock exchange quotation.

These and other concessions and loopholes had led Grundy (1956), quoted by Titmuss (1962), to say that 'as far as estate duty is concerned, the Revenue benefit almost exclusively from the unlucky, the ungenerous and the unwise'. As illustrations, the unlucky would be those who gave away much of their wealth and died within five years, or those who on their death-bed negotiated to buy a farm or woodland (which has an abatement of duty of 45 per cent) and who died before the transaction could be ratified. The ungenerous are those who refuse to part with any of their wealth or to make other provision before they die. The unwise are those who refuse to pay for competent professional advice in setting up their affairs, particularly in setting up discretionary trusts.

CAPITAL TRANSFER TAX (CTT): FINANCE ACT OF 1975

CTT, which replaces estate duty, is a tax on all gratuitous transfers of capital whether they occur during a person's lifetime or at death. It came into force, in effect, from 26 March 1974 for gifts, and 12 March 1975 for death. There are two rates, the higher applying to transfers at death, or within three years of death, the lower referring to gifts.

As Table 17.4 shows, the first £25,000 of transfers is tax free (this

Table 17.4

<table>
<tr><th>Value of transfer
(£)</th><th>Higher rate estates (%)</th><th>Lower rate transfers (%)</th><th>Cumulative tax (lower rate)</th></tr>
<tr><td>0-25,000</td><td>0</td><td>0</td><td>–</td></tr>
<tr><td>25-30,000</td><td>10</td><td>5</td><td>250</td></tr>
<tr><td>30-35,000</td><td>15</td><td>7½</td><td>625</td></tr>
<tr><td>35-40,000</td><td>20</td><td>10</td><td>1,125</td></tr>
<tr><td>40-50,000</td><td>25</td><td>12½</td><td>2,375</td></tr>
<tr><td>50-60,000</td><td>30</td><td>15</td><td>3,875</td></tr>
<tr><td>60-70,000</td><td>35</td><td>17½</td><td>5,625</td></tr>
<tr><td>70-90,000</td><td>40</td><td>20</td><td>9,625</td></tr>
<tr><td>90-110,000</td><td>45</td><td>22½</td><td>14,125</td></tr>
<tr><td>110-130,000</td><td>50</td><td>22½</td><td>19,625</td></tr>
<tr><td>130-160,000</td><td>55</td><td>35</td><td>30,125</td></tr>
<tr><td>160-210,000</td><td>60</td><td>42½</td><td>51,375</td></tr>
<tr><td>210-260,000</td><td>60</td><td>50</td><td>76,375</td></tr>
<tr><td>260-310,000</td><td>60</td><td>55</td><td>103,875</td></tr>
<tr><td>310-510,000</td><td colspan="2">60</td><td>223,875</td></tr>
<tr><td>510-1,010,000</td><td colspan="2">65</td><td>548,875</td></tr>
<tr><td>1,010-2,010,000</td><td colspan="2">70</td><td>1,248,875</td></tr>
<tr><td>Over 2,010,000</td><td colspan="2">75</td><td></td></tr>
</table>

was originally £15,000 but was changed in October 1977), whether this is made by way of gifts during a person's life or at death. The tax is cumulative over a person's lifetime so that this exemption applies only once to each life. However, as we see later, the annual exemption of gifts not exceeding £2,000 per year and other exemptions make the aggregation of transfers less onerous than it appears at first sight.

The last column, headed 'Cumulative tax (lower rate)', shows the amount of tax that would be paid on the appropriate gifts. Thus a first gift of £30,000 would attract tax of £250 (5 per cent of £5,000); at the other end of the scale gifts amounting to £2,010,000 would attract tax of £1,248,875.[1]

The rates shown in the table are marginal rates – the rates due on additional transfers. The average rates are below these because of the initial tax-free slice of £25,000. In the example in the previous paragraph the marginal rate of tax on gifts between £1 and £2 million is 70 per cent, while the average tax on gifts totalling £2 million works out at about 50 per cent. At £110,000 the marginal tax is 45 per cent at death or 22½ per cent for a gift, but average rates are 28.25 per cent and 14.13 per cent respectively.

It was the original intention that only one rate of tax should apply, irrespective of whether the transfer took place in life or at death. Parliamentary pressure resulted in the two-rate scale. The rate for gifts is half the higher death rate up to £110,000, thereafter it tapers off until at £310,000 the rate coincides. Like most last-minute compromises, the decision to have two rates will long be debated.

It is not possible to generalise about the amount of tax estates will pay under the old and new systems for although the rates for CTT are in general lower than the old estate duties, the tax base has been widened to include most gifts. It was the intention that tax receipts should be about the same as under estate duties. However, the change has helped the miser! Using the rates in force when the changeover took place, with no gifts a net estate of £50,000 would have paid estate duty of £11,750, an effective rate of 23.5 per cent. Under CTT it was £7,750 (15.5 per cent). Likewise, an estate of £100,000 would have paid estate duty of £37,250 (37.25 per cent); under CTT it was £28,250 (28.25 per cent).

The idea that a tax covering gifts and estates can be a simple tax is probably an illusion. The following is intended as a guide only to the important features of the current system. The tax is payable on chargeable transfers made after 26 March 1974. A chargeable transfer can arise in a number of ways: a gift; on death; when a transfer is deemed to take place, e.g. if interest is forgone on a loan – the commercial rate of interest is deemed to be transferred; when a capital distribution is made from settled property; where a person omits to exercise a right whereby another person benefits, e.g. an advantageous rights issue where the controlling shareholder 'fails' to take up his rights, which are then taken up by the other shareholders. Exempted from the tax are 'excluded property' and 'exempt' transfers.

The main types of *excluded property* are:

1 Property (other than settled property) situated outside Britain if the beneficial owner is domiciled outside the country.
2 Settled property outside Britain unless the settler was domiciled in Britain when the settlement was made.
3 A reversionary interest in settled property within Britain unless at any time it had been acquired for money or money's worth.
4 A reversionary interest in settled property outside Britain if the entitled person is domiciled outside Britain.
5 British government securities issued as free of tax when in the beneficial ownership of a person neither domiciled nor ordinarily resident in Britain.

The main *exemptions* are:

1 Transfers between spouses; this applies both to gifts and transfers at death.
2 Gifts not exceeding £2,000 per year, the year referred to being the fiscal year to 5 April. In addition, there is a carry-over allowed of the unexpended part of the £2,000 to the next year, but only the next year.
3 Outright gifts to any one person in any one tax year are exempt up to a value of £100.
4 Lifetime dispositions for the maintenance of a former spouse, children, or dependent relatives, if subject to certain conditions.
5 Gifts in consideration of marriage subject to the following limits: (i) £5,000 if given by a parent of a party to the marriage – both the father and mother can use this provision so that for two-parent families £10,000 can be effectively transferred free of tax; (ii) £2,500 if given by a remoter ancestor; (iii) £1,000 from a transferor not in the above categories. The gifts may be outright or by way of settlement except in category (iii), where they must be outright.
6 Gifts to a recognised charity unless made within a year of death, or on death, when the amount is limited to £100,000. Sums above this are dutiable.
7 Gifts to political parties are also treated on the same basis as charities.

However, there are provisions designed to prevent one from setting up one's own political group, in the form of having to have at least one elected member of the House of Commons and not less than 150,000 votes.

8 Transfers for national purposes to so-called 'heritage bodies' are exempt, as are transfers to local authorities and universities.

9 There is provision for 'quick succession relief'. Where a person's estate is increased by a chargeable transfer within four years of his death, the amount of tax charged on that transfer is abated by 80 per cent if the death takes place in the first year after transfer, 60 per cent in the second, 40 per cent in the third and 20 per cent in the fourth.

Gifts – gross and net

It is important for both the donor and recipient to be clear whether a transfer is on a 'gross' or 'net' basis. The gross basis means that the gift is made less tax, whereas on a net basis the gift is the whole amount with the donor liable for tax on this amount.

Suppose a person decided to make a gift of £110,000 and subsequently another gift of £110,000 (see Table 17.5). When a gift is given gross, the donor deducts the amount of tax due to the Inland Revenue. With a net gift of, say, £110,000 it is necessary to ascertain what sum after tax would give this figure; in this case it is £129,483. With the second gift of £110,000, tax is worked out on £220,000 less the tax paid on the first gift.

Table 17.5

	Gross gift (£)	Tax deducted (£)	Net gift (£)	Tax payable (£)
1st gift	95,875	14,125	110,000	19,483
2nd gift	72,750	37,250	110,000	90,205
Totals	168,625	51,375	220,000	109,688

If a donor makes a gift without deduction of tax, or gets an indemnity from the recipient that he will pay, the gift is treated as a net gift. So the gift is grossed up to ascertain its value and the donor is liable for the tax.

It is also important to remember that even a net gift has a contingent liability for three years. If the giver dies in this period, the gift is taxed at the higher rate applicable at death and the recipient of the gift is liable for the extra tax.

In the example we have been using, if the donor died within three years of making the gifts, to his wealth at death is added the gifts of £220,000 in the gross gift case and of £329,688 in the net tax case. If the size of the wealth of the deceased was smaller in the net tax case by the sum of £109,688 extra gifts and tax he had paid, then the amount of tax collected on the gifts and estate would be the same in the two cases. However, as we have seen, the liability for paying the tax may differ.

The distinction between gross and net bequests in a will can be important. If a man makes a bequest to, say, his child of £35,000 with the remainder to his widow, and if the will makes no mention of tax, it is treated as a gross gift. Thus the child receives his portion less tax and the widow the remainder. If, however, the bequest is 'free of tax', the gift of £35,000 is grossed up at the average rate for the estate so that the child receives the £35,000 in full, the tax is paid from the estate and so the widow receives less. The amount of tax paid ultimately may not be very different. The widow will have a smaller estate to leave in the second case which will affect the amount of tax to be paid on her death. However, it is possible that if bequests are made 'free of tax', then the widow or remainder legacee will receive less than the donor intended because tax in this case is borne by the estate and not by the recipient of the other bequests.

The starting rate of tax for death takes into account previous transfers. Thus, if £110,000 has been transferred gross of tax more than three years previously, the estate would start to bear tax at 50 per cent on the first £20,000, that is at the rate applicable to transfers in the £110,000–£130,000 range. Where gifts have been made net, the grossed-up figure is used to determine the starting-point for the appropriate tax rate.

Farming

The old iniquitous position whereby even a death-bed purchase of farmland conveyed substantial tax advantages has been modified. Instead of the old method of a reduction in the rate of tax, an artificial basis of valuation has been introduced of twenty times the rent at which the property could reasonably be let. This relief must be claimed within two years of the transfer at death and the transferor must have for five of the preceding seven years been wholly or mainly engaged in farming. 'Mainly' is satisfied if 75 per cent of his earned income, excluding any income of his wife, comes from agriculture. He must also have occupied the land for two years out of the preceding five years. This concession is limited to the *higher* of (i) £250,000, or (ii) the value of 1,000 acres. For example, assume John Bull farms 1,200 acres and gives them to his son. They are worth £700 per acre. Their agricultural value is £500 per acre and annual rental value is £15 per acre.

Unreduced value = 1,200 X £700	£840,000
deduct	
part eligible for relief = 1,000 X £500	500,000
	£340,000
Part eligible for relief X rental acre value	
= 1,000 X £15 X 20 = 1,000 X 300	300,000
Value deemed to be transferred	£640,000

In this example the market value of the land is £840,000 but because of the relief provisions it is valued at £640,000 for CTT. The usual reasons given for relief of this kind is to prevent the break-up of viable-size farms. Since the main capital asset of a farm is the land, high rates of duty might mean the forced sale of part of the land to meet the tax. It would seem logical if this is the reason for the concession to confine this relief to cases where the recipient of the land continues to farm for some years.

Sole proprietors and partnerships

A substantial concession was made in the Finance Act of 1976 whereby a transfer relating to the business of a sole proprietor, partnership or to a controlling unquoted shareholding would only be taxed on 70 per cent of the transfer value. This was reduced to 50 per cent in October 1977, to give further assistance to small business, when 20 per cent relief was also granted for minority holdings in small companies if these had been owned for more than two years. For each transferor there is a single cumulative limit of £500,000 on transfers capable of benefiting from this relief. This relief applies to all businesses on transfers by gift or at death except that dealers in land and shares or investment concerns are excluded.

The arguments for this concession are the same as those given in the case of farming: i.e. to ensure continuity of the concern by avoiding the need to sell off all or part of the business to meet CTT. Doubts can be expressed about whether this is the most efficient way to ensure dynamic enterprise since the heirs of a proprietor may not have inherited his business talent.

Woodlands

There is a concession whereby growing timber is excluded from the charge on death if this has been owned for five years (unless received by gift or inheritance) and if it is subject to a forestry dedication scheme. However, if the woodland, before it passes on another death, is sold or given away other than to the owner's spouse, tax will be charged. The rate of tax is ascertained by adding the value of the woodland to the value of the estate.

Settlements and trusts

We have seen that settlements and trusts made in the right form provided one of the major ways of lessening the duty payable under the old system of estate duties. CTT attempts to plug this gap, but the provisions are necessarily complicated.

Because the new provisions were seen as particularly harsh to discretionary trusts, the Government reluctantly and controversially made special provision that enabled discretionary trusts made before 27 March 1974 to be wound up and to pay CTT at a reduced rate.

In general a trust will now attract CTT when it is established and when a capital distribution, including the final distribution, is made. In addition, a discretionary trust will be taxed at ten-yearly intervals. The charge will be applied to all capital in the trust, including accumulated income, the charge being 30 per cent of the normal CTT rate. One form of settlement attracts tax only on its formation: that for a child for its benefit and education and to vest in the child on attaining a specified age not later than 25.

CTT and the accretion of income principle

The reasoning behind both the total accretion principle and an expenditure tax is, as we have seen, to tax persons on the increment of spending power that accrues to them per period of time. It is immaterial whether the increment comes in the form of earned or unearned receipts, gifts, bequests, or a change in value of assets held.

Judged in the light of these criteria the CTT is a step forward. Gifts, which on anyone's criteria constitute spending power, which were generally untaxed, are now, if sufficiently large, subject to progressive taxation.[2] Differences remain. These criteria tax receipts in the hands of the recipient, at whatever their marginal rate of tax, whereas CTT taxes according to the position of the donor. If the recipient were taxed on his lifetime receipt of transfers, it is argued that wealthy persons would have a greater incentive to spread their wealth among a larger number of persons. It is clear that some persons would pay less tax under an accretion or expenditure system, while others pay less under the separate taxation systems we now have. It is not hard to formulate examples either way. The practical effect of the two systems may not be great. Transfers between rich persons are taxed more heavily under both systems than transfers between poorer persons, differences are more marked on the rarer transfer between a rich and a poor person.

Wealth taxes

Like the accretion principle of tax, CTT does not directly change the *existing* pattern of wealth ownership. A person with assets of one million pounds which do not change in value is not taxed under either system. He may, of course, have had an income from these assets which will be taxed but the underlying assets are not touched by taxation unless the owner chooses to liquidate some of his wealth in order to pay other taxes. However, the *future* pattern of wealth ownership will be changed since any disposal of wealth by way of gift, or bequest, will be taxed.

The community may decide to impose, in addition to a tax on transfers of wealth, a tax on the possession of wealth. Such a tax can be on an annual or periodic basis with 'low' or 'high' tax rates. The rate or rates of tax may be set 'low' so that the tax may be assumed to be paid from some average level of return that the wealth is assumed to earn. On the other hand, rates may be set higher so that wealth holders whose wealth is earning the assumed return will have to sell some of the assets to meet the tax unless choosing to pay out of income.[3]

If wealth is assumed to yield 5 per cent (which may be high bearing in mind that wealth held in the form of owner-occupied housing, cash, jewellery, works of art, etc. yields no money income), then a wealth tax at 2½ per cent is equivalent to an income tax of 50 per cent, since half of the assumed yield of wealth is taxed away. Similarly, assuming a yield of 5 per cent, a wealth tax of 5 per cent is equivalent to an income tax of 100 per cent, a wealth tax of 7½ per cent to an income tax of 150 per cent and so on. While a high rate of wealth tax may seem a good method of achieving a redistribution of wealth, the consequences for saving in the economy can be serious. Wealthy persons have no incentive to save when the wealth tax results in an erosion of their savings.

One effect of a wealth tax of whatever kind is to give an incentive to hold wealth in forms yielding a high money return – a development of uncertain value.

Undoubtedly the most serious problem with an annual or periodic wealth tax is the practical difficulties of administering such a tax. Valuation is a fairly arbitrary act for assets which are not traded regularly and large-scale evasion by not reporting, or undervaluing assets, is a strong possibility. Proposals for wealth taxes usually fall back on one of two methods for easing the problem: one is to exclude from the tax those assets which are difficult to value, such as works of art; the other is to confine the tax to the very wealthy. The first expedient seriously distorts resource allocation by encouraging the holding of wealth in those forms that escape the tax.

The above account of an annual or periodic wealth tax looks at it as an additional tax, but it is also possible to view it as a tax which could be brought in as a substitute for capital gains tax and the investment-income surcharge. If high rates were charged it can also be seen as a way of enabling income-tax rates to be lowered. For development along these lines, see Fleming and Little (1974), Meade (1975), Sandford (1971), Sandford, Willis and Ironside (1975), and Atkinson (1972; 1975). It remains true that most of the problems that have been pointed out still persist.

A number of countries, including Sweden, Norway, Finland, Denmark, West Germany, the Netherlands, Luxembourg, Austria and the Swiss cantons, impose wealth taxes in some form. For an account of these, see Sandford, Willis and Ironside (1975). In general, the taxes are of long standing, at low rates, and are seen as supplements to income tax. Ceiling provisions whereby the combined total of taxes on wealth and income is limited to a percentage of taxable income is a feature in Sweden and Finland, the two countries with the highest rates.

The closest that Britain has come to a wealth tax is occasional special charges on investment income. The last was imposed for the tax year 1967–8. Although this was a charge on income, it can be treated as a limited wealth tax since when income taxes and the special charge were taken into account the tax was greater than the income on high investment incomes. Disregarding the effect of personal allowances, an individual surrendered more in tax than he received in investment income when that income passed £18,580. A sum of approximately £411,000, invested to produce the average yield on the *Financial Times* share index, would have produced this sum. The first £3,000 on investment income, after deduction of personal allowances, was exempt. The remainder was charged at the following rates: between £3,000 and £4,000 at 10p in the £, between £4,000 and £5,000 at 15p, between £5,000 and £8,000 at 30p, and above £8,000 at 45p. The yield was about £100 million and some 90,000 people were affected.

After considerable discussion, in March 1974 a Green Paper, *Wealth Tax* (1974), was published by the Labour party, who had promised to introduce a wealth tax. In December of that year a Select Committee was set up to consider the Green Paper proposals, and a confused four-volume report, which consisted of five minority reports, was published in November 1975 (see Select Committee on a Wealth Tax, 1975). No majority verdict was reached because of the absence abroad of two Labour party members when a critical vote was taken. The date for implementation of a wealth tax has subsequently been deferred on several occasions, not least because of administrative difficulties. The Green Paper envisaged a wealth tax starting on wealth of £100,000. Two rate bands were used for illustrative purposes, the first starting at 1 per cent, rising in four bands to 2½ per cent on wealth over £5,000,000, the other again starting at 1 per cent but then rising in five bands to 5 per cent on wealth over £5,000,000. It is unlikely that a tax on these lines would be introduced without considerable modification from the proposals put forward in this Green Paper, so further details of the tax will be omitted.

CONCLUSIONS ON A PERIODIC OR ANNUAL WEALTH TAX

The change to capital transfer tax in 1974 for gifts and in 1975 for death has modified many arguments about the need for a wealth tax, since it removed many of the gross anomalies of the old system of estate duty.

Most commentators who now advocate a wealth tax see it as a means whereby capital gains tax and the investment-income surcharge can be swept away if a more comprehensively based wealth tax is introduced. Other commentators go further and see it in addition as a means whereby marginal income-tax rates can be sharply reduced. The administrative costs of such a change are agreed to be high, at least for a considerable time to accommodate the changeover.

Alternative proposals concentrate on modifications to our existing taxes. In particular there is considerable support in the references already mentioned in this chapter for turning capital transfer tax into an accessions tax. Capital transfer tax could operate on the same general lines as at present except that the beneficiary, not the donor, would be subject to tax. The receipt of any gratuitous transfers would be registered during a person's lifetime and subject to a cumulative tax instead of taxing the donor on this basis as at present. It is claimed that such a change would encourage the wider distribution of wealth, since small gifts or bequests, even from very rich persons, would be subject to little or no tax if received by those who had received little in this way already. On the other hand, large gifts or inheritances would be subject to heavy tax.[4] It would be easier to take personal circumstances of the beneficiary into account, such as special relief for minor children who are orphaned. Meade (1975) makes the interesting suggestion that the tax could be higher the greater the excess of the age of the donor over the age of the recipient, on the grounds that the younger a person is when a gift or legacy is received, the more benefit is received. It would seem that before a major change to a wealth tax is introduced, a number of changes could be made to capital transfer tax which would help achieve the same ends as a wealth tax without the same degree of administrative complexity. Besides changing to a beneficiary tax just outlined, the most obvious of these changes would be to scrap the lower rate of tax on gifts and subject all transfers to the higher rate applicable to estates. The exemptions allowed in consideration of marriage clearly help to perpetuate the present structure of wealth, and could be scrapped.

Summary

Information about the distribution of wealth is inadequate, but even if this was not a problem there are very considerable difficulties in interpreting the information. Various definitions of wealth are possible; in particular a narrow definition can be taken which is confined to assets which can be realised by the owner. Alternatively, non-transferable rights such as pensions can be included. Wealth figures on an individual basis show greater extremes than is the case when assumptions are made about the wealth holdings of spouses. Empirical work on wealth holding by families is virtually non-existent because of the difficulties in obtaining the data. Some recent estimates of the Royal Commission on the Distribution of Income and Wealth were given.

A brief resumé of the old system of estate duty, together with its drawbacks, was given before the current system of capital transfer tax was outlined in more detail. Finally, some aspects of an annual or periodic wealth tax were looked at.

Notes

1 The examples assume that the annual exemption has been used up by a previous gift.
2 The annual exemption from tax of the first £2,000 of gifts – which is effectively a limit of £4,000 for husband and wife – does, however, severely limit the efficiency of CTT as a means of redistributing wealth.
3 This assumes that income from wealth is not subject to both income tax and wealth tax. If this is not the case, then the combination of income tax payable on the income received from wealth, and the wealth tax, will result in marginal tax rates of 100 per cent or more in many more instances.
4 The difference is considerable. A large estate will, if transferred other than to a spouse, pay a large amount of capital transfer tax but the residue of the estate, which can be considerable, can be left to one person. We have seen how important inheritance is in the perpetuation of wealth inequality. With an accessions basis of taxation, bequests to only one person will be penalised most heavily.

18
Land

The real property laws of this country, from the period immediately succeeding the Conquest down to the present time, presents a history consistent with itself in one particular, that of a perpetual struggle of rival interests.
C. WREN HOSKYNS, 'The Land-Laws of England', in *Systems of Land Tenure in Various Countries.*

Introduction: the meanings attached to 'ownership'

Mankind, even at a primitive stage of development, shows an acute interest in land and territorial rights. Ownership itself is not a simple issue, it presents a highly complex tangle of privileges, rights and duties. By way of illustration, does ownership confer: the right of alienation, i.e. to sell or give land away; the right of bequest; the right of franchise; the right to mineral wealth below ground; the right to hunt and fish; the right to erect buildings on land; the right to neglect land to the detriment of neighbours and future generations; rights above ground?

In addition: What happens on intestacy? Are services or taxes required of the owner? Does it accord social status? Are improvements made by a tenant the property of the owner, or must the tenant be compensated? Are improvements to land by acts of the community chargeable to the owner, and is spoilation compensated, e.g. acts such as sea defences, drainage, town expansion, siting of airports, roads, etc.? Does the community reserve any public rights, e.g. of access? Has the community the right to acquire the land for the public good?

'Ownership' is the rag-bag into which all aspects are bundled. The history of land and of the privileges, rights and duties that attach thereto exhibits a rich variety of solutions to be found at different times and in different places. Much history is a record of this changing nexus of privilege and responsibility.

The subject of land abounds in legal subtleties. A short summary, or outline, is hardly possible and certainly cannot do justice to the niceties that have developed. In Great Britain the Norman conquest of 1066 brought great changes. After the conquest the normal position was for the Crown to *own* land, and others to hold an estate under various forms of tenure, either directly from the Crown or from an intermediate holder who himself had tenure directly or indirectly from the Crown.[1] Feudal tenure involved the granting of an estate for services. These were in the form of military, spiritual or agricultural obligations. Wills of land were not permitted; descent in the male line predominated.

This situation was gradually changed in a number of ways. Feudal services tended to be commuted into annual money payments or 'rents'. The trust device came to be used to get around the ban on bequeathing land; this right was not legally established until 1540. The freehold, as a freely marketable commodity unencumbered by onerous feudal rights, was achieved by statute in 1660. The system thus established was, speaking very broadly, the one existing until 1947, although there were numerous alterations in the laws affecting land during this time, some of considerable importance. Developments since 1947 will be looked at in more detail later in this chapter.

The economics of land

David Ricardo, an economist of the early nineteenth century, developed the idea that land is in a separate category from other factors of production since its supply could neither be diminished nor increased. He argued that a tax on land could not reduce the available supply and hence could have no adverse effect on production: therefore, 'rent' should be treated differently from other factor payments. Fundamentally, the quantity of land is limited in supply. A community with a growing population is likely to experience an increasing demand for the limited amount of land available for food-growing, dwellings, transport and amenities – which will raise its real value. This 'unearned income' may not accrue to every landowner but it will accrue to landowners *en masse*. We have here the germ of later ideas developed by 'single taxers', such as Henry George, that land need be the only item to bear tax, an idea which today, even if acceptable, would not yield the amount of revenue required.

Ricardo's ideas have been modified on two fronts. The supply of services from land can be increased by, for example, better agricultural methods or increasing the height of buildings; it can also be reduced by, for example, soil erosion. Second, other factors may be akin to land, in that the supply cannot immediately be changed in response to an increase in demand, and these factors will also enjoy an enhanced price, or 'quasi-rent', for a period.

Land has one other attribute which is sufficient to mark it off from most other assets. That is the degree to which the price of land is affected by socially created values (Land Commission, 1965, para. 2):

> There is no novelty in proposals to secure for the community at least a share in the values it has itself created. An act of 1427 sought to recover increases in the value of property attributable to public expenditure on works for sea defence, and in the reign of Charles II, there was statutory appropriation of a part of landowners' unearned enhancement or 'melioration' assessed upon the benefits of street widening in London.

With increased government activity today, the scope for great changes in land values which accrue without effort on the landowners' part is very much increased. Proposals to build new towns, the reconstruction of existing towns, new road links, the closing of railway lines, siting of power stations, airports and seaports, the planning regulations which permit or prohibit certain types of development, are but a few of the more obvious examples of community decisions which can greatly increase, or decrease, the value of land.

Should land be treated differently from other assets?

From the fiscal viewpoint it is necessary to decide whether the relative uniqueness of land, that is its 'fixed quantity' and change in value which can occur through public action, is sufficiently marked to call for special tax treatment. In a country which is sparsely populated, the question may seem an academic one; in a well-populated country like Britain it becomes more acute. The problem, as has been indicated, is made more complex since a wide variety of planning regulations has grown up. The redesignation of land from the 'green belt', that is land that shall not be built upon, to a housing area can increase the price of land many hundredfold. In a similar way, the price may be adversely affected by planning permission which goes the other way.

The author's opinion is that the factors indicated provide clear evidence that land should be taxed. From the account given below for the period since 1947 it is clear that, unfortunately, no political consensus has emerged on the form that such taxation should take. Both Labour and Conservative parties on achieving power have largely undone the work of their predecessors and there is little indication that this situation will change in the near future.

The period 1947–67

Land was considered in the report of the Expert Committee on Compensation and Betterment (1942) under the Chairmanship of Mr Justice Uthwatt. The Land Commission White Paper (1965, paras 3–6) reported as follows:

> The main recommendations of the Uthwatt Committee were implemented by the Labour Government in the Town and Country Planning Act 1947, which vested in the State all development rights in land. Anyone wishing to develop land had to recover the right to develop by payment of a development charge to the Central Land Board. A capital sum of £300 million was available for payments to those who established claims that the value of their land had depreciated as a result of the Act.
>
> The Central Land Board were also given powers to buy land compulsorily for the purpose of disposing of it for development. The Uthwatt Committee had considered that public acquisition, if need be by compulsion, was the only satisfactory answer to the problem of comprehensive development and of securing betterment. In practice, doubts arose about the validity of the powers given to the Central Land Board and they had not been widely used when the Conservative Government changed the situation by abolishing development charges in the Town and Country Planning Act, 1953.
>
> The 1953 Act, a stop-gap measure, was followed by the Town and Country Planning Act 1954, which removed the restrictions on private sales so that those sales took place at market price. A two-price system was thereby created; prices paid when land with development value was sold privately were higher than those paid when such land was acquired compulsorily for public purposes. This two-price system was so clearly inequitable that the Government was forced to eliminate it, and this they chose to do by the Town and Country Planning Act 1959, which restored market value as the basis for compensation on compulsory purchase.
>
> Since the removal in 1959 of the last restraints on the market in land for development, land with planning permission for development or even with the hope of such planning permission, whether stimulated by a development plan or not, has been fetching ever-increasing prices. These prices, which must be paid by public authorities buying land for their essential purposes, place a heavy burden on their financial resources; they are also a deterrent to people wishing to buy their own homes.

Therefore, 1947 sees an attempt to implement some of the recommendations of the Uthwatt Committee report and secure for the State the betterment value of land. This attempt fails because of legislative shortcomings, the complexity of the Act and probably also resentment of a 100 per cent tax on betterment values, and leads to the gradual abandonment of the attempt; by 1959 a return to free-market pricing had taken place.

This period was one in general of steeply rising prices of land. Gains made in this way were, unless caught by the 1947 Act, untaxed until 1962, except when they were undertaken 'by way of trade' and were taxed under normal company taxation. In 1962 capital gains in land and building were taxed if realised within three years. The 1965 Act charged all gains either to a short-term or a long-term capital gains tax.

Land Commission Act of 1967

The Land Commission Act of 1967 was an attempt to re-establish some of the recommendations of the Uthwatt Committee of 1942 but to achieve the aims of the Committee in a different way from the 1947 Act.

The Land Commission, with a head-office in Newcastle and eleven regional offices, administered a tax known as the 'betterment levy', and was invested with wide powers to acquire land compulsorily. Compulsory purchase was based on current market values (less the betterment levy), so it should have been a matter of indifference to a landowner whether he sold to the Land Commission, a public authority or a private purchaser.

The betterment levy was at an initial rate of 40 per cent, and the stated intention of the Government was to increase the rate progressively to 45 per cent and then to 50 per cent at reasonably short intervals. The question of increasing the rate further was not ruled out. The levy thus presents an important change from the 1947 Act, which sought to obtain the whole of the betterment value. Further, the charge was only on the increase in value from existing use to a new use.

Thus, if a piece of agricultural land was originally bought for £300, and was worth £1,000 if sold as agricultural land but worth £3,000 if sold as housing land, no betterment levy was imposed; in the case of continuing agricultural use, it was payable on £2,000 if sold as housing land (current value in existing use deducted from current value in new use). Where the betterment levy was charged, the capital gains tax did not apply, but this tax continued to apply where land was sold for existing use.

In the case of development of land the levy could be payable even though no sale took place, but only *material* development as defined by the Act ranked for levy. Thus a person could rebuild his house and increase its size up to 1,000 square feet, erect a garage or turn his house into flats without incurring a levy. In a like manner, a factory could be rebuilt and enlarged without incurring a levy, provided neither the floor area nor the cubic content was enlarged more than 10 per cent. No levy was imposed on the development or disposal of land held by local authorities for their social services, including comprehensive development and town development, but it applied to land held by them for commercial purposes. Similarly, the levy was not payable by statutory undertakings or endowed charities. An amendment in 1969 exempted from levy cases where the market value of the land did not exceed £1,500. This was expected to reduce by half the number of cases subject to levy. Provision was also made to deal with hardship in cases where a plot of land had been received as a gift and on which the recipient was building a house for his own occupation.

Probably of more practical importance than the yield of the tax on land, if the intentions of the Act had been carried out for long enough, were the powers of compulsory purchase given to the Land Commission. It was envisaged that the Land Commission should be an active body not just acquiring land piecemeal as the need arose but ensuring 'that the right land is made available at the right time'. It was envisaged that the Commission would buy, hold, manage and sell land to developers. These powers were to be gradually given to the Commission.

The period 1970–3

A change to a Conservative Government led to the Land Commission (Dissolution) Act of 1971, which abolished betterment levy with effect from 22 July 1970 and dissolved the Land Commission with effect from 1 May 1971.

After 22 July 1970 gains on land were treated in the same way as other gains and subject to capital gains tax and estate duty.

Development gains tax

A change to a Labour Government in 1973 led to a development gains tax on disposal of land or buildings in the United Kingdom after 17 December 1973. The result was that part of the development gain was taxed as income. This change was seen as a temporary measure before a more thoroughgoing land tax was introduced. Companies' gains were charged to corporation tax but roll-over relief up to 30 per cent of the development gain was available to them.

Gains of no more than £10,000 in any year were exempt for persons; the corresponding figure was £1,000 for companies. Sale of a person's main private residence was also exempt.

A development gain was assessed as the least of: (i) the proceeds less 120 per cent of the cost; (ii) the proceeds less 110 per cent of the 'current-use value' at the time of disposal; and (iii) the capital gain on disposal less the increase in 'current-use value' over the period of ownership, or since 6 April 1965 if then owned.

A development gain could be spread back for up to three years of ownership. A letting of a property for the first time could be treated as making a disposal for purposes of development gains tax.

Development land tax

The new tax promised with the changes in 1973, which were outlined in the previous section, was brought in after 31 July 1976.

The development land tax, as it is called, is charged in respect of the realisation by a person, partnership trust or company of the development value of land in the United Kingdom at the rates shown in Table 18.1 and which are the same for all. From Table 18.1 it will be seen that the first £10,000 of development gain in any year is tax free; there is then a steep jump to a marginal rate of tax of 66⅔ per cent on the next £150,000 of gain, with gains in excess of this being taxed at 80 per cent. It was the stated intention of the Government to have a single rate of 80 per cent payable after the first £10,000 after 31 March 1979. The Conservative party has said, however, they would reduce the tax to 60 per cent and repeal the Community Land Act of 1975, which will be discussed in the next section.

Table 18.1

Realised development value in year	Marginal rate of tax (%)
First £10,000	0
£10,000–£160,000	66⅔
Over £160,000	80

A significant provision of the tax brought in at the parliamentary stage and not intended in the original White Paper is the rule that departs from the usual UK assumption that income of husband and wife is aggregated for tax purposes. For this tax husband and wife are treated separately so that each has the £10,000 exemption and the £150,000 reduced rate band. The exception is that a property obtained from a spouse must be held for a year to gain this concession. The value of this concession, on a gain of £20,000 or more – which is equally split between husband and wife – is a reduction of tax of £6,666 – a stiff price to pay for bachelor status, or meanness on behalf of a spouse who refuses to share the transaction with his or her marriage partner.

The tax is payable on disposal or immediately before a project of material development is begun. In the latter case the land is deemed to have been disposed of at market value. The tax is based on the realised (or deemed realised) value less legal costs, etc. of realisation, minus the relevant base value. Base value is calculated as the higher of the following:

Base A
The aggregate cost of acquisition, plus expenditure on relevant improvements, plus increase in current-use value since date of acquisition, plus a special addition, and a further addition where applicable (see below).

Base B
The aggregate of 110 per cent of current-use value and expenditure on relevant improvements.

Base C
110 per cent of the aggregate of cost of acquisition and expenditure on improvements.

Special addition and further addition
These apply only to land held before 1 May 1977. For land held before 12 September 1974, the special addition is 15 per cent of the original cost for every year of ownership up to a maximum of four years. Thus the maximum that can be added is 60 per cent of cost. For land held after 12 September 1974 and before 1 May 1977, the addition is 10 per cent for every year up to four, so the maximum addition is 40 per cent of cost. (A part of a year counts as a year for these purposes.) The further addition extends the special addition to 'relevant improvements'. These cover amounts spent on enhancing the value of the property, as well as certain legal costs.

The tax does not apply on land passed at death or by gift. In these cases the recipient has the base value that would have applied to the donor.

Local authorities are exempt. Statutory undertakings are also exempt if the development is for their own operations. Charities are exempt in respect of land held by them at 12 September 1974. New acquisitions are chargeable, but development for its own use defers the tax until a disposal is made. Principal private residences are exempt, and, a curious provision, husband and wife are allowed one exemption each.

The development gains tax allows generous relief in respect of other taxes. The part of the gain which is charged to development land tax is not generally charged to other taxes. Thus a sale which realises £50,000 in capital gains and £30,000 in development value will attract development tax on £30,000 but capital gains tax on only £20,000 (50,000–30,000). Relief against any capital transfer tax paid by the donor is even available if the land has been acquired by gift.

Community Land Act of 1975

The Community Land Act of 1975 was passed at the end of 1975 with a promise by the Conservative party to repeal it when the Conservatives came to power. This Act attempts to pick up powers of the old Land Commission which were concerned with land management. Learning from that experience, the new Act departs from the idea of a Central Land Agency and devolves the power to acquire, manage and deal with land suitable for development to local authorities in England and Scotland and to a new Land Authority in Wales.

The intention behind the Act is that the authorities should acquire land which, in the opinion of the authority concerned, is needed for relevant development within ten years from the time at which they are acting. Local authorities have long had some powers to acquire land for their purposes so this Act is an extension of more comprehensive planning. It is envisaged that they will be acquiring development land not just for themselves but comprehensively so as to make it available to others for development as required.

The intention is that the authorities will purchase all land at current-use value – that is to say, its value for its current use excluding any value that may accrue due to the hope of development. If successful in this aim, the development land tax will become redundant since the authorities will be buying all development land at current-use prices.

Summary

Land in a developed community is a scarce resource, and presents two major problems: one is the need for some control or planning of the use of land; and the other is the fact that actions of the community can cause very wide fluctuations in the price of a particular piece of land.

There is now a general parliamentary consensus that some form of planning is required, and that compensation should be paid for those adversely affected by community decisions, while those who receive benefits in this way should contribute to the community. Details of the changes since 1947 were given. Unfortunately, the two major political parties in Britain seem to have devoted more time to undoing the work of the other party when they achieve power than they do in trying to find a permanent solution that would be acceptable to both. This highly destructive process shows no sign of coming to an end.

Note

1 He who held land as tenant of the royal lord could himself become lord by granting the land to another. The primary rung in the feudal tenurial ladder was the tenant in actual possession of the tenement, the tenant *in dominico*. The ultimate rung was the king, the one man in all the realm who was never tenant. Between the two extremes, the rungs were either an ascending series of lordships or a descending series of tenures, according to the view taken. There is no land unowned in all England. Land can be without a tenant, where he who is in possession is the king; but land without a lord there cannot be – *nulle terre sans seigneur* (see Denman, 1958, p. 80).

19

Local authorities' structure, revenue and expenditure

They [local authorities] will be required to assist in both deflation and reflation. They may be called upon to help promote regional policies, to assist selected industries and to help to ameliorate unemployment. Our contributors' comments show how vital the subject is for local government's future, how prominent it is in the minds of those responsible for local government and how incomplete as yet are the arrangements for co-ordination between central and local government. Above all, they bring to light new restrictions on local freedom. They show economic control reinforcing the trend towards centralisation which already exists in so many countries because of the desire for improved and more equal services.

A. H. MARSHALL (1969), *Local Government Finance*, International Union of Local Authorities, The Hague, p. 34.

Introduction

There are very few generalisations that can be safely made about local government. A survey of thirty-three countries (Marshall, 1969) found that local authority expenditure as a percentage of public expenditure varied from 14 to 67 per cent. Some countries had a high proportion of local taxation, others a low proportion. One factor to emerge was that 'Taxes on owners and occupiers of real estate remains the most general kind of local tax. Almost all countries use them.' Canada, Great Britain and South Africa rely almost exclusively upon them, while in the USA about 87 per cent of local taxation came from this source.

Britain in the 1970s is undergoing a series of major constitutional changes. After many years of debate local government was reorganised in London during 1963–5, in Northern Ireland in 1973, in England and Wales in April 1974, and in Scotland in May 1975. In addition, an intense debate about devolution is taking place. In spite of lip-service being paid to the importance of finance in providing local autonomy, the local government reorganisation took place without any major change in finance and the debate on devolution is being conducted in the same manner.

Our main concern is with finance. This chapter outlines the present structure of local government, its sources of finance and its expenditure patterns. The next will be concerned with principles that are applicable whether one has local government or local regions in mind. Chapter 21 looks at local and regional sources of finance.

Local government structure

The structure of local government in England and Wales had remained basically unchanged since the nineteenth century until London was re-organised in 1963–5, while Scotland's pattern was fixed in 1929. The period from the Second World War has been one of intense debate over local government reform, and culminated in a number of Royal Commissions (see Royal Commission on Local Government in England, 1969; Royal Commission on Local Government in Scotland, 1969; and *Local Government Finance in England and Wales*, May 1976, hereafter referred to as the Layfield Report after its Chairman).

The reorganisations differ in a number of ways from the recommendations of the various Royal Commissions, most notably in departing from a single-tier structure. In England most of the old county boundaries were retained and other authorities (except parishes) amalgamated into larger units. Local health, water and main sewage services were taken out of local government control and given to *ad hoc* bodies (for greater details of the new changes, see Redcliffe-Maud and Wood, 1974; *Local Government Finance in England and Wales*, 1974; *New Local Authorities Management and Structure*, 1972; Richards, 1974 and Hepworth, 1976).

Table 19.1 shows the existing structure. From about 1,200 county boroughs, boroughs, urban and rural councils in England and Wales and 430 county, city, burgh and district councils in Scotland has emerged a two-tier structure of county councils and district councils comprising 522 authorities. There are in addition some 10,000 parish councils in England and it is proposed to continue with these and to have similar councils, except in large urban areas, in other parts of the United Kingdom.

In England there are seven large conurbations: London, Tyne–Wear (including Sunderland as well as Tyneside), West Yorkshire, South Yorkshire, Greater Manchester, Merseyside and the West Midlands (including Birmingham, the Black Country and Coventry). In addition, there are

Table 19.1

Structure of UK local authorities

England		
Conurbations		
London		
Greater London Council*	1	
City of London	1	34
London boroughs	32	
Other conurbations		
Metropolitan counties*	6	42
Metropolitan districts or councils	36	
Mixed urban and rural areas		
Counties*	39	
Districts or boroughs	296	336
Isles of Scilly	1	
Wales		
Counties*	8	45
Districts or boroughs	37	
Scotland		
Regions*	9	
Districts	53	65
Island areas (Orkney, Shetland and Western Isles)	3	
		522
Northern Ireland		
Districts		26

*These authorities precept on the others.

three new counties established in estuarine areas: Cleveland (Teesside), Humberside and Avon (Bristol).

The second tier of authorities in the conurbations comprises thirty-two London boroughs and thirty-six metropolitan districts or councils. The ancient and unique City of London is still retained as a separate unit.

The rest of England is divided into thirty-nine counties and 296 districts or boroughs, and the Isles of Scilly. Wales has eight counties and thirty-seven districts or boroughs. Scotland has nine regions, fifty-three districts and three island councils. In what follows attention is concentrated mainly on England and Wales.

The bodies just described are responsible for the main local government services. However, parish councils, which existed in all rural areas, and of which there are some 10,000, have been retained and the principle extended to all except large urban areas. These parish, community or neighbourhood councils, as they are variously called, have rather more power than the old parish councils, but their chief purpose is in channelling public opinion. One important function of these councils is the right to be consulted on all planning applications, and to make representations to higher-level authorities. It is hoped that this level of authority will attract wide public interest and help remove the feeling that local government is something remote and bureaucratic.

Local finance

The above changes resulted in a major restructuring of local government areas and powers, the only sector left much as it was being the financial one. The new local authorities have rates as their only major independent source of revenue; and apart from trading activities, which are normally expected to be self-financing, the balance of current revenue comes from central government grants.

A further matter to complicate the issues of finance was provided by the Royal Commission on the Constitution (1973). Its proposals were discussed in a government paper on *Devolution within the United Kingdom* (1974). The Royal Commission, with its *Memorandum of Dissent*, is not easy to digest. The discussion paper sets out in summary form the seven main schemes of devolution put forward by the Commission. Some of the implications for local government finance of devolution will be considered in Chapter 21.

Local authority current revenue

Local authority current revenue comes from three sources: government grants, rates and other income. 'Other income' comes mainly from housing rents, and receipts from trading activities such as passenger transport, harbours, docks and piers. Although this other income is a sizeable proportion of local finance, it is mainly used to finance the activities giving rise to the revenue; it neither forms a large source of funds for other activities, nor does it constitute a large drain on other revenue. We shall therefore concentrate on income from rates and grants.

THE RATING SYSTEM

The idea of taxing land and property goes back thousands of years and most developed countries use some form of property tax as a source of local revenue. The roots of our present rating system can be traced back to the Elizabethan Poor Law.

Under the rating system each property (strictly called a 'hereditament') is given a rateable value based on the notional annual rent it will command in the open market on the assumption that the landlord is responsible for repairing and insuring the property. For domestic property a deduction is made from gross value for the notional cost of annual repairs and insurance to arrive at a figure of rateable value. Since 1948 the task of valuation in England and Wales has belonged to the Inland Revenue. New valuation lists are supposed to be prepared quinquennially but except in Scotland valuations have always been at longer intervals. Rates are a tax levied on occupiers of rateable property. The rate is fixed annually by the appropriate local council and the occupier's tax is found by multiplying the rateable value of his hereditament by the rate poundage. Thus if the rateable value is £300 and the appropriate rate is fixed at 40p in the pound, the amount payable will be £120.

Property is used in a wide sense to cover land, buildings (domestic and industrial), mines, quarries and fixed plant and machinery. In 1929 agricultural land was derated, i.e. exempted from rate liability, and the rateable values of industrial and freight transport hereditaments were reduced by three-quarters. A general revaluation became effective from 1956. In 1959 industrial and freight transport derating was reduced from 75 to 50 per cent so that their rateable values were approximately doubled. A further general revaluation became effective in 1963 when industrial derating was abolished. The Royal Commission on Local Government in England (1969) thought that the anomaly of agricultural derating ought to be removed, and in the opinion of many people this would help smooth out some of the differences in fiscal capacity between areas that are now apparent. The Layfield Committee considered the arguments for and against derating. In general they favoured rating farming and thought that the Government should offset the burden this would cause to farming in some other way or alternatively introduce rating gradually. The Green Paper on the *Future Shape of Local Government Finance* (1977) follows previous government practice in rejecting these suggestions on the grounds of cost and the likely adverse effects on farming.[1]

RATES – HOW MUCH OF A BURDEN?

Rates have come in for mounting criticism in recent years. When revaluation is carried out it inevitably results in some properties being more highly rated than before; indeed, if no changes take place, the valuation would be largely a waste of time, but inevitably those whose rates have risen relative to others believe they have cause for complaint. Valuation will be looked at in more detail in Chapter 21.

Local authorities, as we saw in Chapter 9, have been increasing their share of government expenditure in response to increasing population and the demand for better public services. Their increase in real expenditures has been faster than the increase in real GNP. Increased grants have made up for a lot of this extra expenditure. Although rates have risen in absolute terms as a percentage of total tax revenue, they now represent a smaller proportion of tax revenue than in the pre-1939 period. In the last decade domestic rates expressed as a proportion of disposable household income show a decline from 2.3 to 2.2 per cent.

These figures should make one pause at the argument which is so frequently put forward that the central government is solely to blame for the revenue plight of local authorities. It could be argued that the central government, as well as having some taxes which have high income and price elasticities, i.e. revenue automatically increases with higher incomes and prices, has been more willing than local governments to raise tax rates so as to protect its revenues. Local authorities are perhaps more vulnerable to pressures from irate ratepayers. The implication that if a tax which serves the central government were to be hived off to local government it will serve them equally well is subject to some doubt.

This conjecture receives support from the information available on revaluation of rateable values. Revaluations took place in 1956 and 1963, neither occasion being used to make a major shift of taxation. Neither was the adoption of some of the recommendations of the Committee of Inquiry's *Report into the Impact of Rates on Households* (1964) so used. It is often alleged that the inequalities of the rating system preclude greater sums being raised from this source, but this no longer seems a powerful impediment, since low-income households are entitled to rate rebates. It is still the case that for many households the cost of rates will be less than the cost of hire of a colour television set. However, it is also true to say that the rating system has a number of defects that have resulted in a great deal of local pressure which has inhibited recourse to more rate financing. These defects and suggested remedies will be looked at in Chapter 21.

Local authority expenditure and revenue

In the context of total government revenue, we have seen in Chapter 10 that rates in the post-1945 period form a smaller proportion of that total than in most of the pre-1939 years. We will now examine in greater detail local government revenue and expenditure. Since expenditure has increased, both in money and real terms, while rates compared with the pre-1939 period have declined as a proportion of finance, the figures will bring out the importance of grants. Results are shown for 1966 and 1976.

Table 19.2 shows local authority revenue and expenditure on current account for 1966 and 1976, indicating, in money terms, over a 4½-fold increase. The price index for general government final consumption increased from 77 in 1966 to 240 in 1976 (with 1970 = 100), more than a threefold increase. So even when allowance is made for price changes there was a substantial increase in real terms. Whereas in 1966 grants accounted for some 41 per cent and rates for 38 per cent of revenue, by 1976 grants were accounting for some 55 per cent and rates for 27 per cent. If we express the money expenditures as a percentage of GNP in each year, we see from the penultimate line of Table 19.2 that expenditure accounted for 9.5 per cent of GNP in 1966 and 13.4 per cent of GNP in 1976. Around 38 per cent of expenditure is for education and educational grants.

Government grants may be *specific*, that is in aid of a particular service or a particular section of a service such as the police grant, or *general*, which are not so tied. The trend has been away from specific grants to a general grant. In particular, there was a switch from certain specific grants to a general grant in 1959–60 and from April 1967 the general grant was replaced by a new form termed a rate support grant. Details will be given in the following sections. Grants may be used to shift revenue to all local authorities or they may be used in whole or in part to direct revenue on some criteria to authorities deemed to be especially 'needy'. A specific grant can be open-ended. For example, if it takes the form of meeting 30 per cent of the cost of a service, the Exchequer contribution depends on the expenditure levels of the local authorities. Grants thus tend to accrue to the richer or higher-spending authorities. With a general grant the Exchequer contribution is fixed. A local authority is free to spend its general grant as it wishes so long as it maintains its legal obligations, but this does not necessarily confer greater freedom on it. This depends not

Table 19.2

Local authority revenue and expenditure on current account

	1966		1976	
	(£m.)	(%)	(£m.)	(%)
Revenue				
Grants				
General	1,168	32.7	7,828	46.0
Specific	313	8.8	1,539	9.0
Rates	1,374	38.4	4,540	26.6
Rent	542	15.2	2,434	14.3
Trading surplus and interest	175	4.9	692	4.1
Total	3,572	100.0	17,033	100.0
Expenditure				
Roads	208	6.5	691	4.7
Environmental*	211	6.6	1,095	7.4
Police	211	6.6	1,024	7.0
Education	1,107	34.7	5,253	35.6
Scholarships and educational grants	106	3.3	420	2.8
Social services†	185	5.8	1,461	9.9
Debt interest				
To central government	171	5.4	1,086	7.4
Other	429	13.5	1,808	12.3
Other	559	17.6	1,906	12.9
Total current expenditure	3,187	100.0	14,744	100.0
Total current expenditure as % of GNP		9.5		13.4
Surplus	385		2,289	

*Sewage and refuse disposal, public health services, land and coast protection, parks and planning.
†Personal social services, school meals and milk.
Source: National Income and Expenditure, 1966–76, *HMSO, London.*

only on the level of the grant but on how stringent other types of legislative and administrative controls are.

The difference between the totals of revenue and expenditure is the current surplus which is used to help finance capital expenditures. These amounts appear in the first line of Table 19.3.

Capital receipts of local authorities are shown at the top of Table 19.3 and capital expenditures are shown on the bottom. Items of a capital

Table 19.3

Local authority expenditure on capital account

	1966		1976	
	(£m.)	(%)	(£m.)	(%)
Capital receipts				
Current surplus	385	27.1	2,289	53.1
Capital grants	82	5.8	208	4.8
Borrowing net				
Central government	546	38.5	481	11.2
Others	414	29.2	1,135	26.4
Miscellaneous	–9	–0.6	192	4.5
Total	1,418	100.0	4,305	100.0
Capital expenditure				
Roads and lighting	112	7.9	327	7.6
Housing	654	46.1	2,222	51.6
Environment	208	14.7	370	8.6
Education	185	13.0	598	13.9
Capital grants to personal sector	20	1.4	167*	3.9
Net lending, mainly for house purchase	54	3.8	144	3.3
Rest	185	13.1	477	11.1
Total	1,418	100.0	4,305	100.0
Total as % of GNP	4.3		4.7	

*Includes in 1976 capital grants of £85 million to public corporations.
Source: National Income and Expenditure, 1966–76, *HMSO, London.*

nature are likely to be spread unevenly over time and this is borne out by the figures. Housing accounts for the largest slice of spending.

A substantial amount of capital receipts comes from the current surplus and a smaller sum by way of capital grants from the central government, of which the bulk has been for road expenditures. Substantial amounts are met by borrowing either from the Government by way of the Public Works Loan Board, or by borrowing on the market. Market borrowing is normally by way of issue of bills, bonds or mortgages or the acceptance of short-term deposits. This market for local authority borrowing grew rapidly after 1955 when the Government ended the automatic access of authorities to the Public Works Loan Board.

In 1975–6 local authorities' net borrowing, i.e. borrowing less repayments, amounted to £2,119 million. The source of these funds is shown in Table 19.4. If we just take borrowing from the market, i.e. exclude the top line of Table 19.4, this amounted to £1,086 million for the year ending 31 March 1976. Of this sum financial institutions and banks provided the bulk. The source of local authority funds from the market changes considerably from year to year.

Table 19.4

	(£m.)	(%)
Net borrowing from central government	1,033	48.7
Other public sector	–6	–0.3
Banking	320	15.1
Other financial institutions	602	28.4
Industrial and commercial corporations	6	0.3
Personal sector	20	0.9
Overseas	–2	–
Bonds, other securities and unclassified	146	6.9
	2,119	100.0

Source: Financial Statistics, *no. 175, November 1976.*

The total debt of local authorities as at 31 March 1976 was some £30,000 million, made up as shown in Table 19.5. Local authorities' short-term borrowing (up to twelve months) is limited to 20 per cent of their total loan debt and must be no more than 15 per cent for loans at three months' notice or less. Table 19.5 shows that with over £2,000 million subject to seven days' notice or less, the collective influence of local authorities in this market is considerable. Although this debt is well below the limit, its management poses considerable problems for local authorities.

Table 19.5

Period to maturity	(£m.)	(%)
Up to 7 days	2,114	7.2
7 days to 3 months	899	3.1
3 to 12 months	943*	3.2
Over 12 months	25,599†	86.5
	29,555	100.0

The figures relate to long-term debt held at 31 March 1975.
*Temporary debt (repayable within twelve months) – includes £382 million of inter-authority borrowing.
†Includes £1,287 million for revenue balances and £236 million for internal advances.
Source: Financial Statistics, *no. 175, November 1976.*

The system of general grants

From 1943 to 1959 Exchequer equalisation grants were payable to county and county borough councils; other types of authority benefited indirectly. There were also a number of specific grants paid.

From 1959 to 1966 this system of Exchequer equalisation grants was changed to a rate-deficiency grant, payable to county and county borough councils, and to many county district and metropolitan borough councils. A limited number of specific grants continued. The grant was initially based on rateable value per head but was subsequently amended to assessing the product of a penny rate per head of population for the local area with the average product of a penny rate per head for England and Wales as a whole. Authorities below the average received the grant. In 1963–4, after the rating revaluations, four out of five local authorities qualified for the grant, reflecting the very skewed distribution of rateable values which are for the most part concentrated in the largest authorities and cities. In that year 222 of the poorer authorities had more than 50 per cent of their rate expenditure met by grants.

The present rate support grant structure came into effect in April 1967 and was modified in 1974. It comprises three parts: the domestic element, the resources element and the needs element. These three elements, together with specific grants and supplementary grants (which are paid in respect of transport services and national parks), are collectively known as the 'aggregate Exchequer grant'.

Payment of the rate support grant

Total grant aid to local authorities – other than specific grants towards mandatory student awards, rate rebates and housing subsidies – is calculated as a proportion of what is termed 'relevant expenditure', i.e. expenditure which is 'relevant' for grant-calculation purposes. Relevant expenditure is broadly equivalent to local authorities' rate-fund current expenditure net of sales, fees and charges. In England and Wales it includes rate-fund contributions to the housing revenue account, but in Scotland it excludes them.

In order that grant aid may be calculated for a following year, service by service, relevant expenditure forecasts for that year are made by joint working groups of officials from local authorities and from central government departments. Grant is thus fixed in November for the following year.

Relevant expenditure is determined annually and the calculation is made on a fixed-price basis (at November prices). However, in order to take account of changing circumstances in the actual year of grant, particularly pay and price variations, local authority associations and central government departments negotiate the impact of these expenditure adjustments. Section 4 of the Local Government Act of 1974 provides for the Secretary of State to vary the amount of rate support grant (RSG) paid to local authorities if their expenditure is likely to be increased substantially. This normally takes the form of an 'increase order'.

As mentioned above, grant aid is calculated as a proportion of relevant expenditure, and since the inception of the present RSG structure, the proportion of relevant expenditure payable as grant has gradually drifted upwards.

Table 19.6 shows the distribution of grant aid in England and Wales in 1976–7. From Table 19.6 it can be seen that 65.5 per cent of relevant expenditure in England and Wales was met by way of grant, of which the bulk came from the rate support grant. In Scotland the corresponding figures are grants accounting for 74 per cent, of which the rate support grant is 68.9 per cent.

In deciding whether to accept for grant the forecast of relevant expenditure for the grant year, the Government takes into account: (i) the latest

Table 19.6

Relevant expenditure and proportion paid as grant in England and Wales 1976–7 (£m. at November 1975 prices)

Total relevant expenditure	10,461	
of which Specific grant	643	6.2%
Supplementary grant	288	2.8%
Rate support grant	5,921	56.5%
		65.5%

Source: Local Government Finance *(1976), p. 211.*

information on relevant expenditure; (ii) the current level of prices, costs and remuneration, allowing for foreseeable changes; (iii) any fluctuation in the demand for the relevant services in the country as a whole; and (iv) the need for, and the ability to develop, the services in the light of the state of the economy.

The provision under (iv) gives Parliament a fairly tight control over local authorities. It has been used on various occasions to restrict expenditure ranking for grant to a figure of growth in real terms. Expenditures in excess of this have to be met by the authorities concerned out of their own resources.

Once the total amount of grant aid has been fixed, the 1974 Act requires the total amount of specific and supplementary grants to be deducted from the aggregate Exchequer grant to local authorities. The residual is the amount of rate support grant.

The arrangements for RSG distribution into its three elements, needs, resources and domestic, are the subject of consultation between representatives of local authority associations and officials of central government departments in the Grants Working Group. The Group presents a report recommending the criteria for distribution for the grant year in question to the Consultative Council on Local Government Finance, chaired by the Secretary of State for the Environment and attended by appropriate Ministers and officials from other government departments and by representatives of the local authority associations. Among the recommendations of the Grants Working Group is included the ratio which should apply between the amount of grant by way of needs and resources elements. This ratio has been held constant in recent years, with 67½ per cent going to needs and 32½ per cent to resources.

(1) The *needs element* aims to equalise the cost per head of providing a standard level of service in each authority. There is a basic payment per head of population, with weightings for such factors as the number of primary and secondary school pupils, persons of pensionable age, population decline and growth, people living in households lacking basic amenities and in shared households, and the number of dwellings started.

The method for distributing needs element between authorities in England and Wales is based on multiple regression analysis – a statistical technique which identifies and weights factors associated with variations in expenditure patterns between authorities and produces a formula which matches, as closely as possible, variations in expenditure. The rationale behind the approach is that the spending patterns of all local authorities in total provide the best indication of their need to spend.

(2) The *domestic element* is a straight subsidy to residential occupiers which amounted to 18.5p in the pound in England, and 36p in the pound in Wales, in 1975–6 and 1976–7. It amounts to a partial derating of domestic hereditaments, and since it is passed on to residential occupiers does not form a source of finance for local authorities. If an English council declared a rate of 80p in the pound, domestic ratepayers would be assessed on a rate of 61.5p in that year. In so far as this is a device to relieve the financially hard pressed it is particularly inefficient since the effect of this subsidy is, of course, to give greatest relief to the highest-rated houses, which will belong to the wealthier sections of the community.

It is also inequitable as between similar properties in different areas which are differently rated. Table 19.7 provides a simple example. Without a subsidy each property would have a £250 rate bill. With the subsidy directly reducing the rate in the pound, the high-rated property with a low rate in the pound benefits much more than the property with a low rateable value but a high rate in the pound.

Having pointed out these anomalies, the Layfield Committee might

Table 19.7

Rateable value	Rate in the £	Total rates without subsidy	Total rates with 16.5p in £ subsidy
500	50p	£250	£167.5
250	100p	£250	£208.75

have been expected to suggest changes. They merely, however, point out that the impact on commercial and industrial uses of rates has not been considered in the same way as with domestic households, and they recommend that this be done. The Green Paper on *Local Government Finance* (1977) proposes to introduce legislation so that ratepayers who lived in mixed commercial and domestic property (e.g. a shop with living accommodation above) who do not at present benefit from the domestic rate relief should do so in future. An absurd system is therefore to be further extended. It would be more equitable, as suggested by Ilersic (1969), to give the amount of the subsidy to authorities for an extension of the rate-rebate scheme.

(3) The *resources element*, in its present form, took over the role of the previous rate-deficiency grant. It is payable to all rating authorities whose rateable value per head is less than a 'national standard rateable value per head of population'. This standard, unlike the old, is higher than the average rateable value and for 1977–8 was £173 per head, and it is revised annually by the Secretary of State for the Environment. Over 90 per cent of rating authorities receive the grant.

Through the combined effect of the needs and resources elements, the objective is to enable individual authorities providing similar standards of service to levy similar rates in the pound whatever their spending needs and rateable resources. The Layfield Committee and the subsequent Green Paper suggest that compensation for relative needs and different rateable resources should be given by way of a 'unitary' grant. This is outlined in the next chapter.

Evaluation of the general grant

We have seen that general grants now account for the bulk of local authority current-account grants, a sum of £6,852 million being received in this form in 1976–7, compared with a sum of £931 million received by way of specific and supplementary grants.

The form of the general grant has been changed on a number of occasions and a brief account of the factors considered in making the grants was given. The appearance of formulae with elaborate weightings might give the impression that the system of general grant has now been refined to a point of near perfection. This appearance is deceptive. In particular, the technique used as the basis for distributing the largest portion of grant, the needs element, has been the subject of some considerable criticism in recent years. The multiple regression approach has been criticised on the grounds that (i) it is fundamentally at fault in assuming that actual expenditure patterns are representative of spending needs – the grant may be attracted to high-spending authorities regardless of whether need exists for the expenditure *vis-à-vis* other local authorities; (ii) it is unpredictable, since variations in expenditure patterns and indicators of need such as those described may lead to significant fluctuations in authorities' needs-element entitlements from year to year, fluctuations which almost certainly do not reflect changes in authorities' expenditure needs – the impact of year-to-year fluctuations has, however, in recent years been dampened by combining the results of one year's formula with that of previous years; and (iii) it is complex and not readily understood.

With these criticisms in mind, preliminary work is currently being pursued by local and central government officials to develop alternative methods of need assessment, such as a service-by-service approach and a unit-cost method.

Summary

Except in the financial field, local government was subjected to a major reorganisation in 1973–5.

Local authority expenditures have increased on current account from being 9.5 per cent of GNP in 1966 to 13.4 per cent in 1976. The increased spending which this represents has partly come from rates but a greater portion has come from grants. Therefore over this period the long-standing tendency for rates to form a smaller proportion of local revenue has continued.

Increasingly grants are being paid in a general rather than specific form, although it is difficult to judge the results of this on local autonomy since the Government uses a wide variety of other forms of control.

On capital account local authority activities have increased their share from 4.3 per cent of GNP in 1966 to a figure of 4.7 per cent in 1976. Housing activities, including net lending for house purchase, account for about 46 per cent of this capital outlay. Nearly 30 per cent of capital receipts come from a current-account surplus, the bulk of the remainder being borrowed from a wide variety of sources.

The total debt of local authorities approached £30,000 million in 1976, of which over £2,000 million was redeemable within seven days. The management of this debt presents considerable problems, as the interest cost had risen to 20 per cent of current-account expenditure in 1976.

Details of the rate support grant were given.

Note

1 The argument on cost grounds simply cannot be substantiated on the evidence of the Layfield Committee. Using 1975 figures, they estimated that the yield from rating agricultural lands and buildings would be £120 million and involve an initial cost of £10 to £15 million. Thereafter the cost would be between 5 and 10 per cent of the initial cost. If we take the worst case: 10 per cent of £15 million gives an annual cost of £1.5 million to collect revenue of £120 million. This compares favourably with the cost of collecting many present-day taxes.

20
Taxes, grants and equalisation

There are no statutory rules or other formal criteria for determining the total of grants. The amount is settled each year by the government following consultation with the local authorities. In the end this is an arbitrary choice. The ratio which grants bear to the yield of rating cannot be related to any objective principles of financing. It is no less than the position reached at any time by an annual series of highly subjective political judgements by successive governments, each reflecting the circumstances appearing to be relevant at the time they were made. In the past few years domestic rate poundages and likely increases in them have strongly influenced the government's decision. Each decision has also been influenced by the proportions of grant paid in the preceding year. The result has been that the cost of expanding local services has been substantially financed from national, not local, taxation.
Local Government Finance (May 1976), p. 210.

This chapter looks at some of the arguments for and against centralisation and some implications that follow for a mixed system. It then examines different types of fiscal arrangement and grant systems. Finally, it takes up the problems associated with equalisation.

The economic arguments for centralisation

The allocative, distributive and stabilisation objects of an economy can normally be more easily performed in a centralised economy. Problems of the co-ordination of different plans of different areas are not likely to be so acute. A highly decentralised society would find it extremely difficult to maintain high employment and stable prices since local areas are open economies and the multiplier effect of local action is likely to be quite small in the area initiating the action.

A serious problem in allocation is posed, as we have seen for so-called public or social goods. Again, a more centralised system is likely to succeed rather better than a decentralised one in providing the right output levels, since in the case of goods with external benefits these are likely to be underproduced as the local areas are concerned primarily with the welfare of its own inhabitants. In a like manner goods which impose external costs are likely to be overproduced since a local area will tend to disregard that part of costs which falls on non-inhabitants of its area. Most expenditures have externalities to some extent. Pollution of the air, rivers and coastline have lately received a good deal of publicity. Much of the work of pollution control is carried out by local authorities but the benefits of less pollution are widely spread. Failure of an upstream authority to purify its waste before putting it in a river imposes greater cost on downstream authorities. Similar types of consideration apply to expenditures on education, justice, health and transport where the costs and benefits spill over to other areas.

The economic arguments for decentralisation

At first sight a highly centralised system has many advantages over a fragmented one. The problems of allocation, distribution and stabilisation can be solved more easily at this level, and since the central government takes the whole country into account, the difficulties associated with externalities are reduced. Likewise, the problems of managing the economy are easier.

The basic drawback of a highly centralised system is its insensitivity to different preferences among its communities. Central provision is likely to be a compromise, based on the decision of the majority, which may nevertheless leave large numbers dissatisfied. For goods with few externalities present, that is where the benefits and costs are largely confined to a local area, effective local government is likely to see a greater diversity according more with local preferences and needs. For example, in the public provision of recreation facilities a centrally decided package per thousand of population would be less likely to fulfil the needs of each area as the same amount of money allocated to recreation facilities as decided by each local area.

This argument is sometimes taken further. Given communities with local autonomy, we are likely to see diversity in the provision of public goods, and in turn individuals will tend to move to a community which satisfies their preferences. Tiebout (1961) and others have generally held that the result of such a process would be an improvement in consumer choice. The individual adapts through moving, in contrast to the collective adoption of the local government area to the wishes of its inhabitants.[1]

Local variations may also increase innovation and efficiency. Local authorities in Britain have a substantial number of innovations to their credit. A far-sighted authority sees a need and tackles it and the process is adopted by others. It may be more efficient to deal with local matters on the spot than have to go through a central bureaucracy. A less tangible benefit is sometimes claimed – that a vigorous local government helps maintain an active interest in politics.

Central-local relations

The arguments which have just been briefly considered are reasons for preferring a system which lies at neither extreme but is counter-balanced with both a central and local structure. For an economic discussion of this issue in greater detail, see Oates (February 1968; and 1972).

There is one view that if adopted has considerable implications for the structure of each level of authority. There are those who argue that the central government should be confined to services whose benefits are felt by the whole nation, regional services provided for regionally and local services accounted for locally. Powerful support on these lines is provided by Musgrave and Musgrave (1973) and Oates (February 1968). While such a division may be of some use as a first approximation, it does not seem to be a useful criterion in actually allocating services. The Musgraves use the example of street-lighting as an example of a geographically limited benefit and therefore one that is ideally suited to local provision. The example seems particularly inept: the light is of course shed locally but its use benefits anyone in the locality – especially, it might be argued, the stranger trying to find his way – and there are good reasons why the lighting of trunk roads is financed centrally in this country, i.e. to ensure some uniformity and thereby help to reduce road accidents.

The static viewpoint, that services can be divided into those with local benefits and those which benefit everybody, is in today's complex urban communities of little relevance. Almost all services have repercussions for good or ill outside a local area. Geographical mobility of the population, the national and international interests of many companies and the increasing interdependence among people everywhere are the stubborn facts that vitiate a good deal of thinking about local provision. The strike of London dustmen imposes not only a nuisance on inhabitants of London but also a health hazard, since germs are no respecters of local boundaries, on the whole country. The box labelled 'services of purely local benefit' turns out to be empty. If this is so it raises the question to what extent it is justifiable to charge activities that local authorities undertake to local inhabitants? Or, to put the matter another way, to what extent do these services justify central grants?

One answer to this problem is to say that since the inhabitants of a country must live in a locality, then it is a simple case of 'gaining on the swings what is lost on the roundabouts'. In modern jargon, 'spill-outs balance spill-ins'. An inhabitant of, say, London will be paying for services that in part benefit people outside London, but in his turn he will benefit by payments made by 'outsiders'. There is a great deal to this contention, and if needs and resources between local areas ever become spread fairly evenly it would be possible, in principle, to rely on local sources of revenue for services run by a local area. However, this condition is not met, and given the fact that some localities are poorer than others, we would find serious underprovision of services in poorer localities if authorities had to rely on local finance. Some form of revenue pooling is needed.

If we consider the other extreme where the central government meets all local expenditures we run into the problem that local areas would have no constraint on keeping expenditures down. A local area may well choose to have a very high level of services – theatres, concert halls, swimming pools, large open spaces, and the like. Many of these services will be of most benefit to those living in the area with smallish externalities. Local autonomy means (at a minimum) that if this is the democratic choice of the community they should be allowed this level of services, but not completely out of the pockets of the general taxpayer.

To summarise, we find that because all services confer some benefit or detriment to a wider community, this does not by itself provide a sufficient reason not to have local taxation. Local taxation serves the purpose of limiting local expenditures. It has both a positive and a negative side. The positive side is that areas which want a high level of services can opt for them. The negative side is that too high a proportion of revenue which has to be met from local sources is likely to result in serious underprovision of resources in poor areas. If we arrange goods on a spectrum with those with few externalities on one side and those with large externalities on the other, we find that a local tax is needed so that goods with few externalities are not overproduced, and state support is needed so that goods with large externalities are not underproduced.

We thus reach an important conclusion that a mix of local and central finance is likely to result in a better community choice of services than either a purely local or a purely central system of finance.

There is no simple answer to the quantitative question of how much finance should come from each source. It depends on a number of factors, such as the extent of inequalities between regions, the form in which central finance is given and other factors which will be discussed.

The Layfield Committee gave considerable consideration to these matters and the majority proposed either a system of responsibilities which frankly recognised the need for strong central intervention – the centralist approach – or that positive steps should be taken to increase the freedom of local authorities to manage their own affairs – the localist approach. A minority of the Committee rejected this polarisation and suggested that the central government should set minimum standards which local authorities would be required to meet, leaving authorities free to provide higher standards if they wished. In the Green Paper the Government rejected all these approaches. It rejected the centralist and localist solutions quite firmly (Green Paper on the *Future Shape of Local Government Finance*, 1971, para. 2.8):

> The central/local relationship is changing all the time because national economic and social priorities can alter substantially even within quite short periods. Any formal definition of central and local responsibilities would lack the advantages of flexibility and rapidity of response to new circumstances. It would be likely to break down under pressure of events. The Government's view is, therefore, that while clarification of responsibilities wherever practicable is desirable, a fundamental redefinition is not necessary as a basis for solving the problems of local government finance. The disadvantages of both the centralist and localist approaches are clear, and the Government do not think there is a case for the adoption of either.

The Government sympathised with the minority view but saw it as too impractical since it would reduce the whole relationship between central and local government to a simply defined form of allocation of responsibilities. Rather they envisaged central–local relationships as a form of partnership, with the balance of responsibilities varying over time.

It will be seen in the next chapter that the minority's view of setting up minimum standards is similar to the suggestions made by the Royal Commission on the Constitution (1973) for regional finance. The latter differed in suggesting that there was no need to enforce standards so long as areas were provided with the means to maintain these standards, and they should be free to spend them as they wished. The Government's suggestion for a unitary grant to local authorities, which is outlined in this chapter, adopts this latter approach, although the extent to which the Government would allow a local authority to depart from national standards in an important service like education is subject to some doubt.

The implications of some central financing

We have just concluded that some mix of local and central finance is to be preferred to either a purely local or a purely central system. What are the implications of part provision from central sources? Effects can be broken down into: (i) the effect on central taxes and expenditures; and (ii) the effect on local taxes and expenditure. The most likely situation under (i) above is the case where central taxes are increased to provide for the subvention to local revenues with the level of central government activity undiminished. It is, however, possible that the central government, by making finance available to local authorities, may be inhibited from raising so much revenue on its own account, and hence has to resort either to debt financing or to cutting its expenditure on goods, services, and/or transfer payments.

Under (ii) above we have the possibility that central finance may form a substitute, or be a complement to, local revenue: if a substitute, the same level of local spending can take place but a bigger proportion will be financed from central sources; if a complement, then the level of local taxation can either be the same (with a higher level of services paid from central finance), or higher if central finance stimulates the level of services and therefore also the level of local taxation. In what follows it will be assumed that provision of revenue by the central government will not inhibit it from carrying out its own programmes and that local authorities will treat the revenue as a complement to their own resources. While these assumptions seem reasonable, the possibility of 'perverse' reactions should be borne in mind.

Types of fiscal arrangement

We deal briefly with the following: rigid separation of central and local sources of revenue; tax-sharing systems; and grants.

RIGID SEPARATION

The rigid separation of central and local sources of revenue is at first sight an attractive proposition. It is simple administratively and it would appear that if a correct division of tax sources is arrived at, maximum freedom is given to all levels of authority.

There are two major problems. One is that such a system lacks flexibility to meet changes in expenditure and revenue over time. If the spending requirements of one level of authority increase more rapidly than the tax base, then either the tax mix is likely to be distorted or expenditures will be curtailed. The second problem is that for most of the taxes that have been put forward for local use, the tax base is spread very unevenly between areas.

TAX-SHARING

In dealing with tax-sharing systems a word will first of all be said on administration of the tax. The mere thought of having two levels of authority taxing the same tax base with *both of them responsible for collecting their own share of revenue* is sufficient to convince most people of the impracticability of the idea. Not, however, all: Hildersley and Nottage (1968) envisage a local income tax being collected by local authorities on the basis of information supplied to them by the Inland Revenue! They say (1968, p. 27):

> The relationship between the Inland Revenue and the local authorities for the personal income tax would thus be essentially the same as for the local property occupation tax. In both cases the Revenue would determine the 'valuation' or 'assessment' and the local authorities would decide the rates of tax to be levied and would collect the sums due.

What is omitted is the essential difference: that the property tax is drawn on only by local authorities, whereas a local income tax would be drawing on a tax base already used by the central government. In what follows it will be assumed that there is no question of duplicate tax-collecting machinery being allowed. If taxes are to be shared in some way, then in principle any level of authority can act as agent for the collection of the tax and so avoid the fatuous duplication in administration. Freedom does not reside in the accident of which body happens to collect the revenue; it is in fact quite possible to imagine the whole of revenue-gathering being farmed out to a public body responsible jointly to central and local governments (or even a return to the days when tax collecting was farmed out to private enterprise). In neither case would this confer power on the tax-collecting body – a mere agent for the transmission of the revenues to the appropriate government body or bodies.

Various types of tax-sharing are possible: for example a split in some proportion; areas free to vary rates; and a tax-credit system.

Tax split

The total proceeds of a tax split are, let us say, split 50/50 between central and local areas, with taxes allocated to areas according to the income produced in that area. There is much to be said against such a system. Besides being complicated to administer, it would tend to perpetuate existing inequalities between regions. Alternatively, the tax share of local areas could be allocated by some formula taking needs and costs into account. This would be similar to a general grant from the central government. With either type of sharing the setting of the tax rate by central government would cause local fluctuations in revenue. Alternatively, mutual consultation on the rate of the tax would be possible.

Freedom to vary rates

Local areas are given freedom to levy their own rates, which are combined with the rate of the central government and collected by the appropriate authority and shared out accordingly.

The result of local areas having different tax rates may be the creation of a 'tax jungle' or the competitive erosion of the tax base. The dangers of not having co-operation has been called a 'tax jungle'. It refers to a situation where an individual or corporation is faced with very high taxes – cases of over 100 per cent of taxable income are not unknown. This can arise where a person has residences in several areas, or is resident in one area and works in another, or a company operates in several areas. If the areas operate different taxes, or both tax the same base with no regard to the taxpayers' other commitments, such inequities can occur. It is not enough to set up a local tax system and leave it at that. Machinery for co-ordination and periodic review are needed.

More common is competitive erosion of the tax base. Some areas, if they have freedom to levy taxes, may, for example, seek to attract industry by giving tax concessions to firms – the end-result can be a situation where local revenues are seriously depleted because each area feels forced to match the concessions given by others, and, of course, the end-result fails in its original purpose of redirecting industry. Areas may compete also, in a negative sense of not putting up taxes, for fear of driving industry or people out of their areas. The result, if local areas are relying on local sources for the bulk of their revenue, can be a severe limitation on their ability to finance services they consider necessary. Variation in local tax rates may well be desirable, and if this is so, it points out the necessity of some permanent form of co-ordinating machinery. Local authorities, because of these difficulties, may find that their interests are better served if in fact they levy a common rate, with this to be decided by consultation amongst themselves. Under this type of tax arrangement it has to be faced that there may be a conflict in policy, with, for example, the central government reducing rates and the local authorities increasing theirs. If these differential changes take place in response to different expenditure trends between the two levels of government, no harm is done, but if the central government is reducing its share of the tax for demand-management purposes, the conflict is a real one.

There are, moreover, similar problems with this type of tax-sharing to those outlined under the section on 'tax split' and equalisation would probably be necessary between areas with both methods.

Tax-credit system

It is possible for the central government to allow a tax credit, or tax deduction, for a locally paid tax against a centrally paid tax. Although systems of this kind are not uncommon in federal systems, they pose considerable administrative complications and problems in equity and stabilisation. If the tax credit covers the whole of the tax paid locally, then there is little incentive for economy at the lower level. The tax credit benefits wealthier regions the most and equalisation will probably be called for. This drawback could be an advantage if the tax credit were confined to development areas where it could boost the resources of those regions, but this implies that a development area and the tax area coincide. If local areas confine their tax to the amount of tax offset by the central government, and there would presumably be strong pressure from the electorate for them to do so, then the tax credit would do little to boost the resources of the localities. It is usually possible to achieve the same ends more simply under the 'tax split' or 'freedom to vary rates' schemes.

GRANTS

There is first of all a basic distinction between conditional and unconditional grants. The former type of grant is payable for the performance of specified things, while unconditional grants may be used for any legal purpose by the recipient. Grants can take on a variety of forms:

1 Grants that cover the whole cost, or almost all of the cost, of provision of a service.
2 Grants that match the revenue contributions of each area.

3 Grants that aim to compensate for differences in fiscal capacity of each area.
4 Grants, on the lines of 2 above, which, in addition, allow for differences in cost of services in each area.
5 Grants that cover the whole cost or almost all of the cost of provision of a public service are sometimes used to encourage authorities to undertake or extend the provision of a particular service. Later, the grant may be merged in a general grant.

General matching grants that mirror the total local revenue contributions of each area have little to be said in their favour. They ensure the perpetuation of inequalities between regions. In this context they do, however, serve the purpose of pointing out that equalisation grants, in whatever form they take, will not be equitable between regions if local efforts to tax their own resources are not allowed for.

The current type of general grant, with its needs, resources and domestic elements, was outlined in the previous chapter. It is the kind of grant which is most likely to preserve the freedom of local authorities to act on their own behalf, although such a judgment is conditional on the fairness of the underlying formula on which the grant is made.

A specific grant for a particular service may cover the whole cost of the service, or it may require revenue matching by the locality. This usually takes the form of the State meeting 75 per cent, or some other proportion of the total cost, with the locality meeting the rest. The latter may be required to provide the service, or it may be voluntary; in the latter case the higher the level of grant, the more likely is the widespread adoption of the service. Variations on straight percentage grants are possible whereby, for example, the State meets the whole of the cost of basic provision of the service and matches expenditure on the service over and above this by a matching grant of, say, 50 per cent.

Specific grants are an obvious way, but by no means obviously the best way, for a central government to stimulate the introduction of a particular service. Given a service with strong external benefits, a high specific grant is likely to see most areas adopt the service. The same aim could be achieved by requiring each area to provide some minimum level of the service and adjusting the unconditional grant upward to assist them to do so. There is probably some administrative gain to be had by keeping the number of specific grants to a minimum. This is likely to involve fewer central government departments in the financial arrangements of local areas and so cut down the amount of detail that needs to pass between them. Against this likely administrative gain must be set the element of compulsion if the alternative of requiring some minimum standard of service is adopted.

Equalisation

It is difficult to better the definition of the purpose of equalisation that is given in the Royal Commission on the Constitution's *Research Paper 9* (1973a): 'Given that an objective of decentralisation is to permit diversity in public services, the objective of an equalisation grant is to eliminate relative poverty as a determinant of diversity.'

EQUALISATION PROBLEMS

It is known that local areas do have unequal resources in Great Britain, and in this section we take up some of the problems associated with attempts to equalise. Not only must the type of taxes and grants be decided on but some measure of local tax effort may be required and some measure of the costs of services in each area. These are contentious matters.

In this country tax effort has received little attention. We mean by 'tax effort' the extent to which a local area makes use of its potential fiscal capacity. Local authorities have rateable value of premises as their only major source of independent revenue. It was extremely difficult to measure local tax effort in the days when each authority assessed its own areas. With the coming of greater uniformity in valuation of premises, the level of rates in the £, in principle, provide a measure of tax effort. In practice, a number of complicated adjustments would have to be made before conclusions could be drawn. For example, the measure of derating afforded to agriculture, and the fact that different types of property are valued in different ways, means that different compositions of these assets in local areas would have to be allowed for. It is also the case that there are still differences in valuation in different areas of the country.

If local areas are to have a substantial addition to sources of finance under their own control, then, in the absence of uniform rates (agreed amongst themselves), the problems of measuring tax effort takes on more importance. A local area should not receive a higher government grant merely by virtue of the fact that it taxes less than other local areas.

Uniform local rates of tax on a uniform tax base overcome the problem of tax effort by curtailing the right of local areas to change rates unilaterally. Against this must be set the advantage that the act of forcing local areas to get together amongst themselves, and presumably presenting a common case to the Government on tax changes, might do much to foster the interests of local areas.

A THEORETICAL MEASURE OF TAX EFFORT

The aim in measuring tax effort is twofold: to ensure, on the one hand, that as far as possible areas should not be penalised because they are poorer than others; and, on the other hand, that areas that choose a high level of services and a high level of local tax should not receive extra subsidies as a result. Let us consider the introduction of a local income tax collected by the Inland Revenue in which areas are free to vary rates, at least within limits.

Neither the level of tax rates, nor the yield from the tax per head, provides a good measure of tax effort. High tax rates could be the result of a very poor area having to set high rates in order to provide the bare minimum of services. On the other hand, it may be a reflection of local interests – collectively the citizens of that particular area prefer to pay more in taxes and receive more in benefit. Alternatively, low taxes may reflect an average level of services and a favourable tax base, i.e. a large number of wealthy citizens.

One obvious method is to make an adjustment for differences in local tax capacity – in the case in point an adjustment to take account of local differences in income. We will work in terms of indices and can express the national average personal income per head as 100. The index for local areas will be above or below the national average in proportion as the average income of their citizens are above or below the national average. In Figure 20.1 this information is plotted on the horizontal axis. On the vertical axis the actual tax revenue per head is plotted. Once again the national average is expressed as 100 and local areas arranged around this. The distance above or below the 45° line in a vertical direction indicates the degree to which an area is making a higher or lower tax effort than average. The position of area *A* has been plotted, and has been found to have an average income per head which is 80 per cent of the national average. If area *A* is at position (1), where receipts are also 80 per cent of the national average, then the area is making an average tax effort. It should receive an equalisation grant to supplement its below-average tax base. At position (3) less than average tax effort is being made – citizens of area *A* may have decided on less local tax and a lower level of local services, in which case its equalisation grant should not compensate for the fact that the area chooses to tax itself less but only for its taxable capacity being below the average. When we come to position (2) we can say that a higher than average tax effort is being made. It has then to be decided whether this is due to the choice of the area to have a higher level of services (in which case no equalisation is called for on these grounds), or whether it is due to increased costs of providing services in that region (in which case equalisation is called for). We have, of course, adjusted for differences in fiscal capacity in the diagram. Local tax rates will differ between areas, therefore, but these differences will reflect differences in taxable capacity.

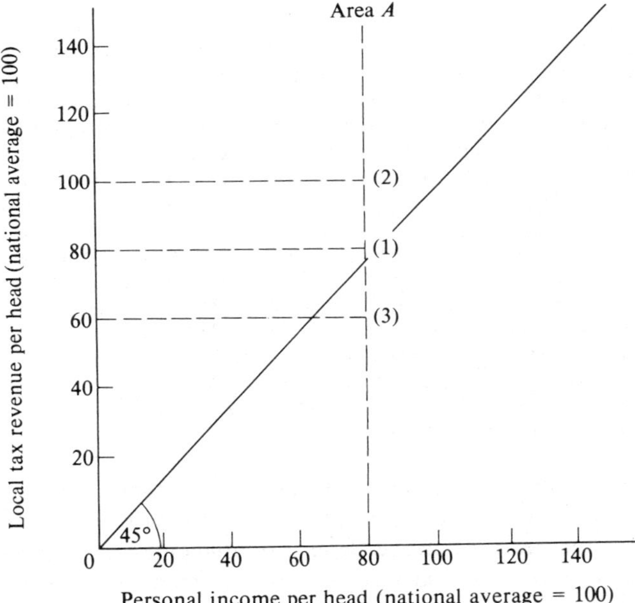

Figure 20.1

The above analysis traced out some important elements that need to be separated if tax effort is to be measured by the spread of personal income.

If local areas are free to levy more than one tax, then tax effort on the above lines could still be worked out, but it would be more complicated to do so. Also, if there are considerable differences in the distribution of income between areas, this would need to be taken into account, since the same average income in two areas could yield different sums from the same tax rate due to this difference in distribution. Figure 20.1 is adapted from Lynn (1964), in which an extensive discussion of this question can be found in relation to the Canadian situation.

The Layfield Committee suggest that the resources element of the rate support grant should be based, not on domestic rateable value as at present, but on aggregate personal income. The reason given for this is the known discrepancies in the valuation of similar houses in different parts of the country.

The Green Paper on the *Future Shape of Local Government Finance* (1971, para. 3.22) rejects this proposal in firm terms:

> There are strong objections to this proposal. Domestic rate bills would become an amalgam of two different bases of taxation; the logic of the system would be difficult to understand and to justify. It would be complex to administer and involve the collection of data on personal incomes for each local authority area. Ratepayers would find it more difficult to see the link between their authority's level of expenditure and its rate poundage. Nor could they see how the rate poundage compared with that of other authorities. Moreover, because only the aggregate of personal incomes in each authority would be taken into account, the effect would be to increase the rate burdens of people with below average incomes living in areas where aggregate income was above the average. It would also reduce the rate burden of people with above average incomes living in areas where aggregate income was below the average. More than a third of all ratepayers might be affected in one or other of these ways; both effects would be contrary to the Committee's concept of taking account of the personal incomes of domestic ratepayers. The Government do not therefore propose to pursue this recommendation.

The proposals to adopt capital valuation of domestic property should result in a more even valuation throughout the country and so reduce this problem. However, there is still a clear difference of opinion, with the Layfield Committee wishing to measure equity, or tax effort, in terms of income, and the Government setting up equity in terms of equal rate poundages for a comparable level of service wherever a person lives. Income is the more usual measure but there would be considerable work involved in getting information on local incomes and their distribution.

Types of equalisation

Equalisation can be considered in terms of equalisation between the groups of citizens comprising the various areas, or in terms of equalisation between citizens irrespective of which local area they happen to live in. (For a full discussion of these issues, see Musgrave (1961).) The choice between them is essentially a political one.

EQUALISATION BETWEEN GROUPS

Equalisation between the groups of citizens comprising the various areas may be based on (1) equalisation of fiscal performance; (2) equalisation of fiscal capacity; or (3) equalisation of fiscal potential. (See Royal Commission on the Constitution, *Research Paper 10* (1973b) on which this section draws.) The differences between these measures can be brought out by a simple example in which we ignore differences in costs and needs between different areas. Let us suppose there are three areas, *A*, *B* and *C*, with *A* the richest and *C* the poorest authority. The yield per head from their respective local tax is given in Table 20.1. For example, area *A* has £60 per head from a tax of 8 per cent, £75 from a rate of 10 per cent and £90 from a rate of 12 per cent.

Table 20.1

Revenue (£ per head) and grants or payments after different equalisation schemes

Tax	Area *A*				Area *B*				Area *C*			
rate (%)	Yield	(1)	(2)	(3)	Yield	(1)	(2)	(3)	Yield	(1)	(2)	(3)
8	60	–	(–15)	(–10)	50	–	(0)	(0)	36	–	(18)	(14)
10	75	(–15)	(–15)	(–15)	60	(0)	(0)	(0)	42	(18)	(18)	(18)
12	90	(–30)	(–15)	(–20)	70	(0)	(0)	(0)	48	(12)	(18)	(22)

(1) Under *equalisation of fiscal performance* the State aims to have equal amounts per head spent in each area and redistributes taxes from authorities whose tax yield exceeds the average to authorities whose tax yield falls short of the average. In order to get the authorities to apply local taxes, a minimum rate will have to be specified. Let us suppose the middle rate of 10 per cent and a desired expenditure of £60 per head: the figures in parentheses under heading (1) give the amount of grant, or if negative the amount of revenue the State collects. No area will in fact apply a rate in excess of 10 per cent since this will result in a direct loss of grant or payment to the State. Thus at the rate of 10 per cent *A* pays £15 per head and *C* receives £18 per head. Here, as stated at the beginning of this chapter, no question of tax effort arises since uniform rates are applied and yields equalised by the grant system.

(2) *Equalisation of fiscal capacity* is based on some decision on expenditure per head and level of tax which is common to all areas. If that level of tax applied to a local area fails to bring in the average revenue the area receives a grant, if more it pays the difference to the State. Local areas are free to tax as they wish, the amount of grant or state payment they have

to make being, however, based on the standard rate of tax. If we again suppose the standard rate of tax to be 10 per cent and average yield £60 per head, we get the figures under (2) in the table. Looking across the table we find that a tax of 10 per cent yields £75 per head for *A* so it pays £15; *B*'s yield is average and so is not affected, and *C* receives £18 per head since its yield is £18 below the average. These grants or payments are the same whatever rates the area chooses to apply. Again no tax-effort problem arises.

(3) With *equalisation of fiscal potential* an area pays a tax or receives a subsidy equal to the difference between the yield obtained by applying its tax rate to the average tax base. Selecting area *B* as average as before, we get the figures under (3) in the table. Since *B* is average, the amount of grant or payment by the other areas is just sufficient to ensure that the net yield (i.e. yield less tax payment or plus the subsidy) from their taxes equals the yield from *B*'s taxes. In terms of tax effort this case is more difficult to judge. The grant or payment made varies with the rate of tax levied and depends on the difference between yields in the area concerned and the average area. A very rich area would find most of its increased revenue from higher taxes payable to the central government, whereas a very poor area, by subjecting itself to rather higher local tax, would find itself in receipt of large grants. In between these extremes lies the whole range of possibilities.

Equalisation of type (1) is unlikely in practice. In effect the local area has no discretion over its rate of tax.

With type (2) equalisation the grant is invariant with respect to the local tax rate, so that if areas tax at the same rate they have the same resources. However, different marginal tax effort is required if areas wish to raise additional finance. Thus the poor area *C*, by taxing at 10 per cent, has £60 per head (£42 tax and £18 grant); to raise £6 of additional revenue per head it would have to raise its tax rate to 12 per cent (£48 tax and the same £18 grant = £66), whereas for the same tax effort of 12 per cent area *A* has £75 (£90 tax less payment of £15).

With type (3) equalisation any areas with the same tax get the same net revenue, and the grant or payment to the central government is proportional to the tax rate. Thus in the case considered in the last paragraph, area *C*, by taxing itself more than average, would receive a bigger grant.

The above illustration has assumed equalisation in terms of the average, which involves redistribution from those above the average. It is possible to envisage levelling up to the wealthiest area, which would only entail redistribution from the State to localities. On grounds of cost to the central government averaging seems the most likely.

The example ignored, or assumed the similarity of, the costs and needs of local areas. In practice, both are likely to vary, and for many years grants to local authorities have attempted in rough and ready fashion to take some account of the most important differences by weighting according to proportion of children and old people, dispersion of the population, etc. To take account of these factors would complicate the example above but add nothing new, so we do not develop this point here. Similarly, we do not develop the example to include more than one tax being available to a local authority.

A UNITARY GRANT

The previous chapter outlined the present system of rate support grant. This aims to equalise between groups of citizens living in different areas but differs from the models just set out in not redistributing revenue from areas with above-average taxable capacity.

The aim of the rate support grant is to enable each local authority to meet its assessed spending needs by levying the same rate poundage. To achieve this it uses the needs element to equalise spending needs per head and the resources element to equalise resources per head. If all authorities' needs and resources were the same, then they could levy the same rate poundage to meet their assessed spending needs. It therefore approaches the equalisation of fiscal capacity model that has just been set out, except that authorities with above-average resources are not required to redistribute revenue to below-average authorities.

The Layfield Committee and the subsequent Green Paper on the *Future Shape of Local Government Finance* (1977) point out the disadvantages of this two-part system and give consideration to bringing in a unitary grant. One disadvantage that we have just noted is that no redistribution from better-off authorities is incorporated in the two-part system and to bring the resources of all authorities up to the level of the richest would mean that grants would have to meet nearly all of local government expenditure.

Under a unitary-grant system compensation for differences in relative needs and rateable resources would still be given but by one grant element. The basic grant would be the difference between the cost to an authority of providing a standard level of service and the revenue it would raise from a standard rate poundage. This is akin to the equalisation of fiscal capacity model with redistribution since above-average authorities would receive a smaller grant by virtue of their higher revenue from a standard rate poundage.

A unitary-grant system means, as the Green Paper points out, that two sets of figures are crucial: the assessment of the cost to each authority of providing a comparable over-all level of services;[2] and the corresponding standard rate poundages. Authorities would be free to spend more or less than the guide-lines provided by the standard level of service, but it is envisaged that additional expenditures would fall more heavily on the local ratepayer than the national taxpayer.

It is clear from the Green Paper that the Government favours a unitary grant and that local authority associations do not. The Government sees the advantages as follows. The grant would be distributed to each county and district council directly, and the standard rate poundage at which an authority could finance its spending on a basis comparable with other similar authorities would be published. This would provide the ratepayer with a guide to judge his authority. If he was paying more than the standard rate, was he getting better services or was his authority less efficient? If he was paying less than the standard rate, was his authority more efficient or was he getting inferior services? It is this aspect that the local authorities fear would threaten the independence of local government. They argue that the inadequacies of the needs assessment system would lead to unfair criticisms of those authorities who do not follow the expenditure guide-lines.

EQUALISATION BETWEEN PERSONS

So far in this chapter we have been relating equalisation to groups of citizens who live in a particular area. The philosophy behind this is that citizens of each area should collectively be placed in more or less equal positions. In the example used income was averaged for this purpose. But two areas may have the same average income but very different income patterns in each community, and the same point can be made whatever tax base is used for the comparison. There is a different idea of equalisation which relates to individuals rather than to areas (for discussion of this issue, see Musgrave (1961) and Buchanan (September 1950). Musgrave (1961, pp. 116–17) says:

> Here, the idea is that the central fisc should neutralize the individual citizen of the federation against the fiscal operations of the particular state in which he resides. This requires direct transactions between the central fisc and the individual citizens of the federation. For this reason it seems more centralist in spirit, but this need not render it necessarily inferior or superior.

If we start from the premise that local areas should be free to opt for better local services out of higher local taxes, then equalisation between persons does not involve equalising the proportion of income taken in tax from persons with the same income. Equalisation requires that persons with the same income pay the same for *the same services* regardless of where they live, and it implies that citizens of local areas that opt for more or better local expenditure will pay a higher proportion of tax than corresponding income groups in other areas that have not so opted. Buchanan (September 1950, pp. 122–9) develops this idea in terms of 'fiscal residuum'. This refers to an individual's total taxes paid, less total benefits received out of that taxation, so the residuum can be negative, meaning a net tax has been paid, or positive, meaning a net benefit has been received, or zero, meaning tax and benefits balance. Buchanan formulates equality in terms of equalising marginal benefits received from government services with marginal taxes paid. In Buchanan's words (September 1950, p. 105), these and 'many other more technical problems make a precise application of the equity principle in the real world extremely difficult, but should not serve to prevent its use as a proximate standard for intergovernmental fiscal policy'.

A considerable amount of work has been done on a national scale in allocating taxes and benefits (see 'Incidence of Taxes and Social Service Benefits', 1976). A number of arbitrary assumptions have to be made about tax and benefit incidence and about how to allocate, or whether to leave out, certain social benefits such as defence expenditures. It is difficult to see this exercise being precise enough to make equalisation between persons for purposes of local taxation anything more than an arbitrary exercise. Professor Buchanan does not explain how a principle difficult to apply can be used as a standard, and it would seem that at the present time equalisation between groups in different areas is the only practical system.

LOCAL EQUALISATION

The equalisation schemes discussed above involve payment to the Government by areas with above-average resources of money and this payment is allocated in a number of possible ways to authorities with below-average resources, or, alternatively, under a unitary-grant system, a smaller grant to richer authorities. It is possible to devise equalisation schemes which local areas operate between themselves.

In this country the only scheme of general local equalisation operates in London, which has had a scheme in some form or another for over 100 years.

LONDON EQUALISATION SCHEME

The present system operates under the Greater London Equalisation Scheme 1968. In 1973–4 the extremes were Westminster making a net contribution of 3.3p of rate poundage, and Lewisham having net receipts equivalent to 6.8p of rate poundage. In London the Greater London Council precepts upon the City and other London boroughs and the transfer of resources resulting from the equalisation scheme is made through this precept. The scheme of equalisation is set out in a White Paper entitled *Greater London Rate Equalisation Scheme* (1968) and in IMTA (1968). The final paragraph of the White Paper indicates that the scheme is somewhat complicated: 'If the Minister is satisfied that an error has been made which is serious enough to warrant a recalculation of all or any of the credits and debts notified to the Greater London Council under paragraph 14 above, he may notify the Council of the revised amounts.'

The scheme, which is based upon the work of Professor A. R. Ilersic, divides London into inner and outer boroughs. Inner boroughs are the City of London and the boroughs of Camden, Greenwich, Hackney, Hammersmith, Islington, Kensington and Chelsea, Lambeth, Lewisham, Southwark, Tower Hamlets, Wandsworth and Westminster. The remaining twenty boroughs form the outer group.

Equalisation proceeds by creating a pool of revenue based upon the boroughs' ability to contribute. The pool is then distributed amongst them by reference to their needs.

Contributions to the pool are calculated for each borough and the City by adding together the aggregated rateable values of all non-domestic hereditaments in the borough and the aggregated rateable values of all domestic hereditaments which have a rateable value of more than £200. From this total is deducted the aggregated rateable values of all domestic hereditaments with a rateable value below £100 for inner boroughs and below £56 for outer boroughs. This gives the base for the tax and the yield of a 10p rate provides the revenue pool.

The pool is first divided to form an inner-borough pool and an outer-borough pool. This division is made on the basis of the total rate revenues in each group, i.e. in accordance with expenditures in each group. Each pool is then divided between its respective boroughs in the same way, so that in what follows we shall merely talk about the division of the pool, when in fact the calculation is being performed twice, once for the inner boroughs and once for the outer boroughs.

The pool is further subdivided into a housing pool and a general expenditure pool. The housing pool is calculated by taking the aggregated housing expenditures as a proportion of total expenditure. The housing pool is then divided between the boroughs on the proportion which the housing costs of each borough bears to the total housing costs of the group. Housing costs are defined as the difference between housing loan charges less the appropriate Exchequer housing subsidy received by each borough.

The balance of the pool after the housing pool has been subtracted is then divided amongst the boroughs on the basis of the need element of the rate support grant adjusted to give additional weight to children under 5, to children under 15 and to persons over 65.

The effect of the equalisation is first to distribute some resources from the inner to the outer boroughs, and second to make a bigger transfer between the inner boroughs themselves.

WIDER EQUALISATION SCHEMES

The conurbation of London is unique because of its size and probably also because of the disparity between the rateable resources of Westminster and the City and some of the poorer boroughs. But disparities in other conurbations and local areas are known to be far from negligible. There seems nothing in principle to stand in the way of applying equalisation to other areas. In practice, it may be more feasible for the central government to even out differences by judicious allocation of its grants.

POOLING

A limited amount of equalisation takes place at the moment by adjustment to the amount of rate support grant payable to an authority. Pooling takes place for teacher-training, advanced further education and pupils who are outside the responsibility of the local education authority. All authorities will benefit by teacher-training but not all authorities will need to set up training facilities. Costs for these services are therefore pooled and apportioned to all authorities on a formula basis.

Summary

Some of the arguments for and against centralisation have been detailed and the implications that follow for a system where part of the finance comes out of central resources and part is raised locally were examined.

Alternative types of fiscal arrangement were given: the separation of central and local sources, tax-sharing systems and grants. The dangers of a tax jungle and the competitive erosion of the tax base were explained.

The problems associated with equalisation were looked at and the meaning of tax effort was detailed and the various types of equalisation that can be attempted were outlined. Finally, details were given of the London equalisation scheme and the details of pooling that takes place for certain services.

Notes

1 There is some doubt as to how far the tendencies listed should be encouraged. If left to themselves the rich would tend to cluster with the rich, and exclude the poor who might become a public burden to them. Similar ghettos built on religion, colour and age would not be unlikely. The result could well be a highly dangerous increase in tension and violence between these self-separated groups. The contrast of a balanced community composed of rich and poor, religious and agnostics, in short a heterogeneous community having a richness of diversity, can itself be held to be a public good.

2 On this crucial issue the Green Paper says: 'The Government will, therefore, as a matter of urgency, explore alternative methods with the local authority associations.' The suggestions made vary from 'common-sense [agreement] about the main factors which determine spending needs' to identifying the main client groups (e.g. schoolchildren, old people) and the national average expenditure per person within each group. Finally, a longer-term approach is mentioned based on detailed analysis of the composition of expenditure on each of a large number of individual operations which go to make up each main service.

21
Local and regional sources of finance

Our general evidence on the other hand, contained very little on finance, reflecting perhaps the difficulties of the subject.
Royal Commission on the Constitution (1973), vol. 1, para. 571.

This chapter examines the need for independent sources of revenue and looks at some of the taxes that are suitable for local and regional use. Finally, it looks at the possible reform of rates. It starts with a recapitulation of the way reorganisation has been carried out, since this has influenced the actual decisions taken.

Reorganisation

The Royal Commission on Local Government in England and Wales (1969) and that for Scotland (1969) were excluded by their terms of reference from considering finance. The subsequent reorganisation of local government in England and Wales departed from the recommendations of the Royal Commissions in not adopting a single-tier structure. Only after vociferous complaints about rates in 1974 was the Layfield Committee on *Local Government Finance* set up. In the midst of this, the most far-reaching changes in the Constitution – devolution to at least some parts of the United Kingdom – was being actively debated in Parliament following the report by the Royal Commission on the Constitution (1973). It is not too strong to say that the mess resulting from this piecemeal approach will be with us for many years.

The Layfield Committee had these rather strong words to say on the subject (*Local Government Finance*, May 1976, pp. 81–2):

We refer in Chapter 2 to the complications arising from the new local government structure containing a variety of two-tier organisations – in the non-metropolitan and metropolitan areas, and in Greater London – with very different distributions of functions and powers. We are bound to say that the heterogeneity of the structure present serious obstacles to any rationalisation of the financial system, and not least to the design of financing arrangements suitable for a situation in which there would be more local responsibility. We have already said that we do not regard our terms of reference as extending to a reconsideration of the structure only recently enacted. If, however, a decision should be taken to recast the financial system to provide greater responsibility, and opportunities should arise for making some changes in the organisation structure which are consonant with responsible local government while easing the introduction of the new financial arrangements, we hope that they would be taken.

Proposals for devolution also clearly impinge on the structure and finance of local government. It is generally true that any tax suitable for local government is also suitable for regional use. This is examined after the need for an independent source of revenue is looked at in the context of local government finance. The same arguments apply in the context of regional finance.

The need for independent local authority revenue?

It is frequently asserted that greater freedom for local government depends on greater independent local revenue, for example the Green Paper on the *Future Shape of Local Government Finance* (1971):

There is a distinction between giving local authorities a share in the proceeds of a central tax as opposed to making them free to fix their own tax rates for their areas. The former is in effect a government grant. It is the latter which adds to local discretion.

More dogmatically Mr Miller, writing on the same subject in the *Local Government Finance Journal* (September 1971) says: 'Retention of a status quo which relies on a continuing and accelerating dependence on central funds is an erosion of local democracy and accountability.' Again Maynard and King (1972): 'The essential lesson, nevertheless, is that local government cannot exercise power if its funds come from the centre.'[1] The Layfield Committee say (*Local Government Finance*, May 1976, p. 79):

A larger local tax base is in our view, an essential first step to increasing local responsibility. But it cannot in itself secure that result. Among other measures needed are: more explicit treatment of local government

> expenditure in the Public Expenditure Survey and greater participation by local government in that exercise; greater certainty over several years in the levels of grant for individual authorities; more stability in grant distribution; and a better integrated time-table for grant determination and local budgeting. . . . Perhaps most important is the need for an effective institution which would among other things keep under review the way in which legislative, administrative and other developments were affecting the balance of power between the government and local authorities.

Underlying many of the above arguments is the assertion that the central government follows up more assiduously by formal or informal means funds distributed from the centre, and that such funds encourage the use of controls generally. It is hard to ascertain what truth there is in this assertion. The Government, by means of the audit, has always been concerned to see that monies are spent in an authorised manner, whether the funds are provided locally or centrally, and this is unlikely to change. The stabilisation objectives of the Government are also likely to ensure that whatever the source of funds the centre will always have a keen interest in both the total of local expenditure and the areas in which the money is to be spent.

Although these views are frequently expressed, it seems the need for greater independent local revenue is far from proven and one that if granted could well disappoint the expectations of its supporters. The feelings of a recent conference on local government were summarised as follows (*Proceedings of a Conference on Local Government Finance*, 1973):

> On the first issue, that of the relationship between local government autonomy and finance, the feeling of the conference was that the two were not closely connected. The argument was that the central government had many instruments at its disposal, both formal and informal, which would enable it to control the activities of the local authorities, whether or not it could operate any financial sanctions. Whether any of these powers were, in fact, used was a matter for political decision. Speakers noted that national policy objectives, such as the management of the economy, or equity in the provision of certain types of services, would in any case require some central control of local authority activities. If the central government wished to exert control it could do so without needing to resort to financial sanctions, and thus it was felt that the source of local finance was not a major determinant of local government autonomy.

Similar conclusions were reached by the Royal Commission on the Constitution (1973, para. 662):

> There seems to be no real connection between the degree of freedom in expenditure exercised by an individual authority and the proportion of its incomes which is derived from independent local revenues. Though on average the proportion of local authority income derived from rates is 40 per cent . . . among individual authorities the range extends from 10 per cent to 60 per cent, and there is no reason to believe that authorities near the top of the scale act in a more independent way than those lower down.

The strong possibility of some form of regional devolution makes the case for greater independent local authority revenue sources even weaker. Not surprisingly the majority report of the Royal Commission on the Constitution gives a rather negative view of providing local authorities with greater tax sources, since any likely taxes in their view should be given to the regions. The views of the minority are stronger (Royal Commission on the Constitution, 1973, para. 269):

> Subordinate public authorities in the area of such intermediate level government – i.e. local authorities and all those concerned with the provision of public services (except the nationalised industries) – will derive their income from their own revenues (e.g. rates) and from the intermediate level government which, as far as the local authorities are concerned, will distribute money along the lines of the present rate support grant system. These subordinate bodies will have no direct financial dealings with the United Kingdom Government.

It was argued in the previous chapter that some degree of local taxation is needed so that goods which have few externalities outside the area are not overproduced and some state support is needed so that goods with large externalities are not underproduced. As the previous quotations imply, the proportion each party bears can vary within wide limits without, it seems, making a great deal of difference to local behaviour.

If the conclusions reached above are valid, it would appear that they also apply to regional government. Although present proposals for devolution are far from settled, it looks as if only very limited financial powers, if any, will be given at the outset to regions. It seems inconsistent and dangerous (see Tait, 1975; and Heald, November 1975) for the Government to say that local authorities need an independent source of revenue as one of the prerequisites of preserving local freedom and at the same time say that regional governments have no such need. It was also argued on economic grounds in Chapter 20 that some source of finance independent of the centre was required. More importantly, a regional assembly with no independent source of finance is likely to be an explosive mixture with a continual source of friction with the central government built into it.

Forms of regional financing

As a background it has to be borne in mind that the present distribution of expenditure per head differs in different parts of the country, with some areas receiving more in benefit than is paid in taxes and other areas receiving less. The Royal Commission on the Constitution commissioned special studies in this area. Although the figures are subject to considerable qualification, they give a general order of magnitude. Expressing expenditure per head in England as 100, it was found that the figure for Wales varied between 113 and 116 during the years 1963–4 to 1969–70. The variation for Scotland was 114 to 131 and for Northern Ireland 102 to 108. The highest figures were recorded for the year 1969–70. In each case, therefore, expenditure per head is considerably higher in Wales, Scotland and Ireland than in England.

The Commission also looked at levels of expenditure on services they considered suitable for devolution and the current variations between planning regions for the year 1968–9. Using expenditure per head in England as 100, they found regional variation from 94 in the West Midlands and East Midlands, to 129 in Scotland. These figures do not show which parts of the United Kingdom are not beneficiaries from the fiscal system, and official data are lacking too. The Royal Commission says (1973, para. 594):

> we believe that a geographical breakdown of revenue and expenditure would show large surpluses of revenue over expenditure in the South East and West Midlands regions of England, and deficits in Northern Ireland, Wales, Scotland and probably all the other English Regions. Some of the deficits would be substantial – areas with low tax revenues also tend to require the highest public expenditure.

In a centralised state there is of course no reason to expect government expenditure and revenue to match on a geographical basis. If the rich tend to cluster in particular geographical areas, then taxes based on income and spending will give greater yields in those regions than in others.

The implications of this for regional finance are fairly obvious: it would be difficult to devise regions that could be self-financing without some form of redistribution. The most likely outcome is to give the regions some tax revenue and to even up resources between them by government grant.

After a survey of federated systems by the Commission, it came to the conclusion that 'the financial arrangements to sustain that division can take many different forms, and that, with varying degrees of efficiency, most of them can be made to work' (1973, para. 572).

The conclusions of the Commission on a practical scheme intended to bring about maximum regional independence was that it should contain the following basic elements:

(a) United Kingdom standards of provision should be determined for all the devolved services.
(b) The degree of equality considered necessary between regions should be achieved not by insisting on the application of United Kingdom standards, but by allocating to each region sufficient funds in total to finance such standards. The cost per head of population would vary from region to region according to local conditions.
(c) Subject to the constraints of economic management, each region could spend its total allocation of funds as it wished. It would have the opportunity to make above-standard provision in some services balanced by substandard provision in other services.
(d) The process of determining United Kingdom standards and measuring regional costs, and of allocating funds between the regions, should not be in the unfettered control of the central government.

This blue-print for regional independence has obvious application to the local authority situation. The unitary-grant system discussed in the previous chapter comes close to this.

Taxes suitable for regional use

Both the majority and minority reports of the Royal Commission on the Constitution were in more or less total agreement on taxes suitable for regional use. Quoting from the minority report (1973, para. 265):

'Candidates' for inclusion in a list of taxes which could be raised independently of the United Kingdom Government by each intermediate level government and which would have a flexible yield are:
(a) A supplementary income tax on individuals resident or working in its area.
(b) A low-rate ad valorem retail sales tax in addition to national levied excise duties and VAT.
(c) Taxes on vehicles and fuel consumption such as the vehicle excise duty and petrol tax, which could be transferred from the central government.

Both reports envisage the possibility of regional governments having new revenue sources. The majority report mentions a hotel tax, while the minority report mentions lotteries.

It would also be possible for regions to levy a tax on firms in their area: either a flat-rate tax for each person employed, perhaps differentiated between males, females and juveniles; or, rather better, in proportion to the total pay-roll of the firm for that area. Administratively, such a tax would be easier if small firms were exempt, say where the number employed was less than 50, or the pay-roll less than £2,500 per week.

Most businesses already have adequate records of wages and salaries so that it should not present very much of a problem for a nation-wide concern to allocate its pay-roll to local areas. The Government could help compensate firms for this charge by allowing the tax to be offset against corporation tax. A uniform minimum rate of tax would enable all areas to obtain revenue from such a tax without causing reallocation of industry. Local variation of the rate over and above this minimum level would be possible so long as rates were not sufficiently spread that they encouraged firms to move to areas where the tax was lowest.

Taxes suitable for local use

The Layfield Committee surveyed the same tax field for sources of finance for local use, but rejected them all as being unsuitable (or as making much of a contribution to local revenue), with the exception of a local income tax. They envisaged this as a supplement to, not as a substitute for, rates.

A local income tax could not be introduced at the level of districts but could, Layfield found, be operated for the non-metropolitan counties, metropolitan districts and probably for the London boroughs in England and Wales and for each of the Scottish regions and islands.

After considering various forms of local income tax the preferred system of Layfield was a local income tax integrated with the national tax system and PAYE. It would be based on the taxpayer's residence, which would entail an additional coding giving the local taxation authority of the individual concerned, and the appropriate rate of local tax. There are some 2 million residence changes each year so considerable work would be entailed in keeping records up to date.

The annual cost of this form of local income tax, the cheapest variant the Committee found, was estimated to be in total £100 million, half estimated to fall on the public sector and half on the private sector (at 1975 costs). It would entail an additional 12,000 Inland Revenue staff.

Simplification of the income-tax system (desirable in any case) would be a prerequisite for the introduction of local income tax.

Not surprisingly, the Government's Green Paper on the *Future Shape of Local Government Finance* rejected the idea of local income tax. As well as concern over cost, the Green Paper (1971, para. 6.11) continues:

> But in any event the Government do not accept that local accountability depends on the proportion of revenue raised locally; or that any clear advantages would flow from the introduction of LIT [local income tax]. The freedom of local authorities to vary the LIT rate would have to be closely constrained so that it did not unduly complicate central government economic and financial management; and there would need to be some equalisation of the proceeds of the tax between richer and poorer areas.[2] Partly for these reasons, it seems highly questionable whether the great majority of electors could be made so aware of the LIT element in their normal PAYE deductions as to achieve the Committee's objective of securing an effective local discipline on local authority expenditure decisions.

It would also appear to be sensible to carry out any devolution proposals before making major changes to the finance of local government. If regions are to be given an independent source of finance, a regional income tax is a strong candidate and is likely to have a number of advantages over a local income tax. Since a regional tax will cover a bigger area than a local authority the administrative difficulties should be considerably diminished.

Assigned taxes

It would be a relatively simple matter for the Government to assign all, or part, of a tax for regional (or local) use. If, say, 10 per cent of income tax was so assigned, regions would automatically have some tax buoyancy built into their revenue. Conversely, a reduction of income tax by the Government would cut regional revenue in the absence of a compensatory change. Any other tax could be assigned in whole or in part; tobacco and alcohol are obvious candidates, but most would not have the advantage of tax buoyancy. Assigned taxes raise the problem of how the proceeds of the tax should be allocated to regions. To allocate them in proportion to the amounts provided within each region raises the objection of not giving sufficient resources to poor regions, as well as the difficulty with some of the taxes of it not being possible to do the regional allocation in the first place. If the proceeds are to be allocated by some formula, then the process of earmarking taxes differs little from a grant. Regions would also have to bear in mind that the yields from assigned taxes would be variable as most yields fluctuate with general economic conditions. While the Government may be in a relatively easy position to compensate for shortfalls in revenue by the issue of debt, this would be more of a problem for regions.

It may be overstating the case to say that assigned taxes allocated by way of some formula differ little from a grant. Regions or local authorities might like the assurance that some fixed proportion of the proceeds of a central tax would be allocated to them as of right. It used to be argued that if part of income tax was assigned, authorities would be assured of some increase in revenue in times of inflation, but this no longer applies with indexed allowances.

Co-ordination between local areas and the Government as to the proportion of a tax take which is to be given to the local sector, or, what amounts to the same thing, agreement each year on the rate of tax that local areas have for their own use, would add considerably to the advantage of an assigned tax. On balance, the Layfield Committee could see little advantage in assigning a tax and did not recommend it.

It seems that Britain, like most other developed countries, will have to continue to rely heavily on a tax on property. This is not to say that the system of local rates in its present form is ideal, rather that a tax on land and property forms a good base for a local tax. In the words of the Layfield Committee, 'there are sound arguments for including a property tax in the totality of taxation, and for it to be levied on a local basis'. The issues of local rating are now taken up.

The structure of rating

Although rates come in for a good deal of abuse they come out rather better than most forms of indirect tax in terms of cheapness of collection, certainty and equity. They can also be varied to suit the needs of the locality. Balanced discussions of rates can be found in Ilersic (1969) and the Layfield Report (May 1976).

For rating purposes property is divided into three categories: domestic, commercial and industrial, and other non-domestic properties. The first two categories are fairly straightforward. 'Other non-domestic properties' comprise for the most part public buildings such as schools, hospitals, town halls, government offices and other Crown buildings. These classes of property have different characteristics which mean that each needs to be considered separately. Common to the classes is the certainty from the ratepayer's point of view, and from the local authorities' viewpoint, that the yield from any particular rate in the pound can be calculated within very close limits. It is also truly a local tax with no problems of apportioning the revenue between authorities. The estimated yield in Great Britain in 1975–6 was:

Domestic (gross of rate rebates)	£1,694 m.
Commercial and industrial	£2,050 m.
Other non-domestic	£ 503 m.
Total	£4,247 m.

Thus almost half of rate revenue in 1975–6 is estimated to have come from the commercial and industrial sector.

DOMESTIC RATING

The cheapness of collection of the tax is partly due to the crude method by which this is done: dumping a demand every six months on a household's door-mat, unless the householder is a council tenant, in which case rates are collected with the rent; or, less frequently, when the owner as opposed to the tenant is rated, known as 'compounding', the owner collects the rate with the rent. Better ways[3] of collecting the tax would add to the cost. For example, it might be possible to get co-operation with employers whereby much of the money could be collected by deductions from pay. Provision for collection by regular payments by a banker's order or Giro over twelve months, instead of ten as at present, would be an improvement from the payee's viewpoint. Extra costs incurred in this way would be unlikely to make it as expensive to collect as most of the existing taxes. This cheapness is due in no small degree to the high yield of the tax and the difficulty of evading or avoiding it so that little has to be spent on 'policing' rates.

The most frequently made charge against rates is that they are regressive (see the Committee of Inquiry into the *Impact of Rates on Households*, 1965; and the Layfield Report, May 1976). This is true, of course, but it is true of nearly all indirect taxes. The fact that supplementary benefits cover rate payments, and the recently introduced system of rate rebates to low-income households, has mitigated the regressive nature of the tax but offsetting this to some extent is the domestic rate relief provided through the rate support grant. Initially the rate rebate to householders was financed nationally to the extent of 75 per cent so that a quarter of the cost fell on ratepayers generally. The proportions have now been altered so that 90 per cent of the cost is paid out by the central government.

The Layfield Committee estimated that some three-quarters of those eligible for all but very small rebates did so. This amounted to 2.5 million households, of which 0.5 million had their rates rebated in full. A further 2.0 million households had their rates paid in full in supplementary benefit. The effect is that almost one-third of all households in England and Wales were eligible for some form of help with their rate bills, and about 85 per cent actually claimed it.[4]

One frequent complaint about rates is that households with similar accommodation but different household income will nevertheless pay the same rates. Particular emphasis is put on the case where there are several income-earners per household. If rates are regarded as a payment for local services, it is by no means certain that the multi-income household will cost more in its use of local services than one which has one income only. For example, a household where the mother, father and two grown-up children all work probably cost an authority less than a household with two children of school age, where a greater use of school, medical and recreational facilities is likely.

If we take two identical houses in one of which live a retired couple with the other occupied by a number of adult earners, it is by no means clear that equity requires a greater contribution from the latter household. Their greater income will have already been subject to tax, and on average 65.5 per cent of local expenditure is now met from general taxation received by way of grant.[5] Rates are a tax on property and the couple have a better standard of accommodation than the household with more adults. The latter may have to share bedrooms, queue up for toilet facilities, and so on. One of the very difficult social problems is the maldistribution of the housing stock. Many couples, whose families have grown up, continue to occupy houses which are too large for their current needs, while many other households have to occupy cramped accommodation. The system of subsidisation of rates unfortunately has the consequence of aggravating this problem. The desire of an old person to continue to live in the house they may have occupied for many years amongst neighbours they know well has to be respected. The theoretical answer to this problem would be not to give rent rebates but to give retired persons sufficient income to maintain themselves properly in suitable accommodation. They would then have the choice, if they decided to continue to live in a bigger house, between having to make other economies, or moving to a smaller house and having more to spend in other ways. The current mess in the housing market – lack of suitable accommodation, the jungle of controlled rents and the various forms of rent and rate rebates, together with mortgage relief – means this market solution is impractical at the present time. It has also been proposed that rate relief should be set against the ultimate sale proceeds of the house, but this would be divisive and penalise the owner as opposed to the renter of a house.

The argument just used, that rates are a tax on property, or on expenditure on accommodation, receives support from the Committee of Inquiry into the *Impact of Rates on Households* (1965, paras 48, 49):

Evidence from the public repeatedly put before us the view that rates ought to have some relation to the services enjoyed by the individual ratepayer. Retired people without children of school age complain that the greater part of the rates they pay is spent on the education of other people's children: others protest that their rates go to subsidise the rents of local authority tenants who are often better off than themselves.

It is not for us to say whether or not rates ought to have some such relation but the claim that they do has had authoritative backing in the past. Edwin Cannan argued 'it happens in practice that the nearest approximation to local rating according to ability and the nearest approximation to local rating according to benefit are one and the same thing, namely, the rating of persons in respect of fixed property in the district'. We cannot easily reconcile this claim with the present facts. It is doubtful whether rates as now levied can be regarded even in part as a charge for services rendered. The essence of local government is that it provides services such as law and order, the benefits of which are indivisible by their very nature. Any charge for those services must be arbitrary and also compulsory, that is, a tax. Although the benefits of many present day local services, particularly the social services which have been developed so notably since the first world war, can be ascribed in a rough and ready way to particular groups and individuals, it is widely accepted that such services should be heavily subsidised. We have, therefore, no hesitation in rejecting the notion that rate payments are other than compulsory exactions, and in all subsequent discussion we treat them as a tax.

If the viewpoint is accepted that rates are a tax on expenditure on accommodation, an argument accepted by the Layfield Committee, it has already been argued in Chapter 19 that rates are amongst the more equitable of indirect taxes since low-income households receive help and better-off people generally pay more in absolute terms than poor households by virtue of living in higher-rated accommodation. The Layfield Committee estimated that for 1975 rating was progressive in its incidence (i.e. it took a bigger share of higher than of lower incomes) up to income levels of about £40 a week, was roughly proportional to income between £40 and £60 a week, and was regressive at higher income levels.

It is also the case that the rent paid by lodgers will be likely to reflect some element of rates which will be payable by the landlord; likewise the cost of hotel or other accommodation will reflect rate charges so that it is not true (in spite of the common belief) that only householders are affected by rates.

From time to time suggestions are put forward that rates could be related to income. The rating system would carry on as at present except that householders' actual rate demands would be weighted according to income. The lowest-income households could, for example, be weighted at 50 per cent so that they would pay only half their rates, and the weights would be increased as income increased. A scheme on these lines would be an improvement in equity terms on the current system of rate rebates where it is known that some of those eligible do not take advantage of the system.

Unfortunately, schemes of this kind have serious drawbacks. Not least is the difficulty of ascertaining the income of the ratepayer since current information is based on place of work rather than residence. It would also probably be necessary to base assessment on the previous year's income, with all the problems this involves.

The idea that rates should be progressive rather than regressive is very attractive to those who wish to see a greater degree of equality in society. It does seem, however, that there would be a very heavy price to pay in terms of administration for what after all is a comparatively small improvement in the revenue system. A similar conclusion was reached by the Layfield Committee. Commensurate resources applied to other areas of the tax system could probably yield far greater equity benefits.

The incidence of rates

The incidence of a tax – who ultimately pays it – is frequently extremely difficult to pin down unless very simplifying assumptions are made (see Appendices 18 and 19 of the Layfield Report, May 1976). This is the case because frequently a tax can be passed on in whole or in part to some other person.

DOMESTIC PROPERTY

As the appendices just referred to point out, rates are a tax on land and property, and traditional economic theory suggests that a tax on land would effectively fall on the landlord since land is in fixed supply and that a tax on property would be passed on to any tenant. We would then have the position that the owner-occupier bears the cost, and with rented property it is shared between landlord and tenant, since rates cover both the house and the land which it occupies.

COMMERCIAL, INDUSTRIAL AND OTHER PROPERTY

With domestic property, rates are normally assessed on the occupier and it seems likely, it has just been shown, that in the majority of cases it stops there. It is more difficult to trace the incidence of rates on shops, industrial and other property. In general, economic theory leads to the expectation that in the long run the charge will be passed on to the customer in the form of higher prices by a process of adjustments of supply and demand for the products concerned and for the inputs to the process. However, since rates on this type of property (but not on domestic property) are allowed as an expense in the computation of corporation tax and income tax, not all of the rate charge falls on the business as a cost and the final adjustment of prices should be the net-of-tax rate charge. In so far as this analysis is valid, then the impact of these rates is borne generally by the customers concerned, who in many cases will have no connection with the area in which the tax is levied. In the short run rate charges may affect rents, profits, prices and possibly wages, and will depend on market conditions and bargaining strength in the sectors concerned.

The impact of rates differs between industries and between different retail outlets. Using the 1968 *Census of Production* figures and expressing rates as a percentage of net output (i.e. value added to materials by the process of production), figures range from about 1 per cent for light industry to nearly 5 per cent in heavy industry, while distributive trades lie in the 3 to 4 per cent range. Retail outlets vary because, for example, shop frontage plays a part in the rating assessment and small shops generally have a higher rateable value *pro rata* to selling space than do large shops.

Rating anomalies

One long-standing complaint against rates is of inequities in the standards of valuing domestic properties, another the continued exemption of agricultural land and property. In both cases the blame lies largely with the central government. Successive governments have managed to postpone or modify these valuations, except in Scotland, so that by the time they are put into effect they are already out of date, or are distorted. Even when valuations take place, the basis for valuation, the rent which the property might be expected to fetch in the open market, is a highly artificial one since a free market in rented housing is now practically non-existent. This method works tolerably well for commercial and industrial property where rental transactions are more frequent. The Layfield Committee report the Valuation Office of Inland Revenue as saying 'the point has now been reached in England and Wales where enough rental evidence for domestic housing to support another revaluation on the present basis will not be available'. This view was supported by all the professional bodies of valuers concerned with rating and the Committee were satisfied that the conclusion was well founded. Alternative methods of valuation will be considered in the next section.

The continued refusal of governments, in spite of very strong contrary advice by successive Committees, to rate agriculture has already received comment in Chapter 19. If farming should be subsidised it would seem more equitable that this should be done out of central taxation and that the subsidy should be brought out into the open. The current domestic resources element in the rate support grant is another example of government interference in the rating system; it gives, as shown in Chapter 19, the most help to the wealthier sections of the community and even this is allocated in an arbitrary manner due to valuation differences.

Under the Rating and Valuation Act of 1961 local authorities must also give registered charities and certain welfare bodies half-relief of rates, and they may at their discretion give more. The sum involved in the relief may be relatively small, in the order of £12 million, but the same point holds as with agricultural derating, i.e. if the Government in its wisdom decides there is a good case for a subsidy, it ought not to farm it out to local ratepayers where the cost will fall very unevenly on different areas. Subsidies, of whatever sort, ought to be open and subject to annual scrutiny so that a rational appraisal can be made of the use the money is serving. Such scrutiny may dictate a lowering or an increase of the subsidy but this decision will be made in the light of alternative uses to which the money can be put.

The Green Paper on the *Future Shape of Local Government Finance* (1977) proposes to compensate local authorities for the rate relief they are required to give charities. If brought into effect, this will overcome the objection of the uneven cost of providing relief but not the objection that regular and rational reappraisal of these and other subsidies should take place.

Other methods of domestic valuation

Given the fact that the present method of assessing rates by means of rental values is now unworkable in the domestic sector, what method should be put in its place? Site-value rating, capital-value rating and a points system have been suggested.

SITE-VALUE RATING

Site-value rating has created some interest in recent years and was the subject of a pilot survey in Whitstable which was published in 1964. Site valuation ignores any value of buildings and assesses sites on their development value. It is therefore asserted that valuation of site value encourages full development of land, and that such valuation is simpler than having to take account of the value of structures on the site. Basing development value on planning and zoning regulations would also, it is claimed, lead to easier, perhaps annual, valuations. It is difficult to hypothesise about the yield from such a method of valuation, but it would not necessarily be less than the yield from the current rating system (given similar rates) since although sites are assessed without buildings on them, they are assessed on their potential development. The experience at Whitstable was to reduce the valuations on housing accommodation, and within this group to reduce the valuation borne by flats and maisonettes the most, followed by reductions on bungalows. Since a general revaluation has taken place since the Whitstable survey, this evidence is not directly relevant to current conditions.

In spite of the advantages outlined above, site-value rating has generally had a hostile reception. The majority of the Simes Committee on Rating of Site Values (1952) rejected this system because they thought it would not be an improvement and would not be easily comprehended by the ratepayer. It was also rejected on these grounds by the Layfield Committee and the Community Land Act, providing for development values to be realised by local authorities, has now effectively removed site-value rating from consideration.

CAPITAL VALUES

Many people have suggested that capital values – the price a property would realise if sold on the open market – would form a better basis for arriving at rateable values since many more properties are sold than let. The Layfield Report says (*Local Government Finance*, May 1976, p. 171): 'Capital Value is now the best measure we have of the benefit people derive from the occupation of their houses. We therefore conclude that the rating system, if it is to continue, will have to be on the basis of capital value for domestic property.' The Report goes on to say that, if adopted, statute would have to specify common assumptions to be made as to tenure and state of repair, and since capital values are more volatile than rental values it regards regular revaluations as essential. It also favours the adoption of a period, rather than a fixed date, for valuation purposes and 'banding' so that properties falling within each band of values are assessed on the same figure. The Green Paper on the *Future Shape of Local Government Finance* (1977) suggests that the next rating revaluation will be on the basis of capital values.

With commercial and industrial property assessed by rental methods and domestic property by capital values, there would be a problem of applying a common tax to properties assessed on different bases. It is proposed that a divisor be proposed to the capital values of houses to produce 'assessed values' to which a rate of tax common to domestic and non-domestic sectors could be applied. This divisor would determine the relative burden of rates between domestic and non-domestic ratepayers and the intention is to review this relative difference only at revaluations, which should be carried out at least at five-yearly intervals. The earliest date by which revaluation could take place is seen as 1982–3.

It is believed that capital-value assessments would result in narrow variations in the rateable values of similar properties in different parts of the country, but (i) they would shift substantially the relative assessments of individual houses; (ii) more expensive houses would be likely to have relatively higher assessments; (iii) some smaller and cheaper properties might rise relative to others; and (iv) they would have uneven geographical effects. The Green Paper indicates that relief would be provided to mitigate the effects of the change in the basis of valuation.[6]

POINTS RATING

It seems very doubtful if valuation by means of capital value would be any less arbitrary than the current system. As experience in the 1970s has shown, house prices are market prices and subject to considerable variation. These variations are particularly sensitive to the ease or difficulty of borrowing funds for house purchase. Even houses which are identical inside and out and next door to each other may sell at very different prices for a wide variety of reasons, for example the need of the seller for a quick sale, or the urgent need of the buyer for a house in that locality. *Valuation is inescapably an arbitrary act.*

Suggestions have been made that this should be recognised explicitly and a points system of valuation adopted. The Layfield Committee seemed to do this idea less than justice and dismissed it in one paragraph. Othick (1973), a chartered surveyor, argued that both rental and capital methods of valuation involved imaginary situations and that 'Perhaps we should be considering something more mechanical, comprehensible and at least mathematically correct.' This led the author to consider the merits of computerised assessment based on such factors as the age structure, floor space, type and location of the property. The great merit of such a scheme is that the ratepayer, with the aid of standardised forms, would be able to work out his rateable value comparatively easily. Indeed, ratepayers' own returns could be used as a basis for preparing the valuation lists. For example, an additional page added to the Register of Electors form which each household has to complete each year would involve very little extra cost of administration in obtaining household returns. Under such a scheme annual revaluations would be a possibility, or alternatively returns could be required, say, every third year. Assessing the factors, and the weights to be attached to them, for a universal rating formula would be a controversial exercise but it would not present great technical difficulties. The difficulty of deciding weights was the reason given by the Layfield Committee for dismissing this method of valuation. The great merit of a points system is that the argument takes place over the components and weighting to be applied in the formula – once this is settled there should be little argument about applying the formula to individual properties, as it is fairly easy to establish the number of rooms in a house, whether it has an inside toilet, etc. In contrast, capital values are easy to agree in principle but likely to result in large numbers of disagreements in practice. The aim would be to keep the number of factors on which rateable values are assessed to a minimum. The current appeal facilities against rating assessments, which appear to work well, could be retained to cover exceptional cases. At the present time a somewhat similar scheme operates for nationalised industries, whose rateable values are decided by a formula reflecting the characteristics of each industry.

The abolition of rates?

Mrs Margaret Thatcher, then Shadow Secretary of State for the Environment, announced in October 1974 the intention of a future Conservative Government to abolish domestic rates within the lifetime of a Parliament. This surprise announcement was made in the run up to an election and no details of any alternative method of finance was given.

In September 1977, Mr Keith Speed, the Conservative spokesman on local government, repeated the pledge to abolish household rates, but warned that it might not be accomplished within the lifetime of a

Parliament. Details were still under consideration at the time of going to press.

Conclusions on the rating system

It has been shown that the rating system has a number of advantages: the tax structure is a relatively simple one; it is easy and cheap to collect; the yield is predictable; evasion is difficult; and above all it is a local tax which is administered locally. The tax is now progressive at low rate income levels because of the system of rebates.

There are a number of disadvantages of rates. If the Green Paper proposals are carried out, some of these will be improved. The long-standing method of assessing domestic rateable values by means of assessing letting values is now admitted to be unworkable because of the paucity of a free market in rented dwellings. Assessing rateable values by means of assessing the capital value of domestic premises has been proposed, and this should ensure more uniform valuation throughout the country at a fairly heavy administrative cost and the likelihood of many disputed valuations at the end of the day. Against the advice of several committees the Government has said it does not propose to abolish the derating of agriculture. The present system of giving domestic rate relief was shown to have serious anomalies: it subsidises the wealthy more than the poor and within each income group the subsidy can vary markedly. No government proposals have been made to correct for these anomalies but the system is to be extended to mixed commercial and domestic property.

Transfer of local expenditures

One often canvassed method for relieving pressure on local resources is for the transfer of the finance of certain services completely to the central government. Educational expenditures, or at least teachers' salaries, the police and fire service and various means-tested benefits such as rent rebates and relief are the most frequently mentioned.

The Layfield Committee considered these suggestions and in general concluded that for the Government to wholly finance these services would seriously weaken local responsibility and there was no case for such a transfer. A few services such as mandatory student awards, police, magistrates' courts and, in England and Wales, the probation and after-care services are already effectively national services. In addition, with some means-tested benefits, local authorities appear to be acting as agents for the Government with again virtually no discretion over the expenditure involved. In these cases the Committee recommends the transfer to the Government of the whole of these expenditures. They stress, however, that rate expenditure on these services is not large, most is already met by way of grant, and that such transfers would have only an insignificant effect on the level of local taxes. Layfield sees no justification for the specific grant for police and recommends that it be absorbed into the block grant, and believes a new basis should be sought for sharing the costs of local authority-administered education. Layfield considered that the transfer of the other services would result in a significant loss of local authority discretion, lead to divided responsibility, and not necessarily lead either to reduced tax burdens or better efficiency.

More radical changes: charging for services

Proposals have been made to finance more local services directly by those who use the services. This raises considerable issues which we shall only touch upon. A selection of those who advocate a market approach includes Peacock and Wiseman (1964), Harris and Seldon (1970), Pennance and West (1971), Maynard and King (1972) and Prest *et al.* (1977). A selection of opponents to the market approach includes Abel-Smith (1964), Titmuss (1967), Collard (1968) and Kaim-Caudle (April 1969). The proposers of the market are usually associated with the political right and opponents with the political left, but this division is by no means general.

The general philosophy of the market approach is that government expenditure should move away from services met out of general taxation and let these services be priced. The Government would channel its resources into helping those people whose private means were insufficient. It is argued that selective help only to those who need it would enable more generous provision to be made. These ideas have been applied to health, education and housing. The implications of these ideas for local finance would be a lowering of the pressure on rates. Opposition to these ideas comes from those who believe that such a market approach would result in less, not greater, efficiency. They point to the possibility of underconsumption of goods with strong externalities if these have to be paid for directly.

The Layfield Committee devoted some time to these issues, and concluded that it did not consider that increased reliance on charges could make a radical difference to the financing of local government services, except as part of a wider national policy applied to other publicly provided services, not least because the required redistribution of income would be a government responsibility.

However, it did see scope for a revision of existing practices. A survey from the Chartered Institute of Public Finance and Accountancy was commissioned which showed diversity and anomalies. The Layfield Report recommended a joint review by the Government and local authorities with the following aims (*Local Government Finance*, May 1976, p. 140):

(i) to determine which charges should be fixed or regulated by the government and which should be left to local discretion;
(ii) to remove anomalies both within and between services and between local authority and other public services;
(iii) to review the statutory levels of charges;
(iv) to recommend which services should normally be expected to cover their full costs.

The Green Paper accepted these proposals and states the intention to set up a review to cover the four points just outlined. It says that since housing rents, transport fares and school-meal charges are already under review in other contexts, these subjects will be excluded from the scope of the review, as will the question of library charges. It will leave activities yielding nearly £800 million revenue each year to be dealt with.

Summary

This chapter started with an outline of the piecemeal approach to local and regional government which has resulted in confusion which will take many years to eradicate. It then looked at some of the arguments about the need for independent local revenue in order to maintain local freedom. Opinions differ: the conclusion supported was that the proportion that the State and the local authority bear was not thought to be critical over a wide level of variation, and what was important was that both parties should bear part of the costs. If these arguments are also valid in the case of regional government, and this would seem to be the case, then present government proposals on devolution fall short in not allocating any independent source of revenue to the proposed regions.

The search for suitable local and regional taxes has gone on a long while with very limited success. The most favoured is some form of local or regional income tax. Although the Layfield Report favoured such a tax for local authorities, it was seen to involve considerable problems and considerable cost. It would in any case appear to be sensible to carry out any devolution proposals before making major changes – a regional income tax is likely to have a number of advantages over a local income tax.

The rating structure was examined, its major faults given and suggestions for improvement outlined. Finally, the role of charges in local services was noted.

Notes

1 This quotation is by the editor on page 5 of the preface; the authors of the booklet are much more cautious in their statements.
2 The implications of this are largely overlooked in the Layfield Committee report.
3 However, the Layfield Committee argued (May 1976, p. 145) that the perceptibility of rates is an advantage: 'The demand, expressed as a lump sum at yearly or half-yearly intervals, brings the tax prominently to the notice of ratepayers; because rates are perceptible, and because deliberate decisions have to be taken to raise rate poundages to meet increased costs, the tax promotes accountability.' They seem in this instance to have ignored the conflict with the tax principle that a good tax should be one that should not exact payment in a manner inconvenient to the taxpayer.
4 The admission that one-third of households are deemed to have incomes that need supplementation speaks for itself as a comment on current social provision, especially for the retired, who form many of these eligible households.
5 This ability-to-pay argument is used for rates but seldom for other indirect taxes such as alcohol or tobacco. It would be possible for the State to have a graduated expenditure tax but this is not likely to lend itself to local operation.
6 Indeed the Green Paper makes the curious statement that: 'In more extreme cases, should they arise, *permanent arrangements* may be made to mitigate the effects of the change in the basis of revaluation' (italics added). This seems to show either a marked lack of faith in the equity of the new system, or a strong desire to perpetuate the existing inequalities.

22
The National Debt

The overall level of government indebtedness gets much less attention than most economic statistics – certainly less than net additions to the level of debt in the form of new borrowings.
D. J. REID (May 1977), 'Public Sector Debt', *Economic Trends.*

Meaning of the National Debt

When the Government spends more than it receives, this results in the issue of some sort of security to cover the deficiency. In like manner a surplus results in a reduction of securities. Roughly speaking the aggregate of securities over time, less redemptions, is called the National Debt. In practice, factors such as currency flows from abroad mean that changes in the National Debt are not identical with the government surplus or deficit in the same period.

In earlier chapters when looking at government spending and revenue it was found necessary to carefully define 'government' in order to avoid misunderstanding. We there included central and local government but excluded the nationalised industries. Unfortunately this division cannot be strictly adhered to since the statistical analysis of the Debt, as currently carried out, blurs these distinctions. The figures of the National Debt cover the sterling liabilities of the National Loans Fund. This fund was set up in April 1968. Prior to this the Consolidated Fund was virtually synonymous with the term 'Exchequer': it received government revenue and made government disbursements. Under the new arrangements, while the Consolidated Fund continues to receive revenue and make disbursements, the National Loans Fund has taken over the responsibility for dealing with any surplus or deficit, and also has the responsibility of servicing the National Debt and receiving interest on loans the Government has made to public bodies. Thus the National Loans Fund, as well as covering borrowing on the Government's own behalf, includes loans made to nationalised industries, other public corporations and local authorities. In addition, the analysis of the National Debt covers nationalised industries' stocks guaranteed by the Government, since these are not usually distinguished separately in the statistical sources.

Statistical data

The analysis of National Debt which follows therefore covers sterling borrowing made on the Government's own behalf and when it is acting as an intermediary to lend to other public bodies. These other public bodies, especially local authorities, borrow from the market on their own behalf, but except for the relatively small amount of guaranteed stock mentioned in the previous paragraph, this other borrowing does not appear in the analysis of the National Debt. The magnitude of this other borrowing will be indicated as appropriate. Also excluded from the analysis is that part of the debt, amounting to £3,444 million at 31 March 1976, which is payable in external currencies.

The Government itself is a substantial holder of its debt. The term *gross* debt is used to mean all debt whether held by the central government itself, termed 'official holdings', or whether it is held outside the government sector. The term *net* debt excludes official holdings. The bulk of the official holdings are held by the Issue Department of the Bank of England, as a counterpart to the note issue, by the Exchange Equalisation Account and the National Debt Commissioners. For many purposes it is the outside holdings which are the significant magnitude.

The left-hand side of Table 22.1 presents information on the gross and net National Debt for selected years. Gross debt has grown in money terms from £7,049 million in 1935 to £54,041 million in 1976. Prices have risen some sevenfold in this period, so in real terms the debt has changed little. Since Gross National Product has risen faster in this period than the National Debt, we see from the last column of the left-hand section that debt as a percentage of GNP shows a significant decrease.

The 'overseas currency' column of Table 22.1 gives figures of government borrowing payable in overseas currencies. This will chiefly cover borrowing from the International Monetary Fund.

The right-hand side of Table 22.1 also gives borrowing by local authorities and public corporations from market sources, i.e. it excludes borrowing from the Government and borrowing guaranteed by the Government which has already been counted in the National Debt figure. Local

Table 22.1

Gross and net National Debt and market borrowing for selected years

Year	Gross and net National Debt (£m. nominal value)				Total outstanding market borrowing (£m. nominal value)		
	Gross debt	Official holdings	Net debt	Gross debt as % of Gross National Product	Overseas currency	Local authorities	Public corporations
1935	7,049	–	6,593	171	–	1,301	164
1955	28,408	–	23,685	183	–	1,505	–
1965	30,461	8,932	21,527	96	1,806	6,403	341
1970	32,366	8,942	23,424	74	2,234	9,355	437
1971	32,806	9,166	23,640	67	2,149	10,104	548
1972	35,400	8,781	26,619	64	1,879	10,599	444
1973	36,526	10,183	26,343	56	1,616	11,500	582
1974	39,490	11,774	27,716	53	1,543	12,955	1,499
1975	44,495	12,785	31,710	47	2,323	–	1,624
1976	54,041	13,634	40,407	–	3,444	–	–

Sources: Figures for 1935 and 1955, Committee on the Working of the Monetary system (1959); Bank of England Quarterly Bulletins; *and* Annual Abstract of Statistics.

authorities are by far the biggest market borrowers but public corporations have been encouraged to make greater use of the market in recent years. In general this borrowing will have a counterpart in the physical assets of local authorities and public corporations, and like the borrowing of these institutions from the Government, will largely be for investment purposes, and should be judged accordingly.

The size of the National Debt by itself tells one little about its importance. We have seen that the apparent enormous sum of £54,041 million for the debt in 1976 is in real terms about the same as that in 1935. About a quarter of this debt, as the breakdown for 1976 (Table 22.2) shows, is held by the Government itself, and the bulk of the remainder is borrowing by the Government for lending to local authorities and public corporations for commercial purposes at market rates of interest.

Table 22.2

	£m.		%
Gross debt in 1976		54,041	
Official holdings	13,634		25.2
Local authority loans	11,477		21.2
Public corporation loans	14,675		27.2
		39,786	
Balance		14,255	26.4
			100.0

Sources: Bank of England Quarterly Bulletin, *vol. 16, no. 4, December 1976; and* Annual Abstract of Statistics.

Figures on debt must be used carefully. In particular, it should be noted that the analysis is frequently made in terms of nominal values. Nominal values are usually taken as the face value of the security, which is usually the value at which it is originally sold, although on occasions a security is issued either at a discount or a premium. Undated and long-term securities have for many years stood at a substantial discount on the stock exchange compared with their nominal values, and for many purposes details in market values would provide more meaningful information.

Table 22.3 shows the broad composition of the Gross National Debt. Although the proportion of debt represented by government stocks does not appear to have altered much, it will be seen later that the post-1945 debt is significantly more liquid than it was in 1935, this liquidity being

Table 22.3

Composition of the Gross National Debt at 31 March (£m. nominal values)

	1935	1973	1974	1975	1976	% 1935	% 1973	% 1974	% 1975	% 1976
Government stocks	5,219	27,069	27,656	30,725	35,580	74.0	74.1	70.0	69.1	65.8
Treasury Bills	371	3,093	5,509	7,522	10,849	5.4	8.5	14.0	16.9	20.1
National Savings	1,003	4,178	4,075	4,014	4,334	14.2	11.4	10.3	9.0	8.0
Tax certificates	–	218	79	27	13	–	0.2	0.2	0.1	–
Ways and means advances	–	634	830	977	1,145	–	1.7	2.1	2.2	2.1
Interest-free loans due to IMF	–	1,120	1,185	1,129	2,059	–	3.1	3.0	2.5	3.8
Other	456*	214	156	101	61	6.4	0.6	0.7	0.4	0.2
	7,049	36,526	39,490	44,495	54,041	100.0	100.0	100.0	100.0	100.0

Note: Because of rounding, figures may not add up to totals shown.

*Includes official holdings of government stocks and Treasury bills.

Sources: Committee on the Working of the Monetary System (1959); and Bank of England Quarterly Bulletins.

indicated by the sharp increase in the number of Treasury Bills. National Savings show a relative decline, this being due, at least in part, to the channelling of savings through institutions, in particular insurance and pension funds, rather than individuals' savings directly.

Table 22.4 shows the estimated distribution of the Gross National Debt as at 31 March 1976. The subdivision of holders will be explained more fully before commenting on the table.

Official holdings. Holdings of the Issue and Banking Departments of the Bank of England, the Exchange Equalisation Account, government departments, the Northern Ireland Government and the National Debt Commissioners, but excluding the National Savings Bank investment account.

Public bodies. Public corporations but excluding the Bank of England, which is included under official holdings, plus local authorities but excluding their superannuation funds.

Banking sector. Comprises the deposit banks, National Giro, discount and acceptance houses, overseas and other banks.

Other financial institutions. Insurance companies, building societies, Trustee Savings Banks' special investment accounts, superannuation and pension funds and unit trusts.

Overseas holders. Identified holdings of international organisations, overseas governments, overseas residents, etc.

Public Trustee and non-corporate bodies. A few identified holders, in particular the Public Trustee, the Church Commissioners and the Charity Commissioners.

Private funds and trusts. Obtained from an analysis of stock registers, this category is very uncertain because of the large number of nominee accounts which conceal the beneficial owners' identity.

Industrial and commercial companies. An estimate based on a sample of large companies.

Other (residual). This will cover the direct holdings of individuals and others. Since this figure is merely obtained by subtracting identified holdings from the outstanding total of debt, it is subject to a large margin of error.

We see from Table 22.4 that the Government itself owns about 25 per cent of the National Debt, and banks and other financial institutions about 35 per cent. Private funds and trusts account for about 19 per cent and

Table 22.4

Estimated distribution of the Gross National Debt at 31 March 1976 (£m. nominal values)

	Treasury Bills	Stocks up to 5 years to maturity	Stocks 5–15 years	Stocks over 15 years and undated	Non-marketable debt	Total	Total as a %
Official holdings	6,021	2,864	1,590	1,978	1,181	13,634	25.2
Public bodies	–	30	9	15	–	54	0.1
Banking sector	2,719	2,118	253		–	5,090	9.5
Other financial institutions	346	3,506	2,907	7,304	–	14,063	26.0
Overseas holders	1,210	996	515	1,543	2,069	6,333	11.7
Public Trustee and non-corporate bodies	28	51	43	145	3	270	0.5
Private funds and trusts	–	2,216	1,150	2,820	4,006	10,192	18.8
Industrial and commercial companies	525	1,972	1,555		4	745	1.4
Other (residual)	–				349	3,660	6.8
	10,849	13,753	6,500	15,327*	7,612	54,041	100.0
Total as a %	20.1	25.4	12.0	28.4	14.1	100.0	

*Of which £3,381 million is undated.

Source: Bank of England Quarterly Bulletin, *vol. 16, no. 4, December 1976.*

overseas holders for a substantial 12 per cent. Even if the categories 'private funds and trusts' and 'other (residual)' comprise substantial holdings by individuals, the share of individuals is less than a quarter of the total, and likely to be substantially below this.

The time structure of debt holdings of each category can change substantially but Table 22.4 shows that at 31 March 1976 the Government held 59 per cent of outstanding Treasury Bills, while 48 per cent of stocks over 15 years or undated were held by 'other financial institutions'.

There has been a very sharp change in the time structure of the National Debt since 1945. For 1935 the Committee on the Working of the Monetary System produced figures relating to the marketable stock, then outstanding at £5,508 million. Table 22.5 compares this with the marketable stock in 1976. In 1935 85 per cent of stock had over 15 years to run to maturity and 61 per cent of the total was undated. Only 3 per cent was redeemable within 5 years. In 1975 53 per cent was redeemable within 5 years, with only 33 per cent having 15 years or more to run or being undated. This represents a massive shift towards liquidity of the National Debt and consequently potential monetary pressures on the economy.

Table 22.5

Year	1935	1976
Amount (£m.)	5,508	46,429
	(%)	(%)
Up to 5 years	3	53
5 to 15 years	12	14
Over 15 years	24	26
Undated	61	7
	100	100

Sources: Committee on the Working of the Monetary System (1959); *and* Bank of England Quarterly Bulletin, *vol. 16, no. 4, December 1976.*

The 14 per cent of non-marketable debt shown in Table 22.4 is from the point of view of government finance no different from the sale of marketable debt; for example a deposit by a member of the public at a National Savings Bank account has much the same effect as a purchase from the Government of a security for the same amount. In the first case the National Savings Bank deposit is credited to the government account and the bank is issued with a government security as collateral; in the second case the individual receives the security directly as collateral. In a similar manner when the public deposits money with the Post Office Savings Bank and the ordinary departments of the Trustee Savings Banks, and when it holds bank notes, this is in effect lending to the Government. Of the official holdings of £13,634 nearly two-thirds represents securities held as collateral by these institutions.

The relevance of the National Debt

The total amount of the National Debt has now been examined, as well as borrowing in overseas currencies and market borrowing by local authorities and public corporations. Borrowings from the central government by local authorities and nationalised industries were listed. The composition of the National Debt for selected years and its time structure have been given and a broad classification shown of the main holders. With this information we are in a position to take up some of the important implications of the National Debt.

Can any valid comparisons be drawn between the debt of a nation and the debt of a company? Briefly the answer is 'yes'; but there are also pitfalls to be avoided.

A company balance-sheet over time will normally show an increase in the liabilities of the company, which will be matched by corresponding increases on the asset side. Before a judgment is made that the increase in liabilities is good or bad, it is necessary to know a great deal more about the changes. For example, it makes a difference if it is the issued capital, reserves or bank overdraft which has increased; and also it makes a difference how the assets have changed: has more been put into plant, or is it that unwanted stocks are piling up?

It is also necessary, within limits, to take account of both sides of the national balance-sheet. The National Debt has been primarily incurred as a result of war expenditure, and there are no physical assets corresponding to this expenditure. However, the public sector has tangible assets and the public debt in the post-1945 period is not the same thing as the debt before 1939. In particular, the nationalisation of industries has resulted in an increase in debt matched by an increase in assets. Loan expenditure of local authorities has been spent on housing and other real assets. A reduction in debt could be achieved by selling these assets to the private sector, but considered solely as a means of reducing the debt the exercise achieves little. Since the Government undertakes 'commercial' activities, there is a case for separating out debt operations of this kind. It may well happen that full commercial criteria should not be applied to all parts of commercial government activity, that, for example, some branch railway lines should be run even though this entails a loss, but separation at least enables a more realistic appraisal of both the National Debt and government commercial activities.

The danger inherent in applying company balance-sheet ideas to the national balance-sheet has been labelled the 'cement and steel' concept. The purpose of business finance is to increase the company's profits and net worth, but this is not the case for government finance (with the possible modification just noted of government commercial activities). Assets held by the firm are the collateral against the firm's debt, but no such reasoning applies to government assets. Applying commercial ideas to the whole of government debt 'reinforces the ancient prejudice in favour of expenditure on hardware as distinct from services', the type of thinking that enjoins the building of schools and hospitals but jibs at paying those that run them adequate salaries. A symptom of this kind of thinking is the fondness of many governments for prestige development rather than undertaking less glamorous but more productive investment.

We can look at this matter from another viewpoint. It is true that the economy will be worse off if the Government increases the National Debt (i.e. borrows) and uses the money wastefully. But this argument has nothing to do with increasing the National Debt; it would be equally valid if the wasteful spending was out of tax revenue.[1]

The technical problems of debt management

So far it has been established that the size of the National Debt by itself is not a good guide to its economic significance. It nevertheless remains true that a large debt poses problems of debt management. These were grouped into five by the Radcliffe Committee (Radcliffe Report, 1959, para. 532):

(a) The Treasury has to deal with maturities of marketable debt, and to make new issues to replace these and to finance new requirements, beyond current revenue, of the central Government.
(b) The markets in outstanding liabilities require 'management', both to facilitate (a) and to avert undesirable repercussions on the wider financial structure of the economy. This requirement applies both to the very short-term liabilities (management of 'the money market') and to the longer-term liabilities (management of the gilt-edged section of the Stock Exchange).

(c) The net capital requirements of the nationalised industries have to be provided; this involves questions on how the money should be raised (which connects with (a) above) and the terms on which it should be made available to the industries.
(d) Similarly the net capital requirements of the local government authorities have to be provided.
(e) The methods of raising funds by the sale of non-marketable securities (e.g. Tax Reserve Certificates and the 'small savings' instruments) have to be determined. All of these tasks are related to each other, and decisions on any one of them must have regard to repercussions on others. In carrying out these tasks the Treasury has always to have regard to the fact that a considerable proportion of the National Debt is held overseas.

The most important problems in the post-1945 period, it has already been indicated, occurred under headings (a) and (b) above.[2] As a result of war-time financing, large blocks of debt became due for repayment. The debt was considerably more liquid and presented a threat of inflationary pressure if the assets, as they matured, were spent on consumer goods rather than reinvested. The period has been labelled one of the 'cult of the equity'; in other words the market for fixed-interest, long-term securities, such as gilt-edged, was not buoyant. Clearly these matters impinge on monetary and fiscal policy and affect rates of interest. A related set of problems was the cost of servicing the debt. In so far as the debt is held by residents of Britain, the problem is not so serious, but high interest costs mean that taxation must be higher than it would otherwise need to be in order to pay the interest charges. The problem may have important considerations concerning the redistribution of income, but this is not our immediate concern in this section. The problem is more serious for that part of the debt which is held by non-residents of Britain (£6,333 million in 1976, about 11.7 per cent of the total gross debt). This implies a payment outflow from this country to the foreign holders, and in so far as they are not content to hold sterling but require their own currencies this is a factor operating to depress the price of sterling on world markets.

The management of the National Debt in relation to the economy

In the words of the Radcliffe Committee (Radcliffe Report, 1959, para. 558):

The most elementary problem of debt management is one that is necessarily solved in some way or other day by day. The previously existing debt, plus any current Exchequer cash deficit, or minus any current Exchequer cash surplus, has to be and is absorbed. Each day the vast majority of holders of Government securities continue to hold those securities at the end of the day, but a fraction of the securities is unloaded during the day: this unloaded fraction, and any currently accruing deficit, must be absorbed either by new holders in the private sector or against release of cash by the monetary authorities. And the same is true of a year's operations: in some way or other the Government's needs are met, and the debt existing at the end of the year must be held by someone, even if this result can only be achieved by allowing cash to constitute a greater part of the debt than before. If the achievement of this result threatens to entail growth of cash or other highly liquid liabilities to a degree thought dangerous, because of the repercussions of this growth of liquidity in the private sector, the authorities have in theory three courses open to them:

(1) they can make long-term securities so much more attractive that the threat is averted (i.e. 'funding' succeeds);
(2) they can increase taxation, so enabling themselves to get the real resources they want without adding so much to, and perhaps even bringing about some reduction of, the National Debt;
(3) they can cut the use of real resources by the public sector (cutting either Government expenditure or investment in the public sector) so reducing the amount of debt to be placed with the private sector in the period.

There have been in the last decade examples of all three methods of adjustment.

This quotation brings out clearly one problem, i.e. that the management of the debt may result in a growth of unwanted liquidity of the debt, in which case a number of alternative (but unpleasant) choices are available. Not brought out quite so clearly is the allied problem; that is, if the debt is changing in total as well as in maturity structure, this implies a different use of real resources. As an example, consider the case of an Exchequer cash deficit (i.e. a need to increase the debt) in a year in which the economy is fully employed.

Even if in these circumstances the most favourable case is taken where the Government is able to make good the deficiency by the sale of long-term securities, it is unlikely that private expenditure will be cut back by the whole amount of the deficiency. Unless additional action is taken on one or more of the ways suggested in (1) to (3) above, inflationary pressure will result.

Similar considerations apply if the economy is not fully employed and the Government is running a surplus (i.e. reducing the National Debt). It is unlikely that the whole of the proceeds will be spent by the private sector on consumer goods or investment projects, and in the absence of offsetting action the economy will be further run down.

It is now possible to understand the statements of the Radcliffe Committee (Radcliffe Report, 1959, para. 535):

For the debt ought not to be regarded as a given total, whose structure alone can be manipulated. If all possible courses in manipulating the structure threaten serious disadvantages this can be a reason for aiming at a bigger Exchequer cash surplus (or smaller deficit), so as to lessen the difficulties of management of the debt. . . . The debt is not, that is to say to be regarded as a residual among the quantities of economic policy. Thus debt management can be regarded neither as something to be, as it were, left to the last and adjusted to all other policy decisions, nor on the other hand as a consideration which should override all other policy decisions; it has to be integrated with a variety of measures in the pursuit of the broad aims of economic policy.

To recapitulate, the management of the National Debt has both monetary implications and implications for the use of the real resources in the economy. Because the propensities of the Government and the private sector will usually differ, the problem of ensuring balance in the economy is not just a simple one of, for example, ensuring that increased government expenditure is matched equally by an increase in taxation or by an increase in debt. In full-employment conditions, a greater sum will normally have to be raised, because private expenditure on goods and services is likely to fall by a smaller magnitude than the changes in revenue brought about by the changes in government spending. Likewise, given a reduction in government spending matched by a cut in taxes, it is unlikely that the whole of this sum will be spent on investment or consumption goods, and it may be necessary for the Government to take some action to maintain a balance in the economy.

If we revert back to the three courses of action open to the authorities, we find that restraints are present on each of them. The success of funding depends on the public's willingness to take up government long-term debt; there may be periods during which the public is not willing to do this. It may be possible to induce the public to hold more debt at a higher rate of interest (the Radcliffe Committee expressed some doubt on this), but even so an increase in interest rates has other implications which must be considered. In particular, rates of interest in Britain that are out of line with other developed countries may result in undesirable flows of money (so-called 'hot money') into and out of the country which are very disturbing to the balance of payments.

Changes in taxation can be aimed primarily either at changing spending in the company sector, or at changing the level of personal spending. The latter is likely to reflect on the company sector if the change continues for any length of time. A variety of other methods can also be used to influence behaviour in these two sectors, for example changing investment allowances or grants, and altering hire-purchase regulations on down-payments and the length of time over which repayments can be made. Much use has been made in the post-1945 period of such policies designed to influence the private sector. This will be taken up later.

Changes in the use of real resources by the Government also has obvious drawbacks. Much of government expenditure is on essential services like roads, hospitals and various kinds of educational establishments. Many people are of the opinion that expenditure on these items should be increased, not decreased. In the words of Professor Galbraith public squalor is contrasted with private affluence. The interruption of capital plans, particularly the capital spending of local authorities and nationalised industries, has been a feature on several occasions in the post-1945 period. It is particularly wasteful and expensive to try and alter capital expenditure once a certain stage of work has been reached, and this type of action is a desperate resort. The recasting of long-term plans is a different matter, but it is the case that planning techniques have not developed to the extent that much reliance can be placed on such forecasts, and altering long-term plans is no remedy for a current imbalance.

Burden of the National Debt

The phrase 'burden of the National Debt' is unfortunately one that seems to be embedded in any discussion about the National Debt. The implication of the word 'burden' is that life would be better if only the burden could be got rid of. Discussion about the debt is thus biased in advance. Confusion is made worse by differences about the meaning of 'burden'.

WHAT DO WE MEAN BY 'BURDEN'?

Burden is sometimes construed to mean the current amount of goods and services which the private sector forgoes in order to enable the public sector to consume. This may be nil in the case of an under-employed economy where the use of resources by the public sector need not be at the expense of private consumption but can come from increased production out of previously unused resources. With full employment of resources, by definition, increased consumption by one sector is at the expense of another if imported commodities remain unchanged. To make sense of the 'burden' argument in conditions of full employment it is necessary, somehow, to evaluate the Government's use of resources and its worth to individuals as opposed to leaving the resources as they were. It is clear that while this line of argument poses important issues, these have nothing specifically to do with debt financing; tax financing raises similar problems.

Another concept of burden relates to the amount of goods and services forgone by people during the period of their lifetimes. Given full employment, capital projects which take a long time to fructify will lessen the amount of currently available consumer goods but increase the amount available, say, ten or twenty years ahead. Again it is clear that important issues are involved which have nothing specifically to do with the National Debt.

The two concepts of burden dealt with approach the question from the side of the use of resources. They can be argued in terms of the money burden on the existing population or in terms of the money burden on future generations. Real economic issues also underlie the discussion in money terms, to be taken up shortly. Again these issues are misleading when confined to a discussion of debt financing, with the implied assumption that financing by other means does not also have similar implications.

Yet another concept of burden relates to the estimated effects that the debt has upon incentives to work, to save, to take risks, and so on.

What emerges from our discussion of the meaning of the 'debt burden' is that government spending raises very important issues. We mentioned the current use of real resources, the stock of capital we should aim to bequeath to the future, and the effect on incentives. The important point emerges that, however the government sector obtains the use of these resources, whether it is by commandeering them, by taxation, or by debt, these important issues remain. To look at the so-called burden of the debt in isolation is a misleading exercise; it is necessary to consider the advantages and disadvantages of alternative methods of obtaining these resources.

INTERNAL AND EXTERNAL BORROWING

An important distinction to be made is between internally and externally held debt – that is, between internal and external borrowing. Internal borrowing is a rearrangement of assets – citizens surrender current purchasing power in return for government securities, and no increase of real resources is directly created as a result. External borrowing, on the other hand, permits an import of real resources, either of consumption or capital goods. Likewise, interest and repayment of internal debt is the transfer of current purchasing power back to holders of the debt. However, interest and repayment of external borrowing means a corresponding outflow of goods and services, unless the external holders choose for a time to reinvest in securities of the country making the repayment. From the point of view of interest and repayment of external debt, it can be said that this constitutes a 'burden' on future output of goods and services. However, it must not be lost sight of that if the borrowing is used to increase the productive capacity of the economy, this may create the capacity not only to do both of these things but also to yield a return over and above this. The application of this to underdeveloped countries is obvious. It may at times be necessary to use foreign loans for purposes of increasing imports of consumption goods; but the use to increase productive capacity is to be preferred, if at all possible, as this will help to create the output to repay and service the loan.

EQUITY ASPECTS OF THE NATIONAL DEBT

Probably the most frequently mentioned aspect of the internally held National Debt is the concern which is expressed over its effects on the distribution of income and wealth. The debt represents a transfer of income from those who pay taxes to those who own the securities, and we have seen that institutions hold the bulk of the securities. Since all citizens pay taxes of one sort or another, it is not easy to work out how much transference in fact takes place, and who pays for it and who benefits from it. If the internally held debt were abolished overnight by decree, the Government would be relieved of the obligation to pay interest on the undated stock and the obligation to pay interest and make repayment of the other obligations. Repayment of stock in practice means the refunding of the debt by making a fresh security issue. The cost to the central government of interest payments is in fact quite small, because of the offset of interest receipts and dividends from public-sector bodies. The cost virtually disappeared in 1970, but has risen since because the increase in the National Debt has exceeded loans to other public-sector bodies.

The real objection that seems to be at the back of this type of argument is an objection to the very unequal distribution of wealth and income in the community. This is a question which is worth discussion in its own right, but interest payments on the National Debt are of only subsidiary importance to the topic.

FUTURE GENERATIONS

We now come to a long-debated question, whether, and in what senses, raising money by debt can be said to burden future generations. Does public debt put a 'chain around the necks' of our children or is it a case of imposing no burden since future generations, as well as having the obligation to pay, also receive the securities on which payment is made? The debt existing at the present time has, as we have seen, the effect of redistributing income from existing taxpayers to existing holders of securities. In 100 years from now both the holders of the debt and the taxpayers will be different people. If we take a shorter time span, say thirty years, the argument can be looked at in terms of inter-generation equity – that sons will be paying for the debts of their fathers. This point has some validity, but does not boil down to anything more than the truism that our actions today will affect the future in a number of ways, some of them calculable and some of them not. *In particular, the argument that raising funds by taxation today, instead of by debt, imposes no burden on the future is clearly false.* If a person's wealth and income is taxed today, while it is true that no 'burden' is left to future generations, it is also true that the assets of the individual to spend on, or bequeath to, his dependants will be less, or, in terms of the father and son argument, that the father will have less to spend on his son. In order to make sense of the argument that raising money by debt finance is a burden on the future, the stream of consequences stemming from raising finance in this way has to be compared with the stream of consequences stemming from raising finance in alternative ways. The number of alternative ways are innumerable, as they can take the form of various combinations of different taxes. In a trivial sense, however we raise the money imposes a burden on the future, in the sense that this question is usually phrased: i.e. that raising money by debt imposes more of a burden on the future than raising it by taxation. The question is not capable of a precise answer, as different assumptions about future behaviour are likely to yield different answers.

In this question we come back once more to a more fundamental question that appears to underlie much argument on this subject; that is, the question of the perpetuation of the existing structure of wealth by inheritance, and once more it seems that discussion of this question directly is more fruitful than a roundabout discussion of imprecise 'burdens' caused by this or that method of financing.[3] We now turn to other meanings of 'burden'.

TAX FRICTION

It is possible that the proportion of taxes needed to be raised to service the National Debt could cause serious disincentives. The argument is valid but trivial. In the context of considering a block of government expenditure financed by taxes or debt, the disincentives of both must clearly be taken into account and are likely to be higher for direct tax finance.

In practice, the interest-payment 'tax bite' is, as we have seen, not serious. Even though the ratio was obviously raised in the war it did not reach the levels of the First World War and its aftermath.

The amount of interest payment is a function of the total amount of debt and the level of interest rates. Although the rise in interest rates has raised considerably the cost of servicing the debt, as we saw previously, the net cost to the Government is low since it lends considerable amounts on to other public bodies who pay market rates.

REDUCED CAPITAL FORMATION

It is possible that debt and tax finance have different effects on investment and hence the growth of the economy. A general presumption would be that taxes are likely to have their major impact on consumption expenditures, while debt would fall more on investment. To the extent that this is true it is implied that the future tax burden lies in having a smaller endowment of capital. This argument appears theoretically sound. Its practical importance lies clearly in the extent to which the two methods of finance have a differential impact on private investment. Both taxes and debt finance are likely to have some impact on investment, and may be said to impose a burden, and the presumption is that debt will have a bigger burden.

The implication is not to rule out debt financing but rather points to the need, if the local circumstances point to this effect being quantitatively important, for some offsetting action to assist private capital formation. Alternatively, it can be argued that this points to tax being called for to finance current expenditures and debt for capital outlays where a stream of future benefits is assumed (see, for example, Musgrave and Musgrave, 1973).

If it is the case that tax finance reduces private expenditures on consumption and investment goods more than debt finance does (and this is a slight modification of our previous assumption that tax finance fell mainly on consumption while debt finance fell mainly on investment), then there are implications for stabilisation of the economy involved which will have implications for the future. The nature of the results will depend on whether the economy was fully employed or not at the time the financing took place. As with the previous case, we may need compensatory action. This will be so where the economy is experiencing inflation and we need to cut real resource use of the private sector to allow for the Government's increased resource use. Debt finance is likely to call for rather greater compensatory action than tax finance if our assumption is true: that debt finance reduces total private expenditure less.

To the extent that domestic borrowing reduces capital formation and income which would be generated therefrom, Musgrave (1959) is able to say that if the cost of borrowing abroad is the same as the domestic rate, then the burden on the next generation is the same whether borrowing is domestic or foreign. In the home case the cost is forgone private capital, in the other the real cost of interest payments (requirement in goods).

Monetary and fiscal implications of the National Debt

In looking at the so-called burden of the debt it was found that merely looking at money transfers obscured rather than illuminated some of the problems. In considering the fiscal and monetary implications it will also be found useful to bear 'real' implications in mind. The following will serve as a summary of points that have been raised earlier.

COMPOSITION OF THE NATIONAL DEBT

The importance of the composition of the debt has been raised on several occasions. In particular, the authorities are concerned with the liquidity of the debt: with the ratio of short- to long-term debt. The important thing, it will be remembered, is that although money can be obtained by selling both types of security on the market, only short-term debt has a fairly certain value. The implications for liquidity are twofold: one is the fear that the private sector will be tempted to convert its assets into spending power; and the second is that the banks and other financial institutions may use the assets as a base on which to expand credit. In both cases what is important is the relationship between the monetary authorities and the private sector. A sale of assets from a private individual to another individual, or a sale from a bank to a private individual, is merely a rearrangement of assets within the private sector, not of monetary importance except in so far as this implies changes in interest rates. If, however, the monetary authorities buy the securities, then this is directly increasing the purchasing power of the private sector. They may have to buy the securities because these are repayable on demand, such as deposits at the National Savings Banks or short-term deposits with local authorities. They may buy marketable securities because they wish to maintain the level of interest rates. They may be forced into raising more money on short-term assets, for example Treasury Bills, because the public is unwilling to subscribe to long-term issues.

TOTAL OF THE NATIONAL DEBT

We have seen that the absolute size of the debt does not as a rule form a big constraint on the Government. If interest payments are a large proportion of the budget it is possible that this will form a constraint on government spending because it fears to put up taxes, but the likelihood of this is, as we have seen, small. In any case interest payments are normally taxed as unearned income and this further reduces the cost.

An increase in the total of the debt is important in so far as it affects the composition of the debt, on the lines indicated in the previous section.[4]

INTEREST RATES

The effect of interest rates on the economy will be discussed in Part III. Changes in interest rates do affect the economy in various ways but these effects are not felt in any simple or direct manner. The monetary authorities must bear in mind the effect on the demand for money by borrowers, on the supply of money, and more directly the effects on the flow of money into or out of the country from overseas.

Minimum lending rate is, as we have seen in Part I, a key rate in the economy which will move most other short-term rates in the same direction as itself. In time this movement is likely to spread to longer-term securities. Also, debt-management policy has obvious implications for affecting the structure of interest rates. It would be possible for the monetary authorities to set the general level of long-term interest rates by making new issues of securities at the interest rate they had selected, and operating in the market day by day to support that rate. If the authorities try to maintain a rate that is clearly out of line with market expectations, undesirable repercussions may follow which will lead them to revise the rate structure they have set. The 'cheap-money' policy pursued after 1945 had this pattern. The authorities had the policy of maintaining low interest rates. An investor who expects the rate of interest to increase (i.e. a fall in the market value of existing securities) not only does not subscribe to new low coupon issues for fear of making a capital loss when interest rates change, but also tends to sell securities and keep liquid in order to take advantage of the investment opportunities when interest rates do change. In the late 1940s the authorities were having to acquiesce in the increasing liquidity of the public, which resulted in their eventual abandonment of the cheap-money policy.

The policy followed in much of the 1950s was to use Bank Rate with other measures which affected short-term rates and indirectly long-term rates, but with no deliberate manipulation of long-term rates. In general, the authorities followed rather than led the rates in the long-term sector. In the words of the Radcliffe Report (1959, para. 429): 'Until the last year or so [i.e. 1958–9] the authorities have not regarded management of the National Debt as an opportunity for working on the structure of interest rates.'

In the 1960s the authorities became more willing to pursue their aims for interest rates throughout the economy by seeking to influence the behaviour of prices and yields in the gilt-edged market; and from 1971, the authorities became more willing to see market rates established.

Summary

Details of the Gross and Net National Debt were given, together with details of borrowing in overseas currencies and market borrowings by the public authorities. Although the debt has increased greatly in money terms, in real terms it is about the same as in 1935, and when expressed as a percentage of Gross National Product it shows a marked decline since 1935. Interest payments on the debt are not a great cost to the Government since it holds some 25 per cent of the total itself and about 48 per cent is lent to public bodies for real investment at market rates of interest.

Besides the technical problems of debt management which were outlined, there are two particular problems which give cause for concern. One is the sharp shift towards liquidity of the debt with, in 1975, half of the marketable debt being redeemable within five years compared with only 3 per cent in 1935; this poses considerable problems for monetary management. The other problem is that over 13 per cent of the gross debt is held overseas, and in addition borrowings in overseas currency are substantial. This debt, even if firmly held by foreigners, adds to the balance-of-payments pressure, and, of more importance in recent years, loss of confidence by foreigners can cause extreme weakness of sterling if they seek to withdraw their funds and convert them into other currencies.

In discussing the so-called 'burden' of the debt, a distinction should be drawn between debt held internally and debt held by foreigners. The discussion of 'burden' unearthed some important problems: the use of resources by the public sector; the amount of capital investment being undertaken; the effect on incentives; the distribution of wealth and income; and the perpetuation of the existing structure of wealth by inheritance.

In all cases it was found that discussion of these problems solely in terms of debt financing obscured rather than illuminated the issues.

The implications of the debt on the use of real resources in the economy are complicated and pose difficult choices. It is necessary to try and trace the effects caused by both the size of the debt, its composition and the structure of interest rates, which are influenced by debt management. These factors affect the liquidity of the economy, the ability of the banks and other financial institutions to create credit, and also have direct effects on individuals and companies. The task is a difficult one and it is not surprising that differences of opinion exist at many points of the analysis. The conclusion reached is that debt management should not be considered as an end in itself but as part of the whole fiscal process.

Notes

1 It would be interesting to know the motives of an anonymous donor who in 1927 made a gift of approximately £500,000 on condition that it should be retained and accumulated until either alone or with other funds it was sufficient to discharge the National Debt (Messrs Baring Brothers and Co. Ltd are trustees). By 1973 the market value of the fund amounted to some £7 million. For this and details of the smaller Elsie Mackay Fund set up for the same purpose, see *National Debt* (1973).

2 The following amounts of stocks were due for redemption in each financial year (*Bank of England Quarterly Bulletin*, vol. 15, December 1975):

1975–6	1976–7	1977–8	1978–9	1979–80	Total
£2,123m.	£2,755m.	£2,552m.	£1,514m.	£2,554m.	£11,498m.

3 The reader interested in pursuing this topic to its metaphysical heights is referred to a collection of writings (Ferguson, 1964).

4 A more diffused effect of the size and composition of the debt may be apparent from its effect on private wealth. An increase in debt among the public itself does not constitute an increase in wealth when aggregation takes place. The assets of some members of the public are matched by corresponding liabilities of other members. To what extent an increase in National Debt is regarded by the public as a net increase in wealth is empirically uncertain. An increase in the National Debt does two things: it increases the public's ownership of claims against the monetary sector; and, at the same time, it increases the tax liability of the public to service the debt. The public's reaction can vary considerably. One extreme is considering the increase in claims it holds as an increase in wealth without making any allowance for the tax liability. At the other extreme, if full offset for tax liability is conceded, no net increase in wealth is apparent. Put simply, in the latter case there would

be no change in aggregate behaviour, due to the wealth effect, if the National Debt was halved or changed by some other fraction. In the context of the present chapter, while it may be true that the wealth effect is important as a long-run determinant of behaviour, it is unlikely to be important as a short-run determinant. This question is discussed in relation to the Federal Debt of the USA by Tobin *et al.* (1963).

23
A critique of public finance

To restrict our Report completely to an analysis of the revenue-raising side would be equivalent to saying that we think it meaningful to ignore one blade of a pair of scissors. There may be some who would say that our efforts should be directed to spreading more equitably the 'burden' of taxation and that we should not concern ourselves with the results of government expenditure. But in many respects one is essential to the other and it is their joint product that must be our concern. Therefore, while we do not attempt to assess government expenditure programmes, we do not ignore them.
Report of the Canadian Royal Commission on Taxation (1966).

Summary of major faults in the present system

This part of the book has outlined the main changes in government spending and revenue during this century. Chapter 13 set up the total accretion principle as a yardstick for evaluating the current system, which was detailed in the following chapters. A summary follows of the major faults found:

1 The complexity and overlapping of the tax and benefit systems.
2 The appearance of high rates of tax which are not in many cases effective rates. This is particularly true of income tax.
3 High rates of tax on income as currently defined for tax purposes, with alleged disincentive effects, the diversion of effort into forms of output attracting low rates of tax, the unproductive use of resources specifically for tax avoidance, and the setting-up of residence abroad by high-rate taxpayers.
4 Lower flat-rate taxes on most other types of spending power.
5 Many social benefits channelled via tax allowances which do not help the most needy.
6 The lack of any consistent principles for company taxation.

These faults add up to a formidable indictment of the system which are likely to have serious economic and social consequences. A recent critique is given by Prest *et al.* (1977). This chapter attempts to suggest remedies. First, the problem of incidence in its traditional form is looked at in more detail. This concept is modified on the grounds that the approach is too narrow. There is a need to look at the total incidence of taxes and benefits, and this is carried out for the income groups for which information is at present available. Second, ways in which the system can be improved are investigated.

Incidence

The classical concept of 'incidence' deals with the problem of trying to sort out who really pays a particular tax and what are the effects of a tax change. The problem has arisen on several occasions. For example, should taxes on companies be considered as being borne by the shareholders, the employees, or the customers of the company? Are capital gains paid by the seller on whom the tax is imposed, or the buyer, or in some measure between them?

Incidence has two aspects: one is concerned with the financial consequences – who actually pays out the money; the other is concerned with a possible transfer of real resources in the economy. If the tax proceeds are spent on real resources, as opposed to making transfer payments, there may well be a loss of resources available for the private sector. This is certain in a fully employed economy, less certain in a less than full-employment situation where government expenditure may be activating what were previously idle resources. If a transfer of real resources is involved, then ideas of burden may try and evaluate the gains and losses resulting from less private and more public activity. Incidence refers to the location of the 'ultimate' as opposed to the 'direct' burden of the tax. The direct location of a tax is the person on whom the legal liability is imposed, the ultimate location the person who finally pays it. 'Shifting' refers to the process by which the direct burden is pushed along through price adjustments from the point of impact (i.e. where statutory liability is imposed) to the final resting place. Adjustments by individuals and firms to their sales and purchases will also affect others. 'Effects' refer to all other changes that the tax may bring about, for example inflation, changes in output or incomes, and transfer effects.

It should be noted that we cannot in any case make practical measurements of the 'ultimate' burden of a tax. Take, for example, a tax on cigarettes. We can measure the consumption of cigarettes and make some assumption about incidence, for example let us say that the consumer pays the whole of the tax. We can then say that this individual pays so much tobacco tax compared with that one. But we cannot catch by this measuring-rod the 'burden' on the person who has had to reduce, or stop, smoking because of the tax.

A great deal of work has been done on incidence theory during the last twenty years. Definitive answers to incidence questions should not be expected, however. The work consists in part of the development of a general theoretical framework used to evaluate specific tax changes. The importance of particular assumptions, for example the degree of monopoly power being exercised, and the elasticities of supply and demand, can then be investigated and empirical work done to establish the actual conditions prevailing in the economy.

A basic distinction is incidence on the sources-of-income side and incidence on the uses-of-income side. The former refers to taxes that alter the returns from wages, interest, profits or rents, the latter to taxes that alter the prices of goods and services. It is known, for example, that the proportion of income that comes from dividends and interest payments increases as one goes up the income scale, and that tax that falls on wages will have a very different incidence, therefore, to an equal yield tax that falls on interest recipients. Taxes that fall on goods and services are generally held to be regressive but for any particular tax such a generalisation might fail to hold. If, for example, the amount spent on alcohol increases with income, then a tax on alcohol may be progressive, at least over some income range.[1]

Incidence can be looked at in different contexts. Following the widely accepted work of Musgrave, we can look at absolute differential and budget incidence. Attempts have also been made to look at dynamic incidence.

Absolute incidence is the examination of the distributional effects of a particular tax, or a change in a particular tax, with no change in government spending or other taxes. Absolute-incidence studies could be used to analyse the effects of a change in taxation on inflation or unemployment. As such, the task is daunting in its complexity and other concepts of incidence have been developed.

Differential tax incidence is the examination of the distributional effects brought about by substituting one tax for another of equal yield while keeping government expenditure constant. This approach therefore avoids the problems associated with a switch of resources to the public sector. Since political decisions frequently involve the decision whether to raise or lower this or that particular tax, efforts on these lines have practical relevance. The concept of incidence that emerges from studies on these lines is a relative one, describing how the incidence of one tax differs from that of some other tax.

Strictly speaking, a differential tax study does not overcome the complexity of the interrelationships in the economy that were referred to in the discussion of the concept of absolute incidence: different taxes are likely to have different impacts on private consumption, and so on. These changes are likely to be smaller than in the absolute-incidence case, but it is an empirical matter in each case whether these effects are small enough to be ignored.

BUDGET INCIDENCE

The concepts of incidence used so far are attempts to look at the effects that flow from government taxation. Even if we assume that such studies yield meaningful results, many would hold that such an approach is seriously misleading. Citizens may benefit from government spending as well as having burdens from the taxes they pay. The concept of budget incidence is thus an attempt to look at the net impact on the individual of government activity: is he a gainer or loser on balance from the incidence of government expenditure and revenue collection? Considerable work has been carried out in recent years on budget studies and the results of British studies will be taken up.

DYNAMIC INCIDENCE

Dynamic incidence was used by Dosser (September 1961) to refer to the effects of fiscal measures on the rates of change of individual and group real incomes, with emphasis on the pattern of change over time. It is possible that a tax measure that succeeds initially in redistributing income to the poor may over time, due to adjustments made because of the tax, have opposite effects. Others have looked at the tax effects on the amount and timing of an individual's lifetime earnings (Polinsky, April 1973). Polinsky points to the possibility that a tax system could be progressive in respect of annual income but regressive looked at from the point of view of lifetime earnings.

It should be clear from this brief introduction to incidence that definitive answers will not emerge from theoretical work alone. The theorist can, for example, try and establish the conditions that must be met for a tax on commodities to be passed on to the consumer. He can construct models with various assumptions about the way the model acts and see how fiscal burdens are distributed. If this is the approach, the model must then be selected which it is thought most closely mirrors the economy. Budget studies which incorporate the benefits that flow from government expenditure must also incorporate ideas about the incidence of these benefits. The problems here may be less acute, but some benefits – those that flow to companies, for example – may be just as difficult to allocate as it is to find the incidence of company taxation. Budget incidence, the attempt to take the effects that flow from the tax and the expenditure side, is so important that these issues will not be examined.

THE INCIDENCE OF TAXES AND BENEFITS: GENERAL CONSIDERATIONS

The study of incidence is thus turned away from an investigation of a particular tax change into a study of the costs (i.e. who pays) and the benefits of the whole fiscal system which can be allocated to individuals. Criticism of this approach has been made on a number of grounds (see Prest, 1968; Peacock and Shannon, 1968b; and Peacock, 1974). The criticisms concern the general methodology used, assumptions about the incidence of taxes and benefits, and the need to improve the data. This method is here put forward as the one that approaches most nearly the concept of the standard of living of a person or family. It does so by taking the income of the unit, adding to it a money value of services received where it is sensible to allocate these on an individual basis, and subtracting taxes paid. The fact that the value of nearly half of government expenditure, on items such as defence and roads, is not allocated and is therefore ignored as a benefit, while a greater proportion of taxation is allocated, is, it is suggested, a useful approach in this context. Alternative assumptions can be made for other purposes, for example Gillespie (1965), in a study of Canadian conditions, has tried allocating defence and other general expenditures on the basis of equal benefit, according to gross income, capital income and disposable income. A similar study for Britain was carried out by Nicholson and Britton (1976) (see also Boreham and Semple, 1976).

There is still the problem of deciding who ultimately pays the tax and receives the benefit. Studies must obviously make assumptions about this and also about what these benefits are worth to the recipient. However, these problems can be seen in perspective. The importance or otherwise of a particular tax or benefit in relation to the whole can be judged. In particular, it would be feasible to set up alternative assumptions about the incidence of various taxes and benefits to see what over-all difference this makes to the 'burden'.

It should be clear that studies of this kind cannot show a comparison with a 'state of nature' where there is no government taxing or spending, because government activity alters incomes, prices, the supply and demand for various factors, and so on. They are likely to be of most use in showing the effect of marginal changes in the level of taxes and benefits, where the secondary effects on factor prices and adjustments are small. Large changes in taxes and benefits need behavioural assumptions to be made about reactions to shifts in the circumstances affecting factors. Budget studies could be broadened out in this way but have not yet been so.

The incidence of taxes and benefits in 1976

Since the early 1960s the Central Statistical Office has published annually in *Economic Trends* detailed tax and benefit figures for particular income categories, divided into single persons and married persons with and without children (see 'Effects of Taxes and Benefits on Household Income, 1976', *Economic Trends*, February 1978). The information is of necessity in terms of averages. It is obtained from the *Family Expenditure Survey* of some 7,203 households. Each household included in the survey is asked to provide detailed information about all forms of income, including National Insurance and other cash benefits received from the State, payments of income tax, the type of dwelling occupied, the kind of education which any member of the household is receiving, and so on.

In any exercise of this nature the inclusion or exclusion of particular taxes or benefits may make a big difference to the results. In 1975 some 60 per cent of total Government receipts and 44 per cent of total government expenditure was allocated to households.

Direct taxes included are income tax, employees' and self-employed contributions to National Insurance. The major taxes not included are corporation tax and taxes on capital. Taxes on capital, i.e. capital gains tax and capital transfer tax, are excluded. Customs and Excise taxes, including VAT, betting tax and local rates, are assumed to be fully reflected in the prices paid by consumers.

Benefits included are subdivided into cash benefits and benefits in kind. Cash benefits include family allowances, pensions, National Insurance and social security benefits, etc., but not scholarship and educational grants. Benefits in kind include the National Health Service, state education, school health services, school meals, milk and welfare foods, scholarships and educational grants. The method of allocating the benefits from state education is to impute to each child the average cost per child of education

Table 23.1

Average incomes before and after the allocation of taxes and benefits, 1976

	Range of original income Under 381	381–	557–	816–	987–	1,194–	1,446–
1 adult							
(1)	102	464	669	903	1,105	1,313	1,587
(2)	1,180	1,300	1,323	1,417	1,441	1,645	1,649
(3)	+1,078	+836	+654	+514	+336	+332	+62
(4) %	+1,056.9	+180.2	+97.8	+56.9	+30.4	+25.3	+3.9
2 adults							
(1)	144	464	694	910	1,094	1,326	1,595
(2)	1,786	1,851	1,987	2,027	2,142	2,204	2,338
(3)	+1,642	+1,387	+1,293	+1,117	+1,048	+878	+743
(4) %	+1,140.3	+298.9	+186.3	+122.7	+95.8	+66.2	+46.6
2 adults 1 child							
(1)							
(2)							
(3)							
(4) %							
2 adults 2 children							
(1)							1,609
(2)							2,617
(3)							+1,008
(4) %							+62.6
2 adults 3 children							
(1)							
(2)							
(3)							
(4) %							
2 adults 4 children							
(1)							
(2)							
(3)							
(4) %							

(1) Original income before taxes and benefits.
(2) Income after all taxes and benefits.
(3) Differences between (1) and (2).
(4) Difference as % of original income (1).

Source: Economic Trends, *no. 292, February 1978, Central Statistical Office.*

(£ per year)

1,749–	2,116–	2,561–	3,099–	3,750–	4,537–	5,490–	6,642–	8,038 and more
1,928	2,331	2,839	3,386	4,096	5,018	5,922	7,383	—
1,659	1,715	1,962	2,110	2,552	3,091	3,525	4,396	—
–269	–616	–877	–1,276	–1,544	–1,927	–2,397	–2,987	—
–14.0	–26.4	–30.9	–37.7	–37.7	–38.4	–40.5	–40.5	
1,933	2,373	2,835	3,414	4,146	5,000	5,986	7,225	10,754
2,238	2,382	2,511	2,658	2,868	3,322	3,884	4,614	6,633
+305	+9	–324	–756	–1,278	–1,678	–2,102	–2,611	– 4,121
+15.8	+0.4	–11.4	–22.1	–30.8	–33.6	–35.1	–36.1	–38.3
1,917	2,390	2,846	3,449	4,131	4,955	6,031	7,150	11,188
2,504	2,545	2,503	2,845	3,319	3,699	4,411	5,066	7,801
+587	+155	–343	–604	–812	–1,256	–1,620	–2,084	– 3,387
+30.6	+6.5	–12.1	–17.5	–19.7	–25.3	–26.9	–29.1	–30.3
1,961	2,374	2,870	3,439	4,135	5,006	5,981	7,221	10,657
2,555	2,568	2,755	3,179	3,523	4,086	4,831	5,529	8,039
+595	+194	–115	–260	–612	–920	–1,150	–1,692	– 2,618
+30.3	+8.2	–4.0	–7.6	–14.8	–18.4	–19.2	–23.4	–24.6
	2,354	2,872	3,439	4,179	4,959	6,052	7,324	11,804
	3,121	3,771	3,916	4,016	4,781	5,090	6,040	8,566
	+767	+899	+477	–163	–178	–962	–1,284	– 3,238
	+32.6	+31.3	+13.9	–3.9	–3.6	–15.9	–17.5	–27.4
			3,373	4,179	4,866			
			4,214	4,921	5,401			
			+841	+742	+535			
			+24.9	+17.8	+11.0			

in the particular category of school he or she is attending. Benefits of the National Health Service are allocated in a similar manner, it being assumed that the total value of all the services (except maternity services, which are allocated separately) is the same for all persons in each of six different categories of the population.

The benefits derived from government expenditure on administration, defence, police, museums, libraries, parks, roads and capital items are not allocated. By their nature, allocation of benefits of these services to individuals would be a haphazard affair.[2]

The value of the analysis is somewhat lessened because the top income range is £8,038 and above. If additional data could be collected to enable information to be given for incomes up to, say, £20,000, it would clearly be of more use. As it is the data are of value only for low- and middle-income ranges. What emerges from this sample? Table 23.1 presents information for the year 1976. Reading down the left-hand margin we have information on family grouping, first for one adult, then for two adults with 0, 1, 2, 3 or 4 children. Across the page information on income range is presented. Beneath each family grouping appear lines numbered (1), (2), (3) and (4). The first line presents the average gross income (termed 'original income') found in each income range, while the second line gives this income after taxes have been deducted and benefits added (this will be termed 'effective income'). The third line gives the difference between original income and effective income, while the fourth line expresses this difference as a percentage of original income. The fourth line thus gives an approximate measure of the progressiveness of the system of taxes and benefits for households of such size; it expresses the net benefits received or net taxes paid.

A recapitulation is in order before commenting on these figures. The estimates gather up the diverse strand present in the British system of taxation and government spending. The Central Statistical Office (CSO) estimate that value-added tax and oil duty are both somewhat progressive taxes, since the demand for the products to which they relate tend to rise more than proportionally with income. Excise duty on tobacco is slightly regressive but that on drink is broadly neutral. However, it is important to remember that these findings would be modified if the range of incomes investigated was extended. Insurance contributions are now largely proportional until an income of £120 a week is reached, while income tax is progressive. On the expenditure side, benefits will normally be progressive – that is, forming a larger percentage of lower incomes than of higher incomes – with the important exception of benefits received via tax allowances.

The picture that emerges is that within the income range considered the over-all impact of taxing and government spending in each family category (1 adult, 2 adults, etc.) is in general progressive. The higher the income the higher the net taxes paid, and the lower the original incomes the greater the net benefit received. The table brings out the sharp progression: thus 2 adults with an average income of £1,933 receive net benefits of 15.8 per cent, and an increase of income to £2,835 means net taxes paid of 11.4 per cent. So the progression is steep and quickly flattens out.

The table also shows the degree of progressiveness between categories. For example, comparing the original-income range of £2,561–£3,099, an average of about £54 a week, with an income about the national average of £80 a week, that is in the range £3,750–£4,537, we get the results set out in Table 23.2.

Table 23.2

	Income £54 per week		Income £80 per week	
	Net tax (–) or net benefit (+) (£)	per annum (%)	Net tax (–) or net benefit (+) (£)	per annum (%)
1 adult	–877	–30.9	–1,544	–37.7
2 adults	–324	–11.4	–1,278	–30.8
2 adults 1 child	–343	–12.1	–812	–19.7
2 adults 2 children	–115	– 4.0	–612	–14.8
2 adults 3 children	+899	+31.3	–163	– 3.9
2 adults 4 children			+742	+17.8

Should we be complacent about these results? That is to say do they accord with current ideas about equity? It may be questioned, for example, whether it is the general wish to impose on a family with one child and earning £54 a week a net tax of over 12 per cent of their rather meagre income. This is a sum that is £19 more than that paid by a couple without children in the same income range, whereas the difference between these two categories in the £80 a week range is a net tax lower by £466. This information gives support to those who advocated paying children's allowances for the first as well as subsequent children, a measure currently being introduced.

While increasing income from £54 a week to £80 a week means that a single person pays about 1.8 times more in tax (from £877 to £1,544) the other categories go up much more steeply. Two adults pay 3.9 times more (from £324 to £1,278), a couple with one child 2.4 times more, while a couple with two children pay 5.3 times more. The categories with three children move from the position of benefiting from an addition to income at the lower income level to one where they pay at the higher level. Once again it can be questioned whether these results are intended.

Proposed reforms

The evidence is overwhelming that our system of taxes and benefits, in spite of a considerable amount of effort, is neither equitable nor succeeding very well in achieving its declared object of relieving poverty. As we saw in Chapter 12, if we take dependants into consideration, some 10 per cent of the population is now eligible for supplementary benefit, although a lower proportion actually claim. This high proportion reflects the fact that basic National Insurance rights, in particular pensions, have never been paid at above subsistence levels. Other rights, most notably unemployment benefit, is paid for only twelve months, forcing many other people to claim supplementary benefit.

In recent years the British tax system has moved much closer to the accretion principle in the sense that the tax base has been widened to include gambling, capital gains, gifts and land. Unfortunately, these items have not been integrated into the income-tax base but, rather, made subject to their own system of taxes that are in general at much more favourable rates than income tax. We thus have a double disadvantage: a complex system of taxing which nevertheless still makes it advantageous to spend time, money and resources in switching assets around for a tax advantage. The high levels reached by income-tax rates, and the fact that averaging income is not possible for most people, seem to have become self-defeating. When the tax base is widened it is felt inexpedient to tax at income rates; consequently, income rates remain at high levels.

The present system of income tax whereby a steeply progressive marginal rate of tax is applied on the one hand and a system of tax reliefs that mitigate these rates on the other is long due for an overhaul. To illustrate the present absurdity we can take the case of a standard-rate taxpayer borrowing £6,000 for house purchase and see how much the top-rate taxpayer can borrow for the same net-of-tax cost (see Table 23.3).

In this example the interest rate has been assumed to be 10 per cent. Because the person paying tax at the standard rate gets tax relief at 33 per

Table 23.3

Sum borrowed (£)	Interest rate (%)	Gross cost p.a. (£)	Marginal rate of tax (%)	Tax saving p.a. (£)	Net-of-tax cost (£)
6,000	10	600	33	198	402
23,000	10	2,300	83	1,909	391
23,000	10	2,300	98	2,254	46

cent, his net-of-tax cost is £402 per annum. The taxpayer with sufficient taxable earned income above £24,000 (at which level he will be paying tax at the marginal rate of 83 per cent) can borrow £23,000 for practically the same net-of-tax cost. If the person with the higher income had been assumed to have more than £2,250 of unearned income, he would be getting relief of tax at the marginal rate of 98 per cent and the net-of-tax cost for him would be £46.

In the above example the tax allowance for housing has been used as an illustration but it needs to be stressed that all tax allowances have this effect: the further up the tax scale one goes, the more the allowances are worth. This absurd system of high tax rates, which nevertheless have their impact greatly softened by tax allowances, came about by accident. When income tax was a flat-rate tax it made no difference in the form in which tax allowances were given; it was only when income tax was made progressive that this anomaly occurred.

There have been a number of suggestions made for changing the system. One possibility is to extend the tax benefit in some other way to those whose incomes are too low to benefit from a tax concession. The present option of a reduced mortgage interest rate is a case in point whereby those on low incomes have the equivalent benefit (obtained by a standard-rate taxpayer) through a reduced interest rate. While such a system helps achieve equity, between borrowers for house purchase in this case, such schemes tend to be administratively complicated and do nothing to even out the value of a tax concession to those paying different marginal rates of tax.

Another possibility is to adopt some form of negative income tax, whereby those on low incomes receive a cash payment for the whole, or some proportion, of tax allowances which they cannot benefit from because of low incomes. At its simplest a married man with two children under 11 was in 1977–8 entitled to a tax allowance of £1,685, taking into account first his married person's and childrens' allowances. If this income is only £1,400, he would, under a negative income tax, be entitled to the difference of £285, or such proportion of this sum as had been agreed. Proposals on these lines in Britain were first put forward by Williams (1943) in terms of a payment of a 'social dividend'. Variations of this idea have been put forward from time to time (see Williams, 1967; Brown and Dawson, 1969; Christopher *et al.*, 1970; Dalton *et al.*, 1976; and Clark, 1977).

Negative income tax schemes have been criticised on a number of grounds. The previous objection that nothing is done to even out the value of tax concessions to those paying different marginal rates of tax still applies. Of more importance is the uncertainty about how successful these schemes would be in relieving low-income persons from the need to seek supplementary benefit. But what probably remains the main dilemma is the probability of very high – sometimes over 100 per cent – marginal tax rates that many of these schemes entail. Marginal tax rates of over 100 per cent are not unknown in our present system. If a low-income earner gets, say, a £5 a week rise, he may find himself paying income tax and at the same time losing many means-tested benefits such as free school milk and dinners for his children and various rent and rate rebates. It is possible that the cash loss in this situation exceeds £5. Under a negative income tax, if differences in tax allowances and income were paid in full, many more people would be subject to at least a 100 per cent tax since for each pound of extra income they would lose a pound of negative income tax. In addition, they could lose or suffer a reduction in any means-tested benefits they were receiving. Suggestions that not all the difference between income and allowances be paid, but say 50 per cent, would reduce the problem of very high marginal tax rates at this end of the income scale but only at the expense of the needy, who would receive less help.

The simplest suggestion for changing the system is to replace tax allowances, which have the effect of reducing taxable income, by tax credits, which reduce taxes by a given amount and so are of equal benefit to taxpayers. Such a scheme enables tax rates to be adjusted, which will help some low-income people and/or enable help to be channelled to those on low income in other ways.

We shall first of all look in more detail at a scheme which has a single income tax in place of the current system of income tax and National Insurance and incorporates a simple tax-credit system. Then we look at proposals made by the Government in 1972 to have a tax-credit system which incorporated a negative income tax since tax credits were to be paid to those below the break-even level of income. A change in government meant that these proposals were not implemented but the ideas still have relevance. The two frameworks provided by these schemes should not be seen as mutually exclusive as various combinations of each scheme are possible.

The example outlined in Table 23.4 uses rates and allowances applicable in the year 1976–7 and assumes a person with a gross earned income of £10,000. The marginal rate of tax on this would be 60 per cent, but the effect of assumed allowances of £1,785 is to produce a taxable income of £8,315, the marginal rate on which is 55 per cent. On 1976–7 rates of tax £3,348 would be payable. Adding in National Insurance contributions the total comes to £3,632.

Table 23.4

Combined income tax and National Insurance scheme with tax credits

Current tax system (£)		Tax-credit system (£)	
Gross income	10,000 (marginal rate of tax 60%)	Gross income	10,000
Allowances	1,785	Tax	3,250
Taxable income	8,315 (marginal rate of tax 55%)	Tax credit	100
Tax payable	3,348	Tax payable	3,150
National insurance	284		
	3,632		

Under the simple tax-credit system shown, the whole of a person's income is subject to tax at the rates which are given in Table 23.5. This produces tax of £3,250. The individual has a tax credit here assumed to be £100, which brings his tax due down to a figure of £3,150. The important point of the system is that the tax credit is invariant to income. Having decided, say, that a married man with two children is entitled to a tax credit of £100, this is the taxpayer's entitlement whether he earns £10,000 or £100,000. Tax rates could be brought down because large-income earners would no longer be receiving large tax allowances.

Table 23.5 gives the rate of tax payable in 1976–7 for a married man when his married person's and children's allowances are taken into account but no other allowances. This is compared with an assumed tax-credit system.

Table 23.5

Comparison of actual tax paid in 1976–7 by a married man with two children under 11, with an assumed tax-credit system

	Actual tax system					Assumed tax-credit system			
(1) Earned income	(2) Taxable income	(3) Marginal rate of tax	(4) Tax bill	(5) National Insurance	(6) Tax and National Insurance	(7) Marginal rate of tax	(8) Total tax	(9) Tax credit	(10) Tax bill
(£)	(£)	(%)	(£)	(£)	(£)	(%)	(£)	(£)	(£)
1,000	–	–	–	58	58	10	100	100	–
2,000	315	35	110	115	225	20	300	100	200
3,000	1,315	35	460	173	633	30	600	100	500
4,000	2,315	35	810	230	1,040	35	950	100	850
5,000	3,315	35	1,160	284	1,440	35	1,300	100	1,200
6,000	4,315	35	1,510	284	1,794	35	1,650	100	1,550
8,000	6,315	50	2,317	284	2,601	40	2,450	100	2,350
10,000	8,315	55	3,348	284	3,632	40	3,250	100	3,150
12,500	10,815	65	4,880	284	5,164	50	4,500	100	4,400
15,000	13,315	70	6,570	284	6,854	55	5,875	100	5,775
20,000	18,315	75	10,236	284	10,520	60	8,875	100	8,775
30,000	28,315	83	18,393	284	18,677	65	15,375	100	15,275
50,000	48,315	83	35,001	284	35,285	65	28,375	100	28,275
100,000	98,315	83	76,501	284	76,785	65	60,875	100	60,775

The first column of Table 23.5 shows various earned incomes. The second column shows the amount of taxable income that a married man with two children under 11 would have when his married person's and childrens' allowances are taken into account but no other reliefs. The third column shows the marginal rate of tax that this level of income attracts, and the next the actual tax payable. The fifth column shows National Insurance contributions and the sixth column the total tax and National Insurance payments combined.

The amounts shown in columns (2)–(6) are those payable in the tax year 1976–7: they are compared in columns (7)–(10) with an assumed tax-credit system where marginal rates are assumed to increase from 10 to 65 per cent. The tax-credit system charges tax on the first pound of income but the combination of a lower rate and tax credit, which is a direct offset against tax, means that tax is not payable until an income in excess of £1,000 is earned, compared with the present system where National Insurance taxes at 6.50 per cent on the first pound of earned income. A comparison of columns (6) and (10) reveals that less tax is payable at all income levels under the tax-credit system and substantially less tax at the upper-income levels. The lower tax at higher-income levels reflects partly the fact that marginal rates have been lowered and partly the fact that the substantial subsidies, because of the current system of tax allowances, no longer apply under the new system. The taxpayer will have a greater after-tax income but he will no longer have some of his expenses paid by the Exchequer.

The rates assumed under the tax-credit system are used to illustrate the principle but they may be regarded as not too unrealistic. The prime justification for lower rates is that considerably more revenue would be forthcoming under a tax-credit system for any particular rate of tax since gross income is the same as taxable income; gross income is not reduced by a system of tax allowances. By way of illustration it was estimated (*Hansard*, December 1975) that the Government's revenue loss from housing and insurance policy tax concessions amounted to £1,200 million, or approximately 13 per cent of total receipts from income tax. If, as equity would seem to imply, the loss of tax allowances for housing is accompanied by a substantial readjustment of subsidies to public-sector housing, there will also be a reduction in government spending to offset, or partly offset, any discrepancy in revenue between the old and new systems.

The system of tax credits could, as at present, differentiate between taxpayers in different circumstances. Since a credit of £100 has been assumed for a married man with two children, a lower sum could be given to unmarried and married couples with fewer children. Greater sums could be given for those with more children and those with exceptional needs such as disability. The point of tax credits is that these would be of equal value to anybody with income sufficient to cause him or her to have a pre-credit tax bill above the credit limit. The break-even assumed in Table 23.5 is at £1,000, where the tax bill for a married man with two children is cancelled out by his tax credit.

An alternative method of treating taxpayers in different circumstances would be to pay out income directly. A preferred method of allowing for children is a continuation of the system of child benefit payments outlined in Chapter 14. In a similar manner, disability could be covered in the form of disability allowances. This change probably has the greatest long-term benefits in terms of simplifying the tax structure and bringing down the present levels of tax. One difficulty with a changeover of this nature is that some individuals, who have made maximum use of current tax allowances, may find themselves adversely affected. There is a precedent in company taxation, where the 1966 change to corporation tax adversely affected companies trading overseas and special tapering provisions were allowed whereby they had a period to adjust to the new tax. Provision could be made for an individual who is worse off under the new system by, say, a figure of 10 per cent or more of his income to have relief on a tapering scale spread over, say, five years.

The new pension provisions in 1978 changed the rate of NI contributions according to whether a person was contracted out of the state pension scheme or contracted into the state scheme. The differential rate could be taken care of in a number of ways. The simplest would probably be to have a two-level system of tax credits, a lower credit applicable to those in the state scheme and a higher credit for those contracted out.

EXTENSIONS OF THE TAX-CREDIT SYSTEM

The original government *Proposals for a Tax-Credit System* (1972), a Green Paper, envisaged a more complicated system of tax credits than has been outlined above, and partly as a consequence of this self-employed and certain other classes of person including those on very low incomes were excluded. In all the scheme was intended to cover some 80 per cent of the adult population in the first instance. The main extensions of the scheme were the abolition of the present system of PAYE, the linking of tax credits to take account of price changes, and possibly also for changes in wage rates, and finally the system allowed payments to those whose incomes were not sufficiently high to exhaust their tax credits. These will be looked at in turn.

In Chapter 12 an outline was given of some of the problems caused by the overlap of social security benefits and the tax system. The proposal to scrap PAYE, which operates on a person's annual income, would overcome some of these problems. It was intended to be replaced by a system of weekly (or monthly, as the case may be) non-cumulative deductions. A person's appropriate weekly or monthly tax credit would be notified to him, and the employer would deduct tax at the basic rate less the appropriate amount of tax credit. At the end of the financial year any over- or underpayment of tax would be settled on the lines of tax paid under Schedule D at present. A person with more than two jobs would operate his tax credit through his main employer, while other employers would deduct tax in full. The scheme of tax credits outlined previously envisaged lower tax credits and a starting rate of tax of 10 per cent, not 35 per cent. To adopt the system of weekly, or monthly, tax credits to this system would involve selecting some average rate of tax for the employee to deduct, which would result in the taxpayer's annual tax payments being more or less in line with his tax bill. For those in regular jobs, and not subject to overtime payments, this would not be difficult. Those with irregular incomes could perhaps apply the average rate that was applicable to their previous year's income.

The proposal to link changes in tax credits to changes in living standards on the lines of adjustment to existing supplementary benefits is designed to integrate the two systems more closely. Tax-credit changes could be linked to movements in prices as ordinary rates of supplementary benefits are, or to movements in earnings, as long-term rates are. There is little difficulty in introducing this proposal.

Perhaps the most radical change proposed in the original government scheme was the payment of the tax credit to those whose income was not sufficient to exhaust the tax credit. If, for example, a person's wage in any week attracted tax of 50p and his weekly tax credit was £4, the scheme envisaged the employer paying out the difference of £3.50, for which he would be subsequently reimbursed. Payment would be made through the employment exchange or social security office for those receiving National Insurance benefit. It was this feature of the scheme that was largely responsible for the exclusion of the self-employed from the proposals because of the complexities of dealing with their tax situations and also of the very low paid on the grounds that they would need more assistance than could be provided in this way.

WHICH WAY?

The large measure of agreement on the faults of the current system of tax and social security unfortunately does not lead to a corresponding measure of agreement of what should be done about it.

Two ways have been looked at in this chapter. The first envisages the amalgamation of income tax and National Insurance contributions into a single progressive tax. This tax scraps the existing system of tax allowances and replaces it by a system of tax credits and lower tax rates. Assistance to those in need could partly take the form of changing the level of tax credit but is largely seen in terms of direct payments to the needy on the same lines as the existing child benefit scheme.

The alternative method suggested in the Green Paper keeps the dual system of income tax and National Insurance contributions and also has the drawback that although some 90 per cent of persons would change to a tax-credit system the remainder would still have the current system of tax allowances. On the positive side this scheme envisages paying out any tax credits not exhausted by tax payments on a weekly or monthly basis to those covered by the scheme. Given a sufficiently generous level of tax credit, many people would no longer have to claim supplementary benefits. However, a study by Atkinson (1973) suggested that the scheme as outlined in the Green Paper would have serious deficiencies in relieving poverty and would indeed make some poor persons and families worse off, largely due to the overlap with other benefits.[3]

The two methods that have been looked at are put forward to stimulate ideas, not as concrete proposals. They present flexible frameworks in which different elements can be combined, for example the basic proposals of the Green Paper could incorporate a unified income and social security tax, and so on. The work of the Select Committee on Tax-Credit (1973) provides considerable information on many of the ramifications of adopting a system along these general lines.

ADMINISTRATION

The provision of benefits, which have been referred to, results in an enormous amount of duplication of government administration, and also of form-filling that has to be carried out by the citizen. Different means tests are applied for rent rebates, rate rebates, school meals, welfare foods, educational allowances, child help, and so on (details will be found in *Social Services for All?*, 1968). Where tests are administered locally, great variation is found in assistance given to families in similar circumstances. With such diversity it is perhaps inevitable that many who are eligible to benefit do not apply; this may be due to a natural pride and the fear of being stigmatised as 'on assistance', or due to ignorance as to their rights, or to the difficulty in establishing whether they are eligible for benefit. We have already stated the opinion of the Supplementary Benefits Commission in Chapter 12. Two simple recommendations there stated that could be carried out quickly are to reduce the number of special benefit rates and more importantly to uprate all benefits on the same day.

More radical suggestions have been made to the effect that a single computerised service could bring large economies in time, money and manpower. Sewill (November 1966) gives a brief outline. Compared with the known technical possibilities we are still in the quill-pen stage; we pay for this in terms of frustration, waste and hardship. Those that object on the grounds that they will be 'just a number' seem to overlook the fact that they already have a National Health Service number and a different National Insurance number as well as a wide variety of codes used in most of their dealings with central or local government agencies.

Improvements and administrative savings could also be made if services were unified under one authority instead of being fragmented over many authorities and departments as at present. Proposals have already been made on these lines. The Ministry of Health issued a Green Paper entitled *Administrative Structure of the Medical and Related Services in England and Wales* (1968) in which it put forward for discussion the idea of a 'unified administration of the medical and related services in the area by one authority, in place of the multiplicity of authorities concerned in the present arrangements'. The *Report of the Committee on Local Authority and Allied Personal Social Services* (1968), known as the Seebohm Report, likewise comes up with similar proposals. This suggests the establishment of one central social-welfare department in each local authority to be responsible for the whole welfare structure administered by local authorities.

The individual vis-à-vis the company

An individual, as we have seen, may be at a serious tax disadvantage compared with a company, whether the latter is incorporated or unincorporated in form. Put the other way, an individual may be able to reap substantial tax advantages by forming a company, and a shareholder may reap tax advantages. This is so because companies are allowed to deduct for the using up of capital before arriving at a figure of taxable profit, whereas individuals do not have this right. Also, a company is in a more advantageous position in being able to claim for expenses. In recent years expense claims have been tightened up, but important differences still remain.

Taxing capital gains as income with averaging allowed would, we have seen, go a long way to achieving equity. Dividends would be taxed as income, and retained profits, if they enhanced the value of the business, would also be taxed as income when the gains were realised.

Difficult questions remain on the extent of company taxation and the treatment of inflation. We noted in Chapter 15 the opinion of the Sandilands Committee that the time is ripe for a Royal Commission to investigate differences in treatment for tax of persons and companies.

Summary

After listing the major faults found in the current system, different concepts of incidence were examined. Some detail was given of the Central Statistical Office studies of the incidence of taxes and benefits on income groups. The advantage of this approach is that the importance of a particular tax, or benefit, in relation to the whole can be judged. Alternative assumptions about the incidence of various taxes and benefits can be made in order to see how great a difference this makes to the 'burden'.

The conclusions reached, from the limited statistical evidence available, is that the present system, in spite of considerable effort, is not very equitable, nor, as we have seen, is it succeeding very well in relieving poverty.

Two alternative frameworks were examined for improvements in the system. These were not meant to be mutually exclusive since various combinations of each scheme are possible. The first looked at a system which combined income tax and National Insurance contributions into a single income tax which incorporated a tax-credit scheme and lower rates of tax. The second looked at government proposals that were made in 1972 for a tax-credit system that envisaged, in particular, the abolition of the present PAYE system and payment of tax credits to those whose incomes were not sufficiently high to exhaust their credits.

While this chapter necessarily concentrated on taxes and benefits, complementary to it was a study of administration. Because of the very fragmented administrative set up, a great deal of waste, frustration and hardship occur at present. Improvement could be expected by reducing the number of benefit rates and of uprating benefits at the same time. More radical suggestions that have been made include the integration of services under one authority, and by using known technical possibilities of computers.

Company taxation still presents many problems, but these would be lessened if capital gains were subject to income-tax rates with averaging allowed.

Notes

1 It is necessary to be cautious in statements about indirect taxes. Implicit in the reasoning is the assumption that all the tax is passed on and that other prices remain the same. If we suppose that alcohol is subject to extra taxation and that this reduces the demand for alcohol, then it is possible that if the production of alcohol is subject to increasing costs, a reduction in output will lower cost and as a result price will rise by less than the tax. If we further supposed that the reduced demand for alcohol results in greater demand for other goods subject to increasing costs of production, then prices of these other goods will rise and the consumers may be said to bear part of the burden of taxation (Krauss and Johnson, November 1972).

2 It is interesting to note that, as with all budget surveys, the amount that people say they spend on alcohol and tobacco is underestimated (by half on alcohol and a quarter on tobacco) and the figures have to be grossed up to allow for this.

3 A basic obscurity of the Green Paper makes informed discussion difficult. The cost of the scheme was estimated at some £1,300 million a year. No discussion was given of the financing of the scheme other than the vague hope that tax buoyancy would be sufficient. Tax buoyancy (automatic increases in tax revenue because of increases in wages and prices while tax rates remain the same) merely confuses the issue. On the figures given, what is entailed is increased taxes in some form of £1,300 million (whether raised deliberately or obtained through tax buoyancy is irrelevant), or corresponding reduction in other public expenditure, or new sources of revenue. To the extent that this increased revenue comes from the poor, then the value of benefits to them are correspondingly reduced. The poor cannot be helped by taxing the poor.

Part III
Policy

24
Introduction to policy considerations

Policy to deal with inflation is a subject on which a great deal has been written and argued by eminent authorities without adding substantially to knowledge, and in some cases subtracting from it.
H. G. JOHNSON (1967), *Essays in Monetary Economics.*

Introduction

In Part I the monetary system was examined, and in Part II government expenditure, revenue and debt. It is now time to attempt to draw these threads together and examine their effects on the economy.

Much has been written about the effects that are likely to flow from different monetary and fiscal changes. The analysis is frequently conducted at great length with an impressive array of geometric and mathematical expertise. Within the assumptions adopted by the author the conclusions can seldom be faulted. As exercises in logic this work probably has value, but as a guide to the best policy to adopt at any one time unfortunately it yields few results. It is seldom that the conclusions can be shown to hold once the restrictive assumptions have been removed.

An added difficulty is the lack of general agreement on a theory explaining the variables usually selected as important for study. The usual variables on which it is desired to see the effects of monetary or fiscal changes are: consumption and saving; investment; prices and output; and work effort. Since the theories explaining these variables are in dispute, it is not surprising that an explanation of the effect of this or that budgetary change is, at best, imprecise and subject to doubt.

This chapter looks briefly at each of these variables. It does not attempt to provide precise answers to the question as to what would happen to each of these if, say, a particular tax was changed. In our present state of knowledge such a precise answer is impossible. Neither does it attempt a detailed assessment of the use of monetary and fiscal methods in the post-1945 period. A number of recent full-scale assessments have been made to which the interested reader can refer (Brittan, 1971; Dow, 1964; Caves, 1968; Hansen, 1969; Cairncross, 1971; and Stewart, 1977). Rather, it looks at some of the problems involved in getting even approximate estimates. We are therefore concerned to look at resource use – the allocation side of the fiscal process. In a fully employed economy resource use by the public sector involves the opportunity cost of less resources available for the private sector. In addition, there may be extra costs because in their adjustment to the taxes economic units may distort their economic choices. There may also be benefits to account for, although the analysis usually concentrates on the 'excess burden', i.e. the excess cost or loss of welfare that results compared with what would have been the burden if a non-distorting tax could have been used to raise the revenue. A lump-sum tax is the only one held to be neutral since the liability to such a tax is in no way related to economic behaviour. All other taxes interfere in some way with choice among consumer goods, or between present and future consumption, or between goods (income) and leisure. On the production side they may cause less than efficient (least factor cost) production.

Other costs associated with taxes are administration and compliance costs: the former are costs of the revenue-collecting agency, the latter of those who have to pay the taxes. VAT and company taxation come in for particular criticism under this head, and an annual wealth tax and a local income tax are likely to have high costs on both levels.

Personal consumption and saving

We have seen in the post-1945 period direct measures, such as rationing and price control, influencing consumption and saving. What of the influence of fiscal and monetary policy?

To get somewhere it is necessary to have a theory to work with, even if it is no stronger than the feeling that 'consumption and saving can be changed by altering income'. Keynes (1936, p. 96) said:

> The fundamental psychological law upon which we are entitled to rely with great confidence both *a priori* from our knowledge of human nature and from detailed facts of experience, is that men are disposed as a rule and on the average to increase their consumption as their income increases, but not by as much as the increase in income.

Since this was written (over forty years ago), this 'law' has been the subject of much debate and investigation. Attempts have been made to modify the law to take account of the structure of wealth as well as of income. It has been suggested that past levels of income need to be taken into account as well as current levels, that it is 'permanent' or normal income which is the relevant concept, or that it is the flow of income over the life-cycle of the individual that matters. Many of these alternative statements are concerned with the long-run trend in consumption and the influences, economic and social, which bear on this. In particular, many of these studies attempt to reconcile studies which use cross-section data on household income, which support the Keynesian viewpoint of a declining marginal propensity to consume as income rises, and time-series data which suggest a constant marginal propensity. Management of the economy, as we are concerned with it, is largely a matter of year-to-year control, and here we are on safe ground in asserting that a change in income will be of major importance and will change consumption and saving in the same direction as the change in income.[1]

The size of the change will depend on many factors. One of the most important is likely to be the way the income change is distributed over different income groups. Budget studies inform us that, as we move up the income scale, out of each addition to income more is likely to be saved – in economic terms, the marginal propensity to save increases with income. It follows that a pound paid in tax by a person with a high income will tend to reduce saving more than a pound paid by a taxpayer with a small income. Thus a progressive income tax is likely to reduce saving more than a flat-rate tax. Put the other way, taxes which fall mainly on the poor are likely to have more impact on consumption, pound for pound, than taxes which fall mainly on the rich. These generalisations are frequently invoked by advocates of tax changes, for example those who advocate reducing the rates of income tax in order to increase savings.

Unfortunately, there is no clear empirical evidence on the effect of the magnitude of the difference on savings or on consumption. If the difference is small, then arguments for tax changes on these grounds can be ignored.[2] If they are large, it is necessary to take them into account. American studies (for example Musgrave, 1959) suggest that although taxes that affect high-income earners are likely to affect savings more than consumption, the effect is easily overstated. Because although low- and high-income earners are likely to have very different *average* rates of saving, their marginal rates differ much less. Dow (1964, pp. 270–5) lists British investigations which in general give more weight to the effect on savings. In view of the uncertain nature of the data and the assumptions that have to be made, authoritative statements on the relationships of changes in tax and effects on consumption and saving must await further investigation.

Let us consider a fully employed economy where the need is to increase saving (i.e. reduce consumption expenditure) in order that resources may be released from the consumption to the investment sector. Even if the argument is accepted that the effect of taxing high incomes is to affect savings to a significant extent, it does not necessarily follow that flat-rate taxes are to be preferred. There is an obvious clash between the objective of control over the economy and of redistribution of income and wealth. Political judgments here come to the fore. From the point of view of controlling the economy, it does not matter whether the savings are undertaken by individuals or the Government. If a decision has been made about the degree of progression of the tax system that is desired, and if it is desired to reduce consumption, then tax rates can be changed. The change can be made so as to leave the degree of progression of the system unchanged. If this results in less private saving, or a slower increase in private saving, this effect can be allowed for in the new rates. This results in the desired level of saving being obtained through a government surplus, or reduced deficit.

It is possible (but not very likely) that this increase in savings of the government sector would result in a shortage of funds for private investment. Numerous ways are available whereby these funds can be channelled back to private investment. The decision is once more primarily a political judgment. The Government could undertake direct investment in firms, or the resources of the Finance Corporation for Industry, or the Industrial and Commercial Finance Corporation, or kindred organisations, could be supplemented. Alternatively, taxes on companies could be reduced or investment grants increased.

One further illustration will be given. At first sight a change in taxing wealth is a clear-cut case of a change in taxation that will affect saving more than consumption. However, it has already been pointed out that one way of avoiding estate duties was to give away one's wealth at least seven years before death, and there is still a tax benefit in lifetime gifts under the new capital transfer tax. To the extent that wealth is given away to younger persons sooner than it would otherwise be given, the consumption patterns of these younger persons are likely to change.

A consideration therefore of the impact of monetary and fiscal changes on consumption and saving should take account of the impact on different income groups because they are likely to have different propensities to consume. Ideally the effects of different amounts of wealth should also be taken into account and allowance made for shifts of money and assets to different age groups who are likely to have different spending habits. Dow (1964, p. 275) has suggested that an important category to separate out is the self-employed, whose propensity to consume is lower than that of comparable income groups because of higher saving to provide investment for their own business.

The above brief discussion shows some of the more important difficulties that have to be faced if 'hunches' about the effects of tax or monetary changes are to be turned into objective facts. In Britain the matter is further bedevilled by a lack of adequate statistical data, in particular in relation to figures of savings. The figures of savings that appear in the *National Income and Expenditure* (the so-called Blue book) tables are completely unreliable. This is so because no attempt is made to arrive at independent estimates of saving. The figure is arrived at by taking estimates of income and deducting estimates of consumption. The resulting residual figure is called 'saving'. Since income and consumption are big magnitudes, even small errors in these estimates can make a large difference in the residual figure. Independent estimates of savings are beginning to be built up but these have yet to be incorporated in the Blue book (see *Economic Trends*, 1965). Uncertainty is therefore present concerning the amount of savings in the community and who undertakes it. There is a need for better statistics of what is actually taking place and for more consideration of the motives for saving, and how these motives change in response to different economic and social pressures. What is certain is that a considerable part of savings has now been institutionalised through pension funds and insurance companies.

Public expenditure can affect consumption and saving as well as changes in tax or monetary policy. The most important part in this respect is likely to be the extent of transfer payments. These, as we saw in Chapter 8, have increased in recent years to a greater extent than other forms of government expenditure. The greater provision of social security payments by the Government, in the form of pensions, children's allowances, and the like, reduce the need for private provision for these needs, although the extent to which the private sector would voluntarily save to provide for these contingencies is uncertain. Similar considerations apply to so-called 'free services', such as medical care, but the effect is weaker in that much would be spent directly on these services by individuals in the absence of schemes financed out of taxation. The overlap of social benefits and taxation, which we have already noted, makes the incentive effects of tax changes even harder to evaluate.

Company saving and investment

The post-1945 period has seen a variety of methods used to influence investment, from direct controls such as licensing and planning permission, to various monetary and fiscal policies. Even if there was agreement about a theory of investment (which there is not), the presence of so many variables makes it very difficult to pin down the effect of any one of them. Investment has been the subject of a good part of recent economic writing (for an advanced study, see Eisner and Strotz, 1963, pp. 61-337, with a selected bibliography of 666 items!).

The 'accelerator principle' makes investment a function of changes in demand. The truth in this principle, that a permanent change in demand calls for a different stock of investment goods, should not blind us to the obvious defects of the principle as a guide to short-term investment decisions. An increase in demand can often be met from previous resources that were idle or not working to capacity. The length of time required to adjust the capital stock, up or down, may run into years. Much investment needs to be planned for a number of years ahead. For example, once a decision has been made in principle to go ahead with a new factory, a suitable site has to be found, planning permission obtained, contractors engaged before work can commence and the construction itself may take one, two or more years. Under these circumstances it might be thought that investment of this type would be insensitive to temporary changes in demand brought about by a government that was pledged to full employment, not intending permanently to alter demand patterns.

Present evidence is far from conclusive, but from surveys of British industry it seems that investment plans do fluctuate considerably according to the current condition of the economy, whether, that is, the period is one of expansion or contraction: 'stop' or 'go'. There are several possible explanations for this. The most unfavourable interpretation to British industry would be that not many firms plan very far ahead or calculate their intended investments in a very rational manner, since many appear not to take tax or investment incentives into account. The White Paper on *Investment Incentives* (1966), quoting an enquiry carried out by the Confederation of British Industry among their members, gave some support to these pessimistic conclusions. However, other factors must also play a part. Some forms of investment have a short time to fruition and it is then more realistic to expect fluctuation in investment according to fluctuations in demand. Again, the cut-back during times of low demand may be due to difficulties in obtaining finance rather than deliberate intentions to cut investment. There is also business confidence to take into account, which may be unduly pessimistic about investment prospects at a time of contraction of demand, and unduly optimistic at a time of buoyant demand.

To the extent that investment does fluctuate with demand, the conclusions for getting growth in the economy are perverse. The intention in cutting consumer demand during times of full employment is frequently to release resources for the investment sector. If the effect is also to cut investment, the required growth will not be forthcoming and employment will fall. If deliberate manipulation of consumer demand in one or more particular sectors can be engineered without too large an overspill to other sectors of the economy, then the non-suppressed sectors of the economy will be able and willing to proceed with their investments.

Other explanations of investment lay more stress on the availability of particular types of saving, for example ploughed-back profits, or the buoyancy of the stock market. British policy, by its frequent discrimination against distributed profits, changes in tax allowances and experiments with initial allowances, investment allowances, investment grants and depreciation provisions, has developed actively in this field. It has been argued in Chapter 13 that the most dubious part of this policy, and also it would appear the least successful, has been the discrimination against dividends. Initial and investment allowances suffered from several drawbacks, as we saw, which it is hoped the new arrangements outlined in Chapter 15 will overcome.

Another theory of investment makes it a function of rate of return on investment compared with the rate of interest. If the return from real investment is above the cost of borrowing (or above the best return that can be obtained from putting surplus funds into financial assets), then the inducement to invest is strong and vice versa. The impact of the rate of interest will be considered in Chapter 26. It is argued there that one way that the rate of interest can be important is via the stock market and its influence on the willingness and ability of firms to raise fresh capital, and on the flow of new money into the market.

Input–output studies approach the problem of investment by trying to unravel the inter-connections between industries. For example, for every £100 of final output in the metal manufacturing trades, a net input is required of £1.8 from coal, £0.7 from other mining, £3 from chemicals, £44.5 from metal, £4.7 from engineering, and so on. If, therefore, a decision is made to expand steel production by so many million tons, the details can be fed into the model and the requirements on the economy can be calculated. The shortfall or over-expansion of investment in particular sectors feeding the steel industry can then be seen and attempts made to get firms to alter their plans accordingly. If industrialists can be convinced of the soundness of the calculations, they have a firmer base on which to plan their own investment. The firm is well aware intuitively that the success or otherwise of its own plans depends to a large extent on what is happening in the rest of the economy – the more facts can replace guesswork, the more steady is investment likely to become. Too much should not be expected from what are admittedly crude models of the interactions in the economy. The hope is that more data will be forthcoming, improvements in method made and the predictions made more reliable.

A number of recent econometric studies of UK investment behaviour have been made and are surveyed by Lund (1975). Eleven out of the twelve studies cited by Lund give a positive role to tax allowances and investment grants in influencing investment, but no consistency on the size of this effect is yet forthcoming.

Alternative assumptions about the incidence of corporation tax can also yield different answers about investment effects. If taxes are fully passed on in changes in prices of goods, then they amount to a sales tax differentiated according to the ratio of profits to sales. Tax should not in this case affect investment. The incidence of tax focuses attention on the degree of competitiveness of the various sectors of the economy and the long-run adjustment mechanisms to changes in demand for particular products. Recent attention has focused on the nature of the corporation tax base and in particular the role of depreciation provisions and the treatment of interest payments in modifying this base. A recent survey is given by Sumner (1976). He points out the violation of neutrality of the present corporation tax, which allows free depreciation of plant and machinery and also allows fixed-interest payments to be an expense to be offset against gross profits, while other investments, buildings and stocks have different depreciation provisions. To allow free depreciation for all assets and to disallow interest payments as a tax offset would be more consistent.

These theories of what determines investment concentrate attention on differing variables that enter into the decision whether or not to invest. They are not independent variables but interact with each other, and their respective importance is likely to change over time. Bearing these facts in mind it is not surprising that evidence of the quantitative effect of government measures on investment is hard to pin down.

In recent years a concept of 'crowding out' has been reintroduced to try and explain the poor British investment performance. The old pre-

Keynesian concept of crowding out assumed full employment and that a pound of government expenditure would crowd out a pound of private expenditure and the economy would be no better off. Modern proponents of crowding out allege that debt finance of the Government that is not accompanied by an increase in money either crowds out business finance or so drives up interest rates as to make private finance prohibitively expensive. While it must be admitted as a theoretical possibility, the evidence for crowding out in British conditions is weak. There is plenty of evidence that businesses see little prospect of profitable returns and little evidence that finance is not available for sound prospects. Indeed, as we have seen, one of the things that went seriously wrong with the economy in the early 1970s was that the boom conditions engendered in the economy resulted in stock market and property speculation rather than industrial investment. Rates of interest in the economy in recent years have generally been below the level of inflation, particularly when the net-of-tax cost to a company of fixed-interest payments is taken into account. (For a fuller discussion of crowding out, see Blinder, Solow *et al.*, 1974.)

Prices and output

The adjustments in prices and output that businesses make in response to government policy changes are at least as difficult to sort out as any that have so far been considered.

At the micro level it is clear that if a manufacturer passes on to his customers the whole of an increase in prices (whether this is due to an increase in purchase tax, in company tax or higher interest charges), the demand for his product may be affected. He may be forced therefore to reconsider his price and so in effect bear part of the increase, at least in the short run. In the long run adjustments can be made to the size of the plant. The industry itself can also expand or contract by the movement of firms into and out of the industry.

Nor are the changes that occur in one sector of the economy likely to be confined to that sector. An increase in the price of, for example, cars may well lead to some substitution of other goods for cars.

The time element has so far been ignored for expositional purposes. Its presence adds considerable practical difficulties in sorting out the effects of a change. For example, after each recent increase in the tax on tobacco, the consumption of tobacco has fallen for a few weeks or months, only to come back to higher levels. One of the difficulties in sorting out the effects of a change is that the market for tobacco, as for many products, has been an expanding one for many years. Most noticeably, population changes and the spread of smoking among women have increased the market. To say that the consumption of tobacco surpasses its old level is not to say that in the absence of the tax change consumption might not be higher than its present level. It is very difficult to separate out statistically the underlying trend in consumption and the change due to the tax measure.

Aggregate changes in price and output inflation/deflation

The above reasoning deals with the response of an individual manufacturer to a change. In trying to account for aggregate movements in prices and output a number of other considerations need to be borne in mind.

The impact of a change will depend in part on the state of the economy. In conditions of full employment the manufacturer is more likely to pass on increases, reasoning that competitors will follow suit, so relative market shares between himself and competitors in the same industry, and also the market share of his industry *vis-à-vis* other industries, will be affected slightly, if at all – an increase in price in one sector may lead, that is, to a broad movement in prices over a wide range of prices.

Many countries have experienced a general rise in prices, or inflation, in the post-1945 period. A number of theories have been developed to explain this phenomenon (see Johnson, 1967; Bronfenbrenner and Holzmann, September 1963, pp. 593–661; Laidler and Parkin, December 1975). Two theories have contended for pride of place: *demand* inflation, which concentrates on the pull which demand can exercise on prices; and *cost* inflation, which lays emphasis on increases in costs forcing up prices. In the latter case an interaction between wages and prices is seen as a process leading to the continual rise in prices. The major emphasis with cost inflation has been put on increases occurring in wages and salaries coming from union pressure. Employers may, however, bid up wages in times of full employment.

The role assigned to fiscal policy in controlling prices is given different emphasis by these two theories, but both have in common the fact that relatively little emphasis is placed on monetary policy. A reaction against this can be discerned in the Johnson, and Laidler and Parkin works just cited.

In general, government policy in the post-1945 period has been seen as aiding, or hindering, other forces which are moulding prices. British government policy came out of this sheltered position in 1966, when in place of exhortation control over prices and wages was directly attempted?![3]

Inflation may be a problem with many similarities to cancer. It seems that cancer is not a single disease, nor has a single cause. Many types of cancer have been recognised and treatment of some of them has been successful. Inflation too may be of different kinds with different causes calling for different treatment.

Work effort

The adjustment in the work effort of a community to a fiscal change has been mentioned on several previous occasions.

In order to get a determinate answer we need to know a great deal. It is worth putting this down if only to evaluate the exaggerated claims that are sometimes made of the effects on work that will follow from a particular change:

1 It is necessary to know how the change affects each group in the community. A group must be defined in some way to make it economically meaningful, perhaps by occupation or income.
2 The numbers in each group must be determined.
3 The average reactions of each group have to be determined.
4 The weighting to be assigned to each group must be determined, for example how should five hours less worked by an accountant be judged in relation to five hours more worked by a dustman?

A determinate answer can only be given if data are available and assumptions made at the relevant points. Clearly, different assumptions about reactions of each group (e.g. that they will work less hard because they have less income because of the tax change, or that they will work harder to make up for the tax change) will yield different answers. In this context groups have to take account not only of the working labour force, but also the potential labour force. Higher taxes have an income effect which increases work effort and a substitution effect (for leisure) which reduces it. Most of the empirical work that has been done has been concerned with income tax, but other taxes will have similar effects if people are concerned with 'real' and not money incomes. Consider an individual's choice between work and leisure and what happens when income tax is increased.

In Figure 24.1 the amount of leisure is plotted along the horizontal axis, the amount of income after tax along the vertical axis. Point *a* represents the amount of leisure a person has if he did not work. Likewise, point *b* represents the amount of income that can be obtained from work.

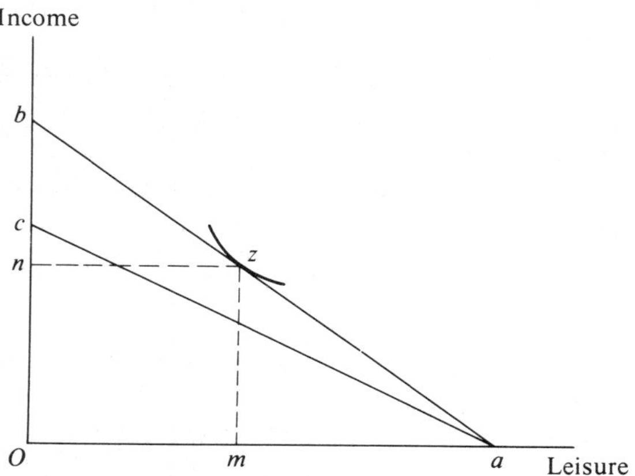

Figure 24.1 *Individual choice between income and leisure*

The straight line joining *a* and *b* indicates the various combinations of each that the individual can obtain by varying his time spent working. Let us assume that the individual chooses point *z*, which gives him a quantity of *Om* of leisure and *On* of income. Into this picture we now introduce an increase in tax which reduces his income to *Oc* for the same hours spent at work. Hence we draw the new line *ac* to indicate the position after the tax change. Where on the new budget line *ac* the individual will settle cannot be determined. The price change has altered the relative prices making leisure cheaper and *substitution* may well take place from work to leisure. On the other hand, the income effect means that the individual will have to work longer if he wants to retain the same after-tax income as before. The position taken up by the individual on the budget line *ac* depends on the combined results of the income and substitution effects. Since the theory is indeterminate, it is necessary to look at empirical work.

A number of studies have been made in this field. For example, appendix 1 of the Royal Commission on the Taxation of Profits and Income (1954) presents the results of an investigation of nearly 1,500 industrial workers. Break (1957) and Fields and Stanbury (1971) later give the results of a study amongst solicitors and accountants. Recent studies by Brown and Levin (December 1974) and Brown (1976) present the results from a sample of over 2,000 weekly paid workers. The results of these and other studies are fairly conclusive that the aggregate number of hours worked are little affected, and if anything the results point to the income effects outweighing the substitution effects, so that higher taxes will be associated with a small increase in hours worked (see a recent survey, *Taxation and Incentives*, 1976; *Fiscal Policy and Labour Supply*, 1977 and Godfrey (1975)). One possible area of exception to this is the reaction of married women to joining the labour force and the number of hours they are prepared to work, but this area is still one that awaits detailed investigation.

Since no study has been able to come up with strong disincentives on the number of hours worked, a number of investigators have postulated other undesirable effects of taxes. These take the form of postulating that the quality of work will be adversely affected, or persons will be less willing to take on more responsible posts, or that tax is a significant cause of the 'brain drain' and that it increases tax evasion and avoidance. While these effects may be important, it has to be pointed out that the nature of these alleged effects are such as to make it extremely difficult to establish to what extent they have any validity. For example, most of us in answer to a questionnaire would probably be glad to blame the tax system, rather than ourselves, for our lack of a better job.

The difficulties in coming to conclusions in this field can be illustrated from the study by Merritt (1968). His book gives a valuable look both at the remuneration of executives and at corporate efficiency. Merritt argues, among other things, that advantages would follow from higher before-tax executive remuneration and also advantages would follow from higher net-of-tax benefits. Giving executives, or some of them, the right to stock options on the American pattern is given as one way of increasing net-of-tax benefits.

Higher before-tax remuneration is seen as a way of forcing companies to be more efficient if profitability is not to suffer. However, this is an argument that can be used to justify giving an increase to any category of worker, or imposing heavy taxes on the employment of labour. Higher after-tax remuneration is recommended on the grounds that it would enable firms to impose stricter work criteria on executives who proved inadequate, since they would have been enabled to provide adequately for this contingency out of their higher net earnings. It seems equally plausible to argue that higher remuneration for executives would make it harder for firms to turn out inefficient executives, since it would be known that they would suffer a larger cut in living standards and larger 'golden handshakes' would be needed.

Even if it could be established conclusively that giving stock options would improve the quality and quantity of executives' work, this does not prove that the change is desirable. Before a change can be recommended on these grounds it is necessary to establish that the reactions of non-executives to this tax privilege would not result in a greater detriment. The change could lead to greater industrial strife by those workers who do not benefit and might more than outweigh the gain in executive efficiency. This increase in strife could occur through a general feeling that the gulf between 'them' and 'us' had widened and general antipathy on the part of the ordinary worker to productivity changes which would put more into the pocket of the executive than into his own. It could also occur because the trade unions used this as a lever to be more militant on behalf of their members. The correctness or otherwise of these reactions, whether they are motivated by feelings of vindictiveness or of social justice, is not important in this context; what matters is the strength of the reaction which needs to be measured against the favourable response expected from the change.

Summary

Before it is possible to analyse the effect of a change in government policy, it is necessary to have a theory about how the economy operates.[4]

In this chapter, consumption and saving, investment, prices and output, inflation, and work effort, have all been examined and treated in isolation from each other. In practice, they are closely interrelated. A change in government policy may cause significant changes in two or more of them. It is the over-all effect that is important. Sometimes changes in different variables will operate in the same direction, for example causing a reduction in investment and in work effort, and sometimes changes will tend to cancel each other out.

In judging the implications for economic policy it has been shown that there is no generally agreed theory to work with. Thus, unfortunately, an analysis, even for an observer who is trying to be impartial, depends a great deal on which theory is selected and on the weight given to each of the variables. More unfortunately still, it leaves the door wide open for those with special interests to defend to select those theories that serve their causes best. This pessimistic conclusion is not intended as an apology for inaction. Given the size of the government sector, it is not possible for the Government to be neutral. It is an indication of the need for care in accepting the claims put forward for this or that particular measure.

Notes

1 An advanced study of the determinants of consumer expenditure is given by Suits *et al.* (1963).

2 Differences may be small in two senses: first, the change makes no perceptible difference to behaviour; second, although the change makes a large difference, the numbers affected by the change are so small, or the amount of money involved is so small, as to make no significant change in over-all saving, e.g. if only 1,000 people are affected by a change, then even though it is assumed they save the whole of the amount involved, this will have an insignificant effect on total savings. Any reactions of those who are not directly affected by the change must also be considered.

3 A chess player will recognise the significance of '?!' In chess notation, a '?' is placed after a doubtful move, a '!' after an excellent move. Both signs placed after a move denote a risky move that has the chance of winning or losing the game according to the play of the opponent. These are symbols that could be adopted, with advantage, in economics.

4 As Shackle writes (June 1961, p. 209): 'When we have no theory about economic affairs, no state of those affairs and no temporal succession of states seems inconceivable. A theory restricts the conceivable states and succession of states to those in which the relations between quantifiable things in the economy conform to some specified rules. Theories differ from each other in the list of quantifiable (not necessarily measurable) things to be considered, and in the precise character of the rules about their interrelation.'

25
Policy (continued)

The British system of public administration, like the universe of Descartes, is in a state of constant flux. Nowhere is this better illustrated than in the evolution of present arrangements for managing and controlling the public sector over the past two or three decades, an evolution which constitutes in my view one of the most interesting and important developments in the practical operation of government in modern times.
SIR SAMUEL GOLDMAN, KCB (1973), *The Developing System of Public Expenditure Management and Control.*

Ideally we set out to ask: If a given change is put into effect, what will be the resulting changes and adjustments in the economy? Or, alternatively, what must be changed in order to achieve some desired objective? The change can be in monetary policy, in government spending, revenue and debt, or in direct type of controls such as hire-purchase regulations. Our ideal has been called 'a state of bliss', and like most states of bliss it is difficult to obtain. The complexity, as the previous chapter indicated, nearly defeats us. There is so much to take into account – so little agreed theory and empirical knowledge to work with.

A recognition of this complexity is in itself an important point. The criticism that an economist will give at least two opinions is understandable.[1] Given an objective, say to increase productive investment, there are usually countless ways of achieving this. There is first of all the decision, a political one, whether it is public or private investment, or both, which shall be increased. If some measure of encouragement of private investment is required, then consumer spending could be encouraged, which in turn would be expected to feed back a demand for investment, or alternatively investment could be encouraged directly. In either case there are numerous combinations of tax changes, monetary changes, or changes in regulations, which can bring this about. No two combinations are likely to have exactly the same repercussions on other parts of the economy. Under these circumstances it would be surprising if a unique 'best' method could be agreed on. A search for a unique solution is likely to be misleading in other ways, for example it is unlikely that a solution which yields a satisfactory solution given full employment of labour will be satisfactory given a large measure of unemployment.

One approach to this problem is the construction of models of the economy which can be put in mathematical terms and programmed on to a computer. Alternatives, for example different tax changes, or a different government borrowing requirement, can then be fed into the model and results compared. Economic models are being used and offer exciting possibilities, but too much should not be expected. A model must be based on assumptions about how the economy works, the incidence of taxation, etc. It has been shown that there is a great deal of uncertainty about these matters and therefore the reliability and robustness of any particular model cannot be taken for granted.

In the context of short-term forecasting, which covers some eighteen months to two years (see below), the centre and focus of forecasting is the estimate of Gross Domestic Product, from which can be derived estimates of demand, of unemployment, and forecasts of the balance of payments. Many of the components of GDP, such as consumption and industrial investment, are of interest in their own right.

In this chapter we look at the main components of GDP before looking at some of the problems of forecasting these magnitudes. Next, various concepts of a 'balanced budget' are examined and rejected. Finally, problems of control and recent changes in public expenditure surveys are examined. Monetary and debt policy is left to the next chapter.

Framework

A look at Table 25.1, which shows Gross Domestic Expenditure in 1976, reveals the magnitudes on which the Government can operate for stabilisation purposes. Some 59 per cent of the total is made up by private consumers' expenditure on goods and services, over a fifth by public current expenditure on goods and services and just under a fifth by gross investment. Of this gross investment, companies and the public sector had almost equal shares, with persons accounting for the remainder.

If we suppose that the Government wishes to cut expenditure by £1,000 million for stabilisation purposes, from Table 25.1 we can establish that this represents a cut in consumers' expenditure of £73,656 million of

Table 25.1

Gross Domestic Expenditure at market prices, 1976

		£ million		%
Private consumers' current expenditure on goods and services		73,656		59
Public current expenditure on goods and services		26,562		22
Gross investment:				
Persons	3,546		3	
Companies	9,769		8	
Public corporations	4,730	23,427	4	19
Central government	1,388		1	
Local government	3,994		3	
Increase of stocks at average prices for the year		359		–
Total GDE at market prices*		124,004		100

*Market prices are increased by taxes on expenditure of £16,660 million and decreased by subsidies of £3,463 million.

Source: National Income and Expenditure 1966–76, *HMSO, London.*

about 1.4 per cent. The same reduction on public expenditure of £26,562 million is a cut of 3.8 per cent. Likewise, if persons' and companies' investment is to bear the whole of the cut, this would amount to a reduction of 7.5 per cent. Correspondingly, if public-sector investment is to bear the whole of this cut, it would amount to a reduction of 9.9 per cent. This simple illustration goes a long way to explain why adjustments are in the main usually carried out on private expenditure: because it is by far the largest component of GNP, a cut of a given magnitude is a smaller proportion of the total, and hence is likely to have a less disturbing effect. There are other reasons for attempting to regulate private consumer expenditure rather than the other components of national income. One is the speed at which measures can be put into effect: investment must be planned for some time ahead and cutting back can prove a very costly process. Another is the argument we have met before that can be summed up by the phrase 'Public squalor, private affluence.' Public spending, whether on current or capital account, is often held to be of an essential nature. There is no need to take this statement at its face-value: government spending needs examining in the same way as other magnitudes and we have seen that in recent years it has come under close scrutiny. Finally, since investment is likely to increase GNP in the future, a cut in current consumption of the private or public sector is usually preferred to a cut in investment, though nevertheless in recent years there have been frequent adjustments to public-sector investment plans.

It will be found that in practice adjustments are much more complicated than the above would imply. For example, whatever measures are used to reduce consumers' expenditure, these are likely to have differential effects on different commodities. Thus to talk of a cut of £1,000 million on consumers' expenditure only amounting to a reduction of 1.4 per cent is misleading. The impact on particular products and services may be severe. Also, of course, there are likely to be repercussions on other components of GNP. Account must also be taken of the extent that persons and companies are able to compensate for the changes by obtaining higher wages or higher prices.

Other economic factors may operate against cutting consumption, such as its expected effect on wage restraint. Political factors must also realistically be taken into account, and at times this may weigh against cutting private consumption. A cut in private consumption is obvious and may be actively resented, whereas a cut in public expenditure may be less obvious. A cut in investment (private or public) is followed by consequences that are remote and not easily related to the original cut.

Practical demand management[2]

The above account has been cast in terms of past figures, but in practice many of the difficulties of demand management arise because estimates are required of the relevant magnitudes for some eighteen months to two years ahead. Forecasts are required for the behaviour of the economy if no policy changes are made and also for the effects of alternative policies.

Several teams of economists are regularly engaged in systematic economic forecasting of this kind. The Treasury and the Bank of England make three forecasts a year. A recent account is given in the *Bank of England Quarterly Bulletin* (June 1977). The National Institute of Economic and Social Research makes a quarterly forecast and publishes it in the *National Institute Economic Review*. The London Business School makes regular forecasts and their main results are published in the *Sunday Times*. The Department of Applied Economics at Cambridge University and a number of industrial consultants and big stockbroking firms also make forecasts. For a critical comment on these forecasts, see Ramsey (1977).

The Treasury and the Bank of England make forecasts before the annual Budget, in the spring, in the summer and in the autumn. They are of world economic prospects, of output and expenditure at constant and current prices, including the current account of the balance of payments, of external capital movements, and of domestic financial flows.

The aim of the domestic financial flows forecast (*Bank of England Quarterly Bulletin*, June 1977):

> is to exhibit the possible implications of the other forecasts for monetary policy, and to provide a plausibility and consistency check which might cause those forecasts to be modified. This role as a consistency check has, indeed, been enhanced and extended by the adoption by the Government in 1976 of formal monetary targets. If, under the conditions predicated by the other forecasts, the financial forecast shows the target variable – whether it be the broad money supply (M3) or domestic credit expansion – failing to meet the objective, this will lead to a reconsideration of the whole set of economic forecasts and, in particular, of the policy assumptions underlying them.

The main requirements for a good forecast are: (i) accurate and up-to-date knowledge of the state of the economy, and of its past history; (ii) where intentions and plans which will take effect in the future are already formed, accurate knowledge of them; and (iii) where the future will be determined by decisions yet to be taken, a good quantitative understanding of the factors which will determine these decisions. The difficulties of forecasting arise from the fact that none of these three requirements is more than very imperfectly met. The statistical information about expenditure, prices and output varies considerably in comprehensiveness, accuracy and up-to-dateness from one sector of the economy to another; in many cases the quality is rather low. This shows itself in the fact that in some cases early estimates are very substantially revised later on, and also in the fact that where a particular magnitude – GNP itself is a good example – can be measured by more than one route, the different approaches commonly yield very different measures of the quarter-to-quarter or year-to-year movements. Knowledge of intentions and plans is confined to certain special cases, in particular (i) government expenditure programmes, and (ii) companies' plans for fixed capital expenditure; in neither case has it been found that subsequent events can be relied upon to conform closely to the reported plans. On the third item, our understanding of the factors which determine spending and other economic behaviour, the achievements of econometric research have been rather modest.

The balanced budget

In the discussion so far no mention has been made about a balanced budget, i.e. the idea that a government is virtuous if it matches expenditure with revenue, but it is still a popular idea: see, for example, Buchanan, Burton and Wagner (1978). It will be clear from this chapter so far that this view is rejected. Our starting-point is that the Government has a role to play in regulating the economy. The size of the government sector today is such that a neutral policy is in any case not possible. Seen in this context there may be strong economic reasons for having either a surplus or a deficit on any particular budget.

Political reasons appear to underlie many objections to departing from a balanced budget. It is argued that government expenditure is too large already and anything which induces caution in government spending is to be welcomed. Give the Government power to spend more than it raises in taxes, so it is argued, and any discipline over its spending is forfeited.

Some time has been spent on looking at government expenditures in detail. The inadequacy of talking of government expenditure as a total, without considering the components of that total, has again been argued. Useful service may be performed by attacking this or that component of government spending as being too high or too low, judging the grounds of the attack on their merits. To argue that there is some fixed percentage of government spending above which inflation or some other evil or evils sets in, as well as being a dubious statistical exercise, is not necessarily an argument for cutting government expenditure, any more than it is an argument for cutting private consumption. What matters, for stabilisation purposes, is the total demands on the economy in relation to the real resources of the economy: if the former is above the latter, it is an indication that the demands from all sectors should be looked at anew. The decision that it is best to cut expenditure in one section or the other does not emerge from the statistics.

It is argued that unbalanced budgets can lead to currency depreciation. The argument is undoubtedly true: there are many examples of governments, unable or unwilling to tax adequately, resorting to the printing press. To argue that a certain consequence *can* happen is not to argue that it *must* happen. If it is feared that the increase in the level of demand causes the inflationary pressure, this only points to the fact that offsetting action is required. If it is feared that deficits over a number of years will so add to the money supply as to be inflationary, a similar reply can be made, i.e. this is a pointer to the need for offsetting action, for example to tighten control of the monetary sector, to fund, or to take action to reduce the deficit, which can be done either by increased taxation or by reducing government expenditure. The latter solution of reducing the deficit does not automatically emerge as the best solution.

A further assertion is that deficits are less painful than current taxes, in the sense that people take account of current taxes and discount future taxes to service debt. It is argued that this leads to over-expansion of government services. A counter-assertion is also put forward, i.e. that traditional concepts of budgeting have hindered the provision of much-needed services and that failure to separate the debt of the nationalised industries and local authorities (which debt will normally result in the creation of real assets) accentuates this trend to under-provision. While either of these assertions may be true for a particular historical time period, they become increasingly hard to demonstrate in a modern budgetary setting.

The concept of the balanced budget has an intuitive appeal to the individual because of the analogy with the economy of the private household. But it has no validity in the accounts of a nation. It is dangerous because it conceals the real issues. In a trite phrase, the real issue is 'the best use of the nation's resources'. The injection of the dogma 'balance the budget' merely helps to cloud the real issue.

THE FULL-EMPLOYMENT BUDGET CONCEPT

While annual budgetary balance is now generally rejected for the reasons given, a new concept has come into vogue: balance at full-employment levels of income (see, for example, Friedman, 1959; Committee for Economic Development, 1972; and Blinder, Solow *et al.*, 1974). The concept played a part in some American presidential budget messages.

The basic idea is that the Government determines the level of government expenditure and then sets tax rates so as to produce a balance at full employment; it is then hoped that the private sector of the economy will also achieve balance of saving and investment at this level. Another variant has suggested that given full employment the over-all budget could be in surplus or deficit but any additional government spending should be of a balanced-budget type.

Objections can be made to rules of this kind on technical grounds: that a budget balance is no guarantee that there will not be deflationary or inflationary pressures in the economy; different types of government expenditure and taxes will, as we have seen, have different effects on the economy. For an elaboration of these differences in the context of the British economy, the reader is referred to Hopkin and Godley (May 1965).

Advocates of budgetary rules rely on the value-judgment that rules like the above, imperfect though they may be, will give better results than the use of discretion. Opposed to this view are those who argue that for any rule it is not hard to find a not too unrealistic set of circumstances that would produce very poor economic results. Discretion in their view enables 'learning by doing', so that future efforts to stabilise the economy should be able to avoid past mistakes.

A less objectionable use of this concept is where it is used, not as a rule but as a way of measuring the effect of the budget on the economy which attempts to abstract from cyclical changes in the economy. However, this involves concepts which are very difficult to measure and its usefulness is therefore suspect.

Problems of control

In trying to regulate the economy the fundamental problem is, as shown, to *diagnose* the trends on which future predictions about the economy will be based. Such diagnosis requires an analysis of plans which have already been made and which will affect the future, as well as an understanding of factors which are likely to affect future expenditures.

On the factual side, of obtaining information about changes in the economy, much has been done to improve the position, although it remains true that a great deal more can and should be done to improve it still further. The question involves not only obtaining information but of obtaining it in time for it to be useful economically. The deficiencies in information make it difficult to evaluate government measures since 1945. It is not easy to decide whether the correct measures were applied in the wrong situation because of faulty information, or whether other elements in the picture were wrong.

After the prognostication, if action is thought to be necessary, the type of action to be taken must be decided upon. Enough has been said to indicate that in most cases a number of alternatives are open which will effect a remedy. The choice of which course of action offers the 'best' solution involves both political and economic judgment. In both cases differences of opinion can occur legitimately. Of particular importance in assessing alternative measures is the *time* scale needed to put the measures into effect, and once put into effect the *time* for them to affect the economy.

The position today is better than it used to be: company taxation has been put on a current-year basis and the Chancellor of the Exchequer has power under the name of the Regulator to vary the principal indirect taxes, in particular VAT and the drink and tobacco duties. The rate of VAT may be varied up or down by 2 per cent, so that the 8 per cent rate can be varied between 6 and 10 per cent by simple parliamentary procedure. Other rates may be varied by up to 10 per cent either way. The maximum value of the change is estimated to be some £1,400 million in 1976–7.

Another important consideration is how *flexible* the proposed action is. If the prognostication is wrong because it has either underestimated or overestimated the effects, can the action be changed so as to allow for these revised estimates?

Effect of changes on the economy

In trying to assess the relative merits of alternative policies it has been shown that it is useful to ask a number of questions, namely how long before the measure can be put into effect, how long before it then makes its impact on the economy, and is it flexible?

Management of the economy, however, is only one aim of government, labelled *stabilisation* in Chapter 10. Policies need also to be judged in relation to their effects on the *allocation* and *distribution* of resources.

Different policies will almost certainly affect the allocation of resources between private and public goods, between investment and consumption goods, and between types of goods in each category. A tax on labour is, for example, likely to lead to the substitution of capital for labour. Tracing the effects of different policies is likely to be difficult because not only is the stock, that is the amount already in existence, likely to be affected, but also the flow, that is the additional amount demanded or supplied over time. Thus one of the effects of the old Selective Employment Tax in its original form was to reduce the demand for part-time workers. Again, a change in tax rates may cause the existing labour force to work less hard, or more hard, and may also encourage or discourage married women into the labour force.

Different policies will also almost certainly affect the distribution of resources and move the economy towards, or away from, whatever degree of equity is considered desirable. For example, consumers' expenditure could be regulated by much greater use of value-added tax, but unless compensating action is taken considerable hardship is likely to poorer persons.

When the aims of government are considered as a whole, this limits the extent to which any one measure can be used. Favourable effects in one direction tend to be counterbalanced by unfavourable effects in other directions. The steps outlined can be summed up in a flow diagram (see Figure 25.1). Once it has been decided that action is required, this leads to a consideration of alternative policies indicated by 1, 2, 3, 4, . . . , *N*. For each policy it is necessary to weigh the time and flexibility elements and their effects on stabilisation, allocation and distribution.

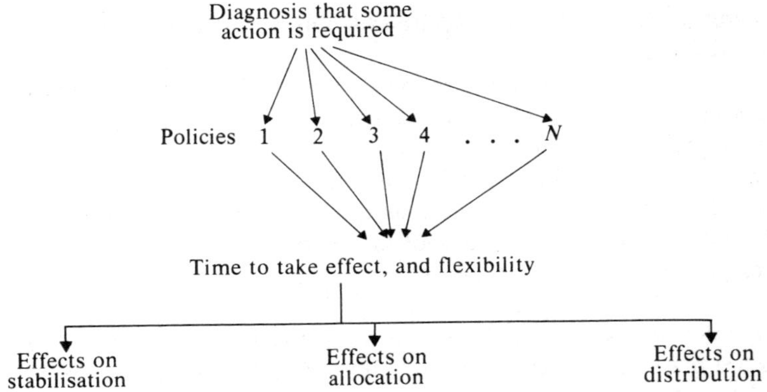

Figure 25.1

Measurement and control of public expenditure

The *Control of Public Expenditure* (1961) report, known as the Plowden Report after its Chairman, recommended that 'regular surveys should be made of public expenditure as a whole, over a period of years ahead, and in relation to prospective resources; decisions involving substantial future expenditure should be taken in the light of the survey'. The system has evolved since, and from 1969 the Public Expenditure Survey Committee (PESC) has published these forecasts as an annual White Paper. The rationale behind the White Papers is explained in HM Treasury (1972) and Goldman (1973).

The main features of the White Papers as outlined by the Treasury are:

1 Annual surveys cover the whole of public expenditure on current and capital account so that Ministers may review and, if necessary, adjust

particular parts in the light of demand-management considerations and the level of prospective resources.

2 The surveys include estimates for each of the next five years; however, the estimates for the last two years in the 1977 estimates are admitted to be 'even more provisional than usual' due to revisions of expenditure plans.

3 The forecasts of expenditure are based on the Government's existing policies and do not anticipate future policy decisions.

4 The figures are presented in constant-price terms. They show whether the Government's proposals have caused or are planned to cause public expenditure to rise or fall, and by how much, for reasons other than price changes.

5 The figures are analysed by function or programme under fifteen headings, such as defence, health and education.

6 The figures are also analysed by economic category, such as wages and salaries, grants and public capital formation.

7 The figures are given separately for central government, local authorities and public corporations, because of the differing degrees to which their expenditure is subject to parliamentary control.

As mentioned in 4 above, attempts are made to adjust for price changes. Figures are presented in two ways: at 'survey prices', and 'in cost terms'. The figures at survey prices are based on prices that ruled at the base date and assumes these prevail for the years covered by the survey. They therefore give an index in volume terms. Because of the difficulty of measuring the output of services, they are measured in terms of input – that is, by numbers employed and services purchased, etc.

Figures presented 'in cost terms' attempt to take account of future relative price movements by extrapolation of the average movements in five basic price indices. Figures on this basis thus attempt to take account of the fact that even if the volume index for certain services is the same the relative cost of the services may differ because of relative price changes.

Table 25.2 presents figures at 1976 survey prices and is therefore an attempt to illustrate the change in government expenditure in volume terms after price changes are netted out. Figures for 1971-2 and 1975-6 are given for comparison, as well as projected expenditures up to 1978-9. The provisional estimates for 1979-80 and 1980-1 are omitted. Total expenditures in the period 1971-2 up to 1975-6 showed a large increase (most of the increase occurred in the four periods before 1975-6). The large increase in grants and subsidies is mainly due to the restraint of

Table 25.2

Public expenditure by authority and category (£m. at 1976 survey prices)

	1971–2	1975–6	1976–7	1977–8	1978–9
Central government					
Goods and services	14,544	15,794	16,170	15,787	15,764
Grants and subsidies	13,160	16,837	17,718	17,539	17,615
Lending to nationalised industries	1,924	1,146	800	750	900
Other lending	292	1,362	766	68	536
Local authorities					
Goods and services	11,599	13,646	13,507	12,600	12,291
Grants and subsidies	646	1,384	1,444	1,594	1,644
Lending	270	406	54	-92	-75
*Public corporations**					
Capital expenditure	1,028	1,241	1,439	1,306	1,255
Debt interest†	1,075	1,128	1,800	2,300	2,300
Contingency reserve	–	–	–	650	900
	44,538	52,944	53,698	52,502	53,130

*Excluding nationalised industries.
†New basis, i.e. excluding interest, which is covered by trading income or interest receipts.
Source: The Government's Expenditure Plans, *HMSO, London, 1977.*

electricity, gas and postal charges under a Conservative Government and food and rent subsidies under a Labour Government. The restraint in nationalised industries' prices has now been phased out. The envisaged reduction in public expenditure reflects the Government's determination to restrain the growth of public expenditure. Goods and services, rather than transfer and subsidy payments, have been cut, with substantial adjustments in lending provisions.

In response to criticism of its expenditure plans, which will be looked at below, the Government has now instituted cash limits to the system. Expenditure plans at survey prices have to be translated into cash figures for the year immediately ahead. Wherever possible, control figures for the year ahead are now expressed as cash limits. These express the extent to which the Government is normally prepared to adjust the base prices to allow for pay and price increases. In 1976–7 cash limits have been applied to over 65 per cent of expenditure, including the grants paid to local authorities. The services omitted from the cash-limit system are mainly those which are demand-determined, i.e. where the Government has an obligation to meet claims. The contingency reserve, which appears for the last two periods in Table 25.2, is one of the means used to try and keep actual expenditure within the totals laid down. Claims on the reserve are mainly intended for demand-determined services where provision for new measures cannot be met within existing programmes, or increased costs cannot be corrected or offset by reductions elsewhere in the estimates. The debt-interest figures are shown on the new basis, i.e. they are net of receipts which the public sector earns on its borrowing through prices, rents or interest payments. On this basis the figure for debt interest represents that portion which must be financed either by taxation or by further borrowing.

While there is general agreement that the Public Expenditure White Papers represent a considerable advance in managing government expenditure, and that successive White Papers have been much improved, there is still considerable criticism of the scope and detail of the estimates (for a recent evaluation, see *Growth and Control of Public Expenditure*, 1976).

The most far-reaching criticism is one that reflects on long-established parliamentary procedures: that expenditure decisions are largely taken in isolation from revenue decisions. While the detailed linking of expenditure and revenue plans is unlikely, and may be undesirable, the total revenue implications of government spending plans would enable a more realistic evaluation of choices. Thus, if the Government is envisaged as spending, say, £300 million more in the next period than it did in the previous period, the implications of this on possible tax changes could be indicated on various assumptions about changes in growth, prices and incomes. Tentative as such estimates would have to be, they would at least enable changes in total spending to be related to the tax implications of the spending decisions.

More detailed criticism of the spending estimates concerns the use of survey prices, which are unique to the PESC system and, furthermore, are not uniform throughout the estimates. It has given rise to the saying that the accounts are expressed in 'funny' money, but this disparagement goes too far, as any index is subject to some degree of ambiguity. The use of these survey prices does, however, make it very difficult for outsiders to compare one year's White Paper with another year's.

The casting of estimates and authorisation of expenditure in terms of constant survey prices, or in cost terms that take the 'relative price effects' into account, give rise to concern that future expenditures are effectively isolated, at least for a time, from market pressures caused by relative price changes. One of the advantages claimed for cash limits is that they may force a reconsideration of spending if there have been strong relative price changes.

Finally, we note the important point that the spending estimates do not attempt to evaluate the different impact on the economy that different categories of expenditure may have.

Summary

The main components of Gross Domestic Product were looked at as these are critical for short-term forecasting. Some of the difficulties in forecasting the relevant magnitudes were examined.

Ideas about a balanced budget were then taken up. These ideas have an intuitive appeal to the individual because of the false analogy often made between the economy of the State and that of the private household.

Practical difficulties in establishing just what is happening in the economy, and what measures should be taken if something needs correcting, were outlined and summarised.

Finally, an examination and evaluation was made of the Government's measurement and control of public expenditure as detailed in their annual Public Expenditure White Papers.

Notes

1 For a recent lively account of the role of economists in advising governments and the constraints they work under, see Peacock (March 1977).
2 I am indebted to Professor Sir Bryan Hopkin for this section.

26
Monetary and debt policy

[E]conomists have had little difficulty in verifying that monetary policy can influence interest rates and credit conditions, and great difficulty in detecting the influence of the latter, or of the quantity of money itself, on economic activity. Nevertheless, very few economists would be prepared to assert, and certainly none has ever attempted to prove, that monetary policy has no influence whatever on the economy.
H. G. JOHNSON (1967), *Essays in Monetary Economics.*

Monetary and debt policy aims at influencing the economic activity of the community by acting on the quantity and composition of money and assets. Indissolubly linked with this is policy on interest rates. Policy is concerned with internal stabilisation and external balance-of-payments considerations. The last ten years have seen much work in this field at both the empirical and theoretical level (for a concise account see Bain, 1976). This chapter attempts no more than to state some of the main issues, many of which have still to be resolved.

Introduction

Monetary policy differs from fiscal policy in an important aspect that is easy to overlook. A fiscal change such as a change in taxes is a policy instrument in the hands of the Government – there may be difficulties of an administrative or technical nature but all that has to be ascertained is the effect of the change on the goals the Government is pursuing. The money supply is not a policy instrument in the same way. The Government may decide it wants the money supply to change; it can only attempt to do this indirectly and may be thwarted in its attempts. With monetary policy the instruments at its disposal operate on intermediate targets which in turn are expected to affect the goals. We thus have goals, intermediate targets and instruments.

Goals: full employment, growth, price stability, a satisfactory balance of payments or exchange rate, equity.

Intermediate targets: money supply, credit, interest rates.

Instruments: open-market operations, reserve requirements, requests, direct controls such as wage and price controls.

The goals may be mutually unattainable, trade-offs may be needed between them, but once these have been decided fiscal policy just has to establish the difficult question of how the fiscal change affects the goals and the nature of the time lags involved. With monetary policy we have another layer of ambiguity: monetary instruments only operate on intermediate targets, so that as well as uncertainties between the targets and goals we have uncertainties between instruments and targets.

The above account has made an over-sharp distinction between fiscal and monetary policy. It is hard to imagine a pure fiscal change, i.e. one with no monetary overlap, and similarly it is hard to imagine a pure monetary change that has no fiscal ramifications. Management policy is more complicated than the above account would imply and a successful policy needs to take these mutual influences into account. The intermediate stage in the operation of monetary policy has a further important consequence: the target variables may change autonomously and policy mistakes may be made as a consequence.

Questions about the quantity of money fall into those dealing with how this quantity can be controlled, and if control can be achieved, is it successful, or does the presence of liquid assets nullify in whole or in part the attempt at control? From a different standpoint, questions may be posed on the relation of the quantity of money to prices. Once the simple, but incorrect, idea that there is a direct relation between the two is rejected, it is necessary to look at the reasons for holding money and the effect of other assets on money holdings.

The importance of the composition of assets has been commented on several times. The monetary authorities for much of the post-1945 period were concerned to reduce the liquidity of the banks for fear that they would use this as base for extending loans. Also, they aimed to reduce the liquidity of the public in general so as to reduce the potential spending power in the economy. The quantity of assets, that is whether the total is increasing or decreasing, will have repercussions on liquidity and make it easier or harder for the authorities to maintain the level of liquidity and structure of rates they require.

Monetary policy therefore involves a study of money, assets and interest rates. It is not possible, without drastic simplification, to separate out one of these components for study independently of the other components. Indeed, by trying to do so we may obscure the effects we are trying to trace. Monetary and debt analysis thus becomes an attempt to trace the impact of money, assets and interest rates. An important part of this impact is the action of each of these components on the other.

Money

The conclusion was reached in Part I that the quantity of coin and notes in the British system is not an important policy variable; they are not issued as a means of financing government expenditure. As a last resort the Government issues Treasury Bills, which – in the absence of countervailing action – can be used by the banks to expand deposits. Control of bank deposits is open to the authorities by a variety of means; the limitations were dealt with in Chapter 7. These methods were:

1 Open-market operations } (both have direct effects on other rates
2 Changing MLR } of interest)
3 Use of directives or moral suasion
4 Special Deposits, and Supplementary Special Deposits
5 Prudential examinations and ratios.

Open-market sales to the public will tend to depress prices and so drive up the yield on existing securities; conversely, open-market buying will lower yields. Also, the issue of new securities will have to take account of the change in yield on old securities. Open-market operations are concerned with government fixed-interest securities and thus will not automatically affect company finance. However, if the change in yield on government securities is expected to be one that will last for some time, it is usual to expect sympathetic changes in other rates, otherwise money will tend to flow to that sector which now offers better terms. As with most relationships, this can be a two-way affair. The yield on existing securities may be used as a guide by the authorities as to the interest rates to be charged on new government debt. In the words of the Radcliffe Report (1959, para. 552) the authorities, 'Over much of the period [1945–59] were therefore entirely passive, indeed fatalistic, in their attitude to the movement of long-term interest rates.'

The dilemma is clear: the authorities can set out to control the rates of interest by being willing to buy and sell on the market as required, in which case they cannot have control over the quantity of assets; or they can control the quantity of assets, in which case they have to forgo control over the rate of interest and let this find the level at which the quantity of assets they have decided on will be held.

Changing the MLR operates initially on the short end of the market. Given a change in MLR that is expected to continue for some time, it is likely that the long end of the market will be influenced to some extent.

It may be the case that a change in MLR and open-market operations are undertaken together in an attempt to reduce bank deposits and enforce a contraction on banks. By selling securities to the public, the authorities cause the public to exchange some of their bank deposits for government securities – a leakage as far as the banking system is concerned, if the authorities do not return the money to the system. The success of this policy depends, as shown earlier, on the willingness of the public to take up new government issues, how they finance these securities and on the ease with which the banks can recoup them.

Changing interest rates may influence the amount of money people are willing to hold, i.e. the demand for money. The higher the rates of interest the more is forgone by keeping a balance in a current banking account. This effect is not thought generally to be very strong.

The use of moral suasion and of Special Deposits do not directly act on interest rates; they are an attempt to restrict the supply of credit that the banks can extend. In Britain it is clear that sufficient pressure can be brought on the banks to make a credit squeeze on the banks effective. The critical question is whether this means an effective squeeze or whether other institutions take up the running.

The conclusion reached earlier was clear cut: the presence of other financial institutions with quasi-money assets does to some extent nullify the attempt to limit credit; the expansion that can take place in trade credit and economising on money balances also help to limit the effectiveness of a squeeze. However, this is not to say that a squeeze on the banks can be completely counteracted. In particular, certain sectors of the economy – those that traditionally rely on bank credit – are likely to be more seriously affected and find it more difficult to find substitute finance. In general, small firms and private individuals will be squeezed more than large firms; for example, house purchase, where bridging loans from a bank play an important role, will be affected. Monetary policy has in the past been recommended because its effects were thought to be impersonal, compared with, say, changing Customs and Excise duties, where a decision has to be made as to which articles shall bear the tax. This is seen to be false. A monetary squeeze no less than other measures has directional effects which may be desired, or not desired, but cannot be avoided. It remains true, however, that monetary policy has widespread effects on the economy; these are hard to quantify and depend on a number of circumstances, for example how long the credit squeeze is expected to last.

The recognition of the importance of controlling other financial institutions was shown in the financial history of the early 1970s leading up to the White Paper (*Licensing and Supervision of Deposit-Taking Institutions*) which proposes control over all deposit-taking institutions.

Control of the money supply is, as has been shown in Chapter 7 and above, subject to considerable uncertainties. Theoretically the money supply can be maintained at a desired level by sufficient use of the measures just outlined, but the cost of doing so – high interest rates, bankruptcies, unemployment and fluctuations of the economy – may at times be thought to be unacceptable. Since 1976, as outlined in the last chapter, monetary aggregates have become one of the target variables and if forecasts show this target is not being met it may lead to a reconsideration of policy.

For Monetarists control of the money supply is seen as a key factor in controlling the economy and in particular in controlling inflation. Because of uncertain time lags they do not recommend the use of monetary policy for short-term control of the economy but rather believe that a steady growth in money supply will lead to long-term stability in the price level.

Keynesians tend to stress not the quantity of money side of the coin but the interest-rate side. The next sections look in more detail at interest rates.

Monetary assets and rates of interest

We have seen that the monetary authorities are concerned with both the quantity of monetary assets and the composition of them. They are concerned because of the effect on their ability to control the banks and the financial sector, rates of interest, and consumption and investment generally.

The line marked '1' in Figure 26.1 represents the so-called 'normal yield curve'. It shows the relationship that is usually found between yields and issues of securities of varying maturity, but similar risk in respect of default, for example it represents the normal relationship of yield on government securities of varying maturity: other fixed interest securities will again, as a rule, stand in some stable relationship to yield on government securities.

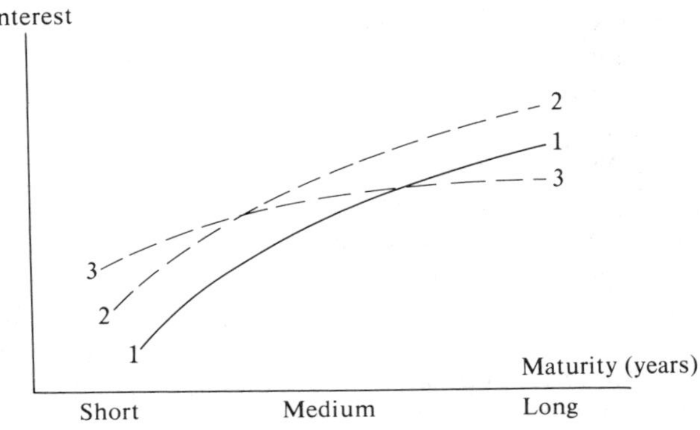

Figure 26.1 *Normal yield curve*

The yield curve moves sharply up at the short end and then tends to flatten out. The nearer the security is to maturity, the more certain is the capital value of the security, the higher yield on longer securities reflecting the greater uncertainty as to capital value. An increase in interest rates from, say, 10 per cent to 12 per cent is not going to make all that difference to the value of a Treasury Bill that in any case will be worth its face-value in three months. It will make a substantial difference to the market price of a security that is not redeemable for a number of years. Nobody is going to purchase an old security at £100 that yields 10 per cent when a new security that gives 12 per cent can be purchased for £100. The market value of the old security will fall so as to bring its yield into line.

It has already been shown that the monetary authorities can influence the rates of interest in various ways. Here we are talking of a *shift* in the yield curve, say from curve '1' to curve '2' in Figure 26.1. They can confine their attention to the short end of the market by changing the MLR, letting their influence work its way to the longer end of the market. They can conduct open-market operations in longer-term securities and so influence the longer term directly. Thus selling long-term securities will tend to depress the price and raise the yield; if this is accompanied by an increase in the MLR, the yield curve will shift in the direction of curve 2. Selling short-term debt and buying long-term debt will tend to increase the yield on short-term and decrease it on long-term, in the manner indicated by curve 3.

One reason why it is necessary to say 'tend to' in any account of influences affecting interest rates is the impossibility of knowing in advance the effects of the influence on expectations and confidence. If a change in MLR, for example, is expected to be reversed in the near future, it is likely to have different results than if it is expected to remain at its new level for some time, and different results again if it is expected to be changed soon in the same direction as the original move.

Two innovations were witnessed in 1977. One was the successful issue of partly paid stocks. This was the first issue of government stock payable by instalments since 1940. In the first two issues £15 was payable on application, with two unequal instalments payable approximately one month and three months from the time of issue. Such issues help ensure a substantial volume of future funding and so it is hoped will lead to confidence that monetary targets can be achieved.

The second innovation was the issue of floating rate stocks. The interest rate is fixed at ½ per cent over the average Treasury Bill rate during each half-yearly interest period. These innovations are seen as additions to the usual type of security intended to give the authorities a greater degree of flexibility in managing the markets.

Other fixed-interest securities, for example company debentures, will normally have a slightly higher yield than government securities in order to provide a premium for the risk of default. Again, the action of the market can be expected to keep the yield on government securities and other fixed-interest securities more or less moving together.

When we move to ordinary equity shares of companies, it may be felt intuitively that there should be some connection between yields on fixed-interest securities and yields on equities; but so many other factors play their part in determining the market price of equities that a simple stable relationship is unlikely. In general, we should expect a change in long-term rates on government securities that is expected to last for some time to be reflected in the market for equities by the channelling of some new money, and the channelling of some of the proceeds from the sale of existing securities, towards the fixed-interest sector of the market rather than towards the equity market. If such a movement does take place, we have lower prices (i.e. greater yields) in the equity market and the opposite movement in the fixed-interest market. Because risk of default, and hopes of gain in the form of dividends paid out by the company and capital value of the equity shares, vary so much between companies, and because these hopes and fears need not be linked (although they may at times be related) to changes in fixed-interest rates, the relationship between equity prices and other security prices is not a direct one. This should not be taken as saying that prices in the two markets are completely independent of each other.

Influence of interest rates

It has been established so far that the monetary authorities can influence the structure of interest rates in the economy. They do this primarily by MLR and by market operations in their own debt. These effects are fed back by the market and move other rates in the same direction as the movement in government security rates.

It has now to be decided what influence the level of interest rates has on the economy. Here we again enter controversial territory.

Those that hold that interest rates are important have to demonstrate not only a connection between various interest rates (on the lines of the previous section) but a connection between interest rates and real variables in the economy, i.e. between interest rates and consumption and/or investment.

At several points we have discussed the influence of interest rates. Attempts to link changes in the rate of interest with changes in the supply of money via the locking-in effect were discounted for Britain. In general, consumption also seems to be relatively insensitive via any direct effect of a change in interest rates. Consumers are known to alter their purchase of goods when the down-payment and/or period of hire-purchase agreements are altered, but little change is noticed if interest rates are changed. However, empirical work on the wealth effect of a change in interest rates yields more positive results. When interest rates fall, the value of long-term, fixed-interest debt, and sometimes other financial assets such as equities, increases and the value of real assets such as housing may rise. The owners of such instruments may increase their consumption for a time out of this increased wealth. Even if the asset is not sold, the owner, feeling wealthier, may save less and be able to consume more by this means. The reverse situation can apply when interest rates rise and, hence, capital values fall.

Many factors are present in a decision whether or not to undertake real investment, and because many investments are required to pay for themselves over a period of a few years, a change in interest rates is not likely to alter significantly many of these plans. Increases in interest rates are also softened because some fixed-interest charges, for example debenture interest and bank overdraft charges, can be offset against tax by companies. However, as the projected life of an investment goes up, the interest component of the finance involved becomes a greater proportion of the cost of the project and it would be expected that long-term investments would be more sensitive to changes in interest rates. Empirical studies seem to confirm this view.[1]

There may also be an important influence via the impact on company finance. The stock of financial assets in the economy is very large in relation to the flow of new financial assets coming on to the market in any financial period, say a year. Now the stock of assets must be held by somebody or some institution. Securities can only be sold if somebody else is willing to purchase them. The prices of existing securities will affect the price at which new securities will find willing holders.

It is submitted that, because the amount of existing securities is very large in relation to new issues in a year, the causation runs from the yield on existing securities determining the conditions under which a new issue can be successful, rather than from new issues influencing to any great extent the yield on old securities. It is now possible to distinguish two important ways that current yields can influence investment.

First, if current holders of existing securities are content with low yields (i.e. prices of securities are 'high'), firms find the stock market buoyant, and issues of new securities are easier and more profitable, easier because the market is buoyant, and more profitable because the securities can be issued at a higher price (lower yield). The reverse situation also holds: a depressed market makes it harder and more costly to raise new money by the issue of securities. Thus investment which has to be financed by the issue of securities can be influenced if the stock market can be influenced.[2] It has been argued in the previous section that a change in interest rates on government securities which compete on the market with company issues can have this effect.[3]

As an example, the case of an increase in MLR will be taken. Two strands of influence can be picked out: (i) the relative effect – that because rates on government securities have increased, rates on company securities will have to adjust in the same direction; and (ii) effects on confidence. If raising MLR is taken as a sign that a period of restriction is on hand (and particularly if it is accompanied by other measures which depress the economy or particular sectors of it), then (i) and (ii) taken together may operate to have a sizeable effect on stock exchange prices as a whole or of the particular sectors concerned. In addition, the authorities can influence the market in other ways, for example by asking for dividend restraint or altering company tax or allowances.

Second, if the return which a firm is receiving from its existing real investment is below the average yield on financial assets, incentive to undertake further real investment will be low. The prudent firm will hold any funds it has in financial assets which will give it a greater return than putting it into real assets. Also, it will not attempt to raise money on the market at a cost which exceeds the expected return. This reasoning will not hold in every individual case; it is not difficult, for example, to imagine circumstances where a firm can find profitable real investment outlets even though the yield from its existing real capital is low. However, as an explanation of aggregate behaviour of the real investment market this influence is likely to be a powerful one. This has lead to the suggestion (for example, Brainard and Tobin, May 1968) that a target of monetary policy should be the real return on equity.

Other monetary effects

Roe (June 1973) makes an important distinction between the *control* over the money supply function and the *support* function. The latter is the concern that monetary authorities must have to ensure the viability of firms, institutions and markets. It is the need to protect them from undeserved insolvency – due, for example, to the collapse of confidence in a particular security market. A large-scale example of assistance given for this reason was the 'lifeboat' operation organised by the Bank of England in 1974.

Monetary policy is thus seen as having two aims, and these may conflict at times. It would be foolish to press a restriction in the money supply so that a wholesale loss of confidence and collapse of the financial sector ensued. A more likely danger highlighted by Roe is that abrupt changes of policy can have similar effects. He outlines the position in Britain before 1969 when there was no real restriction on the growth of the money supply, the gilt-edged market was being supported, thereby guaranteeing liquidity, and direct financial assistance to industry was being provided on a large scale by the Industrial Reorganisation Corporation. The change in attitude to all three helped contribute to the cash-flow crises of 1970–1. We have already detailed the next cycle of monetary expansion which followed this and its subsequent reversal which led to the more serious crises of 1973–4.

External considerations

For a country like Britain, which is one of the world's financial centres and is also involved heavily in international trade, monetary and debt policy has major implications for the balance of payments. To put it another way, balance-of-payments considerations are one of the major factors determining monetary and fiscal policy.

Under the present system of floating exchange rates, the Bank of England still intervenes in the foreign exchange markets to ensure that the exchange rate is not pushed to unrealistic levels.

The authorities are concerned that interest rates do not get too far out of line with financial centres in other countries. A major part of the more recent emphasis on monetary magnitudes is again to maintain foreign confidence in the management of the economy.

Direct effects come from that part of the National Debt which is held by other than British residents. Servicing this part of the debt therefore results in a flow of payments overseas and pressure on the balance of payments. There is thus a possibility that rates of interest considered desirable for internal purposes clash with rates considered desirable for external reasons. The effect on the balance of payments of the external debt depends on a number of considerations. In particular, it depends on whether the overseas holder is prepared (for a time) to hold sterling balances, that is in effect to reinvest in sterling securities, or whether these holders convert into gold or foreign currencies. It also varies a great deal depending on the amount and type of debt held abroad, the reactions of these holders and the extent to which transactions are covered in the forward exchange market.

A relative change in interest rates between countries, or changes in confidence, may cause flows of money between financial centres. So-called 'hot' money is money invested short term for speculative reasons and in order to take advantage of differentials in interest rates. A change in confidence or in interest differentials will reverse the flow. The danger of these flows of short-term money is that they may cause (taking Britain as an example) a 'run on the pound', i.e. in present conditions an excessive depreciation of sterling. Since there is nothing to distinguish 'hot' money from other sterling balances (although some idea of the magnitudes involved may be built up from a knowledge of the lenders), an adverse balance of payments caused by the outflow of these volatile funds may so unsettle other foreign holders that they, too, seek to convert their sterling holdings into gold or foreign currencies, and a run on the pound is under way. We see therefore why rates of interest in one country need to take account of rates ruling in other financial centres.

Flows of money between countries depend on much more than differential interest rates; these other influences are usually summed up by the word 'confidence'. In the post-1945 period Bank Rate was usually changed only as part of a 'package deal'; that is to say, other things are altered at the same time. For example, an increase in Bank Rate could be accompanied by all, or some, of the following measures: restrictions on the banks; hire purchase made less attractive by increasing the down-payment and decreasing the period over which payments could be spread; restrictions on currency movements; and tax increases. In these circumstances the 'package deal', of which Bank Rate formed a part, could restore confidence that sterling was not going to be devalued and result in a substantial improvement in the reserve position, i.e. foreign holders were willing to retain their sterling holdings and many of those who caused the adverse outflow by exchanging sterling for gold or other currencies were induced to return to sterling. As we have seen, the position since 1971 has changed, and MLR is now much closer to a market-determined rate and is changed frequently.

With a floating rate of exchange there is still the possibility of conflict between internal and external policy. Pressure against sterling which results in a falling exchange rate improves our price competitiveness abroad but makes imports more expensive and so leads to inflationary pressure at home. Intervention to stabilise exchange rates offers the same constraints on internal policy as is felt with fixed rates. With the ending of a formal pay policy in 1977, the Government hoped to see average earnings rise by no more than 10 per cent over the following twelve months and settlements made only once in a twelve-month period. It indicated that it was not prepared to see the exchange depreciated to compensate for excessive wage increases since this would merely add to inflationary pressures.

Conclusion

The monetary authorities, because of the size and importance of their operations, are not in a position to adopt a completely 'neutral' policy where they can leave market forces to determine interest rates and the size and composition of money and assets.

Although policy changes in this field have effects on the internal economy, these effects are not precise, nor can their magnitude be predicted very accurately. Reasons for this stressed the part played by expectations and the effects on confidence. Thus rates of interest above traditional levels may yet stimulate, rather than depress, economic activity if it is generally thought that rates will go higher and remain higher for some time. Similarly, rates of interest below traditional levels may depress rather than stimulate activity if it is thought that rates will shortly go lower and remain lower for some time. Abrupt changes of monetary policy from ease to restriction were shown to have been very disruptive to the economy in recent years.

External effects of changes in policy are, unlike internal effects, often very quick to take effect, but they share with internal effects the difficulty of predicting the magnitude of the change. Maintaining confidence in the currency is the most important external role of monetary and debt policy, but monetary and debt policy is only one (although an important one) of the factors affecting confidence.

Summary

This chapter started with a resumé of how effectively the monetary authorities can control the supply of money. As with so much economic policy there may be trade-offs between the money supply, interest rates, bankruptcies, unemployment and economic fluctuations in the economy which involve unpleasant choices.

Monetarists stress control over the money supply as a key factor in long-term management of the economy, in particular in controlling inflation. Since 1976, under the influence of the International Monetary Fund, Domestic Credit Expansion has become one of the targets of policy, and the emphasis has changed in the 1970s from a prime emphasis on interest rates to a greater emphasis on monetary magnitudes. However, for an open economy like Britain it is unrealistic to suppose that the authorities can completely neglect the effect of interest rates and only pursue a monetary target.

The influence of interest rates on the economy is important because it will attract or repel funds from abroad, and has effects on long-lived capital investment. Other effects on the economy are harder to establish empirically. One of the most important ways is if the stock market can be influenced; this is likely to affect companies thinking of raising new money by a stock or share issue. Also, rates of return on real investment need to be above average rates of return on financial assets if real investment is to be encouraged. The impact of a change in interest rates is difficult to measure because it depends so much on whether the change affects, and in what direction it affects, confidence and business expectations. It is easier to pin-point the harmful effects that have followed abrupt changes of policy from monetary ease to monetary stringency.

This part of the book set out with the limited aim of showing just how difficult management of the economy, whether this is attempted by fiscal or monetary means, is. It is not just that our theories about how the economy operates are imperfect and our knowledge of the facts imprecise. Given perfection in both cases there would still be disagreement, because value-judgments enter as to which way, out of numerous possible ways, should be selected to achieve any particular end.

Notes

1 This account has abstracted from the effects of a credit squeeze as such. If credit is squeezed, there are obviously direct effects on the economy which will vary according to the severity of the squeeze. Changes in interest rates need not be accompanied by tighter monetary conditions, although in practice higher interest rates may be coupled with calls for Special Deposits or other measures designed to restrict lending.

2 The crucial assumption in this sentence is 'investment which has to be financed by the issue of securities'. Little evidence is available on the extent to which investment intended to be financed by an issue of securities is deferred or abandoned when the stock market becomes unfavourable. The alternative is to go ahead with the investment, if temporary finance is available, with the intention of repaying this when an issue can be made on more favourable terms. Temporary finance is usually costly and is likely to deter the use of this method.

3 The oral evidence of the representatives of the Issuing Houses Association to the Radcliffe Committee (Minutes of Evidence, Questions 4001–167) is germane. Three strands can be distinguished: Did a change in interest rates affect new issues: (i) by freezing the market for technical reasons, i.e. because of interruption of the mechanism for making new issues; (ii) by affecting the supply of capital; or (iii) by affecting the demand for capital? The effects under (i) and (ii) were generally discounted; but the third heading raised some interesting replies: 'The whole terms of an issue depend on the Bank Rate and gilt-edged prices, and if we thought there were likely to be very wide or large fluctuations in the Bank Rate we should just have to be more careful' (Question 4039); 'Presumably it is part of the job of the issuing house, advising their clients, to consider that economic climate, and they would be considering their assessment, in the light of that and of the possibility of a movement in the Bank Rate' (Question 4044); 'But, generally speaking, I would think that the actual mechanical fact of raising the Bank Rate merely means a mechanical adjustment of rates. It might in certain cases make borrowing too expensive; and some people might say that they would not go ahead' (Question 4045).

References

ABEL-SMITH, B. (1964), *Freedom in the Welfare State*, Fabian Society, London.

ACCOUNTING STANDARDS COMMITTEE (November 1976), *Exposure Draft 18*, London.

Administrative Structure of the Medical and Related Services in England and Wales (1968), Ministry of Health, HMSO, London.

ARTIS, M. J. (1965), *Foundations of British Monetary Policy*, Blackwell, Oxford.

ASSOCIATION OF MUNICIPAL CORPORATIONS (1965), *Reform of Rating*.

ATKINSON, A. B. (July 1971), 'The Distribution of Wealth and the Individual Life-cycle', *Oxford Economic Papers*, Oxford University Press, London.

— (1972), *Unequal Shares: Wealth in Britain*, Allen Lane, The Penguin Press, London.

— (1973), 'Low Pay and the Cycle of Inequality', in F. Field (ed.), *Low Pay*, Arrow Books, London.

— (September 1973), *The Tax Credit Scheme and Redistribution of Income*, Institute for Fiscal Studies, Heinemann, London.

— (1975), *The Economics of Inequality*, Oxford University Press, London.

— and HARRISON, A. J. (June 1974), 'Wealth Distribution and Investment Income in Britain', *Review of Income and Wealth.*

— and HARRISON, A. J. (1977), *The Distribution of Personal Wealth in Britain*, Cambridge University Press.

BAIN, A. D. (1976), *The Control of the Money Supply*, 2nd ed., Penguin, Harmondsworth.

Bank Charges (1967), Report No. 34, National Board for Prices and Incomes, HMSO, London.

Bank of England Quarterly Bulletins

(September 1961 and June 1968), 'Overseas and Foreign Banks in London', vol. 1, no. 4; and vol. 8, no. 2.

(June 1962), 'Inflows and Outflows of Foreign Funds', vol. 2, no. 2.

(December 1962), 'Bank Liquidity in the United Kingdom', vol. 2, no. 4.
(March 1963), 'Management of Money Day by Day', vol. 3, no. 1.
(March 1965), 'Note Circulation', vol. 5, no. 1.
(June 1965), 'Financial Institutions', vol. 5, no. 2.
(June 1966), 'Official Transactions in the Gilt-edged Market', vol. 6, no. 2.
(June 1968), 'Control of Bank Lending: the Cash Deposits Scheme', vol. 7, no. 2.
(June 1970), 'The Importance of Money', vol. 10, no. 2.
(June 1971), 'Competition and Credit Control', vol. 11, no. 2.
(September 1971), 'Competition and Credit Control: the Discount Market', vol. 11, no. 3.
(March 1972), 'The Demand for Money in the UK: A Further Investigation', vol. 12, no. 1.
(September 1974), 'The Demand for Money in the UK: Experience since 1971', vol. 14, no. 3.
(June 1975), 'The Supervision of the UK Banking System', vol. 15, no. 2.
(September 1975), 'The Capital and Liquidity Adequacy of Banks', vol. 15, no. 3.
(March 1977), 'DCE and the Money Supply: A Statistical Note', vol. 17, no. 1.
(June 1977), 'Financial Forecasts in the United Kingdom', vol. 17, no. 2.
(June 1978), 'The Secondary Banking Crises and the Bank of England's Support Operations', paper presented by the Bank to the Research Panel of the Wilson Committee, vol. 18, no. 2.

BARR, N. A., JAMES, S. R. and PREST, A. R. (1977), *Self-Assessment for Income Tax*, Institute for Fiscal Studies, Heinemann, London.

BARRO, R. J. and FISCHER, S. (April 1976), 'Recent Developments in Monetary Theory', *Journal of Monetary Economics*, vol. 2, no. 2.

BELL, K. (1975), *Research Study on Supplementary Benefit Appeal Tribunals*, HMSO, London.

BEVERIDGE, W. H. (1944), *Full Employment in a Free Society*, Allen & Unwin, London.

BLINDER, A. S., SOLOW, R. M. *et al.* (1974), *The Economics of Public Finance*, The Brookings Institution, Washington, DC.

BLUNDEN, G. (1976), 'Recent Developments in British Banking', Speech at the Cardiff Business Club, 25 October 1976.

BOREHAM, A. J. and SEMPLE, M. (1976), 'Future Development of Work in the Government Statistical Service on the Distribution and Redistribution of Household Income', in *The Personal Distribution of Income*, ed. Atkinson, A. B., Allen & Unwin, London.

BRACEWELL-MILNES, B. (1976), *The Camel's Back: an International Comparison of Tax Burdens,* Centre for Policy Studies, London.

— (1977), *Short Measure from Whitehall*, Centre for Policy Studies, London.

BRAINARD, W. C. and TOBIN, J. (May 1968), 'Pitfalls in Financial Model Building', *American Economic Review*, Papers and Proceedings, vol. 58.

BREAK, G. F. (September 1957), 'Income Taxes and Incentives to Work', *American Economic Review*, vol. 47.

British System of Taxation (1977), Central Office of Information, Pamphlet 12, HMSO, London.

BRITTAN, S. (1971), *Steering the Economy: the Role of the Treasury*, Penguin, Harmondsworth.

BRONFENBRENNER, M. and HOLZMAN, F. D. (September, 1963), 'Survey of Inflation Theory', *American Economic Review*, vol. 53, no. 4.

BROWN, C. V. (1976), 'Taxation and Labour Supply – Weekly Paid Workers', in *Taxation and Incentives*, Institute for Fiscal Studies, London.

— and DAWSON, D. A. (1969), *Personal Taxation, Incentives and Tax Reform*, Political and Economic Planning, London.

— and LEVIN, E. (December 1974), 'The Effects of Income Taxation on Overtime: The Results of a National Survey', *Economic Journal.*

BRUNNER, K. and MELTZER, A. H. (December 1971), 'The Uses of Money: Money in the Theory of an Exchange Economy', *American Economic Review*, vol. LXI, no. 5.

BUCHANAN, J. M. (September 1950), 'Federalism and Fiscal Equity', *American Economic Review*, pp. 583–600; reprinted in *Readings in the Economics of Taxation*, ed. Musgrave, R. A. and Shoup, C. There is a subsequent discussion by Jenkins, N. P. and Buchanan, J. M. (August 1951), *Journal of Political Economy*, pp. 353–9.

— (1968), *The Demand and Supply of Public Goods*, Rand McNally, Chicago.

— (1977), *Democracy in Deficit: The Political Legacy of Lord Keynes*, Academic Press, New York and London.

—, BURTON, J. and WAGNER, R. E. (1978), *The Consequences of Mr. Keynes,* Hobart Paper 78, IEA, London.

— and TULLOCK, G. (1962), *The Calculus of Consent*, University of Michigan Press.

CAIRNCROSS, A. (ed.) (1971), *Britain's Economic Prospects Reconsidered*, Allen & Unwin, London.

Catalogue of Social Security Leaflets, Department of Health and Social Security, HMSO, London.

CAVES, R. E. (ed.) (1968), *Britain's Economic Prospects*, Allen & Unwin, London, for The Brookings Institution, Washington, DC.

CENTRAL OFFICE OF INFORMATION (1977), *The British System of Taxation*, Pamphlet 112, HMSO, London.

CHRISTOPHER, A. *et al.* (1970), *Policy for Poverty*, Research Monograph no. 20, Institute of Economic Affairs, London.

Circumstances of Families (1967), Ministry of Social Security, HMSO, London.

CLARK, C. (1977), *Poverty before Politics*, Hobart Paper 73, Institute of Economic Affairs, London.

CLAYTON, G. *et al.* (eds) (1971), *Monetary Theory and Monetary Policy in the 1970's, Proceedings of the 1970 Sheffield Money Seminar*, Oxford University Press, London.
CLOWER, R. E. (ed.) (1969), 'The Keynesian Counter-Revolution: A Theoretical Appraisal', in *Readings in Monetary Theory*, Penguin, Harmondsworth.
COLLARD, D. (1968), *The New Right: A Critique*, Fabian Tract 387, Fabian Society, London.
COMMITTEE FOR ECONOMIC DEVELOPMENT (1972), *Taxes and the Budget: A Program for Prosperity in a Free Economy*, New York.
COMMITTEE OF INQUIRY ON THE IMPACT OF RATES ON HOUSEHOLDS (1965), *Report*, Cmnd 2582, HMSO, London.
COMMITTEE ON FINANCE AND INDUSTRY (1931), Cmnd 3897, HMSO, London.
COMMITTEE ON THE WORKING OF THE MONETARY SYSTEM (1959), *Report*, Cmnd 827, HMSO, London.
COMMITTEE ON TURNOVER TAX (1964), *Report*, Cmnd 2300, HMSO, London.
COMMITTEE TO REVIEW NATIONAL SAVINGS (1973) (Page Committee), Cmnd 5273, HMSO, London.
Conditions Favourable to Faster Growth (1963), National Economic Development Council, London.
Conference on Proposals for a Tax-Credit System (1973), Institute for Fiscal Studies, London.
Control of Public Expenditure (1961), The Plowden Report, Cmnd 1432, HMSO, London.
Corporation Tax (1965), Cmnd 2646, HMSO, London.
CRAMP, A. B. (February 1963), 'Banks and Their Competitors', *Banker*.
— (June 1966), 'Control of the Money Supply', *Economic Journal*.
— (October 1967), 'The Control of Bank Deposits', *Lloyds Bank Review*.
CROCKETT, A. (1973), *Theory, Policy, Money and Institutions*, Nelson, London.
CROUCH, R. L. (December 1964), 'The Inadequacy of "New Orthodox" Methods of Monetary Control', *Economic Journal*.
— (August 1965), 'The Genesis of Bank Deposits, New English Version', *Bulletin of the Oxford Institute of Statistics*.
DALTON, A. *et al.* (1976), *A Chancellor's Primer*, Bow Group, London.
DALTON, H. (1959), *The Inequality of Incomes*, Routledge & Kegan Paul, London.
DENMAN, D. R. (1958), *Origins of Ownership*, Allen & Unwin, London.
DEPARTMENT OF ENERGY (1976–7), Energy Discussion Documents, HMSO, London.
Development Areas Regional Employment Premium (1967), Cmnd 3310, HMSO, London.
Devolution within the United Kingdom: Some Alternatives for Discussion (1974), HMSO, London.
DOSSER, D. (September 1961), 'Tax Incidence and Growth', *Economic Journal*, vol. 71, pp. 572–91.

DOW, J. C. R. (1964), *The Management of the British Economy, 1945–60*, Cambridge University Press.

DOWNS, A. (1956), *An Economic Theory of Democracy*, Harper & Row, New York.

DREES, W., JR (1967), 'Efficiency in Government Spending', *Public Finance*, vol. XXII, nos 1–2.

Economic Trends (1965), HMSO, London.

'Effects of Taxes and Benefits on Household Income: 1976' (February 1978), *Economic Trends*, no. 292, Central Statistical Office, HMSO, London.

EINZIG, P. (1970), *The Eurodollar System*, 4th ed., Macmillan, London.

EISENSTEIN, L. (1961), *The Ideologies of Taxation*, Ronald Press, New York.

EISNER, R. and STROTZ, R. H. (1963), 'Determinants of Business Investment', in *Impacts of Monetary Policy*, Prentice-Hall, Englewood Cliffs, NJ.

Employment Policy (1944), Cmnd 6527, HMSO, London.

EXPERT COMMITTEE ON COMPENSATION AND BETTERMENT (1942), *Report*, Cmnd 6386, HMSO, London.

FEIGE, E. L. and PEARCE, D. K. (June 1977), 'The Substitutability of Money and Near-Monies: A Survey of the Time-Series Evidence', *Journal of Economic Literature*, vol. XV, no. 2.

FERGUSON, J. M. (ed.) (1964), *Public Debt and Future Generations*, University of North Carolina Press.

FIELD, F. (1975), *Poverty: The Facts*, Child Poverty Action Group, London.

FIELDS, D. B. and STANBURY, W. T. (June 1971), 'Income Taxes and Incentives to Work: Some Additional Empirical Evidence', *American Economic Review*, vol. 61.

Financial Accounts of the United Kingdom (annual publication), HMSO, London.

Financial Statistics (monthly publication), Central Statistical Office, HMSO, London.

Financing Strikes (1974), Conservative Political Centre, London.

Fiscal Policy and Labour Supply (1977), Conference Series No. 4, Institute for Fiscal Studies, Heinemann, London.

FLEMING, J. S. and LITTLE, I. M. D. (1974), *Why We Need a Wealth Tax*, Methuen, London.

FOGARTY, M. P. (1976), *Pensions – Where Next?*, Centre for Studies in Social Policy, London.

FRIEDMAN, M. (ed.) (1956), *Studies in the Quantity Theory of Money*, University of Chicago Press.

— (1959), 'A Monetary and Fiscal Framework for Economic Stability', in *Essays in Positive Economics*, University of Chicago Press.

— (1962), *Capitalism and Freedom*, University of Chicago Press.

— (1968), 'Money: Quantity Theory', in Sills, D. L. (ed.), *International Encyclopedia of the Social Sciences*, Collier-Macmillan, New York, vol. 10, p. 434.

— (1969), 'The Optimum Quantity of Money', in *The Optimum Quantity of Money and Other Essays*, Macmillan, London.

— (1974a), *Monetary Correction*, Institute of Economic Studies, London.

— (1974b), *Milton Friedman's Monetary Framework: A Debate with his Critics*, in Gordon, R. J. (ed.), University of Chicago Press.

GILLESPIE, W. I. (1966), 'The Incidence of Taxes and Public Expenditure in the Canadian Economy', study no. 2 for the Canadian Royal Commission on Taxation, Queen's Printer, Ottawa, Canada.

GODFREY, L. (1975), *Theoretical and Empirical Aspects of the Effects of Taxation on the Supply of Labour*, OECD, Paris.

GOLDMAN, S. (1973), *The Developing System of Public Expenditure Management and Control,* HMSO, London.

GOODHART, C. A. E. (1975), *Money, Information and Uncertainty*, Macmillan, London.

Greater London Rate Equalisation Scheme (1968), HMSO, London.

Green Paper on *The Future Shape of Local Government Finance* (1971), Cmnd 4741, HMSO, London.

Green Paper on *The Future Shape of Local Government Finance* (1977), Cmnd 6813, HMSO, London.

Green Paper on *Reform of Corporation Tax* (1971), Cmnd 4630, HMSO, London.

GRUNDY, J. M. (1956), *Tax Problems of the Family Company*, Sweet & Maxwell, London.

Growth and Control of Public Expenditure (1976), Report of a Conference by the Institute for Fiscal Studies.

HANSEN, B. (1969), *Fiscal Policy in Seven Countries, 1955–65*, OECD, Paris.

HARBURY, C. and McMAHON, P. (September 1973), 'Inheritance and the Characteristics of Top Wealth Leavers in Britain', *Economic Journal.*

HARRIS, R. and SELDON, A. (1970), *Choice in Welfare*, Institute of Economic Affairs, London.

HEALD, D. A. (November 1975), 'Financing Devolution', *National Westminster Bank Review.*

HEMMING, M. F. W. (August 1965), 'Social Security in Britain and Certain Other Countries', *National Institute Economic Review*, no. 33.

— and DUFFY, H. (August 1964), 'The Price of Accommodation', *National Institute Economic Review*, no. 29.

HEPWORTH, N. P. (1976), *The Finance of Local Government*, Allen & Unwin, London.

HICKS, J. R. (1939), *Value and Capital,* OUP, London.

HILDERSLEY, S. H. H. and NOTTAGE, R. (1968), *Sources of Local Revenue*, Royal Institute of Public Administration, London. A paper of the same title appears in *Local Government Finance* (1973), Proceedings of a Conference, Institute for Fiscal Studies, London.

HINES, A. G. (1971), *On the Reappraisal of Keynesian Economics*, Martin Robertson, London.

HM TREASURY (1972), *Public Expenditure White Papers Handbook on Methodology*, London.

HOCKMAN, H. M. and RODGERS, J. D. (September 1969), 'Pareto Optimal Redistribution', *American Economic Review*, vol. 59.

HOPKIN, W. A. B. and GODLEY, W. A. H. (May 1965), 'An Analysis of Tax Changes', *National Institute Economic Review*, no. 32.

Housing Policy: A Consultative Document (1973), Cmnd 6851, HMSO, London.

'How the Banks Compete for Deposits' (July 1967), *Banker.*

HOWELL, R. (1976), *Why Work?*, Conservative Political Centre, London.

HYDE COMMITTEE (1977), Accounting Standards Committee of the Various Professional Accounting bodies, Box 433, Chartered Accountants Hall, London.

ILERSIC, A. R. (1969), *Rates as a Source of Local Government Finance*, IMTA, London.

IMTA (1968), *Rate Equalisation in London*, London.

'Incidence of Taxes and Social Service Benefits' (February 1976), *Economic Trends*, no. 268, HMSO, London.

INFLATION ACCOUNTING COMMITTEE (1975), *Report* (Sandilands Report), Cmnd 6225, HMSO, London.

INFLATION ACCOUNTING Guide (1975), *A Brief Guide to the Report of the Inflation Accounting Committee*, Department of Trade, HMSO, London.

INVESTMENT INCENTIVES (1966), Cmnd 2874, HMSO, London.

Investment Incentives Survey (1965), Confederation of British Industry, London.

JACKMAN, R. and KLAPPHOLZ, K. (1975), *Taming the Tiger*, Institute of Economic Studies, London.

JOHNSON, H. G. (June 1962), 'Monetary Theory and Policy', *American Economic Review*, vol. 52, no. 3.

— (1967), *Essays in Monetary Economics*, Allen & Unwin, London.

KAIM-CAUDLE, P. R. (April 1969), 'Selectivity and the Social Services', *Lloyds Bank Review.*

KALDOR, N. (1955), *An Expenditure Tax*, Allen & Unwin, London.

KEYNES, J. M. (1930), *A Treatise on Money*, Macmillan, London.

— (1936), *The General Theory of Employment, Interest and Money,* Macmillan, London.

— (1940), *How to Pay for the War*, Macmillan, London.

KRAUSS, M. B. and JOHNSON, H. G. (November 1972), 'The Theory of Tax Incidence: A Diagrammatic Analysis', *Economica*, new series, vol. 39, p. 373.

LAIDLER, D. (1977), *The Demand for Money: Theories and Evidence*, 2nd ed., Dun-Donnelley, New York.

— and PARKIN, J. M. (December 1975), 'Inflation – A Survey', *Economic Journal.*

Land Commission (1965), White Paper, Cmnd 2771, HMSO, London.

LEIJONHUFVUD, A. (1968), *On Keynesian Economics and the Economics of Keynes,* Oxford University Press, London.

LEISNER, T. and KING, M. (1975), *Indexing for Inflation*, Institute for Fiscal Studies, London.

Licensing and Supervision of Deposit-Taking Institutions (1976), Cmnd 6584, HMSO, London.

LISTER, R. (1975), *Social Security: The Case for Reform*, Child Poverty Action Group, London.

Local Government Act 1974 (1974), chapter 7, HMSO, London.

Local Government Finance (The Layfield Report) (May 1976), Cmnd 6453, HMSO, London.

Local Government Finance (May 1977), Cmnd 6813, HMSO, London.

Local Government Finance in England and Wales: Consultation Paper (June 1973), Department of the Environment and the Welsh Office, HMSO, London.

Local Government Finance in England and Wales (1974), Department of the Environment, HMSO, London.

'London Money Market' (May 1966), *Midland Bank Review*.

LUND, P. J. (1975), 'The Econometric Assessment of Investment Incentives', Department of Industry, Proceedings of a Conference. To appear in *The Economics of Industrial Subsidies*, HMSO, London (forthcoming).

LYNN, J. H. (1964), *Studies of the Royal Commission on Taxation. No. 23 Federal-Provision Fiscal Relations,* Ottawa.

McNAIRN COMMITTEE ON THE RATING OF PLANT AND MACHINERY (1974), *Report,* HMSO, London.

MARSHALL, A. H. (1969), *Local Government Finance*, 33 national reports and a general report prepared for the 1969 IULA Congression, Vienna, International Union of Local Authorities, The Hague.

MAYNARD, A. H. and KING, D. N. (1972), *Rates or Prices*, Hobart Paper 54, Institute of Economic Affairs, London.

MEADE, J. E. (1975), *The Intelligent Radical's Guide to Economic Policy,* Allen & Unwin, London.

— (1977), *Committee on Taxation*, Institute for Fiscal Studies, London.

MERRITT, A. J. (1968), *Executive Remuneration in the UK*, Longmans, London.

— and MONK, D. A. G. (1967), *Inflation, Taxation and Executive Remuneration*, Hallam Press, London.

MESSERE, K. (1975), 'Recent and Prospective Trends in Tax Levels and Tax Structures', Lecture Series No. 2, Institute for Fiscal Studies, London.

MILLER, W. G. (September 1971), 'The Future Shape of Local Government Finance', *Local Government Finance Journal*, no. 9.

MISHAN, E. J. (1967), *The Costs of Economic Growth*, Staples Press, London.

MODIGLIANI, F. (May 1975), '25 Years After the Rediscovery of Money: What Have We Learned?', *American Economic Review*, vol. 65, Papers and Proceedings, p. 179.

'More Light on Personal Saving' (April 1965), *Economic Trends*, HMSO, London.

MONROE, J. G. (December 1956), 'Annual and Other Periodical Payments', *British Tax Review*.

MORGAN, D. R. (1977), *Over-taxation by Inflation*, Hobart Paper 72, Institute of Economic Affairs, London.

MUSGRAVE, R. A. (1959), *The Theory of Public Finance*, McGraw-Hill, New York.

— (1961), 'Fiscal Theory of Political Federalism', in *Public Finances: Needs, Sources and Utilization*, Conference Report of the National Bureau of Economic Research, Princeton University Press.

— and MUSGRAVE, P. B. (1973), *Public Finance in Theory and Practice*, McGraw-Hill, New York.

— and SHOUP, C. S. (eds) (1959), *Readings in the Economics of Taxation*, Allen & Unwin, London.

MYRDAL, G. (1960), *Beyond the Welfare State*, Duckworth, London.

National Debt (1973), Cmnd 5488, HMSO, London.

National Income and Expenditure (Blue Book) (1976), Central Statistical Office, HMSO, London.

National Superannuation and Social Insurance Proposals for Earnings-Related Social Security (1969), Cmnd 3883, HMSO, London.

New Local Authorities Management and Structure (1972), HMSO, London.

NEWLYN, W. T. (June 1964), 'The Supply of Money and Its Control', *Economic Journal.*

NICHOLSON, J. L. and BRITTON, A. J. C. (1976), 'The Redistribution of Income', in *The Personal Distribution of Incomes*, ed. Atkinson, A. B., Allen & Unwin, London.

NOBAY, A. R. and JOHNSON, H. G. (June 1977), 'Monetarism: A Historic Theoretical Perspective', *Journal of Economic Literature*, vol. XV, no. 2.

North Sea Oil and Gas (1972–3), First Report of the Committee of Public Accounts, House of Commons Paper 122, HMSO, London.

OATES, W. E. (February 1968), 'The Theory of Public Finance in a Federal System', *Canadian Journal of Economics*, vol. 1.

— (1972), *Fiscal Federalism*, Harcourt Brace Jovanovich, New York.

OTHICK, F. (1973), 'Rating Valuation', paper in *Proceedings of a Conference on Local Government Finance*, IFS Pub. no. 10.

PAGE, SIR H. (1977), 'The Saver of Slender Means: Whatever Happened to the Page Report?', *Three Banks Review*, no. 114.

PATINKIN, D. (1965), *Money, Interest and Prices*, 2nd ed., Harper & Row, New York.

— (1972), *Studies in Monetary Economics*, Harper & Row, New York.

PEACOCK, A. T. (January 1964), 'Problems of Government Budgetary Reform', *Lloyds Bank Review.*

— (1974), 'The Treatment of Government Expenditure in Studies of Income Distribution', in *Public Finance and Stabilization Policy: Essays in Honour of Richard Musgrave*, ed. Smith, W. L. and Culbertson, J. M., North-Holland, Amsterdam.

— (March 1977), 'Giving Economic Advice in Difficult Times', *Three Banks Review*, no. 113.

— and SHANNON, R. (August 1968a), 'Problems of Government Budgetary Reform', *Lloyds Bank Review.*

— and SHANNON, R. (August 1968b), 'The Welfare State and the Redistribution of Income', *Westminster Bank Review.*

— and WISEMAN, J. (1961), *The Growth of Public Expenditure in the United Kingdom*, Oxford University Press, London.

— and WISEMAN, J. (1964), *Education for Democrats*, Hobart Paper 25, Institute of Economic Affairs, London.

PENNANCE, F. G. and WEST, W. A. (1971), *Housing Market Analysis and Policy*, Hobart Paper 48, Institute of Economic Affairs, London.

POLINSKY, A. M. (April 1973), 'A Note on the Measurement of Incidence', *Public Finance Quarterly*, vol. 1, pp. 219–30.

PREST, A. R. (1968), 'The Budget and Interpersonal Distribution', *Public Finance*, vol. XXIII, nos 1–2.

— *et al.* (1977), *The State of Taxation*, Reading 16, Institute of Economic Affairs, London.

Proceedings of a Conference on Local Government Finance (1973), Institute for Fiscal Studies, London.

Proposals for a Tax-Credit System (October 1972), Cmnd 5116, HMSO, London.

RADCLIFFE COMMITTEE (1959), *see* Committee on the Working of the Monetary System (1959).

RAMSEY, J. B. (1977), *Economic Forecasting – Models or Markets?*, Hobart Paper 74, Institute of Economic Affairs, London.

Rate Rebates in England and Wales 1971–72 (1972), Department of the Environment and the Welsh Office, HMSO, London.

REDCLIFFE-MAUD, LORD and WOOD, B. (1974), *English Local Government Reformed,* Oxford University Press, London.

Reform of the Exchequer Accounts (1963), Cmnd 2014, HMSO, London.

Regeneration of British Industry (1974), Cmnd 5710, HMSO, London.

Regional Development Incentives (1975), Cmnd 6058, HMSO, London.

REID, D. J. (November 1976), 'National and Sector Balance Sheets', *Statistical News*, no. 35, HMSO, London.

— (May 1977), 'Public Sector Debt', *Economic Trends*, HMSO, London.

Report into the Impact of Rates on Households (1964), Cmnd 2582, HMSO, London.

Report of Committee on Housing in Greater London (1965), Cmnd 2605, HMSO, London.

Report of the Canadian Royal Commission on Taxation (1966), Queen's Printer, Ottawa.

Report of the Committee on Local Authority and Allied Personal Social Services (Seebohm Report) (1968), Cmnd 3703, HMSO, London.

Report of the Committee on the Taxation of Trading Profits (1951), Cmnd 8189, HMSO, London.

Report of the Expert Committee on Compensation and Betterment (Chairman Mr Justice Uthwatt) (1942), HMSO, London.

Report of the US Commission on Money and Credit (1961), Prentice-Hall, Englewood Cliffs, NJ.

REVELL, J. (1973), *The British Financial System*, Macmillan, London.

— (1975), *Solvency and Regulation of Banks*, University of Wales Press.

Revenue Statistics of the OECD Member Countries 1965–74 (1976), OECD, Paris.

RICHARDS, G. (1974), *The Reformed Local Government System*, Allen & Unwin, London.

ROBINSON, J. (1962), *Economic Philosophy*, Penguin, Harmondsworth.

ROE, A. R. (June 1973), 'The Case for Flow of Funds and National Balance Sheet Accounts', *Economic Journal*, vol. 83, no. 330.

ROYAL COMMISSION ON THE CONSTITUTION 1969–73 (1973), *Report*, vols 1 and 2, Cmnd 5460 and 5460–1, HMSO, London.

ROYAL COMMISSION ON THE CONSTITUTION (1973a), *Research Paper 9*, Dawson, D., HMSO, London.

— (1973b), *Research Paper 10*, King, D. N., HMSO, London.

ROYAL COMMISSION ON THE DISTRIBUTION OF INCOME AND WEALTH (July 1975), *Report No. 1*, HMSO, London.

ROYAL COMMISSION ON GAMBLING (July 1978), *Final Report*, Cmnd 7200, HMSO, London.

ROYAL COMMISSION ON LOCAL GOVERNMENT IN ENGLAND AND WALES (1969), Cmnd 4040, HMSO, London.

ROYAL COMMISSION ON LOCAL GOVERNMENT IN SCOTLAND (Chairman Lord Wheatley) (1969), Cmnd 4150, HMSO, London.

ROYAL COMMISSION ON THE TAXATION OF PROFITS AND INCOME (1954), *Second Report*, Cmnd 9105; and (1955) *Final Report*, Cmnd 9474, HMSO, London.

RUBNER, A. (June 1964), 'The Irrelevancy of the British Differential Profits Tax', *Economic Journal.*

SANDFORD, C. T. (1965), *Taxing Inheritance and Capital Gains*, Hobart Paper 32, Institute of Economic Affairs, London.

— (April 1967), 'The Swedes can do It, Why Can't We?', *Banker.*

— (1971), *Taxing Personal Wealth*, Allen & Unwin, London.

— (1975), *An Annual Wealth Tax*, Institute for Fiscal Studies, London.

—, WILLIS, J. R. M. and IRONSIDE, D. J. (1975), *An Accessions Tax,* Institute for Fiscal Studies, London.

SANDILANDS COMMITTEE (1975): *see* Inflation Accounting Committee.

SCHULTZ, W. J. and HARRIS, C. L. (1965), *American Public Finance,* 8th ed., Prentice-Hall, Englewood Cliffs, NJ.

SCOTT, M. F. G. (1976), 'Some Economic Principles of Accounting: A Constructive Critique of the Sandilands Report', Lecture Series No. 7, Institute for Fiscal Studies, London.

SELECT COMMITTEE ON TAX CREDIT (1973), *Session 1972–3, Report and Proceedings*, HC 341–II, 341–III, HMSO, London.

SELECT COMMITTEE ON A WEALTH TAX (November 1975), *Session 1974–5, Vol. I Report and Proceedings of the Committee; Vol. II Minutes of Evidence; Vol. III Minutes of Evidence; Vol. IV Appendices to Minutes of Evidence*, HC 696, vols I–IV, HMSO, London.

Selective Employment Tax (1966), Cmnd 2986, HMSO, London.

SEMPLE, M. and BOREHAM, A. J. (1976), 'Future Development of Work in the Government Statistical Service on the Distribution of Household

Income', in *Proceedings of The Royal Economic Society Conference on The Distribution of Income and Property*, London.

SEWILL, H. (November 1966), 'Automatic Unit for National Taxation and Insurance', *Conservative New Techniques*, no. 6.

SHACKLE, G. L. S. (June 1961), 'Recent Theories Concerning the Nature and Role of Interest', *Economic Journal.*

— (1967), *The Years of High Theory: Invention and Tradition in Economic Thought 1926–1939*, Cambridge University Press.

— (1972), *Epistemics and Economics*, Cambridge University Press.

— (1974), *Keynesian Kaleidics*, Edinburgh University Press.

SIMES COMMITTEE (1952), *Report of the Committee of Enquiry on Rating of Site Values*, Ministry of Health, HMSO, London.

SIMONS, H. C. (1938), *Personal Income Taxation*, University of Chicago Press.

Social Insurance and Allied Services (1942), Cmnd 6404, HMSO, London.

Social Services for All? (1968), Fabian Society Tracts, nos 382–5, London.

STAFFORD, D. C. (November 1976), 'Government and the Housing Situation', *National Westminster Bank Review.*

Statistical Abstracts of the United Kingdom, HMSO, London.

STEWART, M. (1977), *The Jekyll and Hyde Years: Politics and Economic Policy Since 1964*, Dent, London.

STONE, R. *et al.* (1962), *A Computable Model of Economic Growth*, Chapman & Hall, London.

STONE, R. and STONE, G. (1964), *National Income and Expenditure*, Bowes & Bowes, London.

SUITS, D. B. *et al.* (1963), 'The Determinants of Consumer Expenditure: a Review of Present Knowledge', in *Impacts of Monetary Policy*, Prentice-Hall, Englewood Cliffs, NJ.

SUMNER, M. (1976), *The Effect of Taxation on Corporate Saving and Investment*, Lecture Series No. 4, Institute for Fiscal Studies, London.

Supplementary Benefits Commission Annual Report (1975), Cmnd 6615, HMSO, London.

TAIT, A. A. (1975), *The Economics of Devolution – A Knife Edge Problem*, Fraser of Allander Institute, Glasgow.

Tax Statistics (1976), Statistical Office of the European Communities, Brussels.

Taxation and Incentives (1976), Conference Papers, Institute for Fiscal Studies, London.

Taxation of North Sea Oil (1976), Conference Papers, Institute for Fiscal Studies, London.

Taxation of Trading Profits (1951), Cmnd 8189, HMSO, London.

TEW, B. and HENDERSON, R. F. (eds) (1959), *Company Income and Finance, 1949–53*, Cambridge University Press.

TIEBOUT, C. M. (1961), 'An Economic Theory of Fiscal Decentralization', in *Public Finances: Needs, Sources and Utilization*, National Bureau of Economic Research, Princeton University Press.

TITMUSS, R. M. (1962), *Income Distribution and Social Change*, Allen & Unwin, London.

TITMUSS, R. M. (1963), *Essays on 'The Welfare State'*, Allen & Unwin, London.

— (1967), *Choice and the Welfare State*, Fabian Tract 370, Fabian Society, London.

TOBIN, J. *et al.* (1963), 'An Essay on Principles of Debt Management', in *Fiscal and Debt Management Policies*, Prentice-Hall, Englewood Cliffs, NJ.

TOWNSEND, P. (1974), 'Poverty as Relative Deprivation: Resources and Style of Living', in *Poverty, Inequality and Class Structure*, ed. Wedderburn, D., Cambridge University Press.

TULLOCK, G. (1976), *The Vote Motive*, Institute of Economic Affairs, London.

VICKREY, W. (1974), *Agenda for Progressive Taxation*, Ronald Press, New York.

WAGNER, A. (1890), *Finanzweissenschaft*, 3rd edition, Leipzig.

Wealth Tax (1974), Cmnd 5704, HMSO, London.

WHITTINGTON, G. (1974), *Company Taxation and Dividends*, Lecture Series No. 1, Institute for Fiscal Studies, London.

WILLIAMS, B. R. (1967), *The New Social Contract*, Conservative Political Centre, London.

WILLIAMS, LADY RHYS (1943), *Something to Look Forward To*, Macdonald, London.

WILLIS, J. R. M. and HARDWICK, P. J. W. (1978), *Tax Expenditures in the United Kingdom*, Heinemann, London, for the Institute for Fiscal Studies.

Index